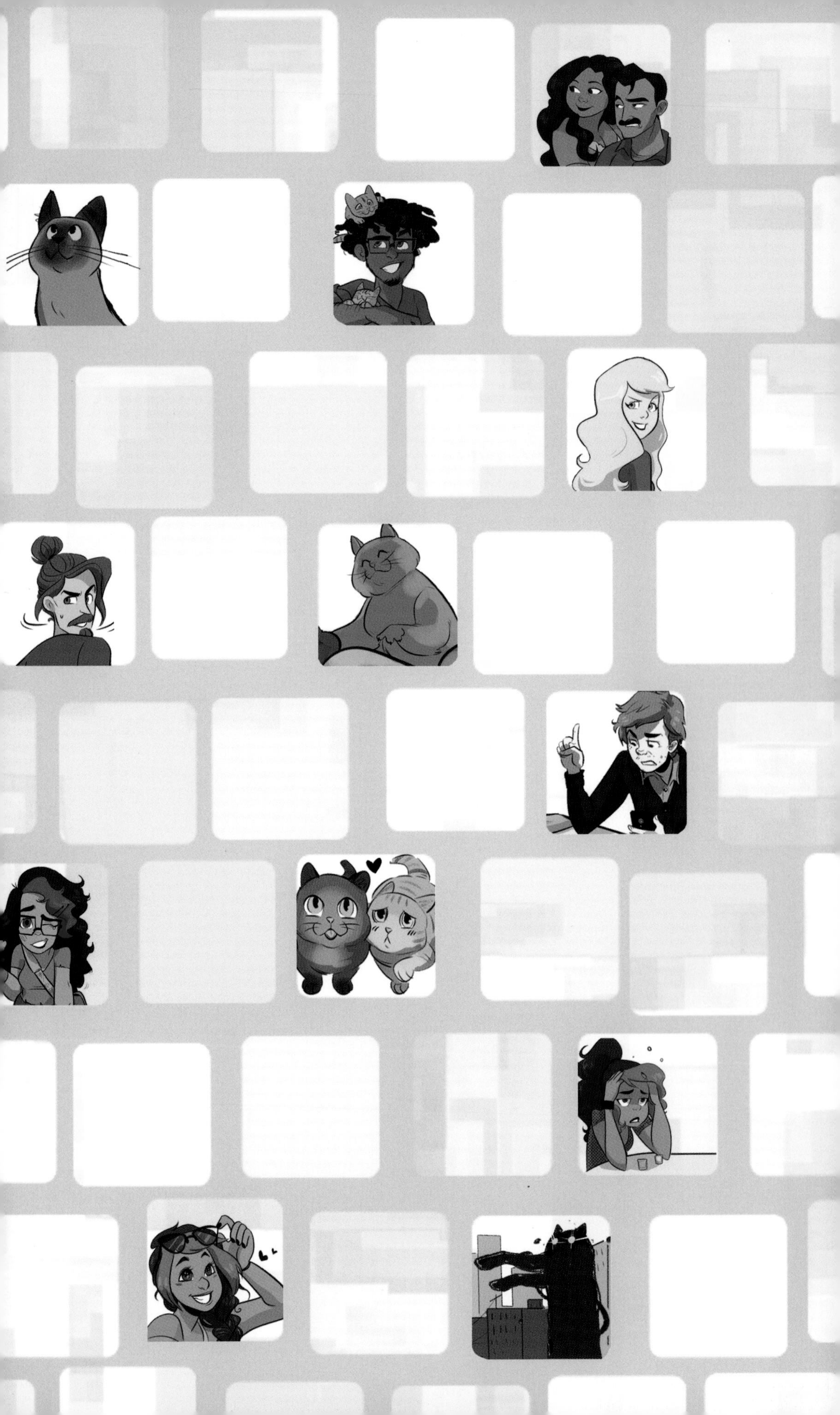

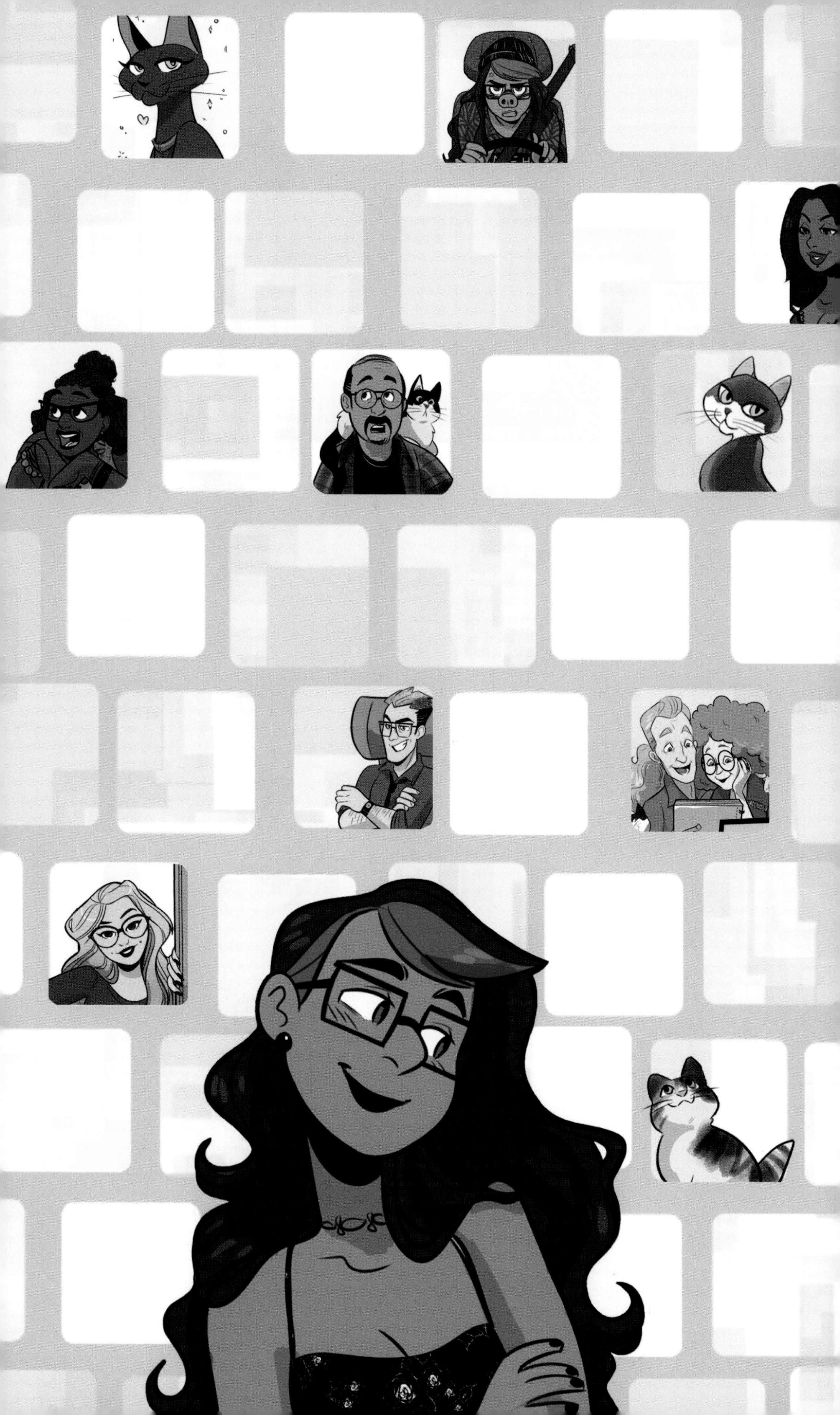

WRITTEN AND CREATED BY

JUSTINE PRADO

ART BY

JENN ST-ONGE

COLORS BY

CAREY PIETSCH

LETTERS BY

JOYANA MCDIARMID

COVER BY

JENN ST-ONGE

PUBLISHER

MAYTAL GILBOA

GRAPHIC DESIGNER

CARLA BURGOS

SPECIAL THANKS

MARIA LLORENS

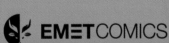 EMETCOMICS

First Published in the US in 2017 by Emet Entertainment, LLC.
LCCN: 2016955233
ISBN: 978-0-9981799-0-2
Order from emetcomics.com

Finding Molly

An Adventure in Catsitting

JUSTINE PRADO

JENN ST-ONGE

 EMETCOMICS

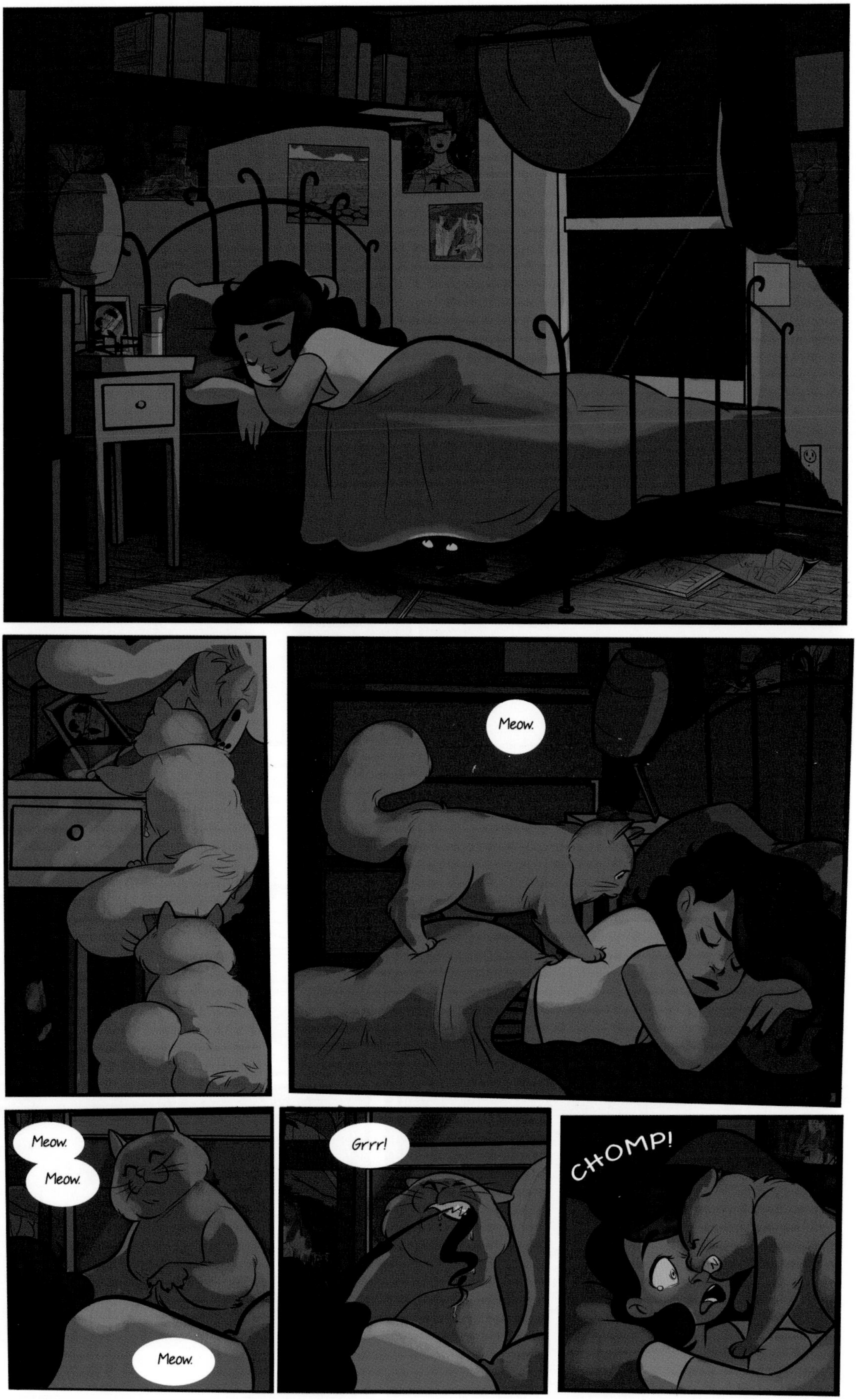
Meow.
Meow.
Meow.
Meow.
Grrr!
CHOMP!

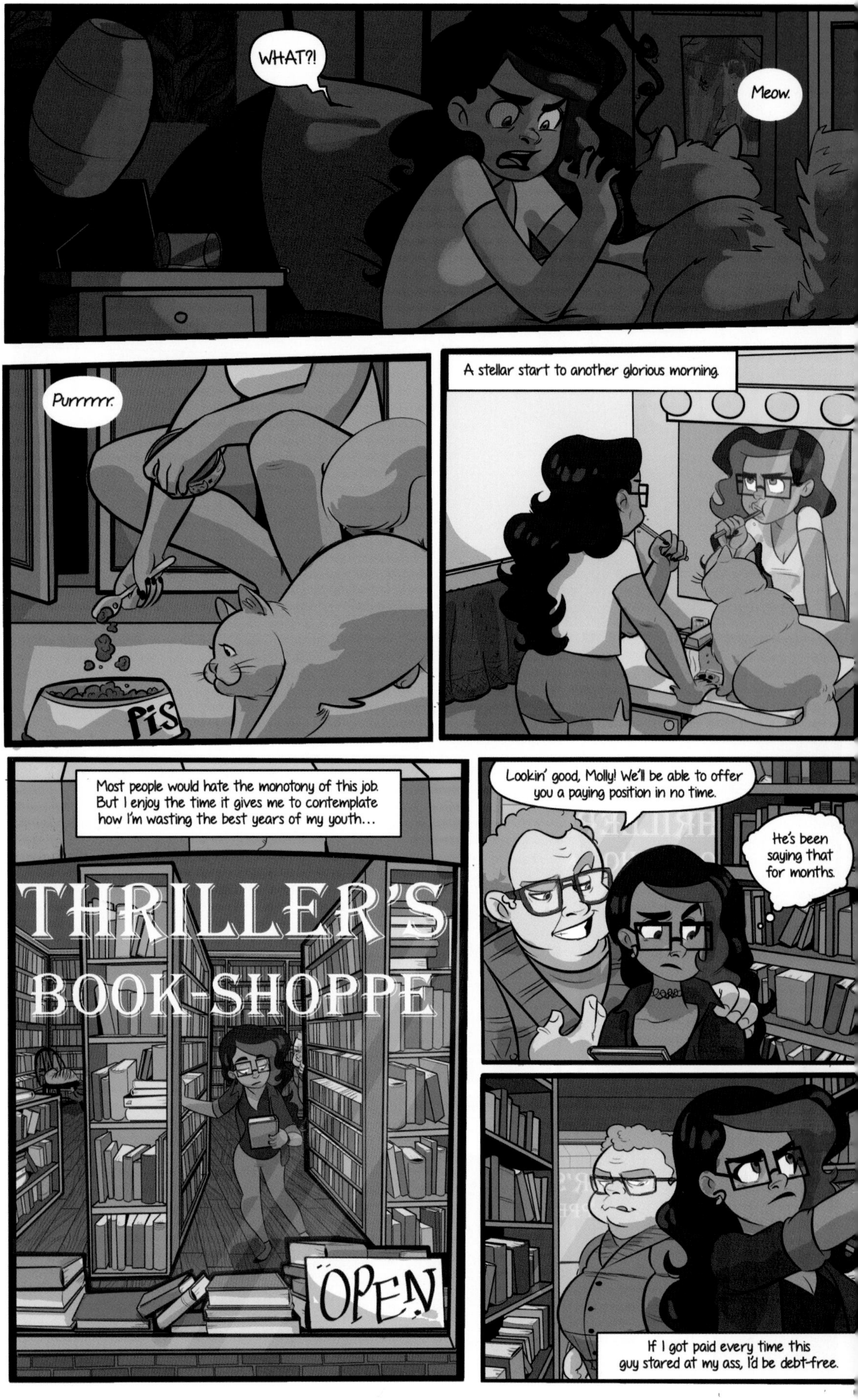
WHAT?!
Meow.
Purrrrr.
PIS
A stellar start to another glorious morning.
Most people would hate the monotony of this job. But I enjoy the time it gives me to contemplate how I'm wasting the best years of my youth...
THRILLER'S
BOOK-SHOPPE
OPEN
Lookin' good, Molly! We'll be able to offer you a paying position in no time.
He's been saying that for months.
If I got paid every time this guy stared at my ass, I'd be debt-free.

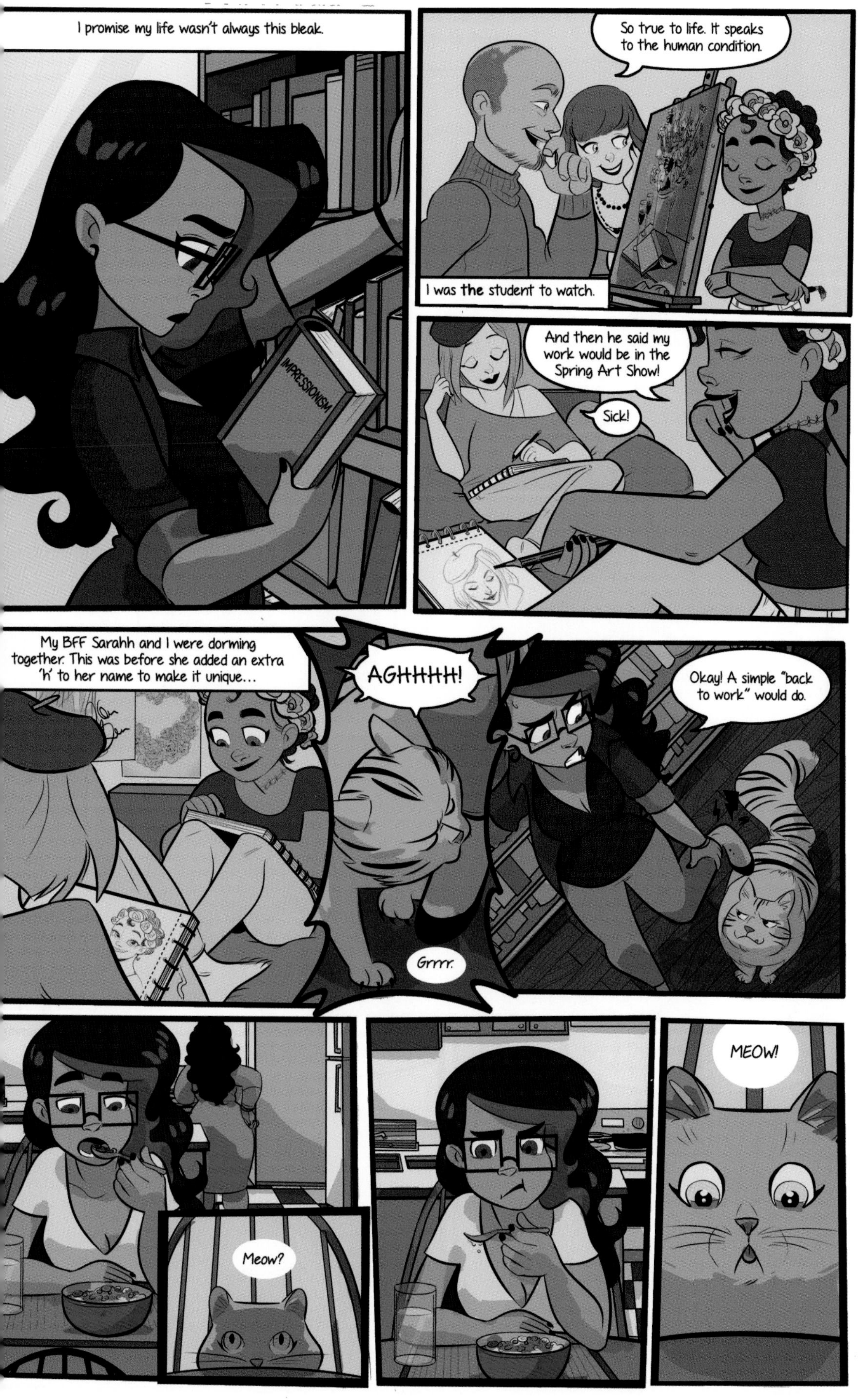
I promise my life wasn't always this bleak.
IMPRESSIONISM
So true to life. It speaks to the human condition.
I was **the** student to watch.
And then he said my work would be in the Spring Art Show!
Sick!
My BFF Sarahh and I were dorming together. This was before she added an extra 'h' to her name to make it unique...
AGHHHH!
Okay! A simple "back to work" would do.
Grrrr.
Meow?
MEOW!

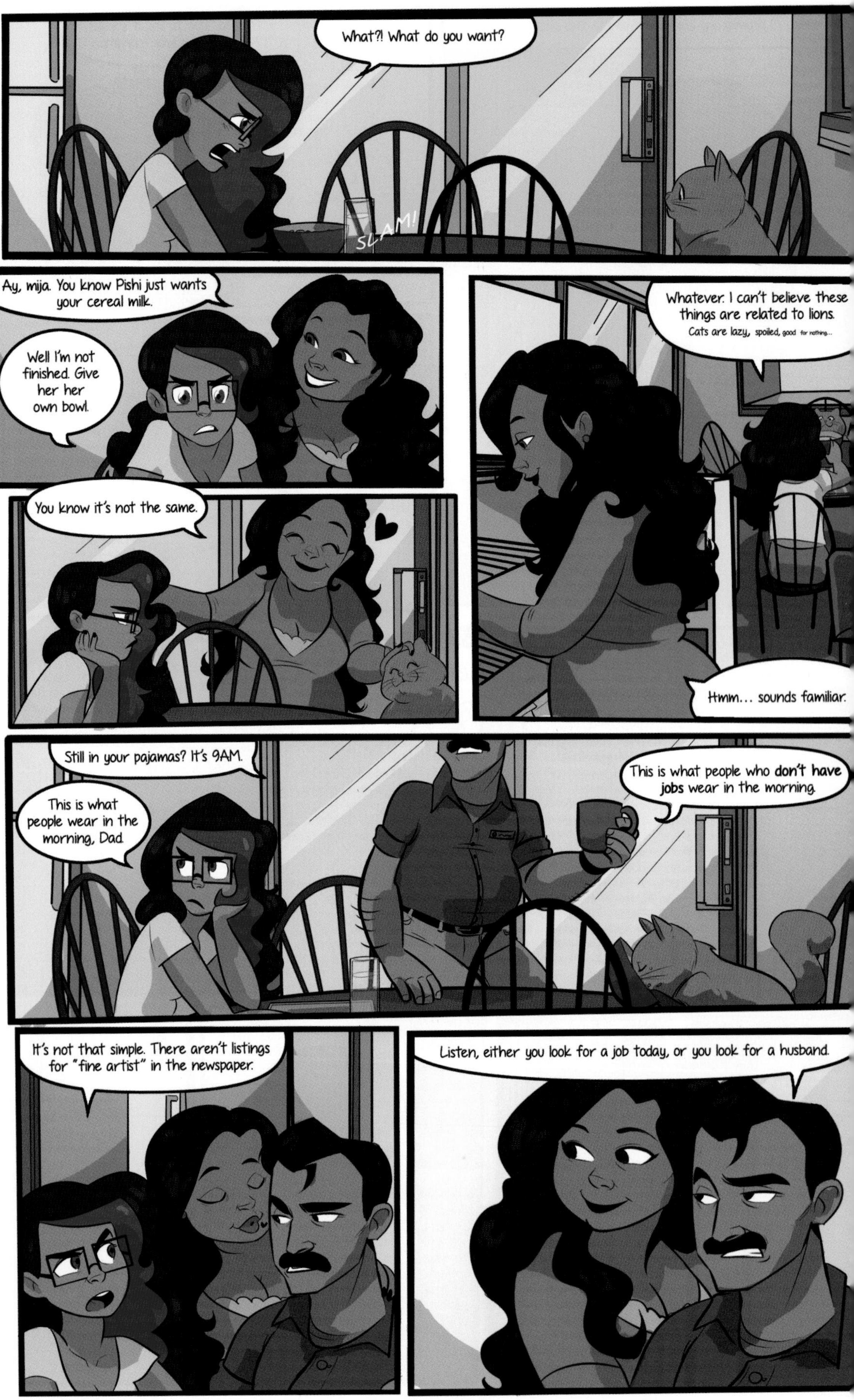
What?! What do you want?
SLAM!
Ay, mija. You know Pishi just wants your cereal milk.
Well I'm not finished. Give her her own bowl.
You know it's not the same.
Whatever. I can't believe these things are related to lions.
Cats are lazy, spoiled, good for nothing...
Hmm... sounds familiar.
Still in your pajamas? It's 9AM.
This is what people wear in the morning, Dad.
This is what people who **don't have jobs** wear in the morning.
It's not that simple. There aren't listings for "fine artist" in the newspaper.
Listen, either you look for a job today, or you look for a husband.

OMG. This isn't the old country.

And boy are you lucky. You'd be past your prime.

A weird old *bruja* who rides her bike around town. They'd say, go get a big jar so we can pickle the witch before she spoils! *Torshideh!*

Which **old country** are we talking about, Dad?

Doesn't matter. You're a problem everywhere.

Is it any wonder I became an artist?

There's nothing that says you can't be a great artist **and** a wife. Even Frida Kahlo was married!

Oh, Jesus.

You two need to chill. I'm going to figure it out, I promise. And as much as I love these **daily** pep talks, I think it's time I start my day.

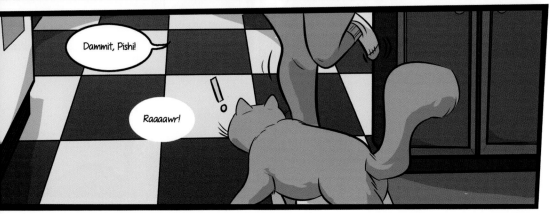

Dammit, Pishi!

Raaaawr!

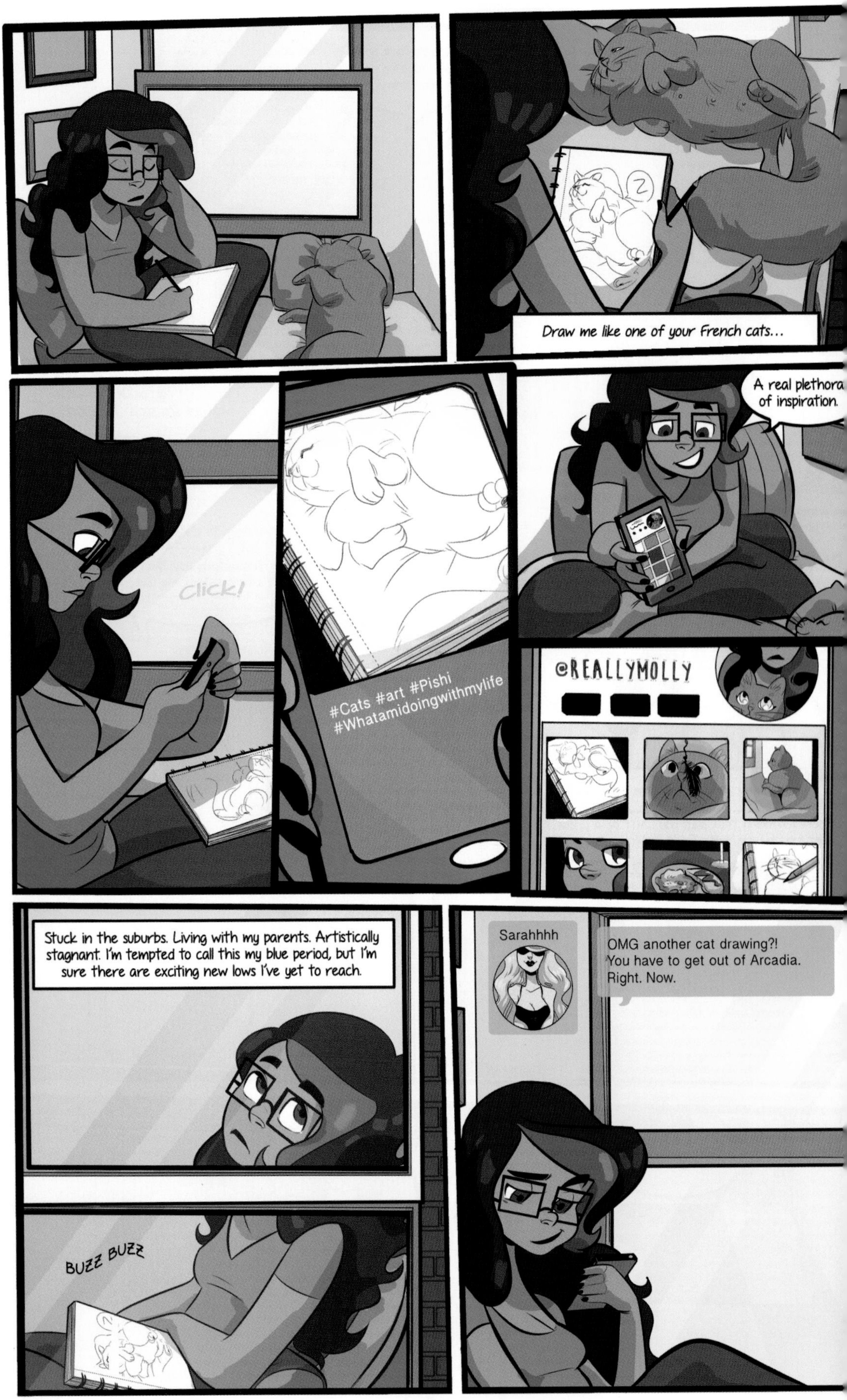

Draw me like one of your French cats...
Click!
#Cats #art #Pishi
#Whatamidoingwithmylife
A real plethora of inspiration.
@REALLYMOLLY
Stuck in the suburbs. Living with my parents. Artistically stagnant. I'm tempted to call this my blue period, but I'm sure there are exciting new lows I've yet to reach.
BUZZ BUZZ
Sarahhhh
OMG another cat drawing?!
You have to get out of Arcadia.
Right. Now.

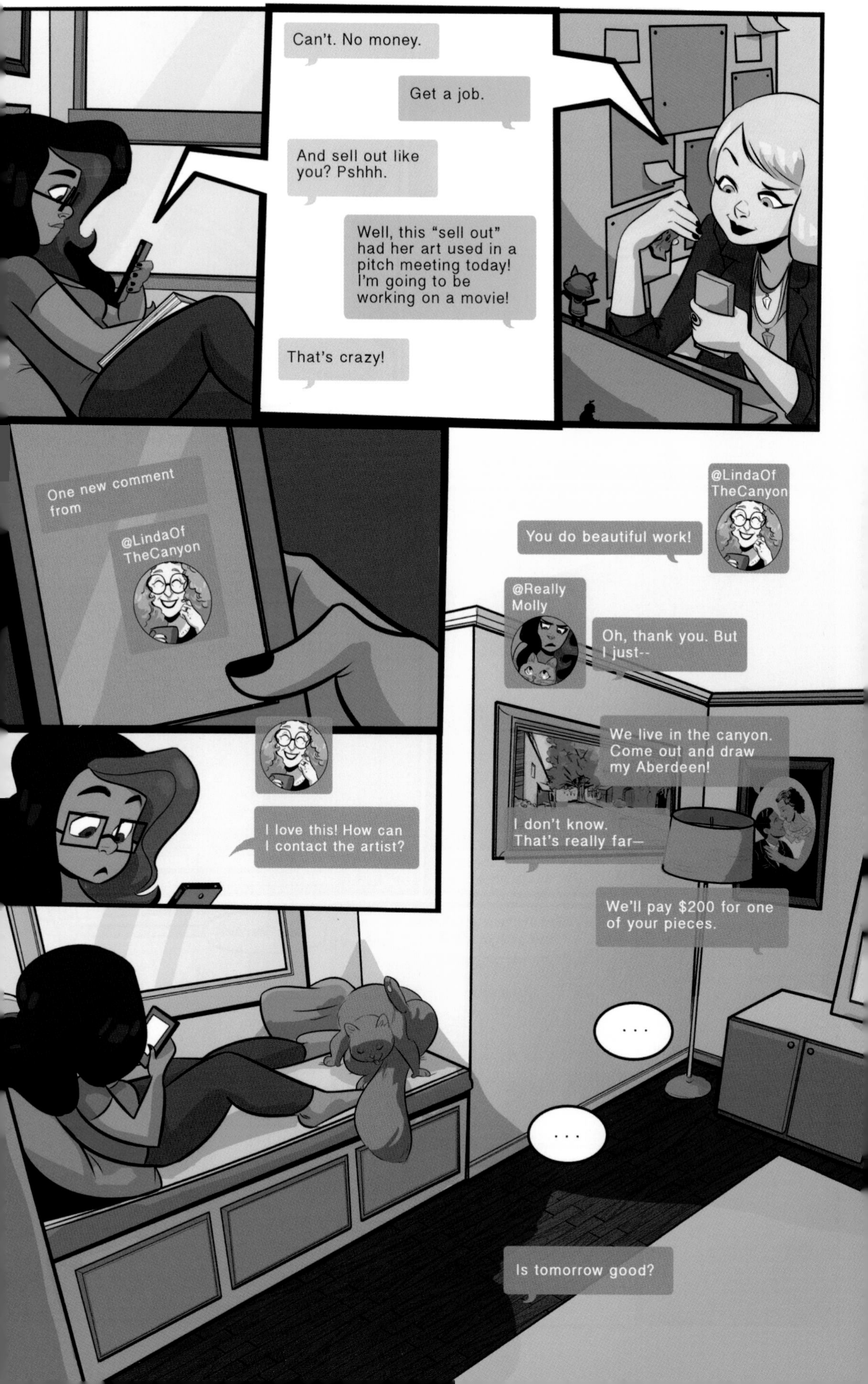
Can't. No money.
Get a job.
And sell out like you? Pshhh.
Well, this "sell out" had her art used in a pitch meeting today! I'm going to be working on a movie!
That's crazy!
One new comment from
@LindaOf TheCanyon
@LindaOf TheCanyon
You do beautiful work!
@Really Molly
Oh, thank you. But I just--
I love this! How can I contact the artist?
We live in the canyon. Come out and draw my Aberdeen!
I don't know. That's really far—
We'll pay $200 for one of your pieces.
. . .
. . .
Is tomorrow good?

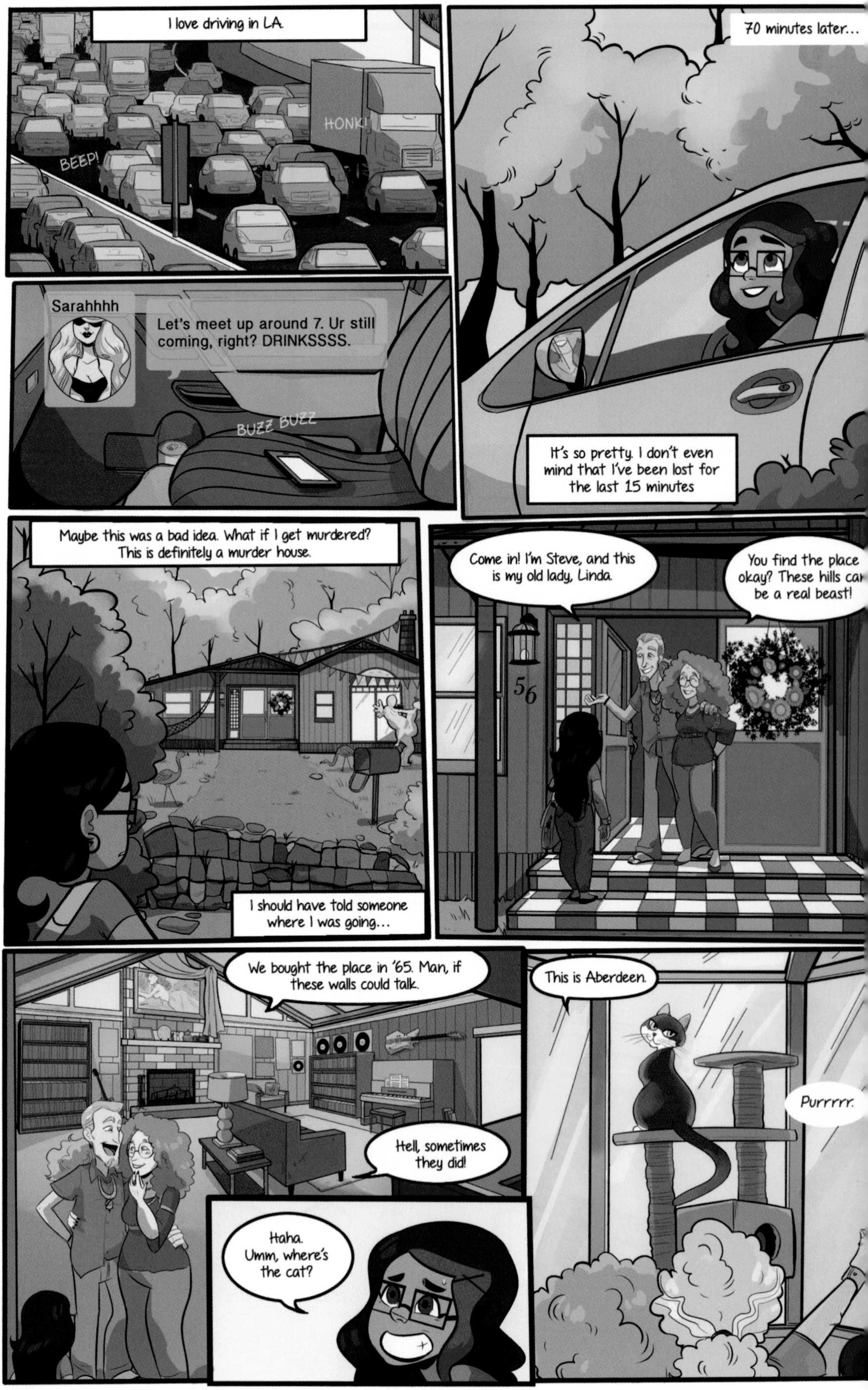
I love driving in LA.
BEEP!
HONK!
Sarahhhh
Let's meet up around 7. Ur still coming, right? DRINKSSSS.
BUZZ BUZZ
70 minutes later...
It's so pretty. I don't even mind that I've been lost for the last 15 minutes
Maybe this was a bad idea. What if I get murdered? This is definitely a murder house.
I should have told someone where I was going...
Come in! I'm Steve, and this is my old lady, Linda.
You find the place okay? These hills ca
be a real beast!
56
We bought the place in '65. Man, if these walls could talk.
Hell, sometimes they did!
Haha. Umm, where's the cat?
This is Aberdeen.
Purrrrr.

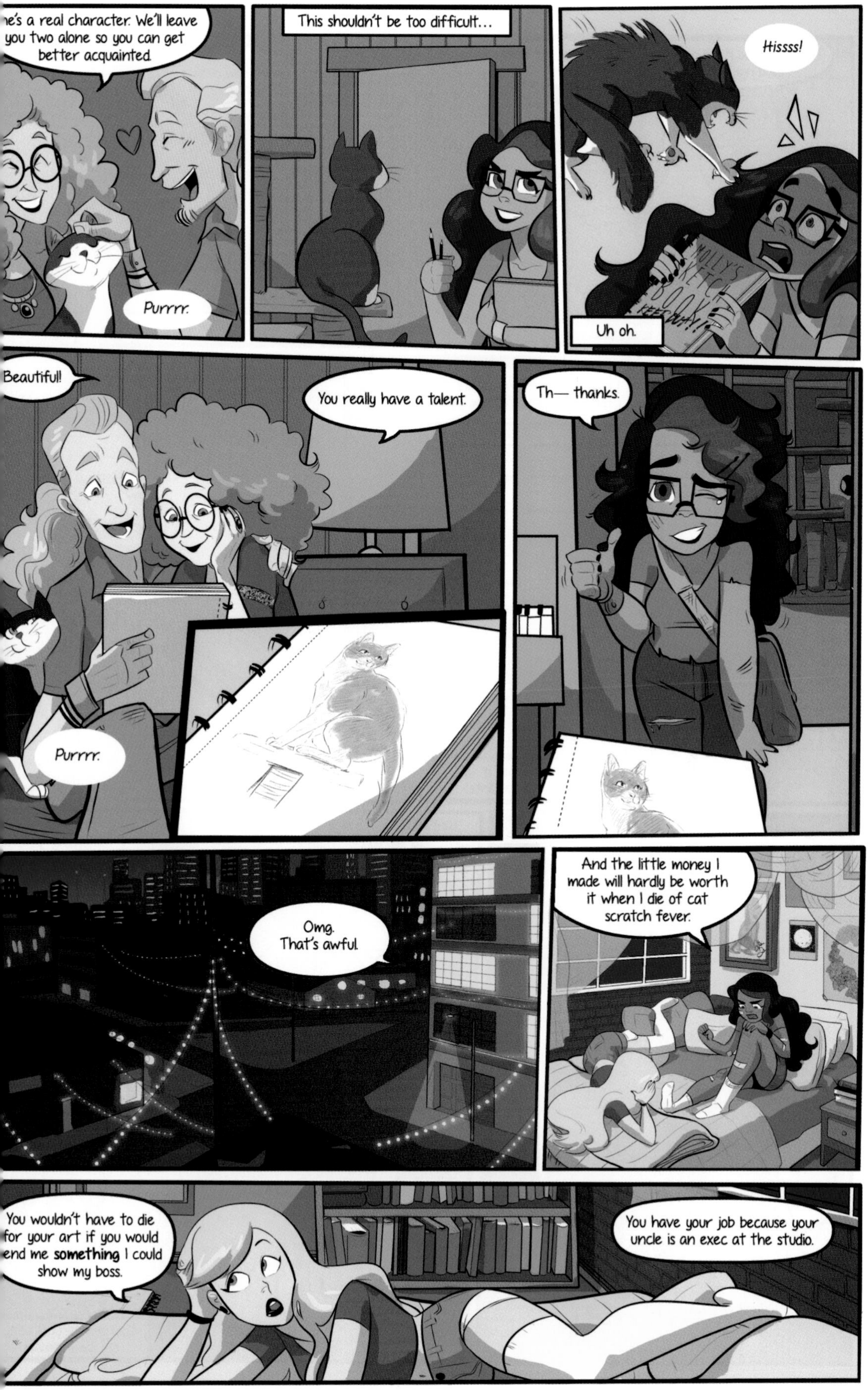

he's a real character. We'll leave you two alone so you can get better acquainted.
Purrrr.
This shouldn't be too difficult...
Hissss!
MOLLY'S SKETCH BOOK KEEP OUT!!
Uh oh.
Beautiful!
You really have a talent.
Purrrr.
Th— thanks.
Omg. That's awful.
And the little money I made will hardly be worth it when I die of cat scratch fever.
You wouldn't have to die for your art if you would end me **something** I could show my boss.
You have your job because your uncle is an exec at the studio.

The art world if full of nepotism. Even your girl Frida used her husband's fame to get a leg up.

This place is amazing.

That's how artists get work.

MATEO'S STUDIO

Not all artists...

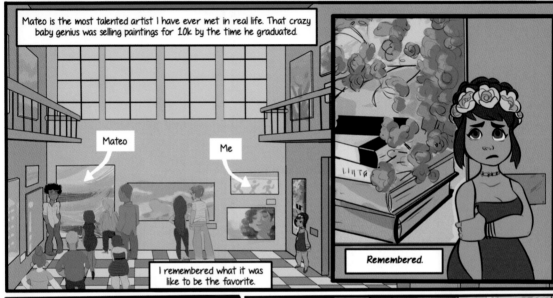

Mateo is the most talented artist I have ever met in real life. That crazy baby genius was selling paintings for 10k by the time he graduated.

Mateo

Me

I remembered what it was like to be the favorite.

Remembered.

Hey, Mateo. How's life as the art scene darling?

He-hey Molly. It's nice to see you.

Likewise.

I can't believe you guys live here.

Cool artists. Cool lofts. It's like a dream.

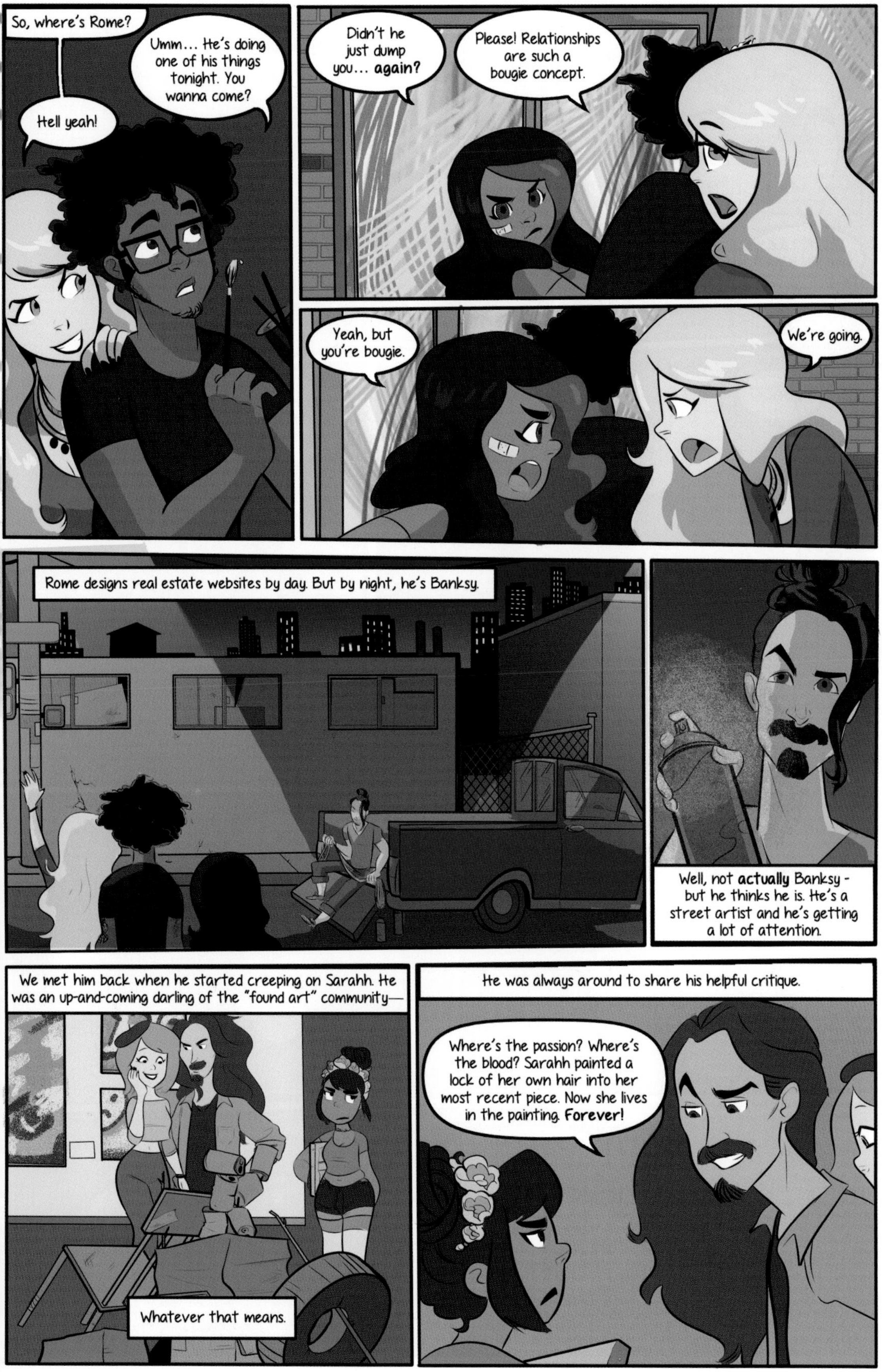
So, where's Rome?
Umm... He's doing one of his things tonight. You wanna come?
Hell yeah!
Didn't he just dump you... **again?**
Please! Relationships are such a bougie concept.
Yeah, but you're bougie.
We're going.
Rome designs real estate websites by day. But by night, he's Banksy.
Well, not **actually** Banksy - but he thinks he is. He's a street artist and he's getting a lot of attention.
We met him back when he started creeping on Sarahh. He was an up-and-coming darling of the "found art" community—
Whatever that means.
He was always around to share his helpful critique.
Where's the passion? Where's the blood? Sarahh painted a lock of her own hair into her most recent piece. Now she lives in the painting. **Forever!**

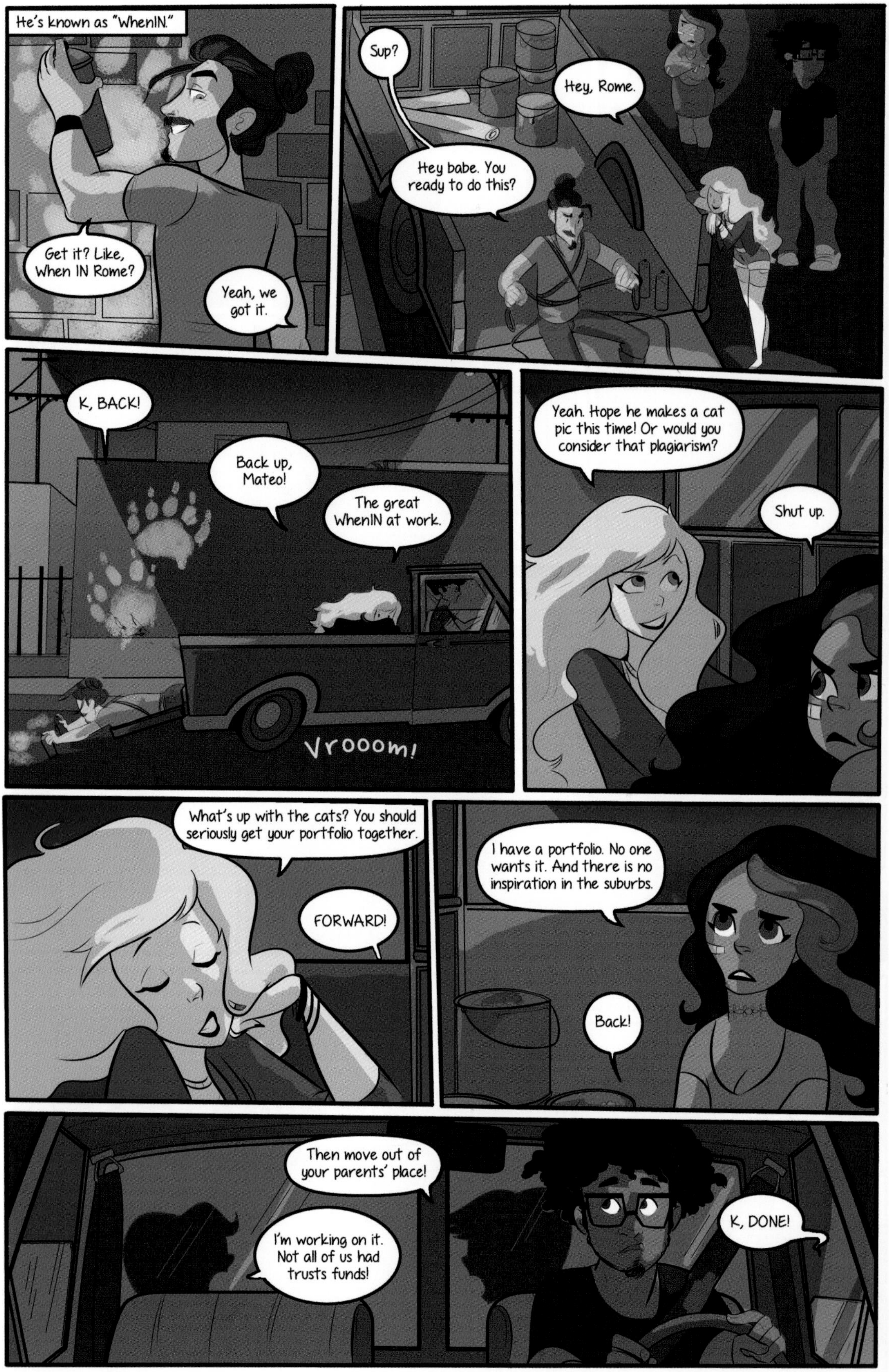
He's known as "WhenIN."
Get it? Like, When IN Rome?
Yeah, we got it.
Sup?
Hey, Rome.
Hey babe. You ready to do this?
K, BACK!
Back up, Mateo!
The great WhenIN at work.
Vrooom!
Yeah. Hope he makes a cat pic this time! Or would you consider that plagiarism?
Shut up.
What's up with the cats? You should seriously get your portfolio together.
FORWARD!
I have a portfolio. No one wants it. And there is no inspiration in the suburbs.
Back!
Then move out of your parents' place!
I'm working on it. Not all of us had trusts funds!
K, DONE!

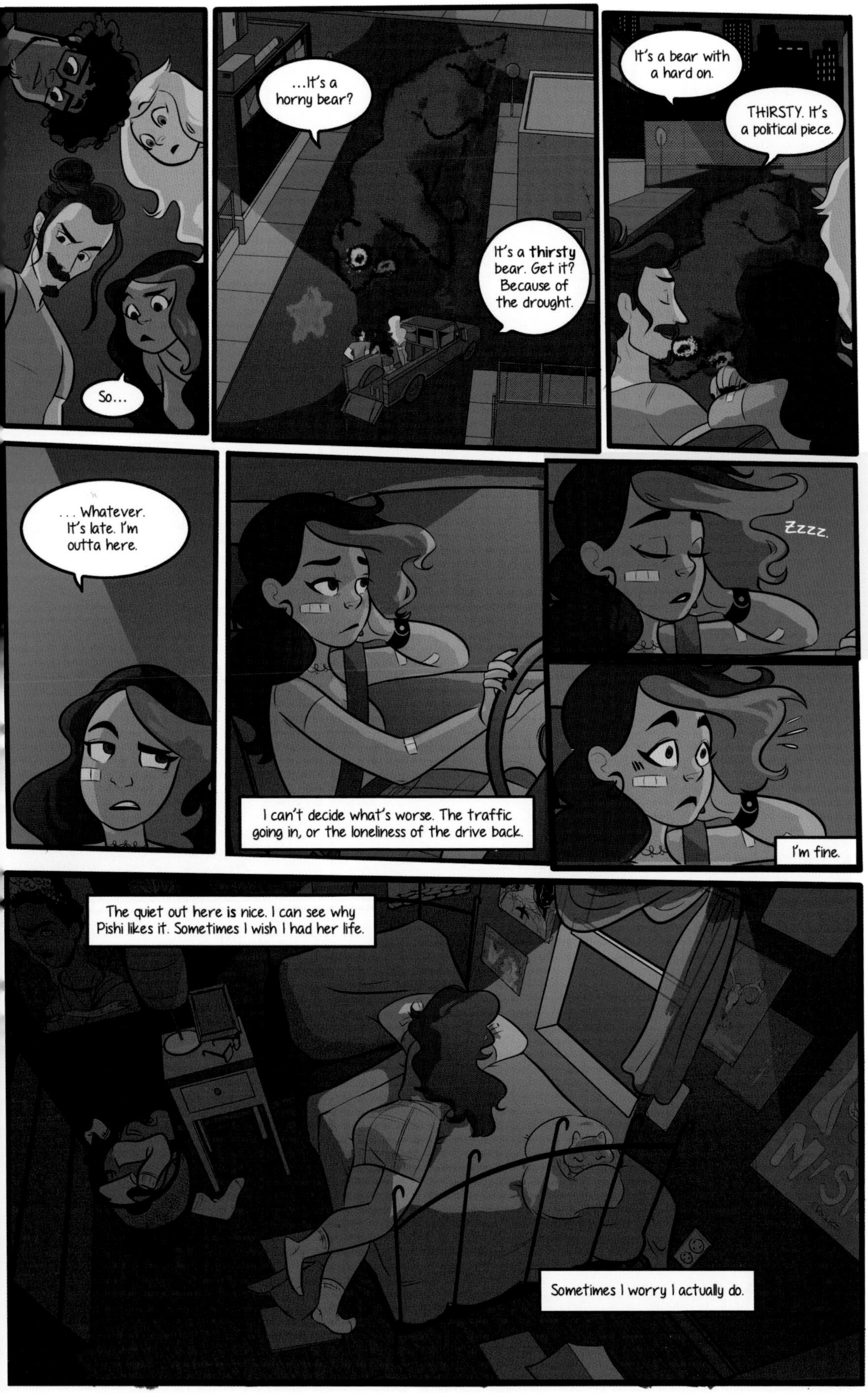
So...
...It's a horny bear?
It's a thirsty bear. Get it? Because of the drought.
It's a bear with a hard on.
THIRSTY. It's a political piece.
. . . Whatever. It's late. I'm outta here.
I can't decide what's worse. The traffic going in, or the loneliness of the drive back.
Zzzz.
I'm fine.
The quiet out here is nice. I can see why Pishi likes it. Sometimes I wish I had her life.
Sometimes I worry I actually do.

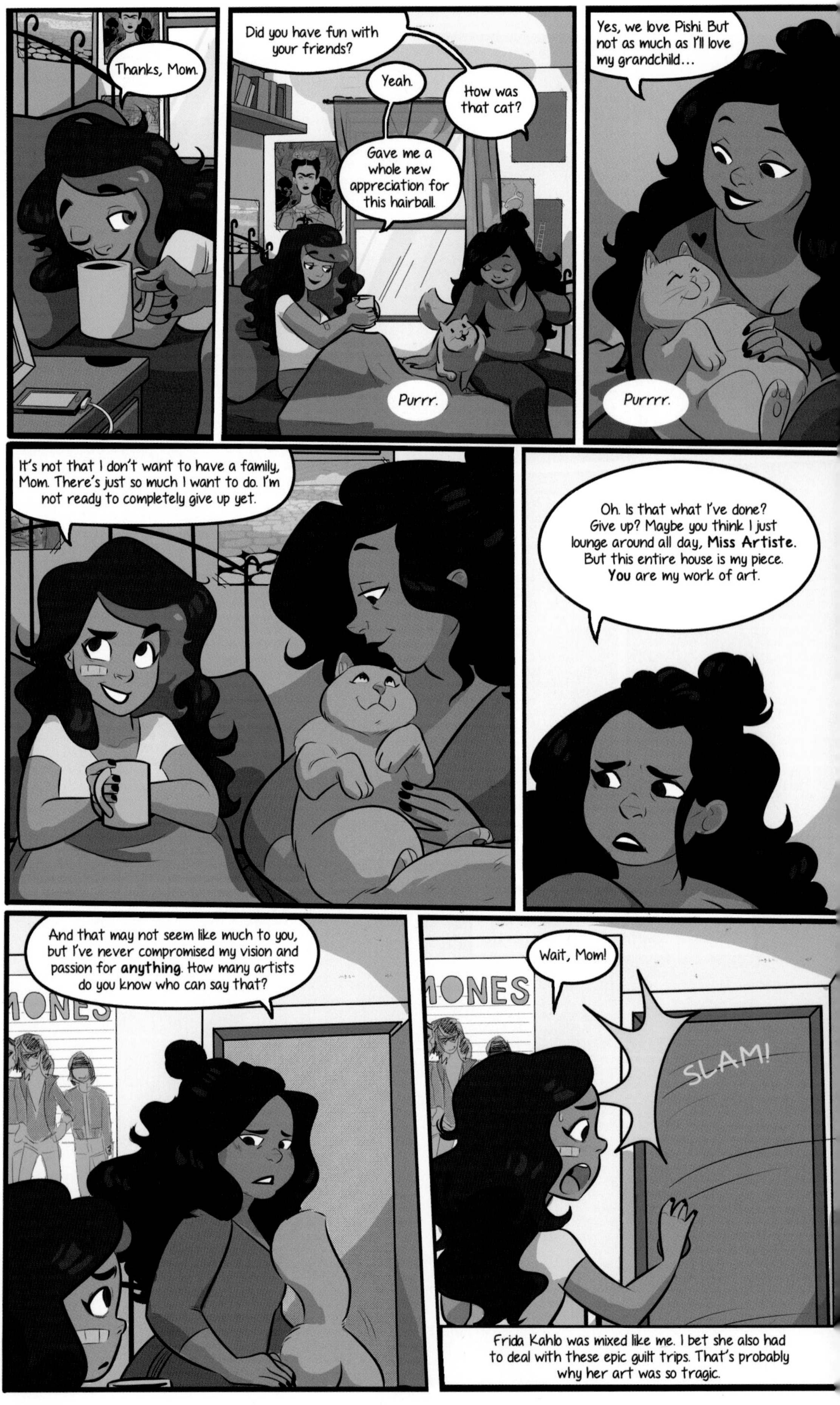

Thanks, Mom.
Did you have fun with your friends?
Yeah.
How was that cat?
Gave me a whole new appreciation for this hairball.
Purrr.
Yes, we love Pishi. But not as much as I'll love my grandchild...
Purrrr.
It's not that I don't want to have a family, Mom. There's just so much I want to do. I'm not ready to completely give up yet.
Oh. Is that what I've done? Give up? Maybe you think I just lounge around all day, Miss Artiste. But this entire house is my piece. You are my work of art.
And that may not seem like much to you, but I've never compromised my vision and passion for anything. How many artists do you know who can say that?
MONES
Wait, Mom!
MONES
SLAM!
Frida Kahlo was mixed like me. I bet she also had to deal with these epic guilt trips. That's probably why her art was so tragic.

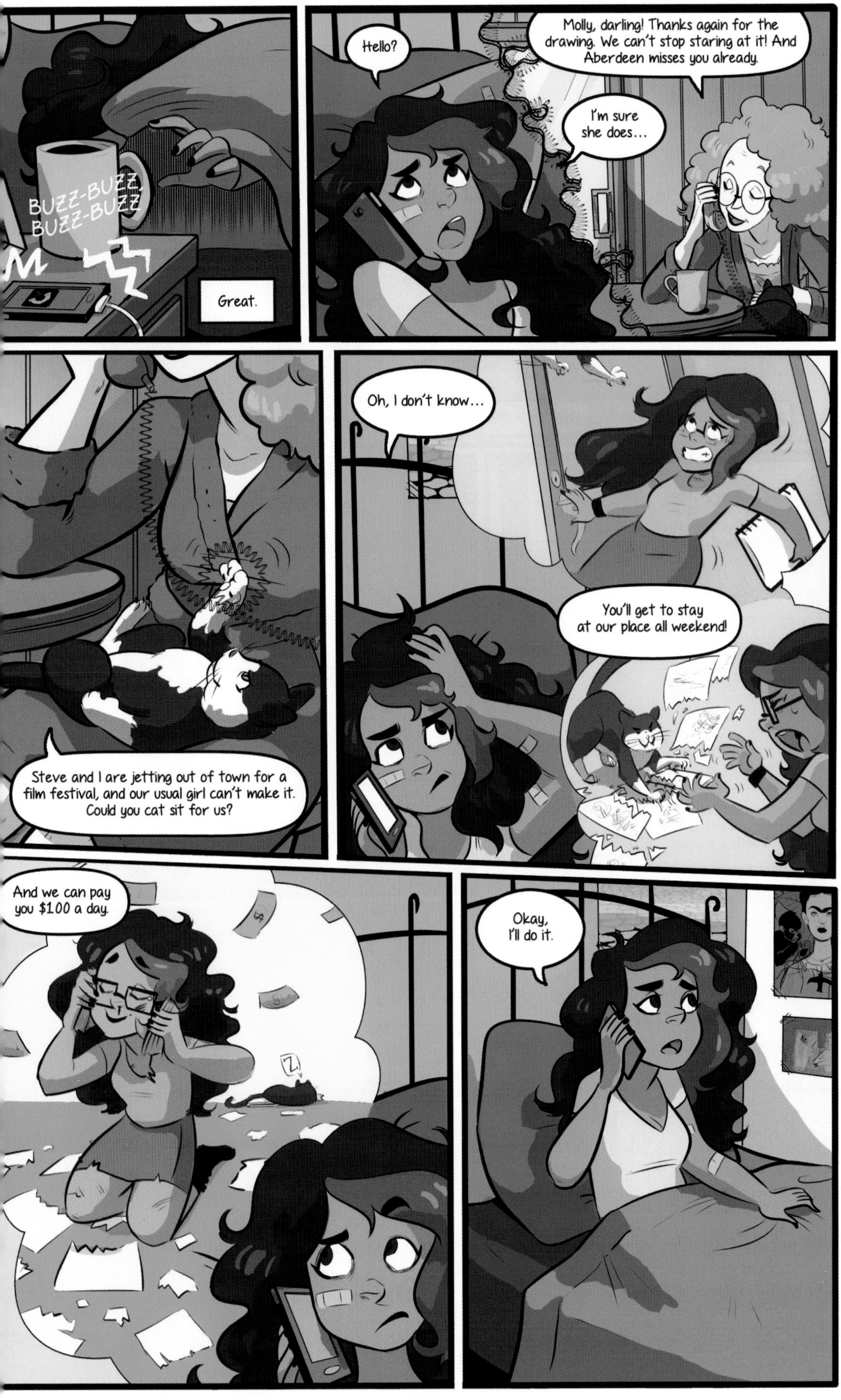
BUZZ-BUZZ, BUZZ-BUZZ
Great.
Hello?
Molly, darling! Thanks again for the drawing. We can't stop staring at it! And Aberdeen misses you already.
I'm sure she does...
Steve and I are jetting out of town for a film festival, and our usual girl can't make it. Could you cat sit for us?
Oh, I don't know...
You'll get to stay at our place all weekend!
And we can pay you $100 a day.
Okay, I'll do it.

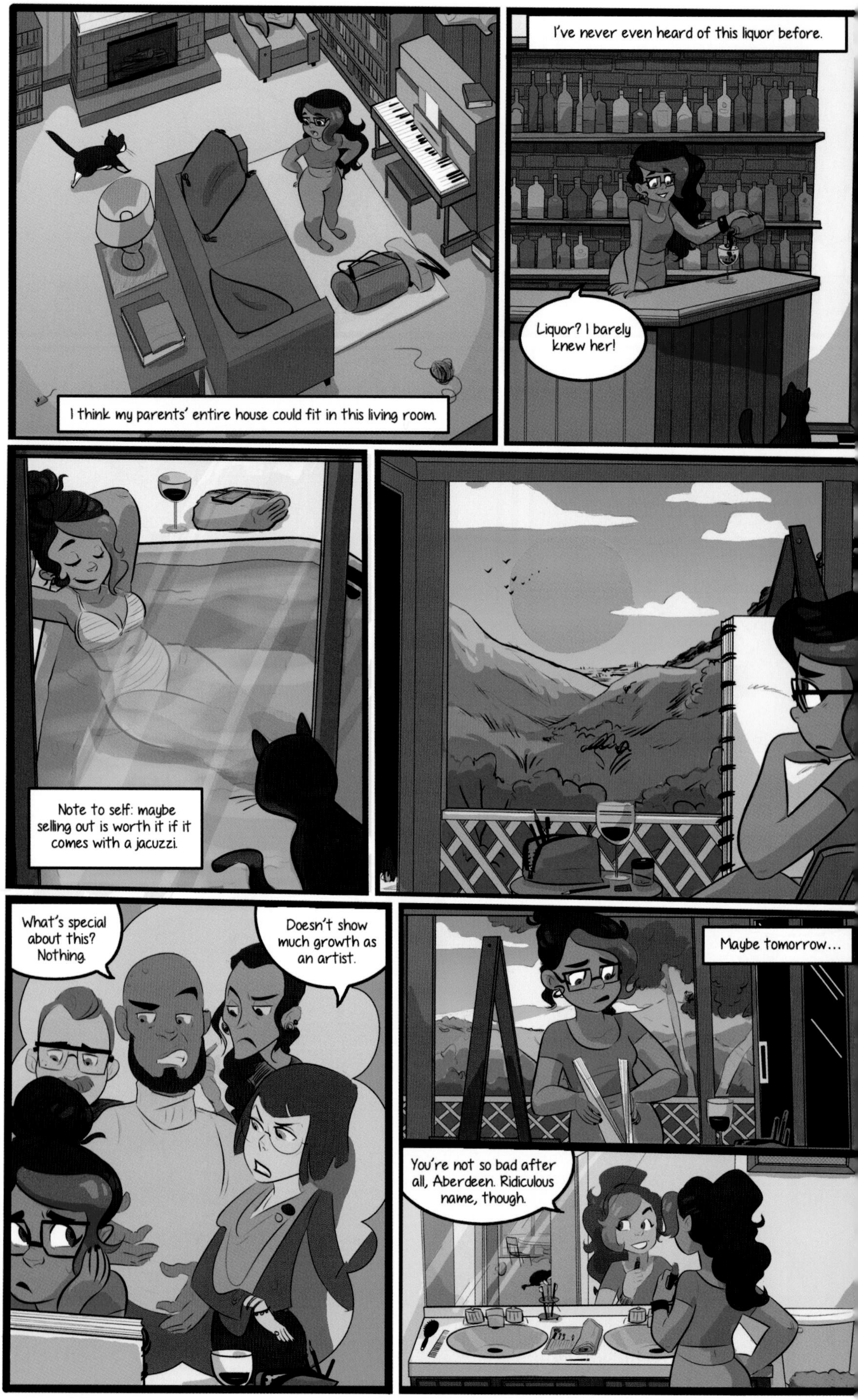
I think my parents' entire house could fit in this living room.
I've never even heard of this liquor before.
Liquor? I barely knew her!
Note to self: maybe selling out is worth it if it comes with a jacuzzi.
What's special about this? Nothing.
Doesn't show much growth as an artist.
Maybe tomorrow...
You're not so bad after all, Aberdeen. Ridiculous name, though.

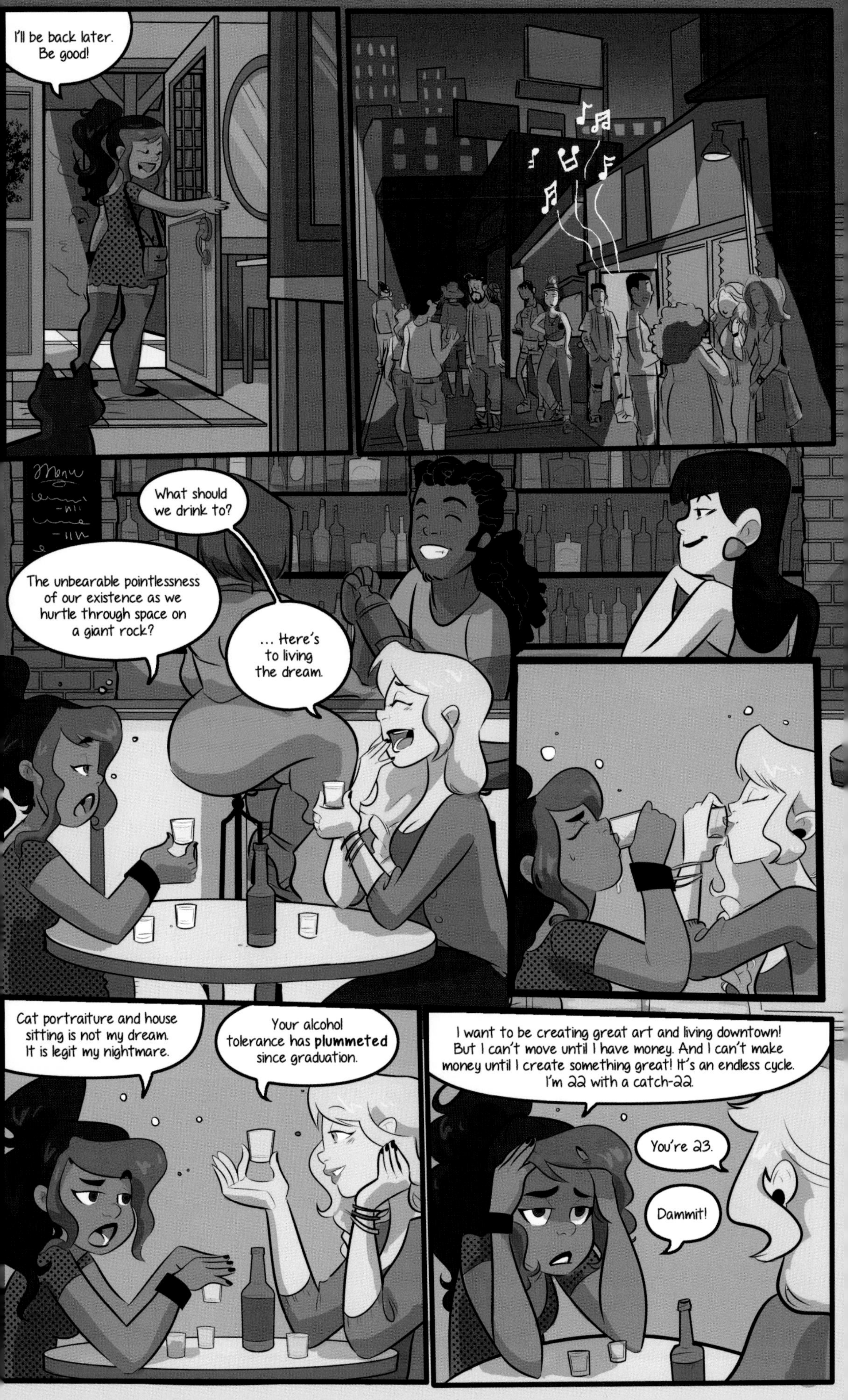
I'll be back later. Be good!
What should we drink to?
The unbearable pointlessness of our existence as we hurtle through space on a giant rock?
... Here's to living the dream.
Cat portraiture and house sitting is not my dream. It is legit my nightmare.
Your alcohol tolerance has **plummeted** since graduation.
I want to be creating great art and living downtown! But I can't move until I have money. And I can't make money until I create something great! It's an endless cycle. I'm 22 with a catch-22.
You're 23.
Dammit!

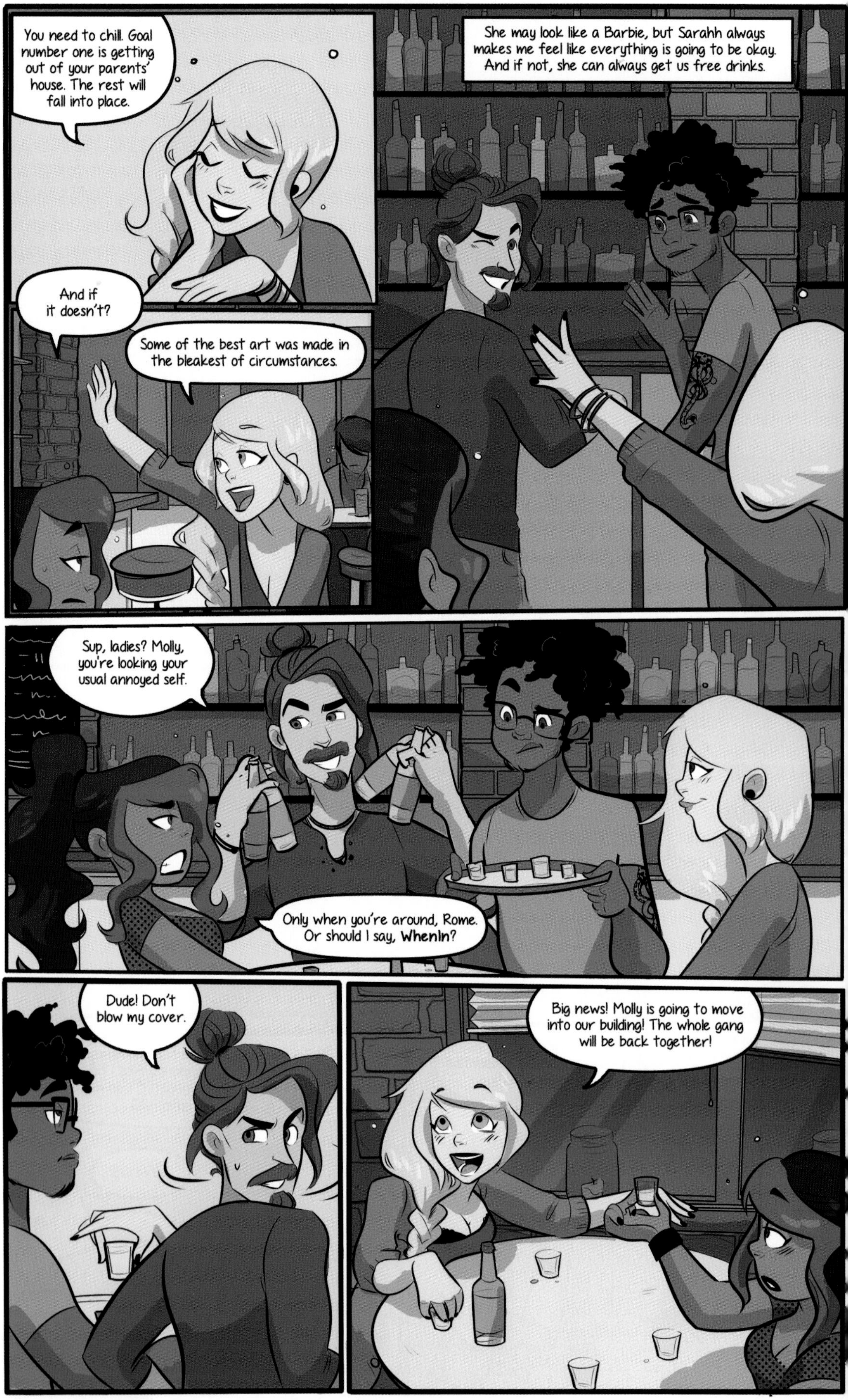
You need to chill. Goal number one is getting out of your parents' house. The rest will fall into place.
And if it doesn't?
Some of the best art was made in the bleakest of circumstances.
She may look like a Barbie, but Sarahh always makes me feel like everything is going to be okay. And if not, she can always get us free drinks.
Sup, ladies? Molly, you're looking your usual annoyed self.
Only when you're around, Rome. Or should I say, **WhenIn**?
Dude! Don't blow my cover.
Big news! Molly is going to move into our building! The whole gang will be back together!

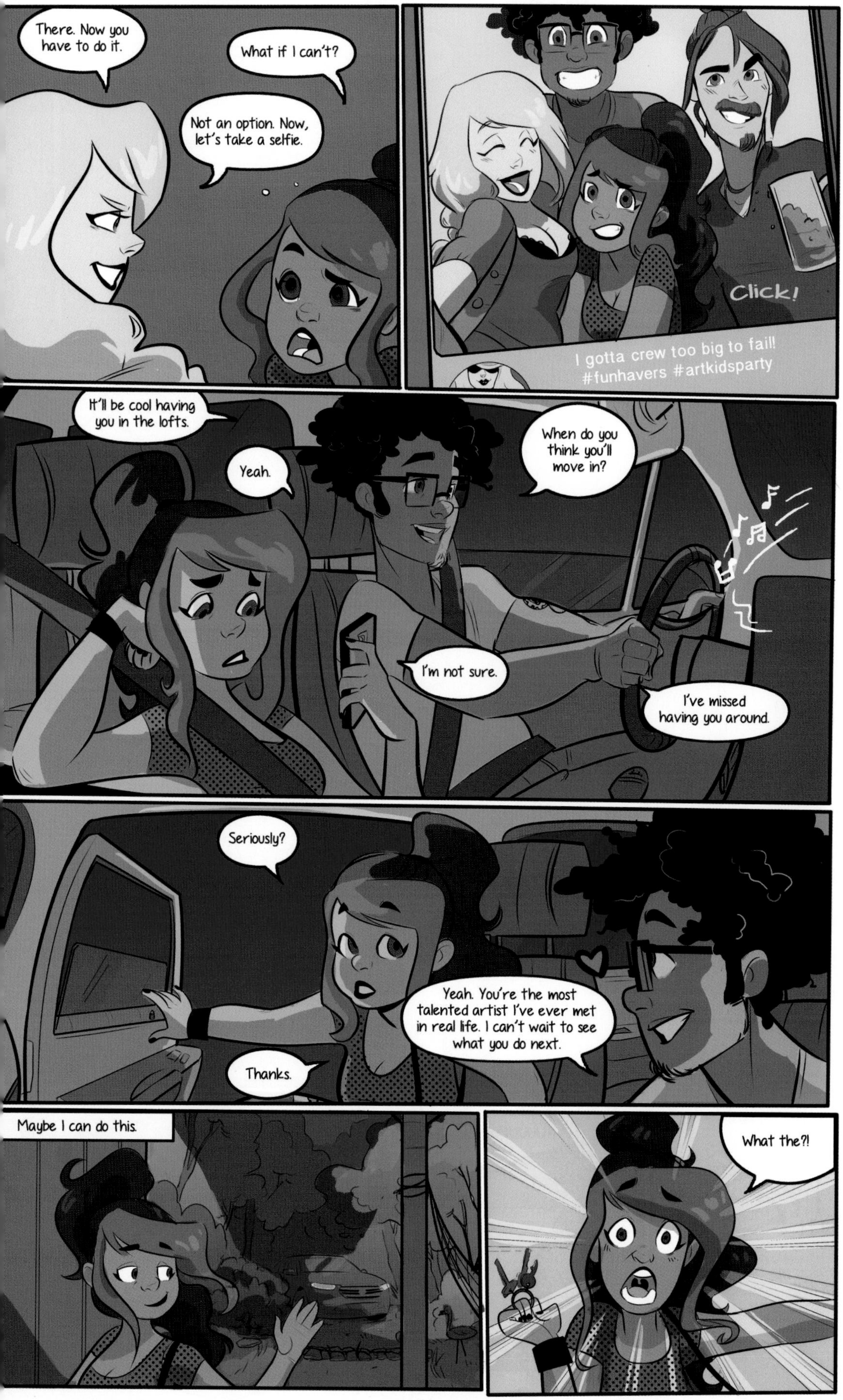
There. Now you have to do it.
What if I can't?
Not an option. Now, let's take a selfie.
Click!
I gotta crew too big to fail! #funhavers #artkidsparty
It'll be cool having you in the lofts.
Yeah.
When do you think you'll move in?
I'm not sure.
I've missed having you around.
Seriously?
Yeah. You're the most talented artist I've ever met in real life. I can't wait to see what you do next.
Thanks.
Maybe I can do this.
What the?!

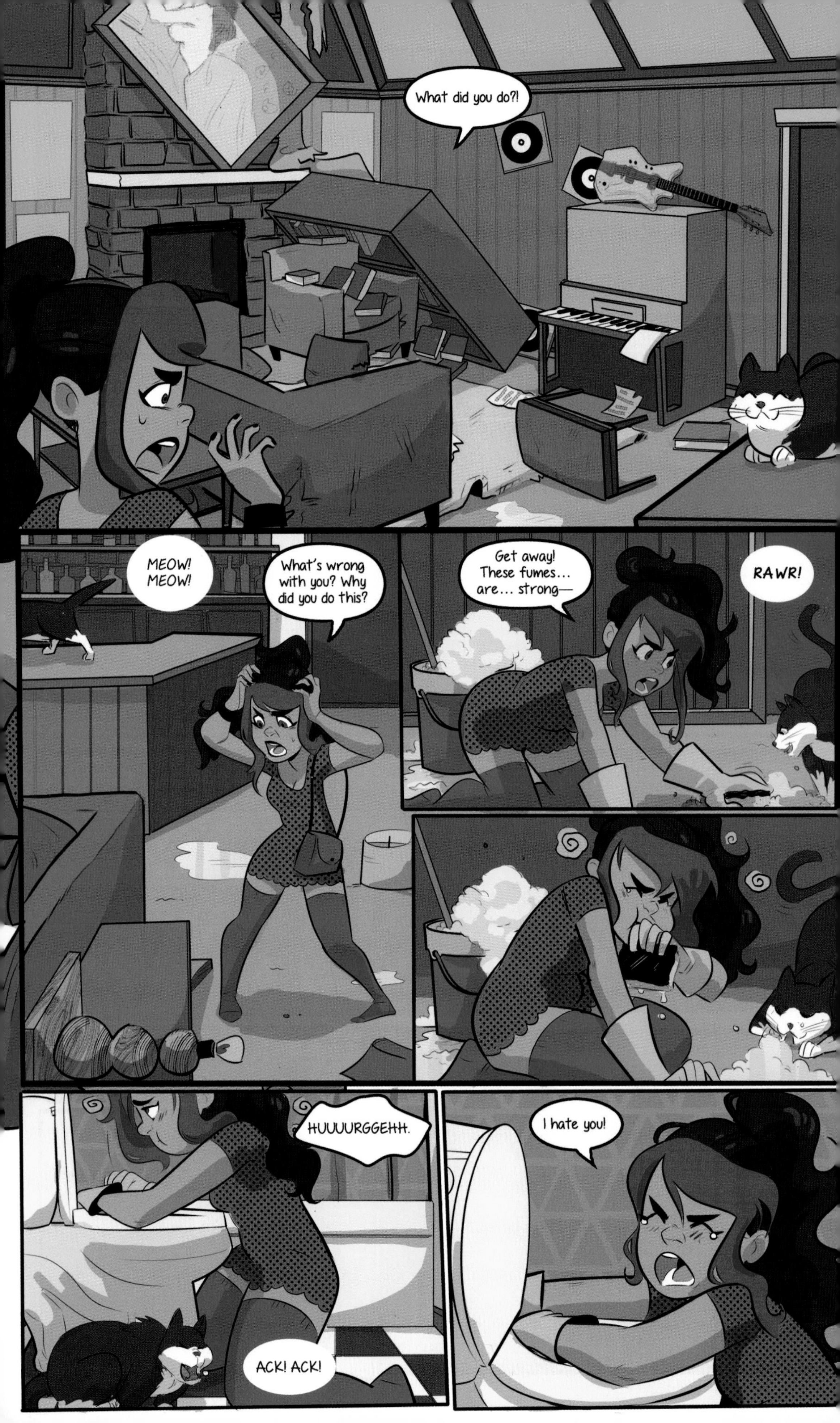
What did you do?!
MEOW! MEOW!
What's wrong with you? Why did you do this?
Get away! These fumes... are... strong—
RAWR!
HUUUURGGEHH.
ACK! ACK!
I hate you!

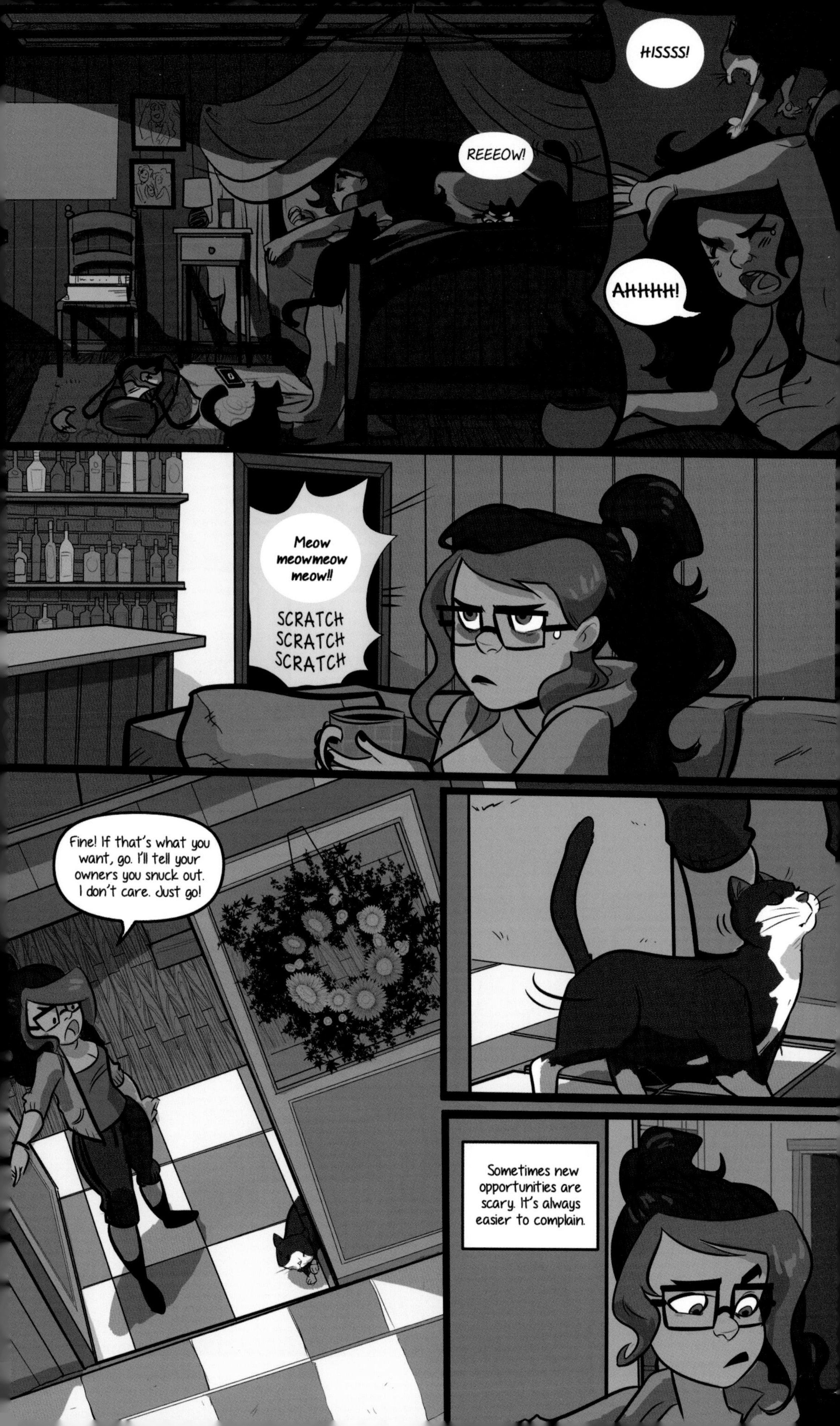
HISSSS!
REEEOW!
AHHHHH!
Meow meowmeow meow!!
SCRATCH SCRATCH SCRATCH
Fine! If that's what you want, go. I'll tell your owners you snuck out. I don't care. Just go!
Sometimes new opportunities are scary. It's always easier to complain.

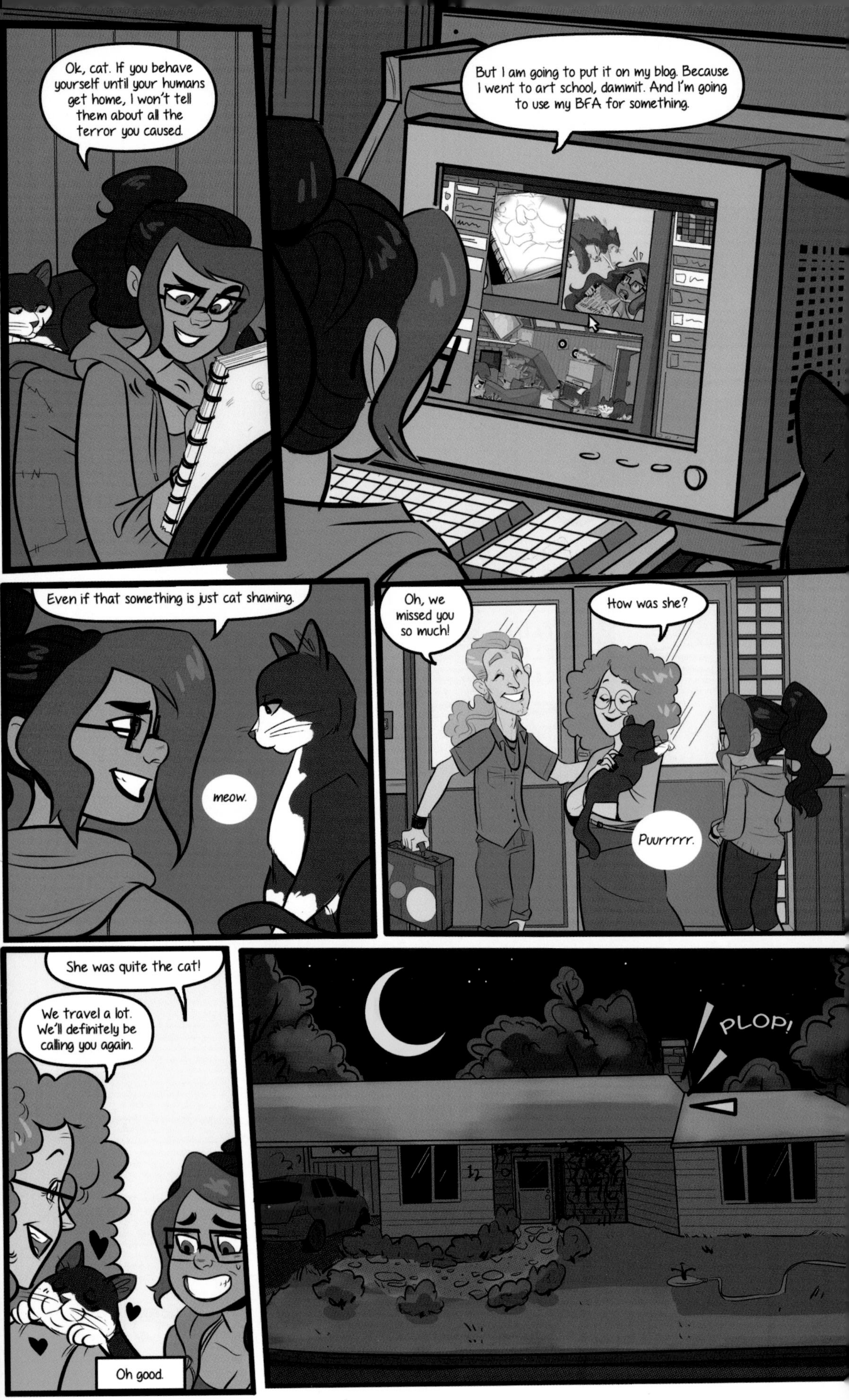
Ok, cat. If you behave yourself until your humans get home, I won't tell them about all the terror you caused.
But I am going to put it on my blog. Because I went to art school, dammit. And I'm going to use my BFA for something.
Even if that something is just cat shaming.
meow.
Oh, we missed you so much!
How was she?
Puurrrrr.
She was quite the cat!
We travel a lot. We'll definitely be calling you again.
Oh good.
PLOP!

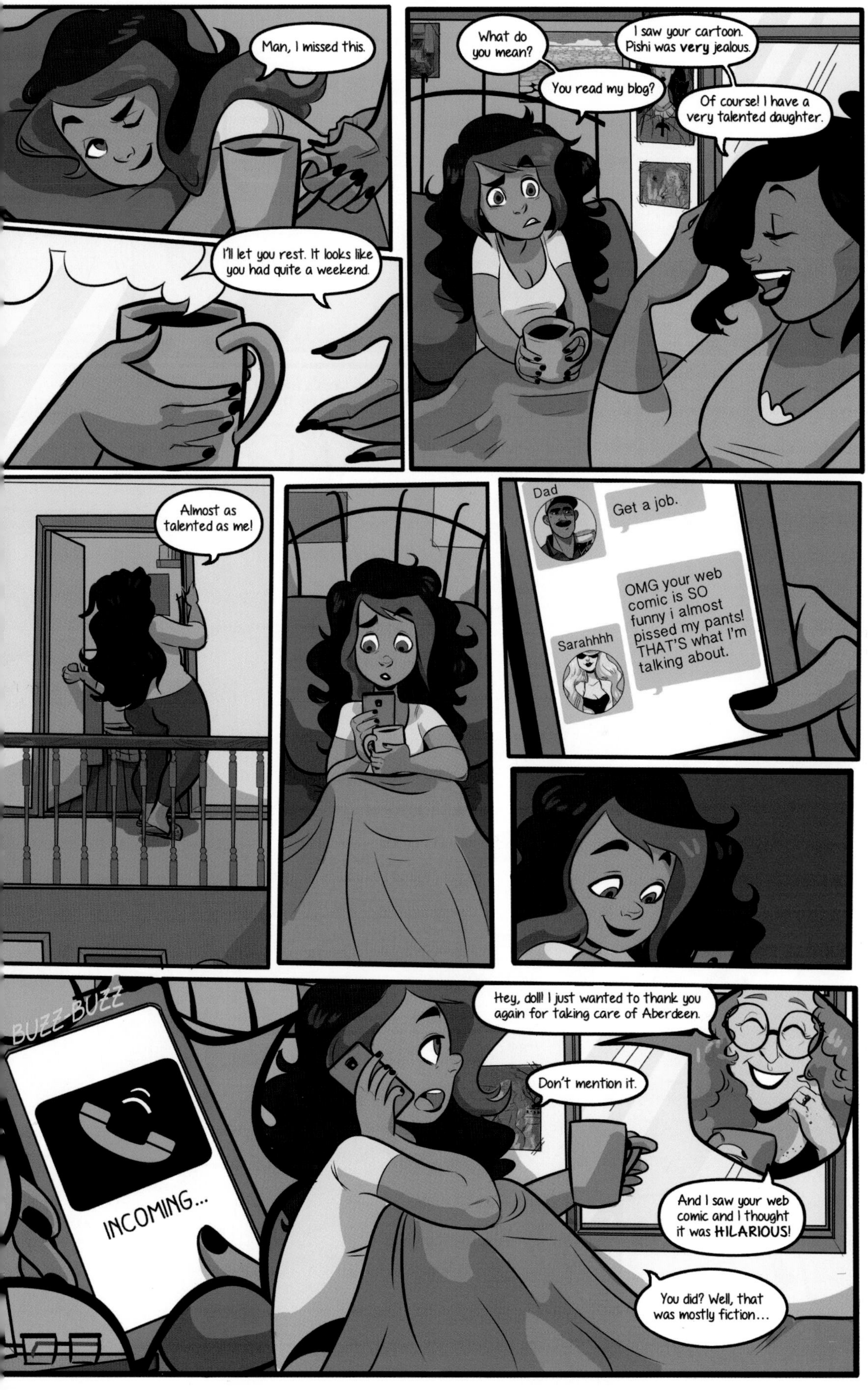
Man, I missed this.
I'll let you rest. It looks like you had quite a weekend.
What do you mean?
I saw your cartoon. Pishi was very jealous.
You read my blog?
Of course! I have a very talented daughter.
Almost as talented as me!
Dad
Get a job.
Sarahhhh
OMG your web comic is SO funny i almost pissed my pants! THAT'S what I'm talking about.
BUZZ-BUZZ
INCOMING...
Hey, doll! I just wanted to thank you again for taking care of Aberdeen.
Don't mention it.
And I saw your web comic and I thought it was HILARIOUS!
You did? Well, that was mostly fiction...

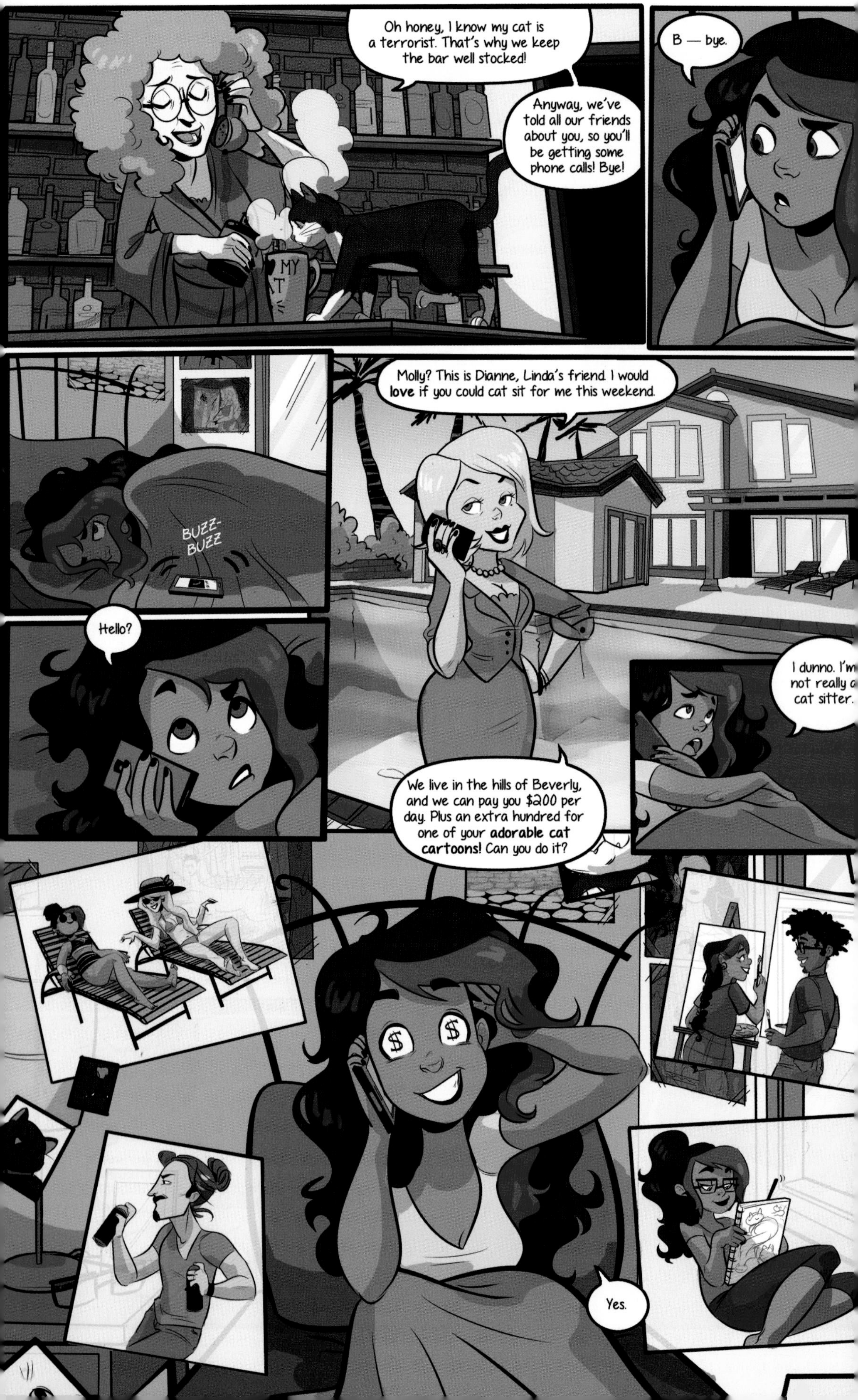

Oh honey, I know my cat is a terrorist. That's why we keep the bar well stocked!
Anyway, we've told all our friends about you, so you'll be getting some phone calls! Bye!
B — bye.
BUZZ-BUZZ
Molly? This is Dianne, Linda's friend. I would **love** if you could cat sit for me this weekend.
Hello?
I dunno. I'm not really a cat sitter.
We live in the hills of Beverly, and we can pay you $200 per day. Plus an extra hundred for one of your **adorable cat cartoons!** Can you do it?
Yes.

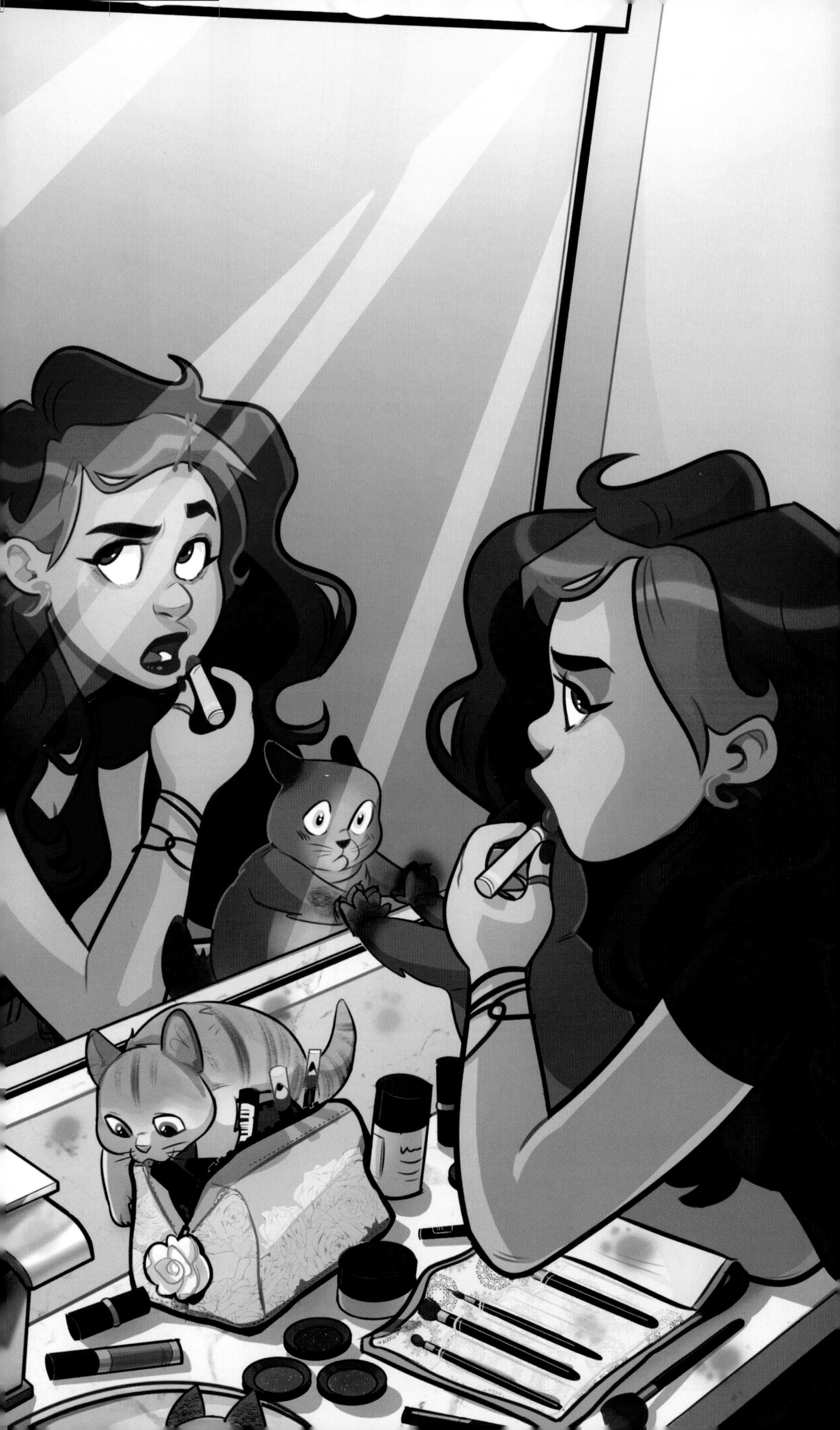

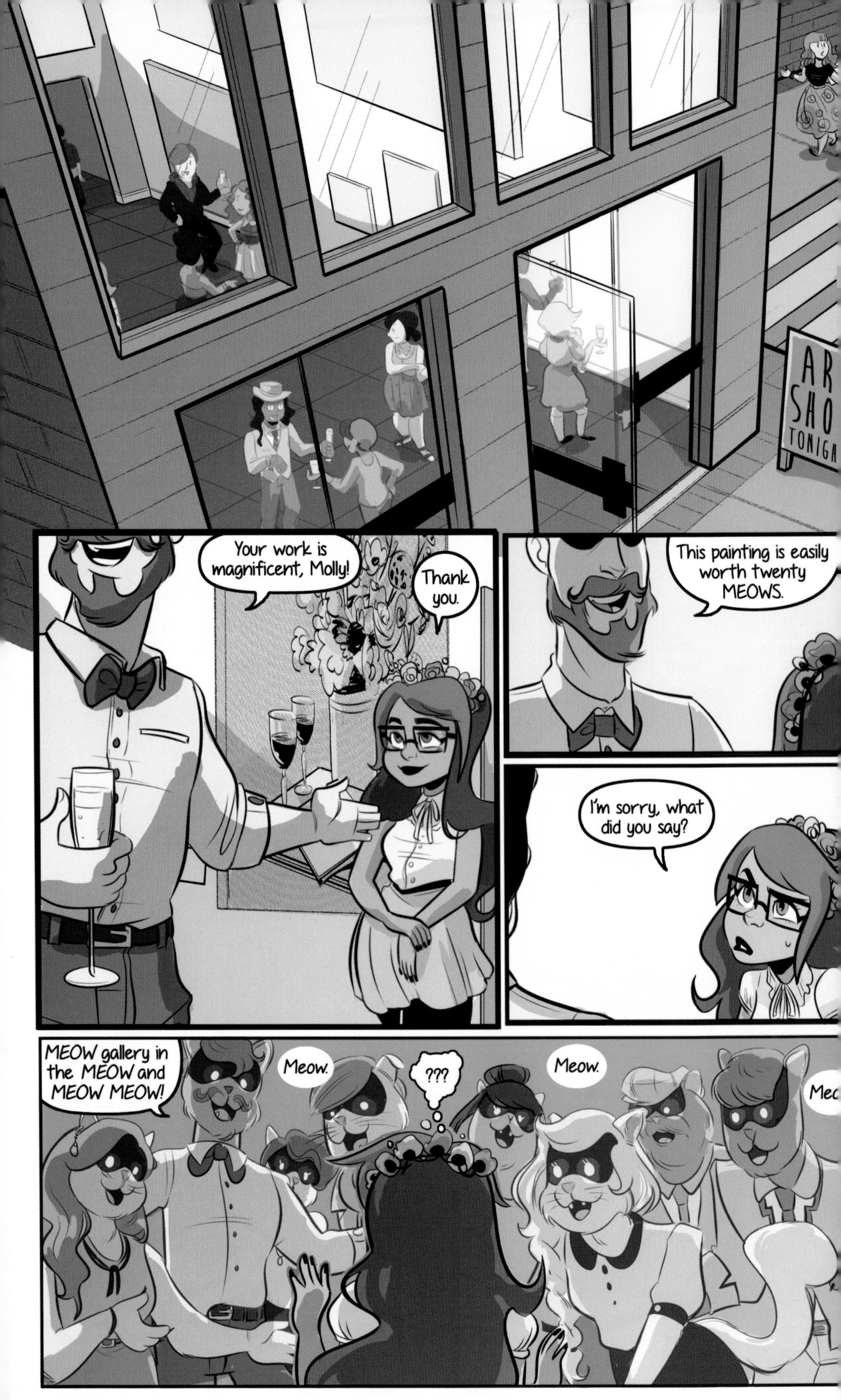
AR
SHO
TONIGH
Your work is magnificent, Molly!
Thank you.
This painting is easily worth twenty MEOWS.
I'm sorry, what did you say?
MEOW gallery in the MEOW and MEOW MEOW!
Meow.
???
Meow.

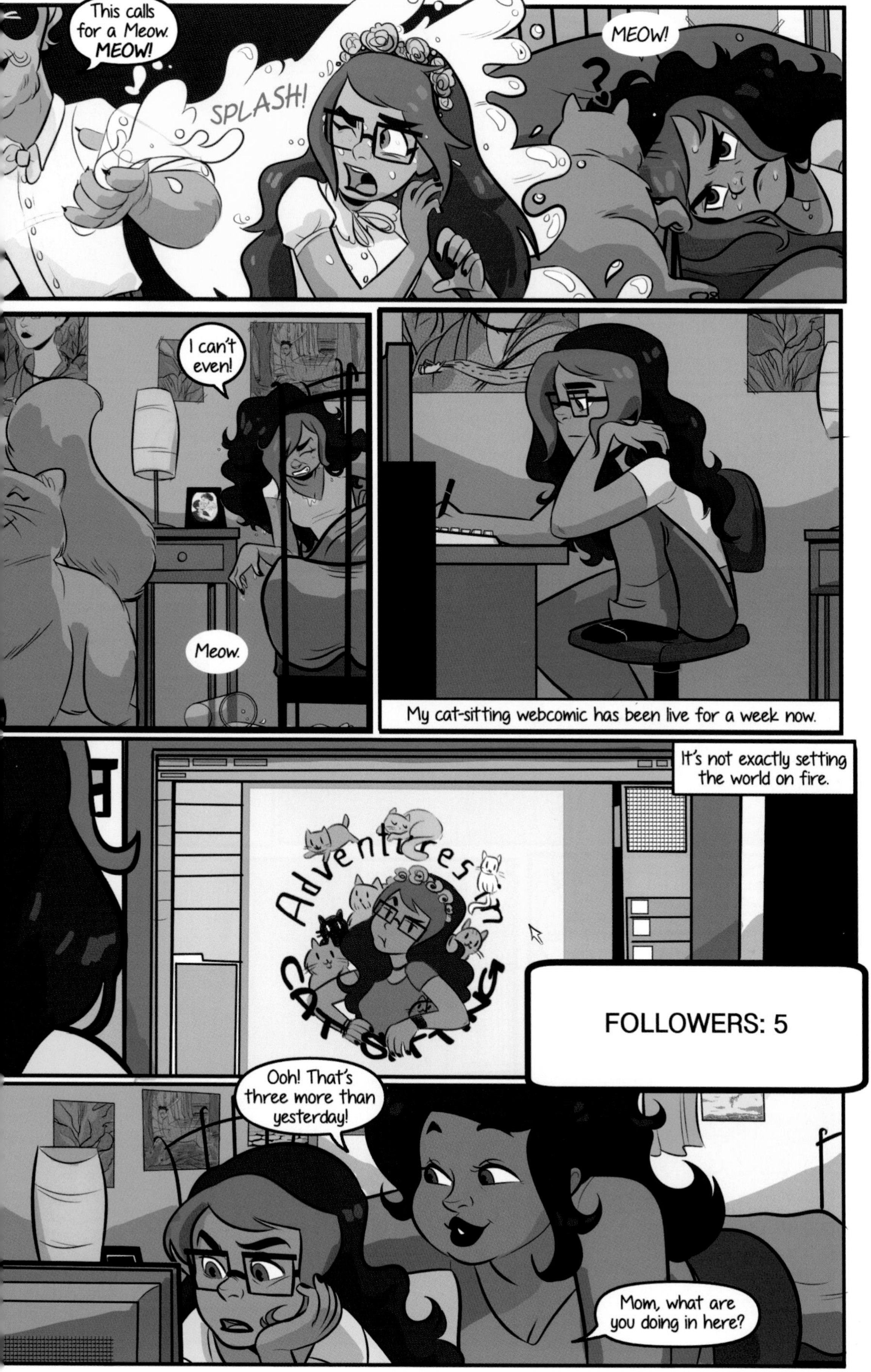

This calls for a Meow. MEOW!
SPLASH!
MEOW!
I can't even!
Meow.
My cat-sitting webcomic has been live for a week now.
It's not exactly setting the world on fire.
Adventures in Cat-Sitting
FOLLOWERS: 5
Ooh! That's three more than yesterday!
Mom, what are you doing in here?

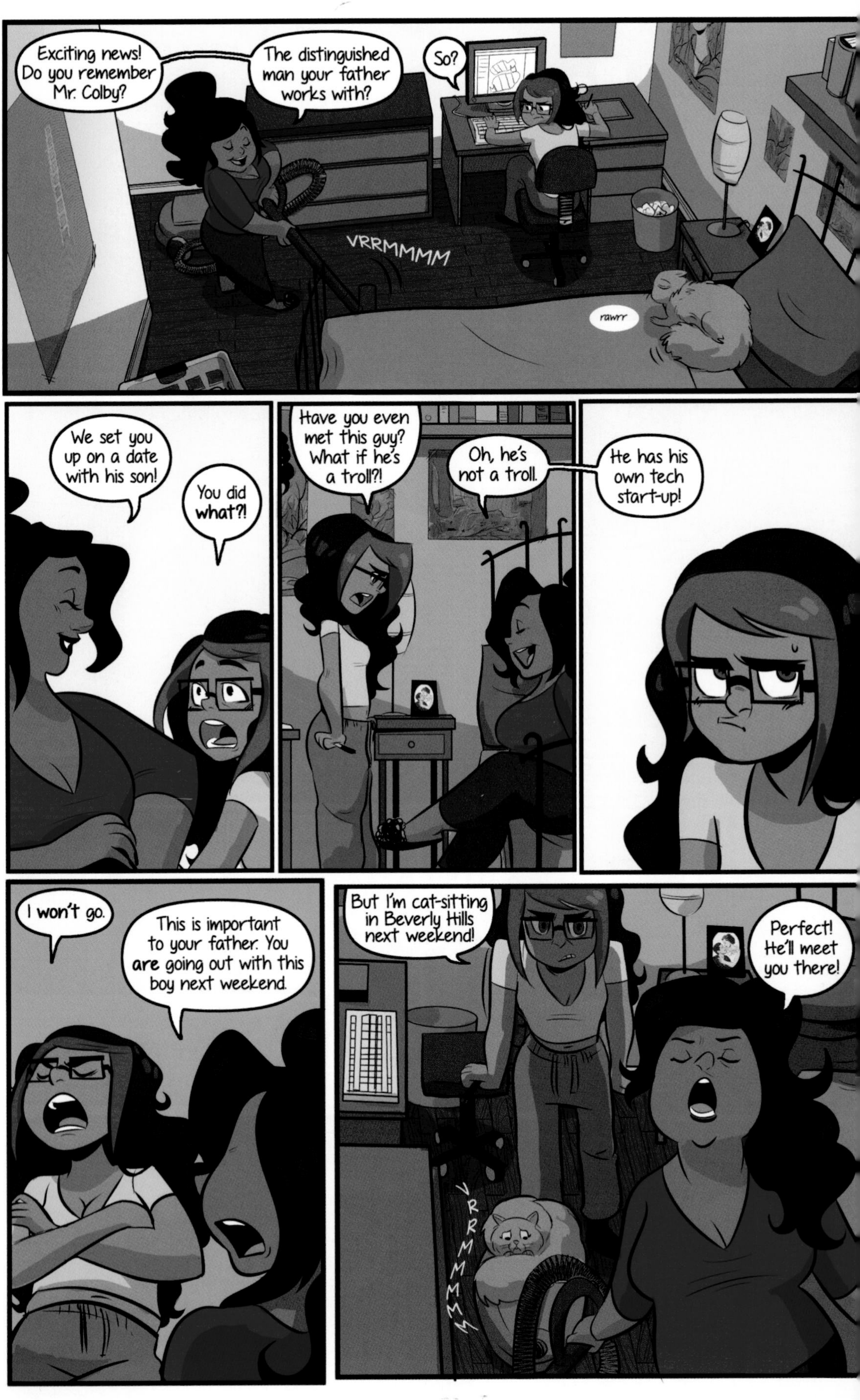
Exciting news! Do you remember Mr. Colby?
The distinguished man your father works with?
So?
VRRMMMM
rawrr
We set you up on a date with his son!
You did **what**?!
Have you even met this guy? What if he's a troll?!
Oh, he's not a troll.
He has his own tech start-up!
I **won't** go.
This is important to your father. You **are** going out with this boy next weekend.
But I'm cat-sitting in Beverly Hills next weekend!
Perfect! He'll meet you there!
VRRMMMM

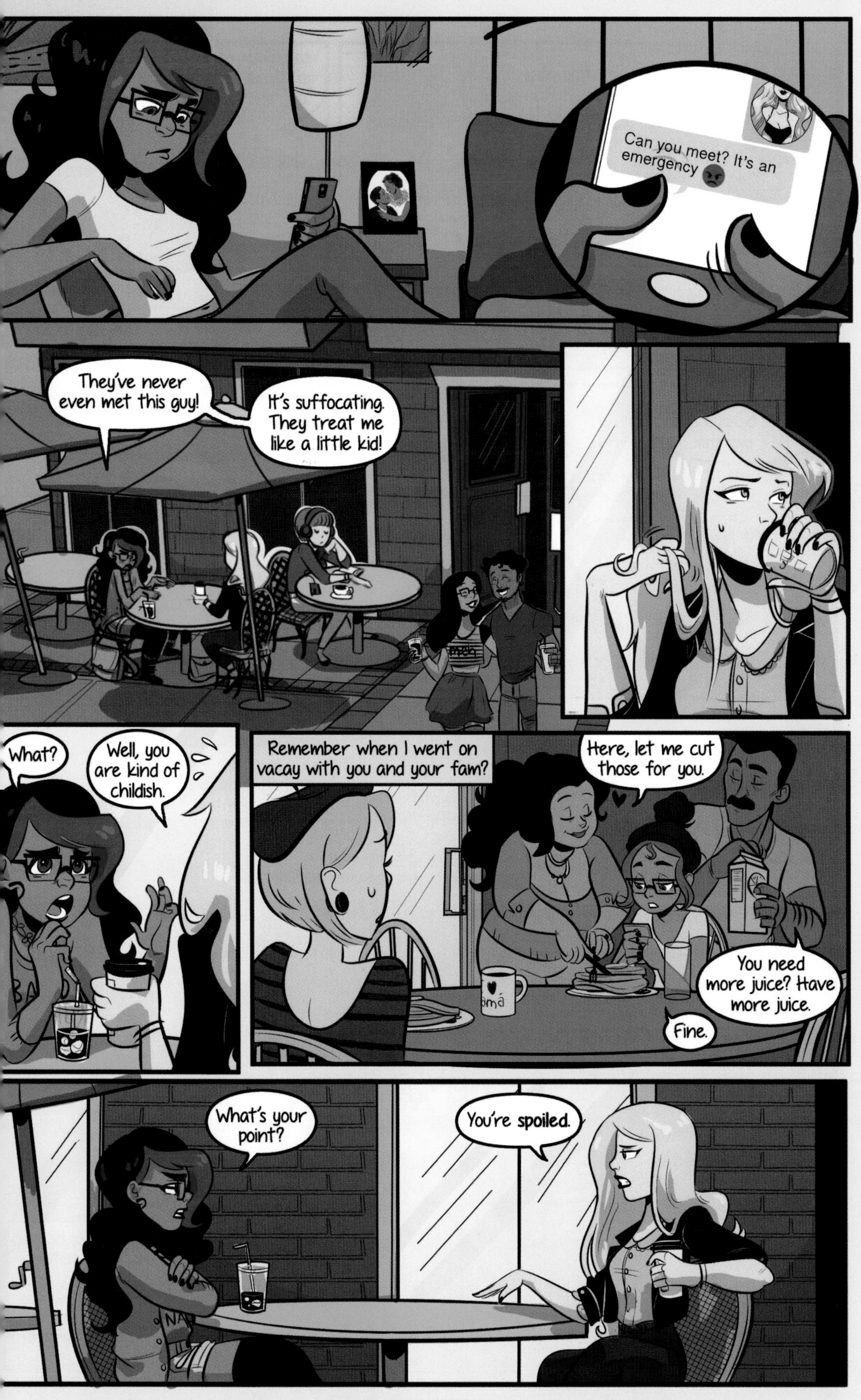

Can you meet? It's an emergency
They've never even met this guy!
It's suffocating. They treat me like a little kid!
What?
Well, you are kind of childish.
Remember when I went on vacay with you and your fam?
Here, let me cut those for you.
You need more juice? Have more juice.
Fine.
What's your point?
You're **spoiled**.

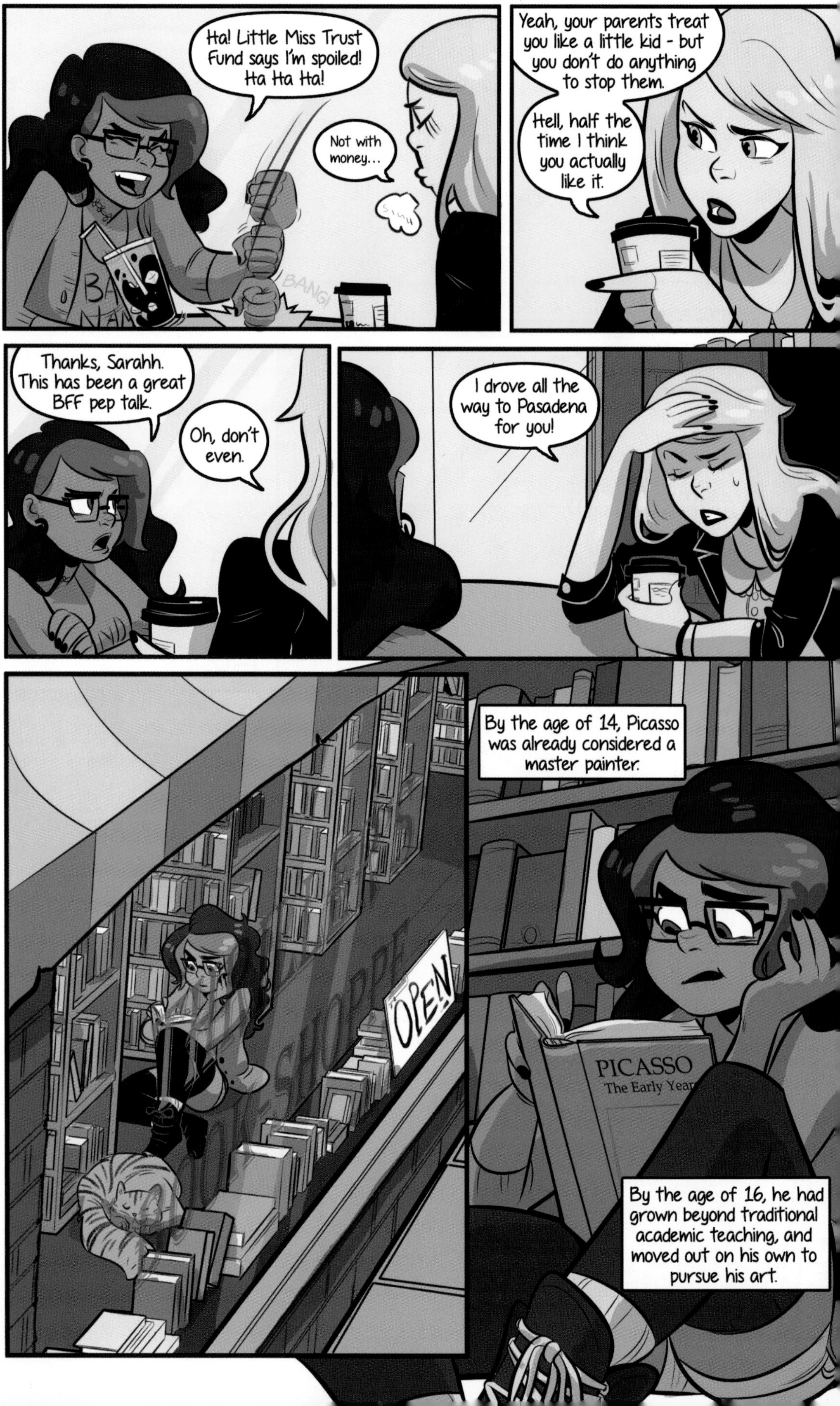

Ha! Little Miss Trust Fund says I'm spoiled! Ha Ha Ha!
Not with money...
BANG!
Yeah, your parents treat you like a little kid - but you don't do anything to stop them.
Hell, half the time I think you actually like it.
Thanks, Sarahh. This has been a great BFF pep talk.
Oh, don't even.
I drove all the way to Pasadena for you!
By the age of 14, Picasso was already considered a master painter.
OPEN
PICASSO
By the age of 16, he had grown beyond traditional academic teaching, and moved out on his own to pursue his art.

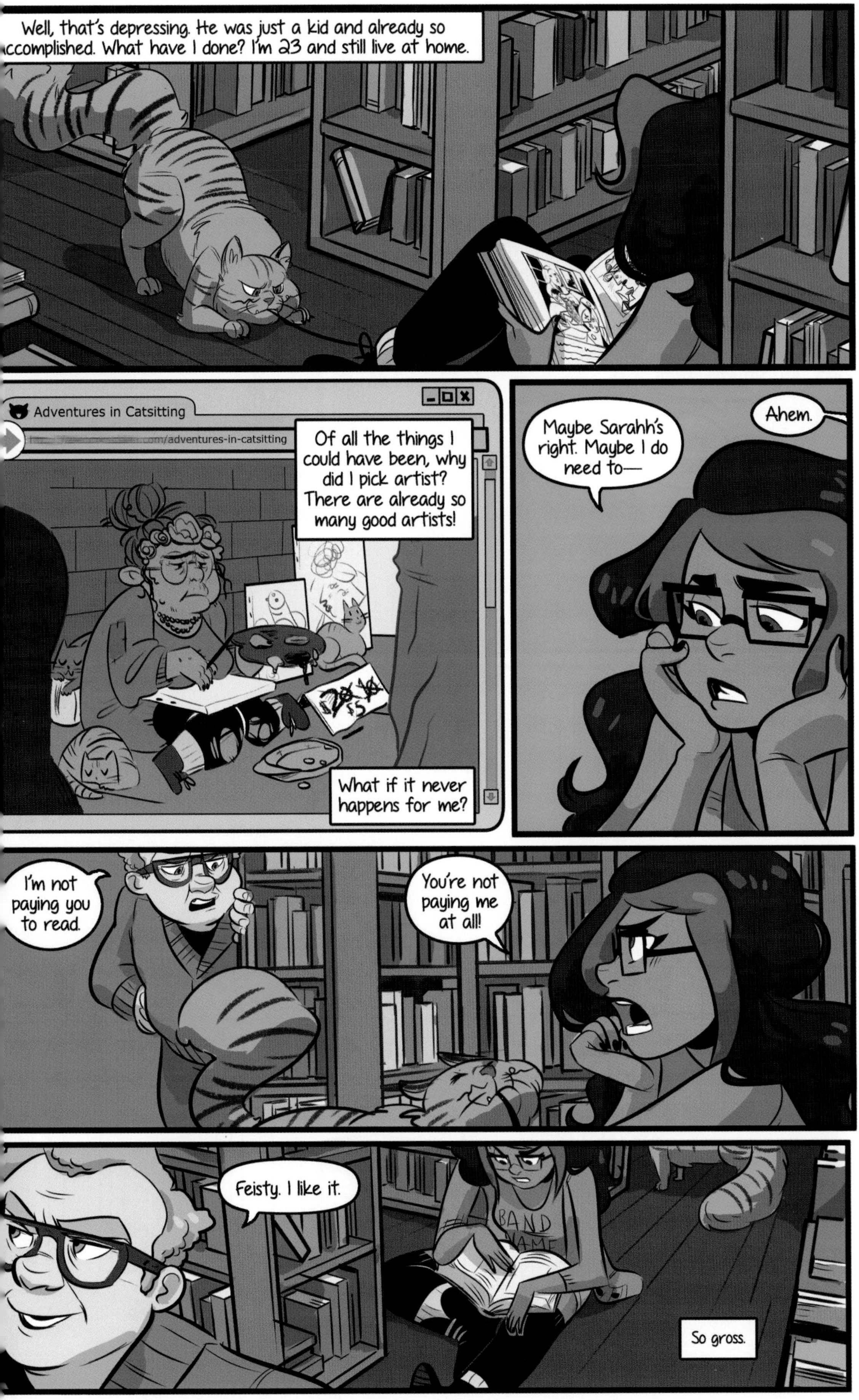
Well, that's depressing. He was just a kid and already so accomplished. What have I done? I'm 23 and still live at home.
Adventures in Catsitting
.com/adventures-in-catsitting
Of all the things I could have been, why did I pick artist? There are already so many good artists!
What if it never happens for me?
Maybe Sarahh's right. Maybe I do need to—
Ahem.
I'm not paying you to read.
You're not paying me at all!
Feisty. I like it.
BAND NAME
So gross.

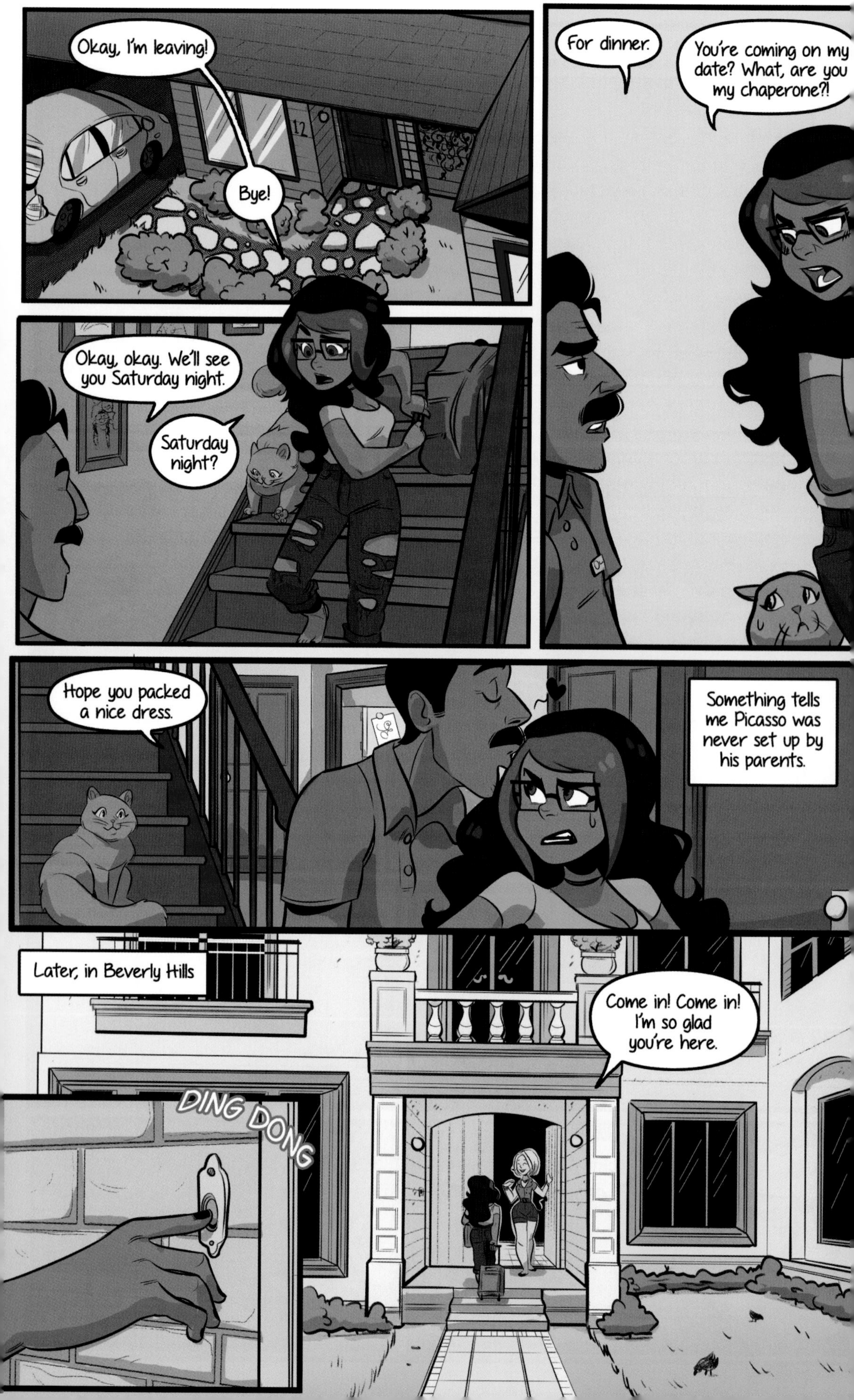

Okay, I'm leaving!
Bye!
Okay, okay. We'll see you Saturday night.
Saturday night?
For dinner.
You're coming on my date? What, are you my chaperone?!
Hope you packed a nice dress.
Something tells me Picasso was never set up by his parents.
Later, in Beverly Hills
DING DONG
Come in! Come in! I'm so glad you're here.

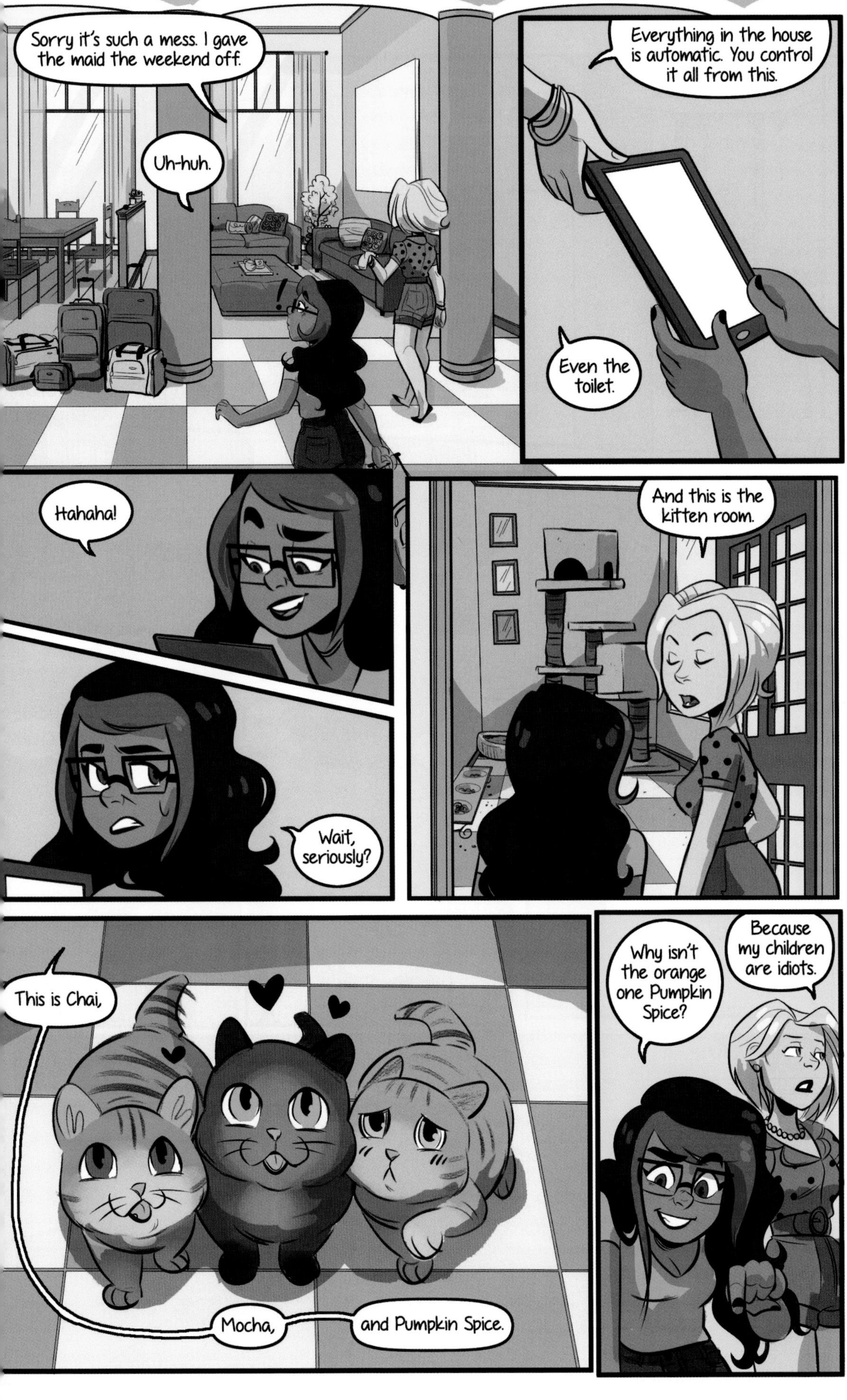
Sorry it's such a mess. I gave the maid the weekend off.
Uh-huh.
Everything in the house is automatic. You control it all from this.
Even the toilet.
Hahaha!
Wait, seriously?
And this is the kitten room.
This is Chai,
Mocha,
and Pumpkin Spice.
Why isn't the orange one Pumpkin Spice?
Because my children are idiots.

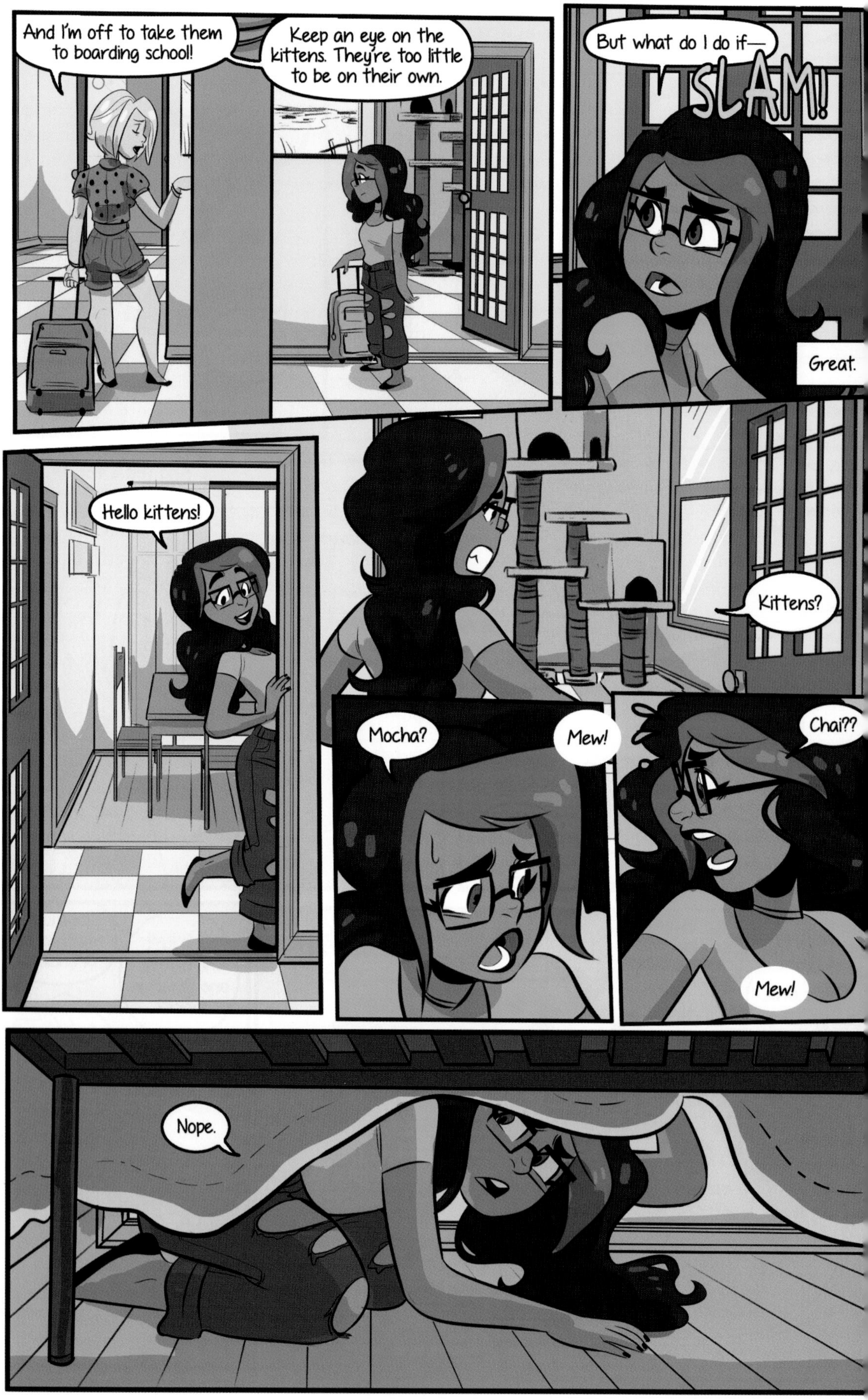
And I'm off to take them to boarding school!
Keep an eye on the kittens. They're too little to be on their own.
But what do I do if—
SLAM!
Great.
Hello kittens!
Kittens?
Mocha?
Mew!
Chai??
Mew!
Nope.

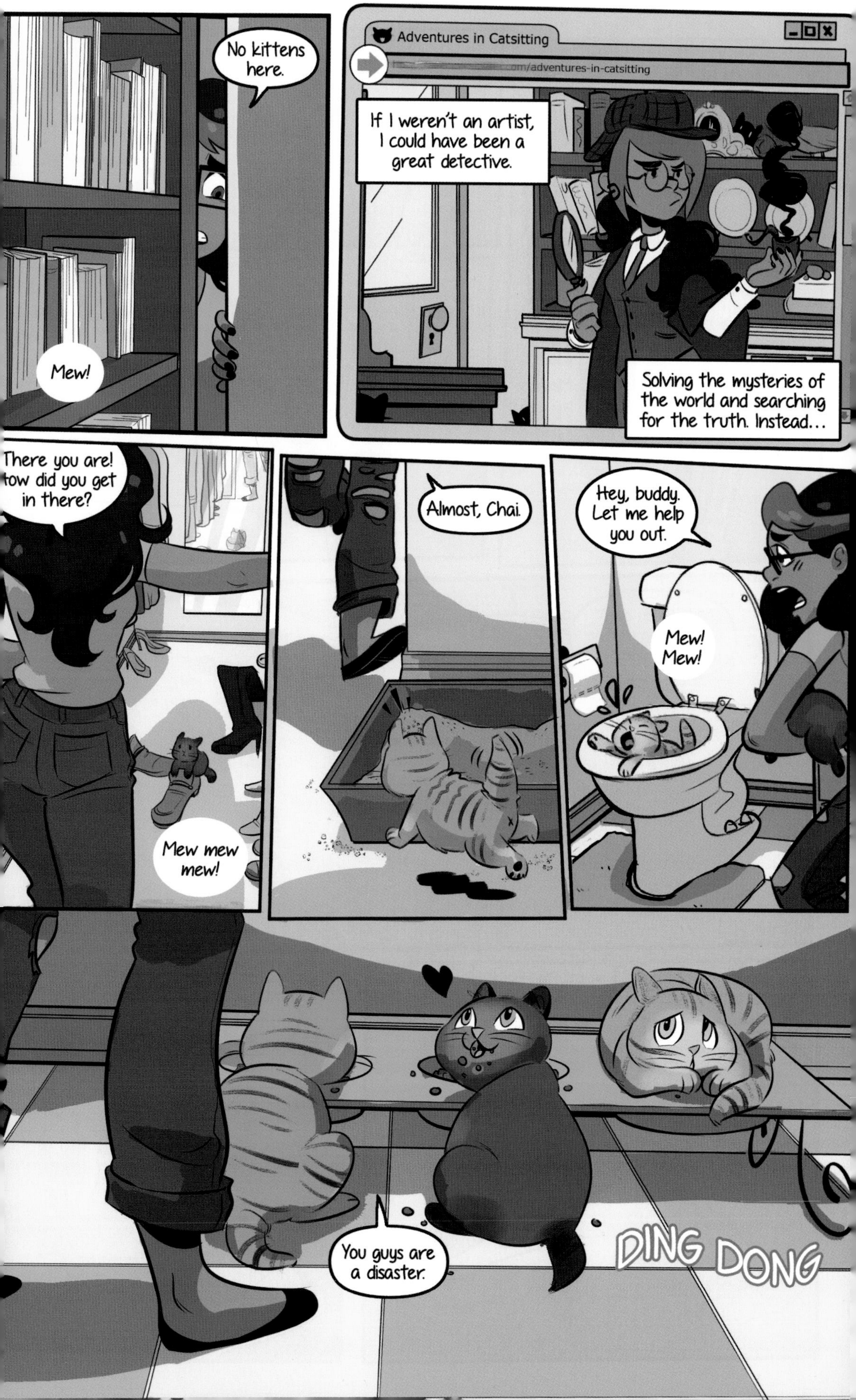

No kittens here.
Mew!
Adventures in Catsitting
com/adventures-in-catsitting
If I weren't an artist, I could have been a great detective.
Solving the mysteries of the world and searching for the truth. Instead...
There you are! ow did you get in there?
Mew mew mew!
Almost, Chai.
Hey, buddy. Let me help you out.
Mew! Mew!
You guys are a disaster.
DING DONG

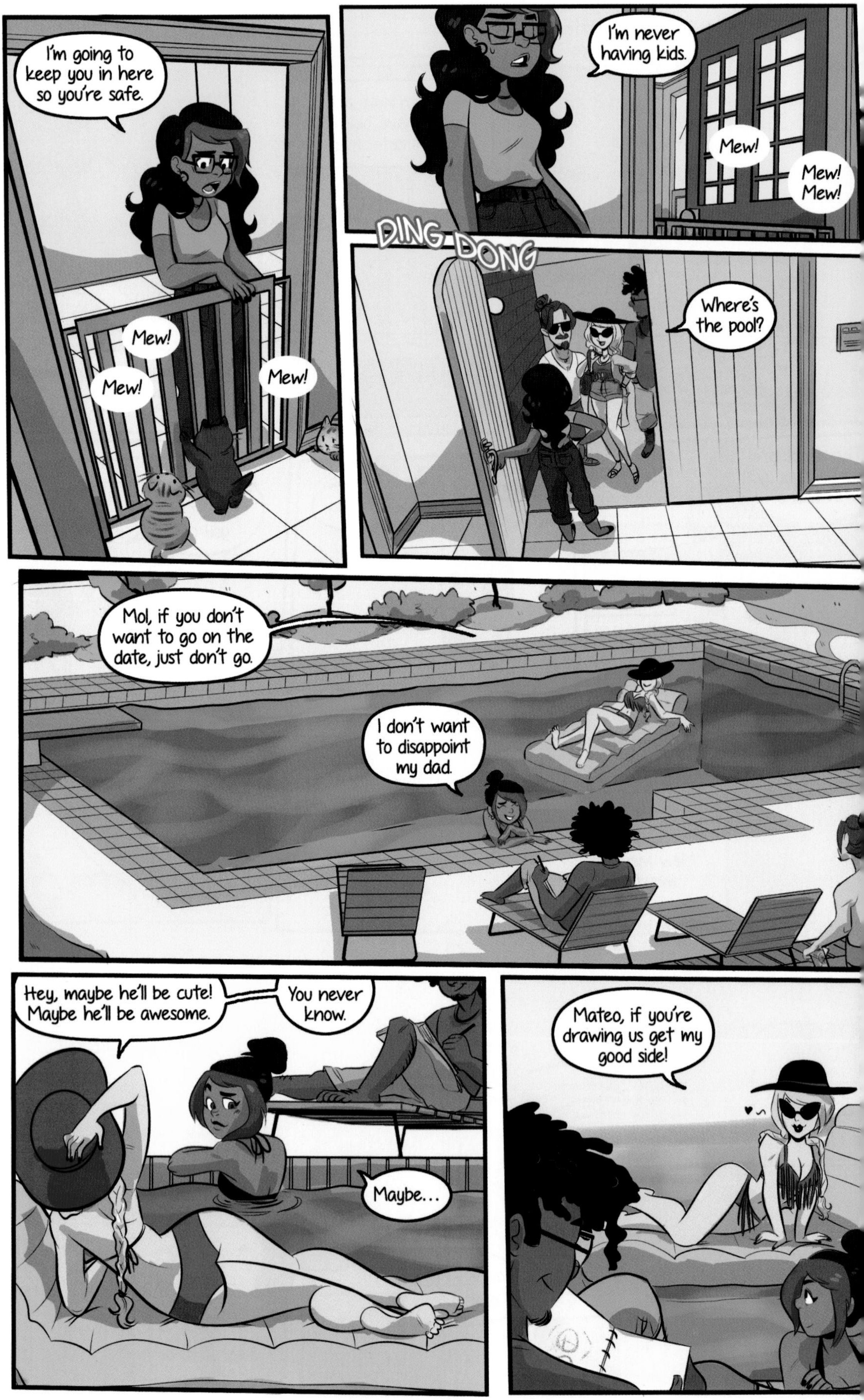
I'm going to keep you in here so you're safe.
Mew!
Mew!
Mew!
I'm never having kids.
Mew!
Mew! Mew!
DING DONG
Where's the pool?
Mol, if you don't want to go on the date, just don't go.
I don't want to disappoint my dad.
Hey, maybe he'll be cute! Maybe he'll be awesome.
You never know.
Maybe...
Mateo, if you're drawing us get my good side!

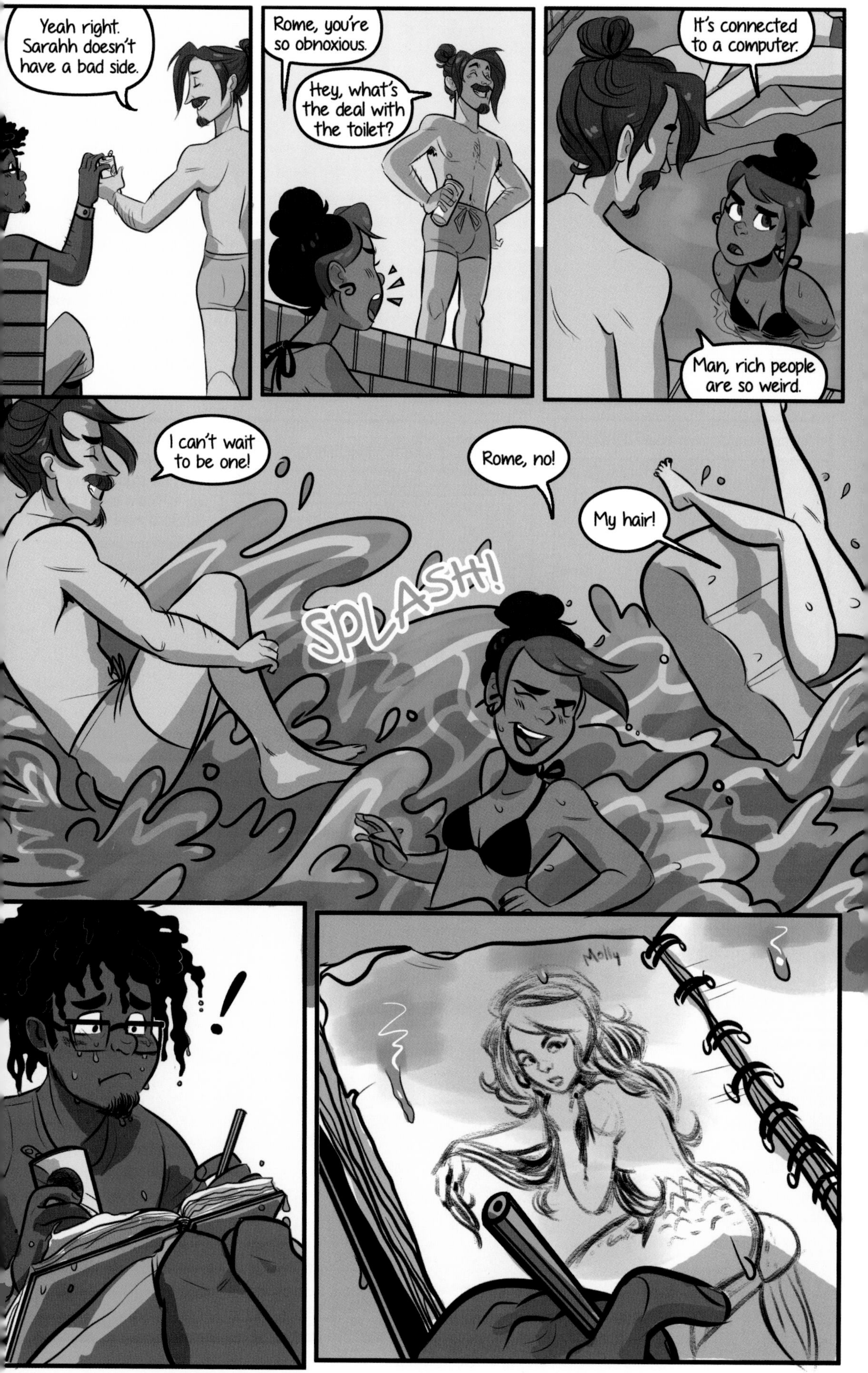
Yeah right. Sarahh doesn't have a bad side.
Rome, you're so obnoxious.
Hey, what's the deal with the toilet?
It's connected to a computer.
Man, rich people are so weird.
I can't wait to be one!
Rome, no!
My hair!
SPLASH!
!
Molly

Mew!

Mew!

Mew!

What? What do you want?

Mew mew mew mew mew

Maybe I could have been a hero...

Adventures in Catsitting

om/adventures-in-catsitti

Leading my troops into battle and saving the world from evil. I could've made a real difference.

You have to sleep. It's bedtime.

You're lucky you're cute.

Puuurrrrr.

Puuurrrrr.

Don't poop on me.

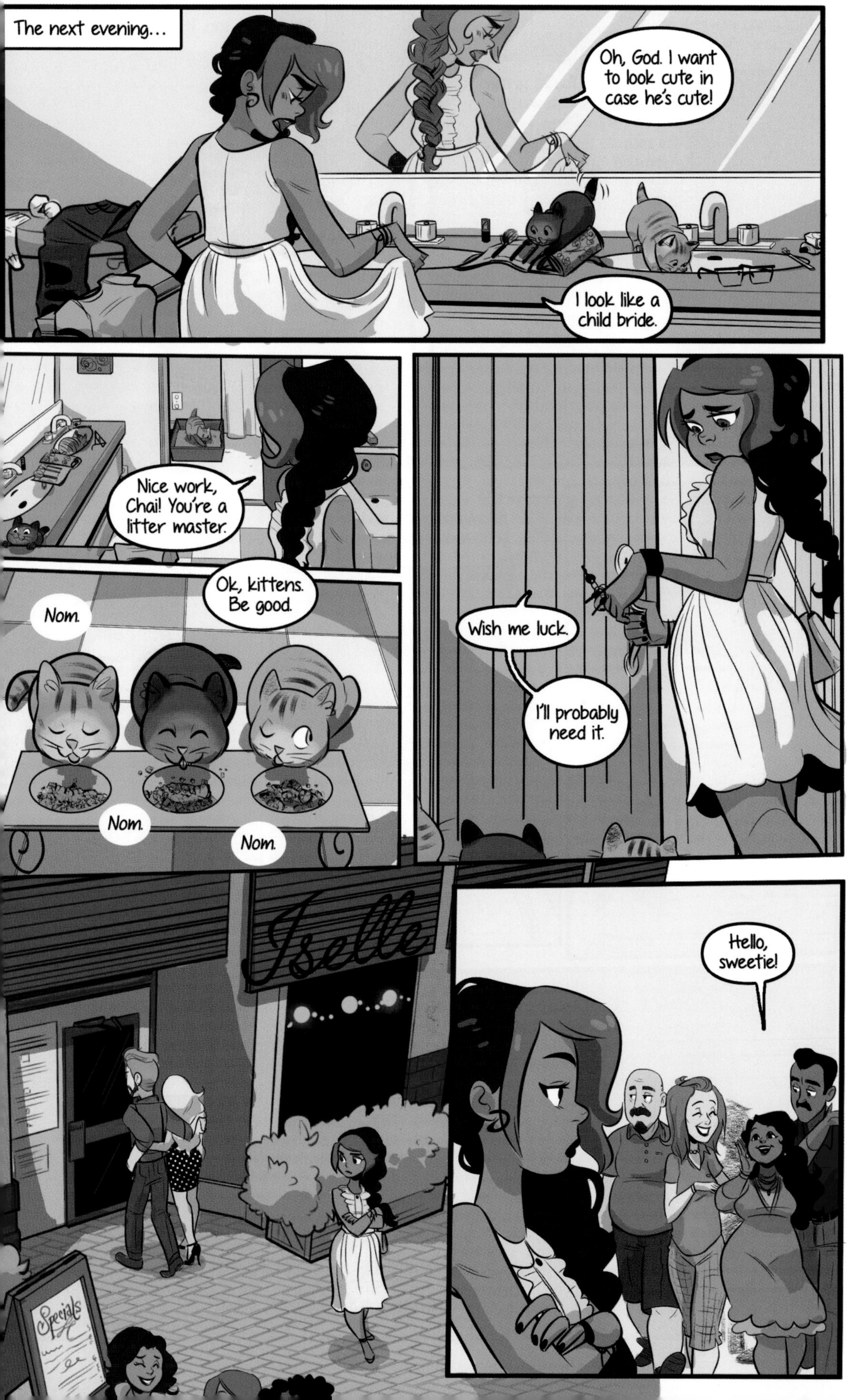
The next evening...
Oh, God. I want to look cute in case he's cute!
I look like a child bride.
Nice work, Chai! You're a litter master.
Ok, kittens. Be good.
Nom.
Nom.
Nom.
Wish me luck.
I'll probably need it.
Iselle
Specials
Hello, sweetie!

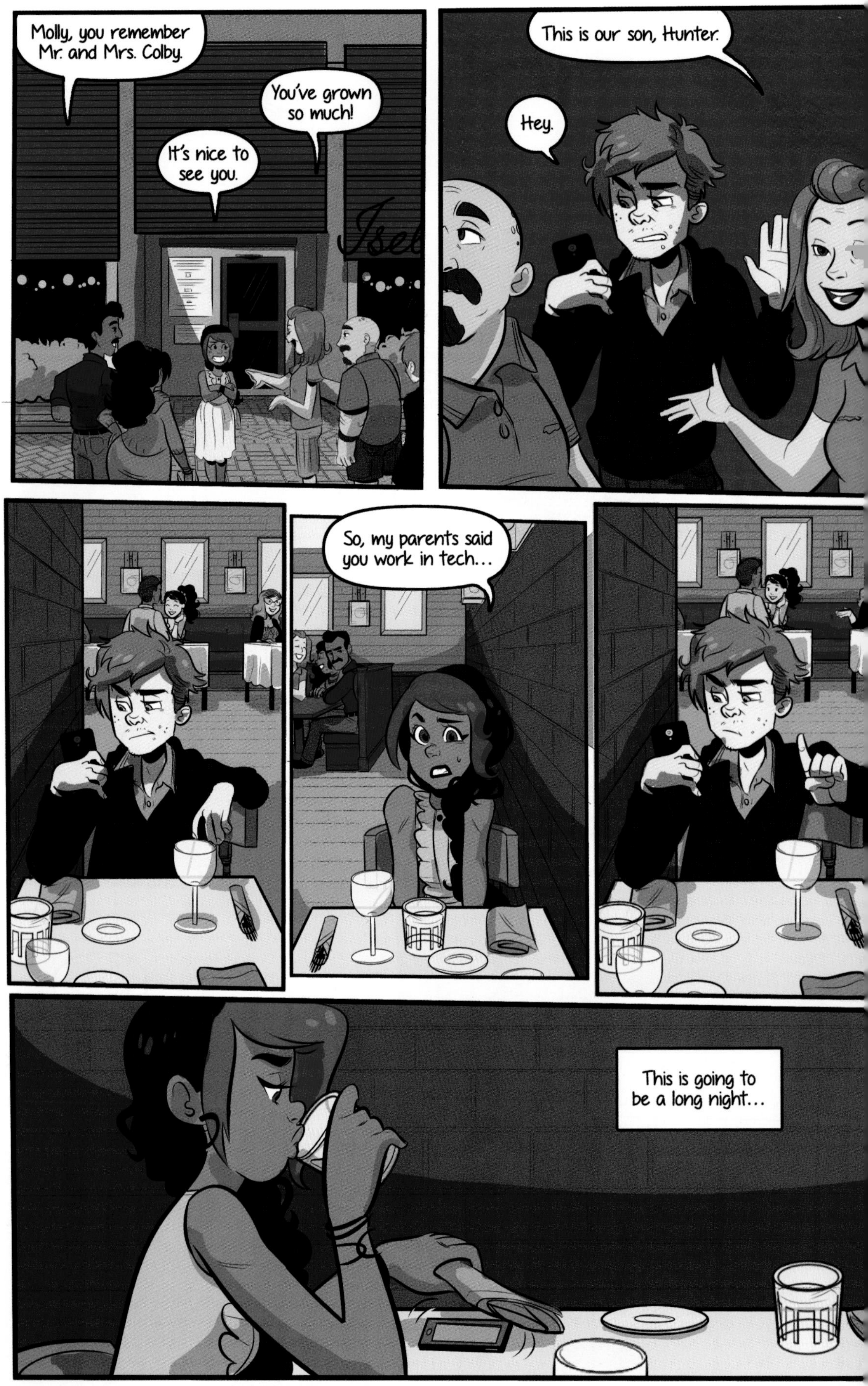
Molly, you remember Mr. and Mrs. Colby.
It's nice to see you.
You've grown so much!
This is our son, Hunter.
Hey.
So, my parents said you work in tech...
This is going to be a long night...

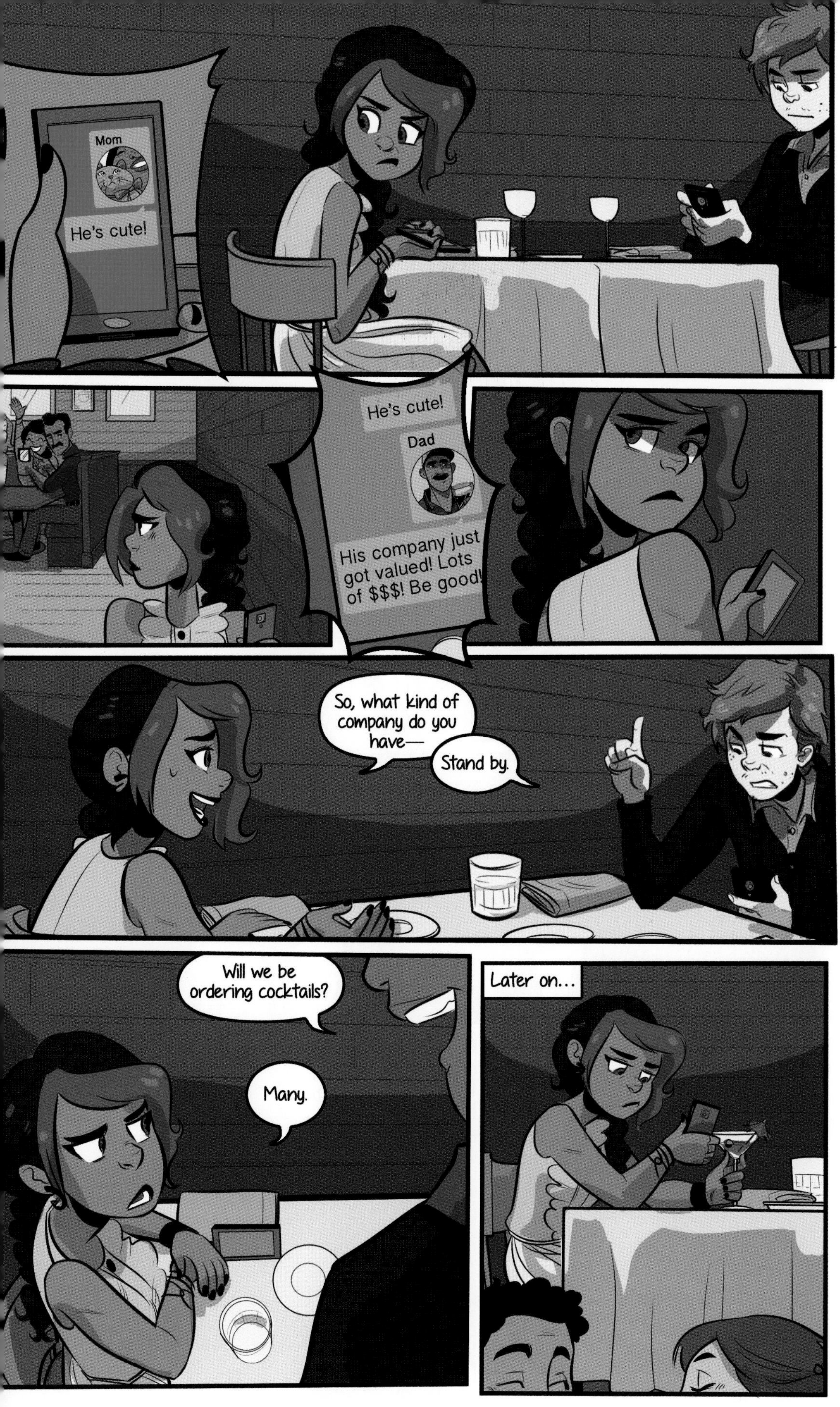

Mom
He's cute!
He's cute!
Dad
His company just got valued! Lots of $$$! Be good!
So, what kind of company do you have—
Stand by.
Will we be ordering cocktails?
Many.
Later on...

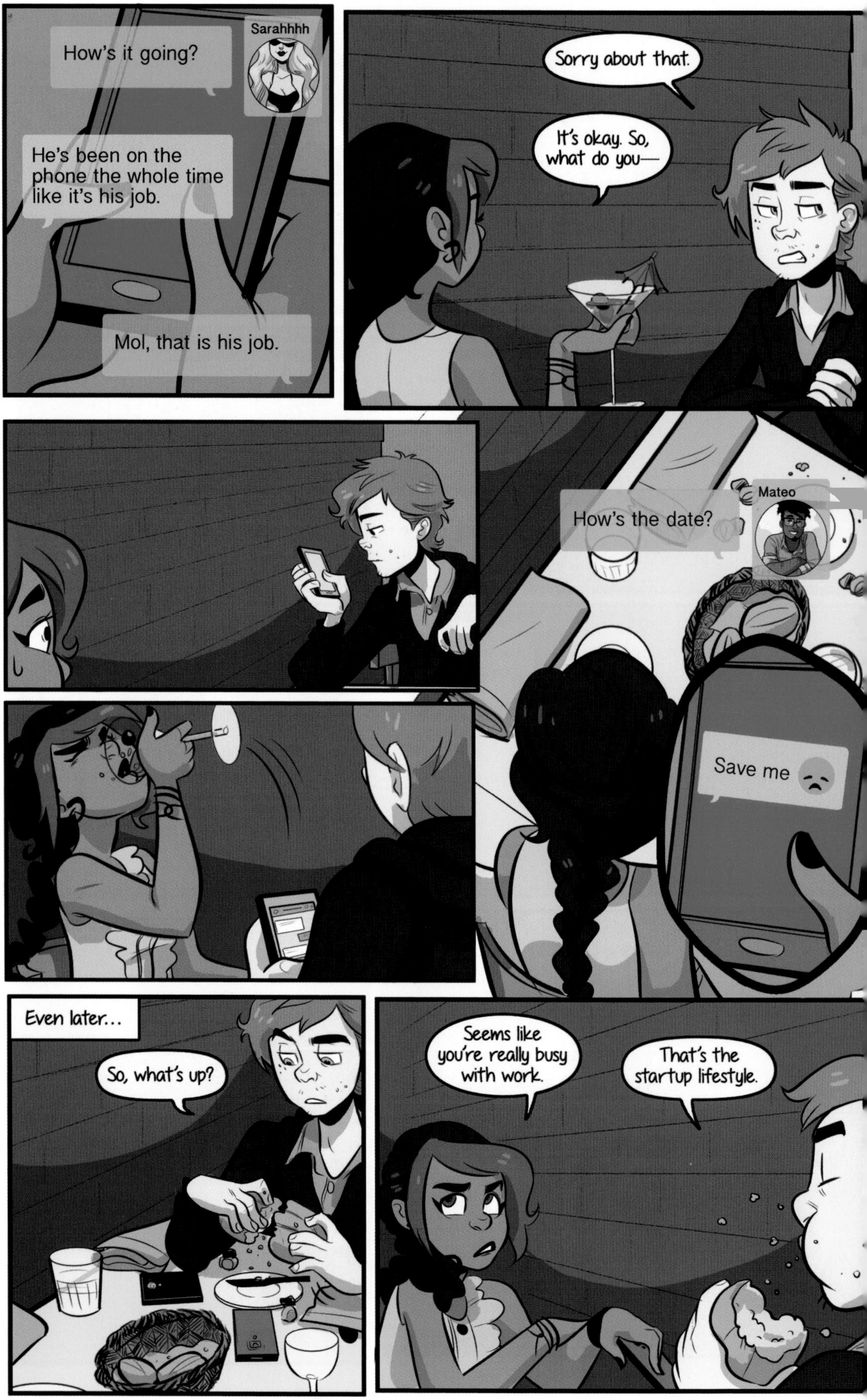
Sarahhhh
How's it going?
He's been on the phone the whole time like it's his job.
Mol, that is his job.
Sorry about that.
It's okay. So, what do you—
Mateo
How's the date?
Save me
Even later...
So, what's up?
Seems like you're really busy with work.
That's the startup lifestyle.

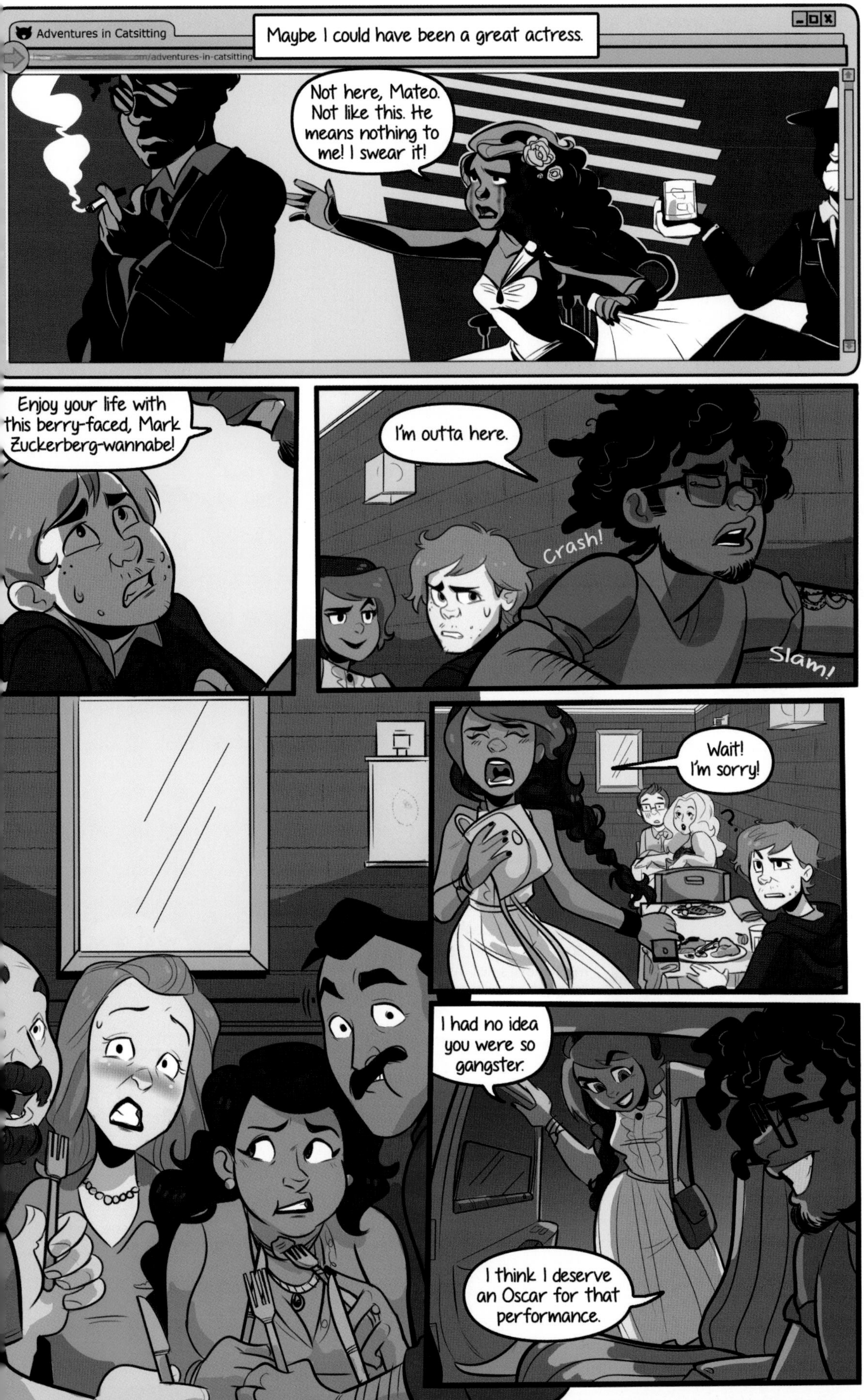
Adventures in Catsitting
m/adventures-in-catsitting
Maybe I could have been a great actress.
Not here, Mateo. Not like this. He means nothing to me! I swear it!
Enjoy your life with this berry-faced, Mark Zuckerberg-wannabe!
I'm outta here.
Crash!
Slam!
Wait! I'm sorry!
I had no idea you were so gangster.
I think I deserve an Oscar for that performance.

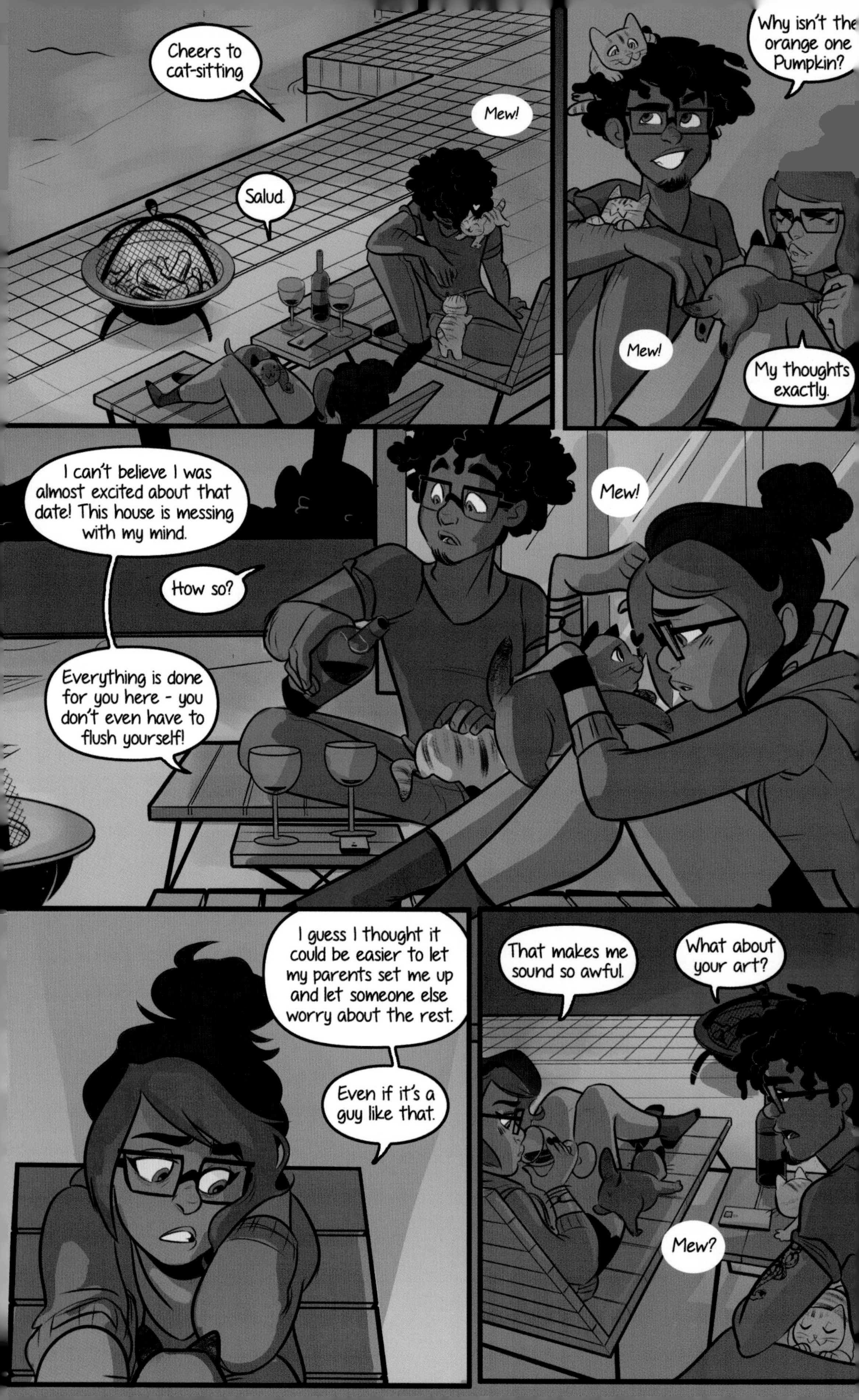
Cheers to cat-sitting
Mew!
Salud.
Why isn't the orange one Pumpkin?
Mew!
My thoughts exactly.
I can't believe I was almost excited about that date! This house is messing with my mind.
Mew!
How so?
Everything is done for you here - you don't even have to flush yourself!
I guess I thought it could be easier to let my parents set me up and let someone else worry about the rest.
Even if it's a guy like that.
That makes me sound so awful.
What about your art?
Mew?

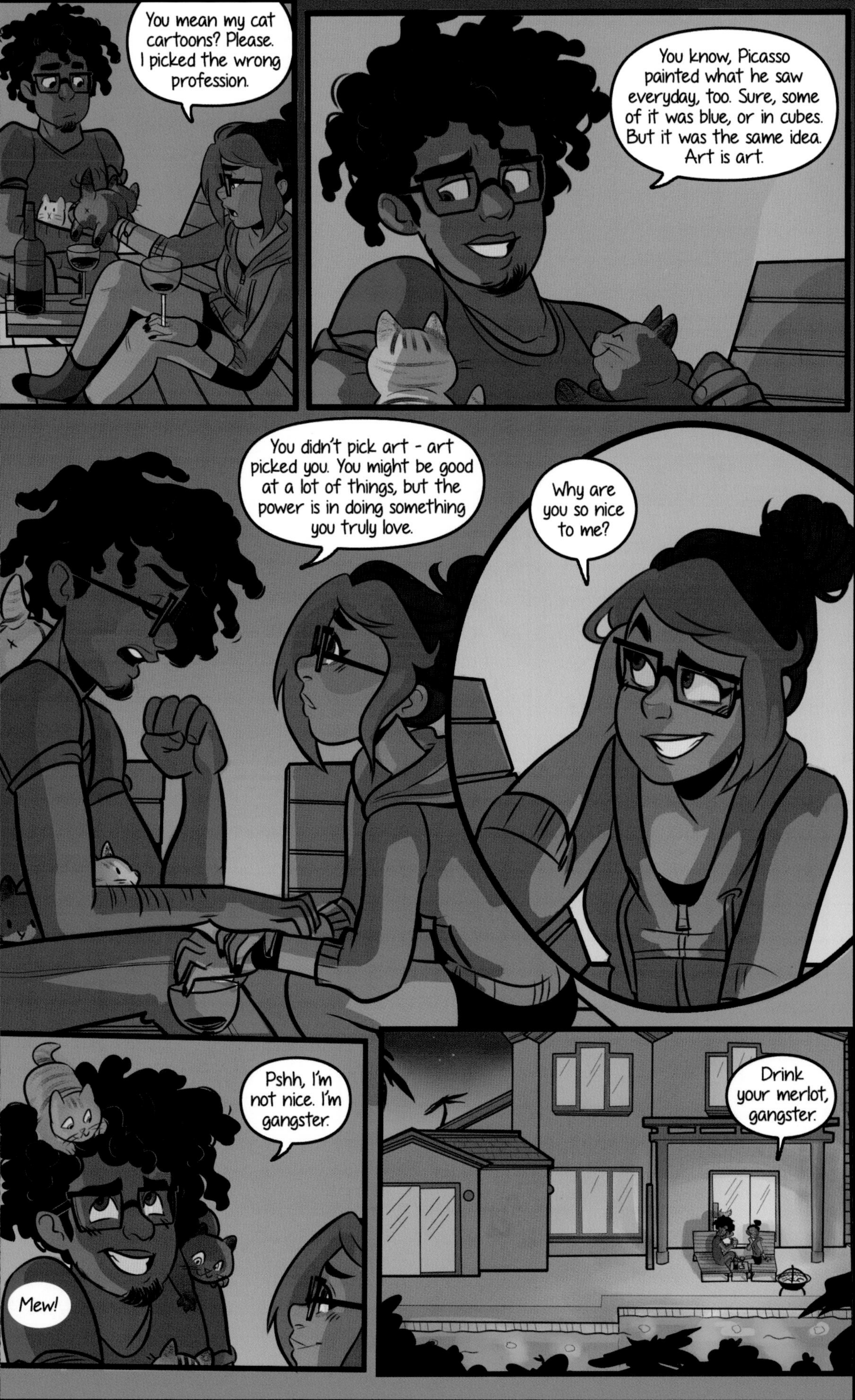
You mean my cat cartoons? Please. I picked the wrong profession.
You know, Picasso painted what he saw everyday, too. Sure, some of it was blue, or in cubes. But it was the same idea. Art is art.
You didn't pick art - art picked you. You might be good at a lot of things, but the power is in doing something you truly love.
Why are you so nice to me?
Pshh, I'm not nice. I'm gangster.
Mew!
Drink your merlot, gangster.

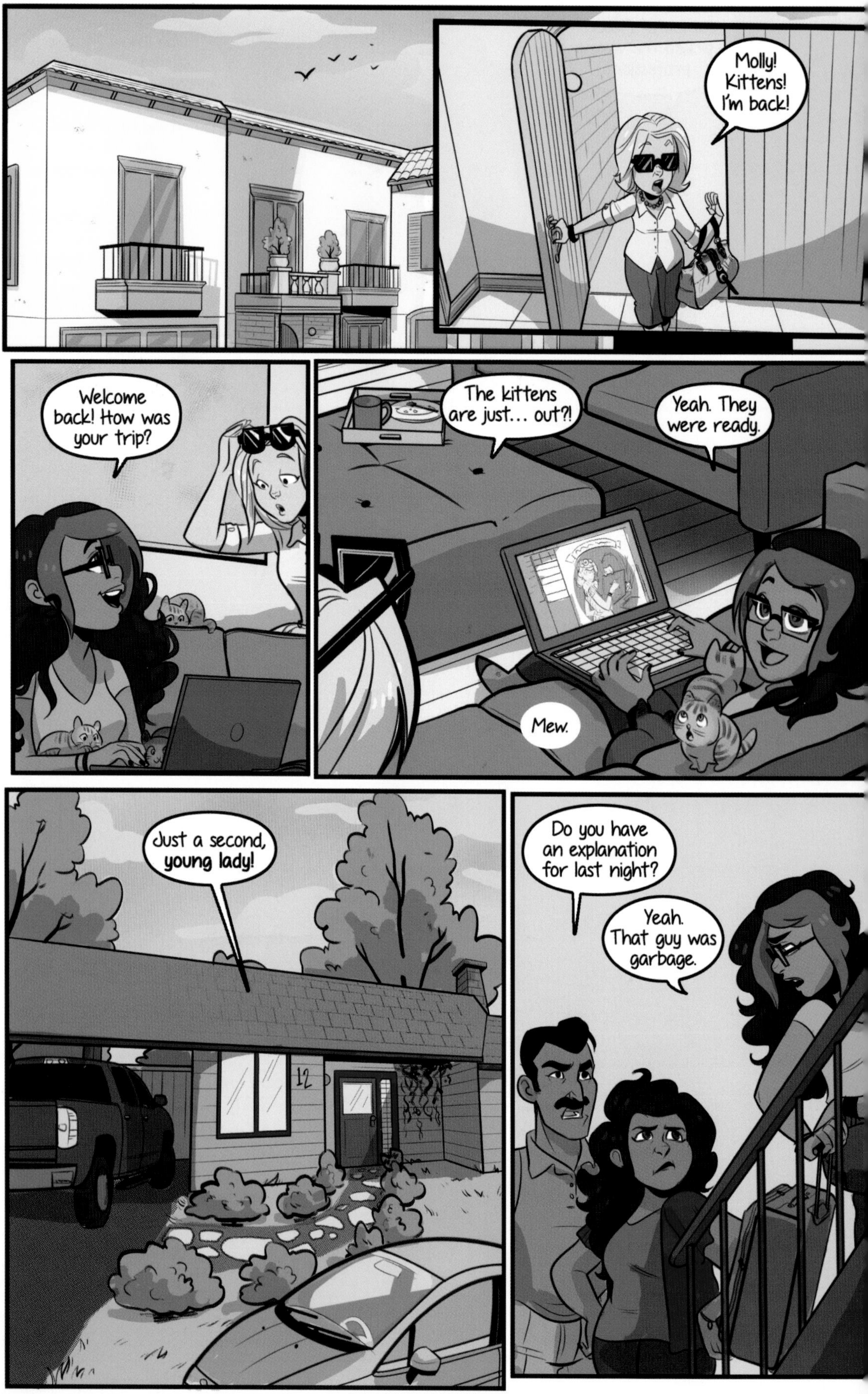
Molly! Kittens! I'm back!
Welcome back! How was your trip?
The kittens are just... out?!
Yeah. They were ready.
Mew.
Just a second, **young lady!**
Do you have an explanation for last night?
Yeah. That guy was garbage.

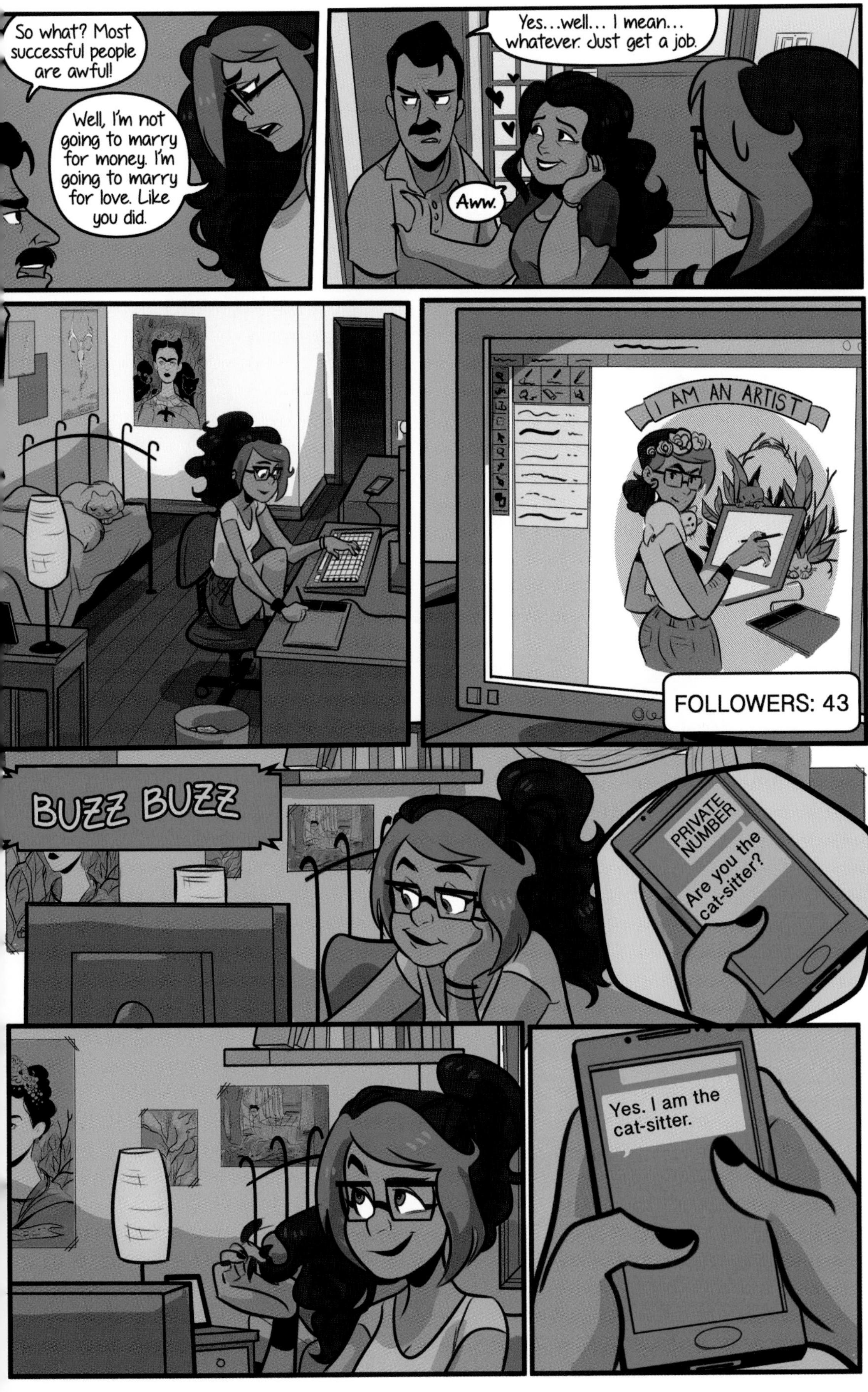
So what? Most successful people are awful!
Well, I'm not going to marry for money. I'm going to marry for love. Like you did.
Yes...well... I mean... whatever. Just get a job.
Aww.
I AM AN ARTIST
FOLLOWERS: 43
BUZZ BUZZ
PRIVATE NUMBER
Are you the cat-sitter?
Yes. I am the cat-sitter.

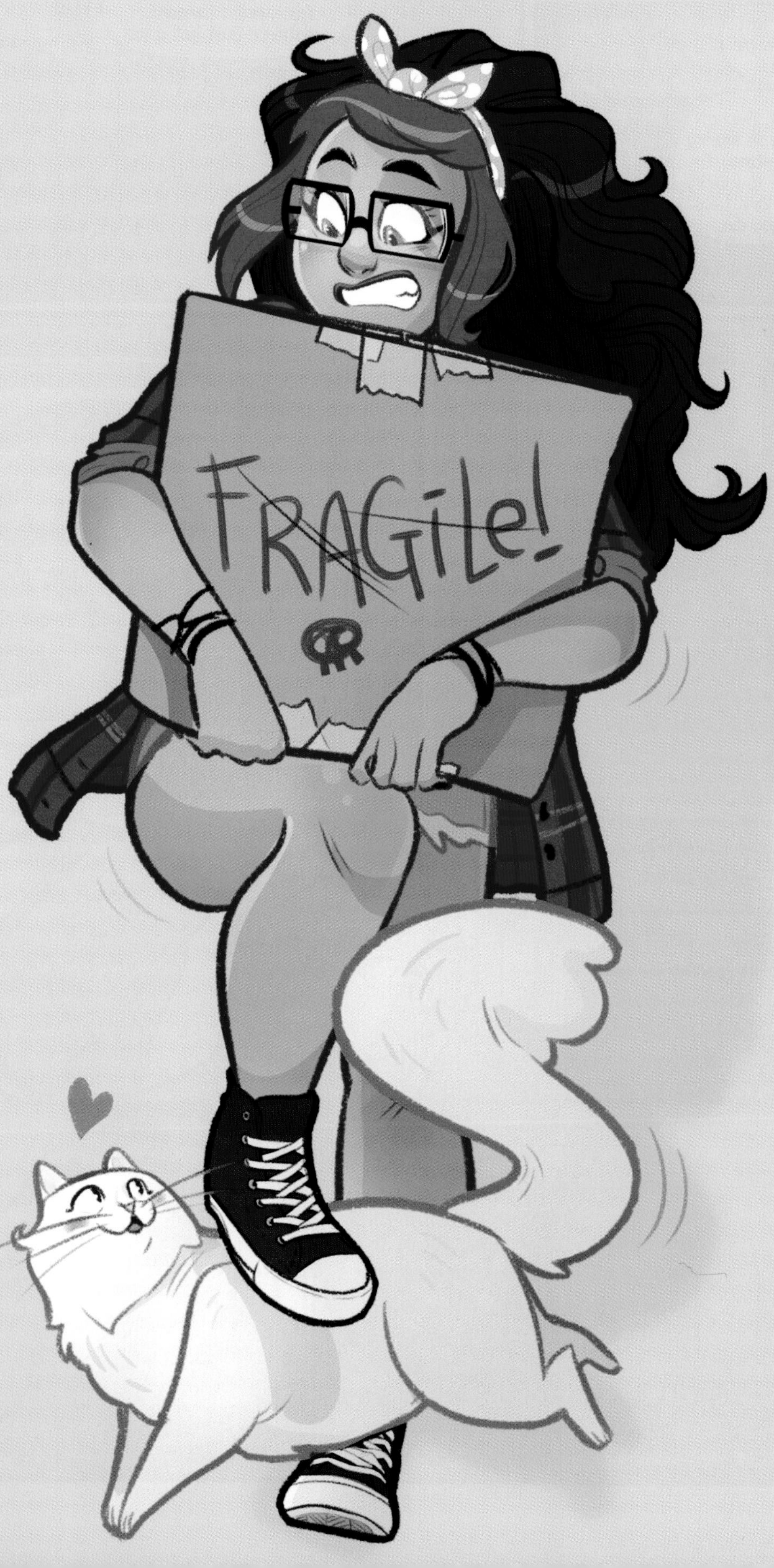
FRAGILE!

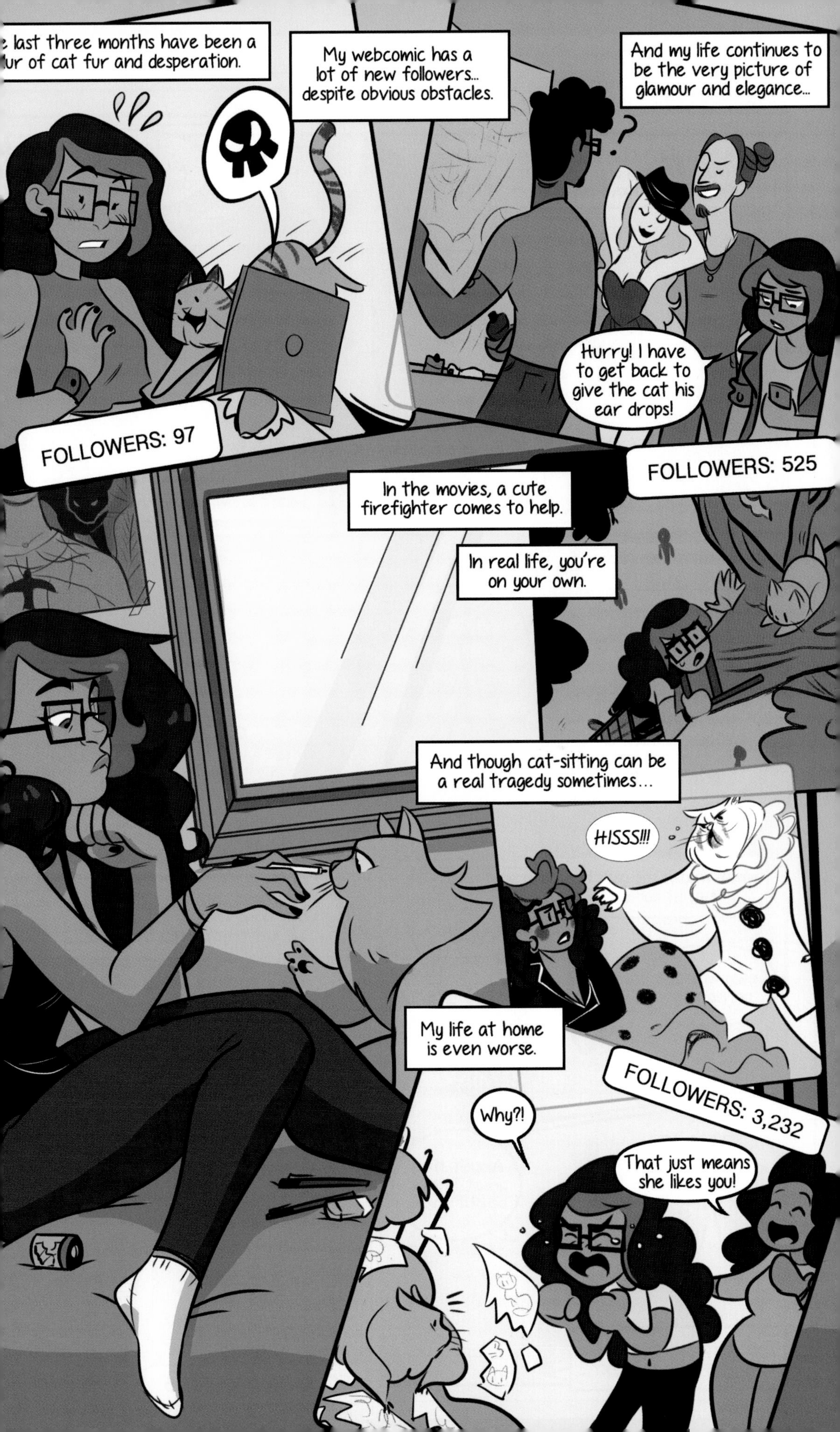

e last three months have been a
lur of cat fur and desperation.
My webcomic has a lot of new followers... despite obvious obstacles.
And my life continues to be the very picture of glamour and elegance...
Hurry! I have to get back to give the cat his ear drops!
FOLLOWERS: 97
FOLLOWERS: 525
In the movies, a cute firefighter comes to help.
In real life, you're on your own.
And though cat-sitting can be a real tragedy sometimes...
HISSS!!!
My life at home is even worse.
FOLLOWERS: 3,232
Why?!
That just means she likes you!

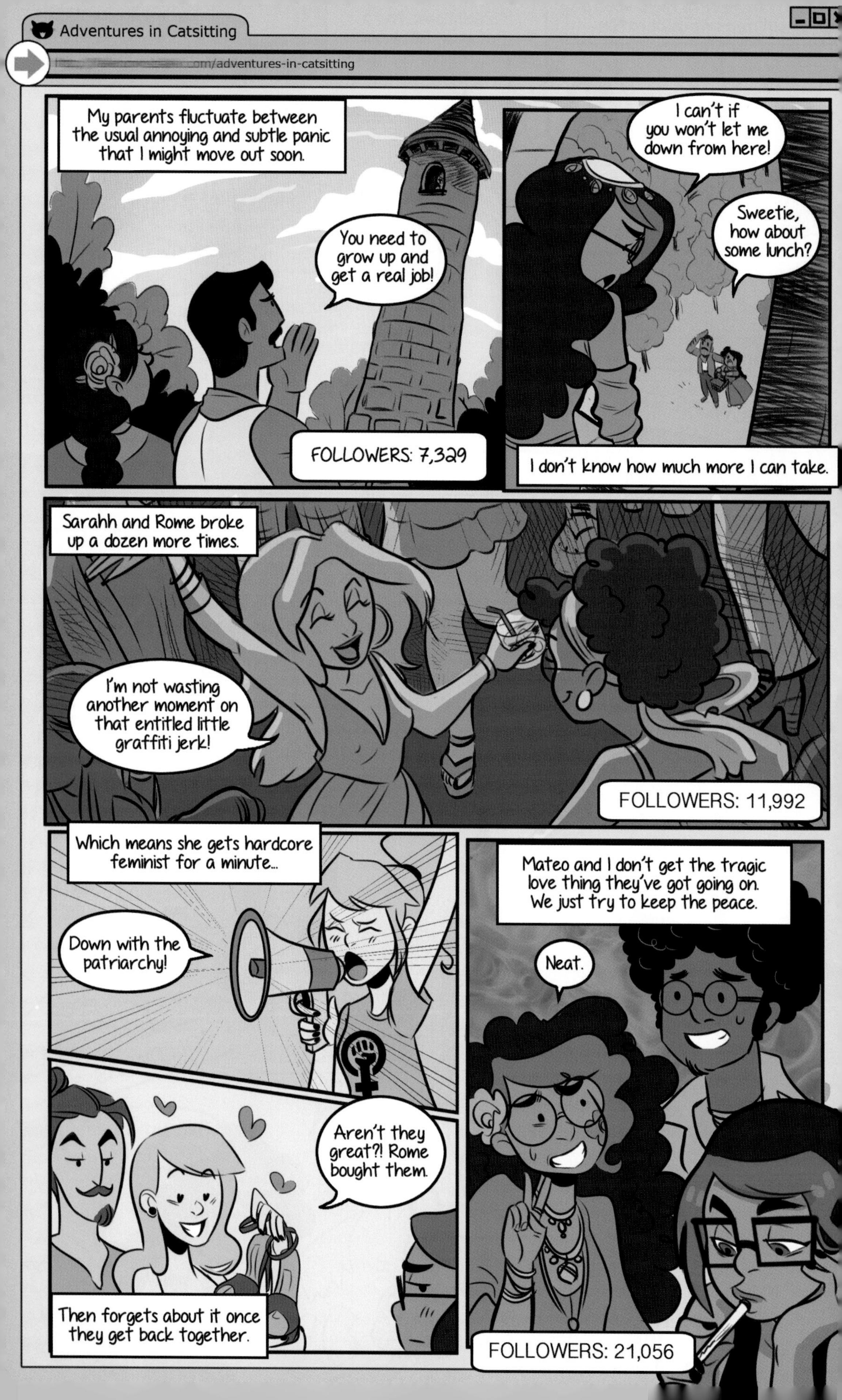
Adventures in Catsitting
om/adventures-in-catsitting
My parents fluctuate between the usual annoying and subtle panic that I might move out soon.
You need to grow up and get a real job!
FOLLOWERS: 7,329
I can't if you won't let me down from here!
Sweetie, how about some lunch?
I don't know how much more I can take.
Sarahh and Rome broke up a dozen more times.
I'm not wasting another moment on that entitled little graffiti jerk!
FOLLOWERS: 11,992
Which means she gets hardcore feminist for a minute...
Down with the patriarchy!
Aren't they great?! Rome bought them.
Then forgets about it once they get back together.
Mateo and I don't get the tragic love thing they've got going on. We just try to keep the peace.
Neat.
FOLLOWERS: 21,056

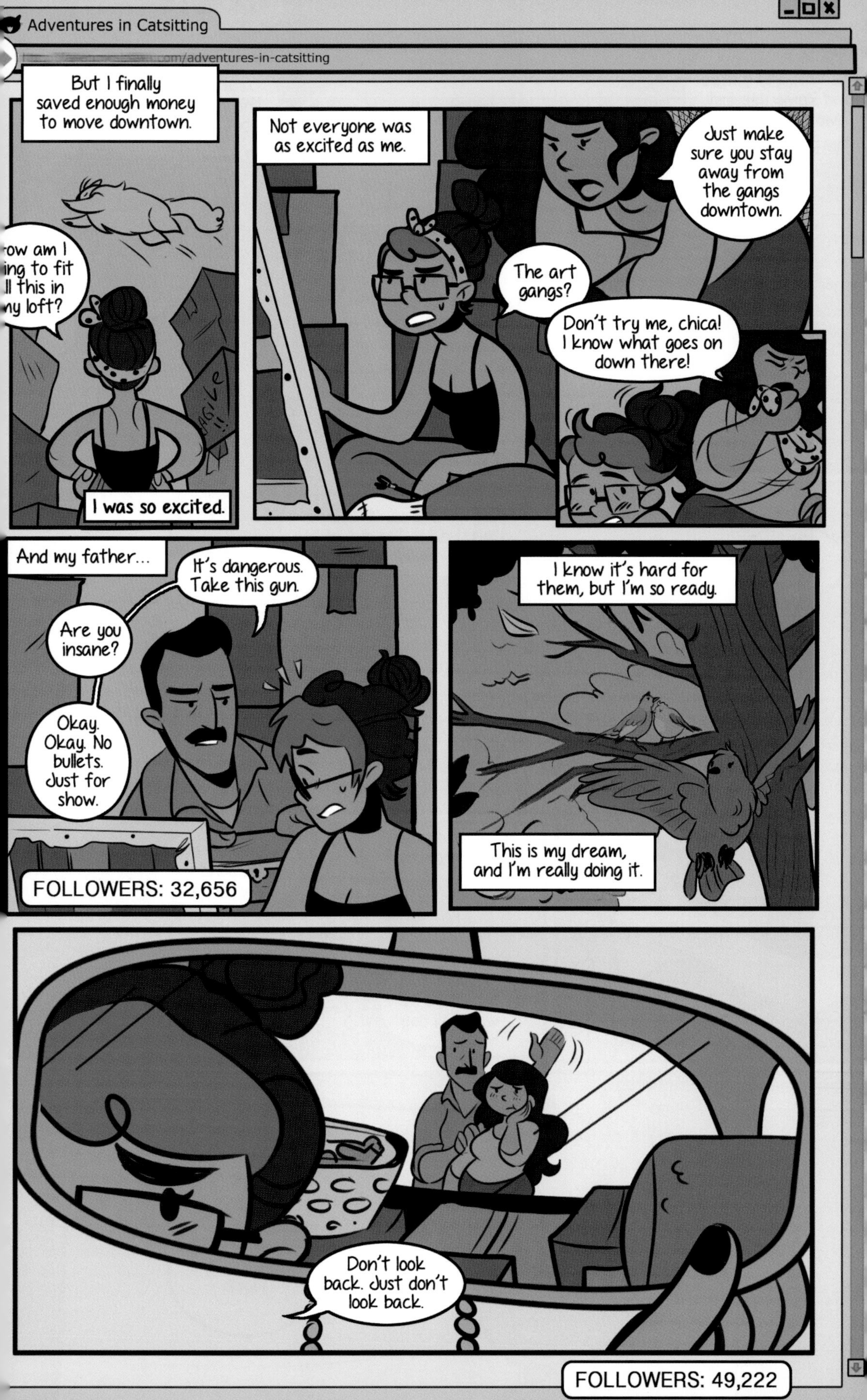

Adventures in Catsitting
com/adventures-in-catsitting
But I finally saved enough money to move downtown.
ow am I ing to fit ll this in ny loft?
I was so excited.
Not everyone was as excited as me.
Just make sure you stay away from the gangs downtown.
The art gangs?
Don't try me, chica! I know what goes on down there!
And my father...
It's dangerous. Take this gun.
Are you insane?
Okay. Okay. No bullets. Just for show.
FOLLOWERS: 32,656
I know it's hard for them, but I'm so ready.
This is my dream, and I'm really doing it.
Don't look back. Just don't look back.
FOLLOWERS: 49,222

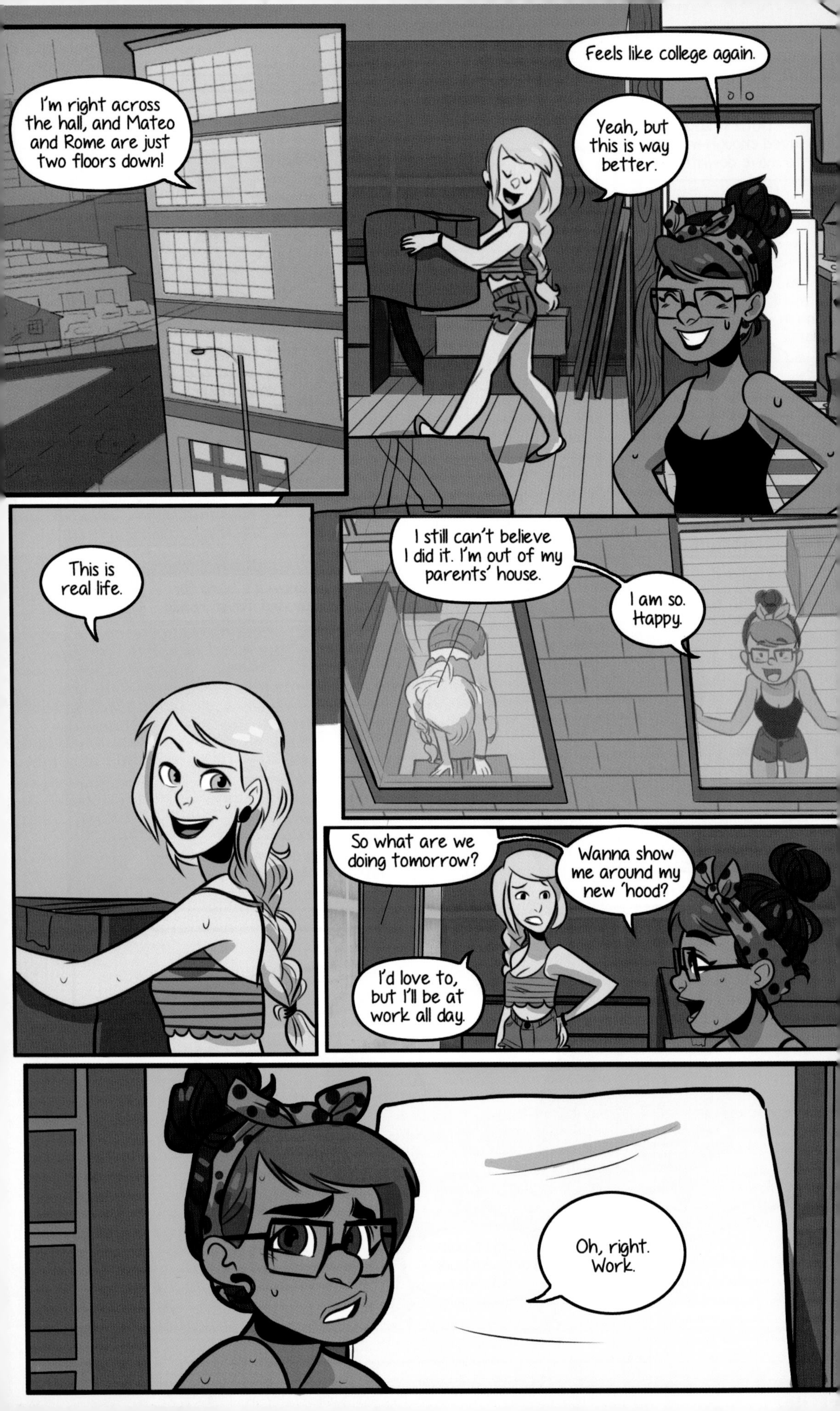
I'm right across the hall, and Mateo and Rome are just two floors down!
Feels like college again.
Yeah, but this is way better.
This is real life.
I still can't believe I did it. I'm out of my parents' house.
I am so. Happy.
So what are we doing tomorrow?
Wanna show me around my new 'hood?
I'd love to, but I'll be at work all day.
Oh, right. Work.

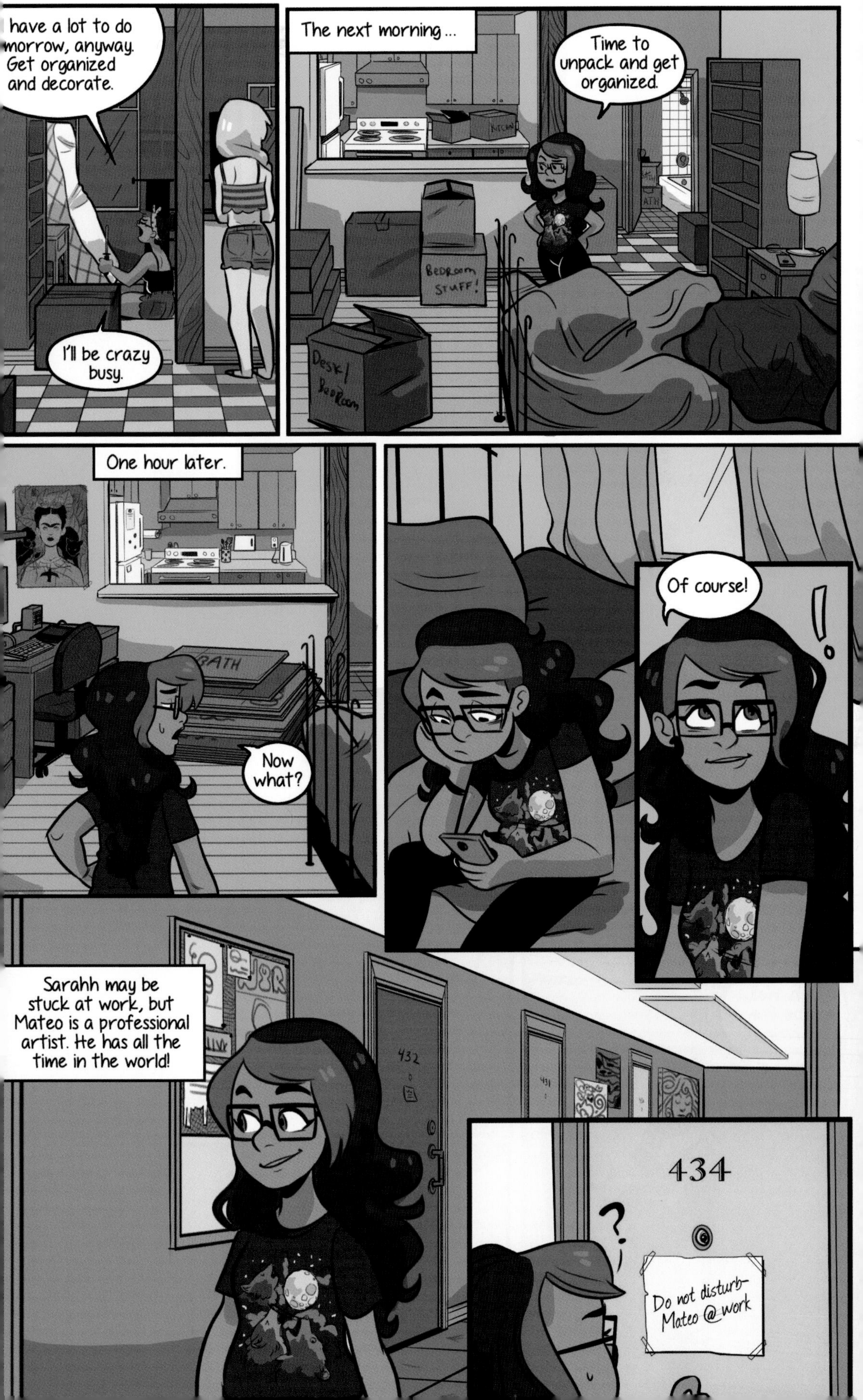
have a lot to do
morrow, anyway.
Get organized
and decorate.
I'll be crazy
busy.
The next morning...
Time to
unpack and get
organized.
BEDROOM
STUFF!
Desk/
BedRoom
One hour later.
Now
what?
Of course!
Sarahh may be
stuck at work, but
Mateo is a professional
artist. He has all the
time in the world!
432
434
?
Do not disturb–
Mateo @ work

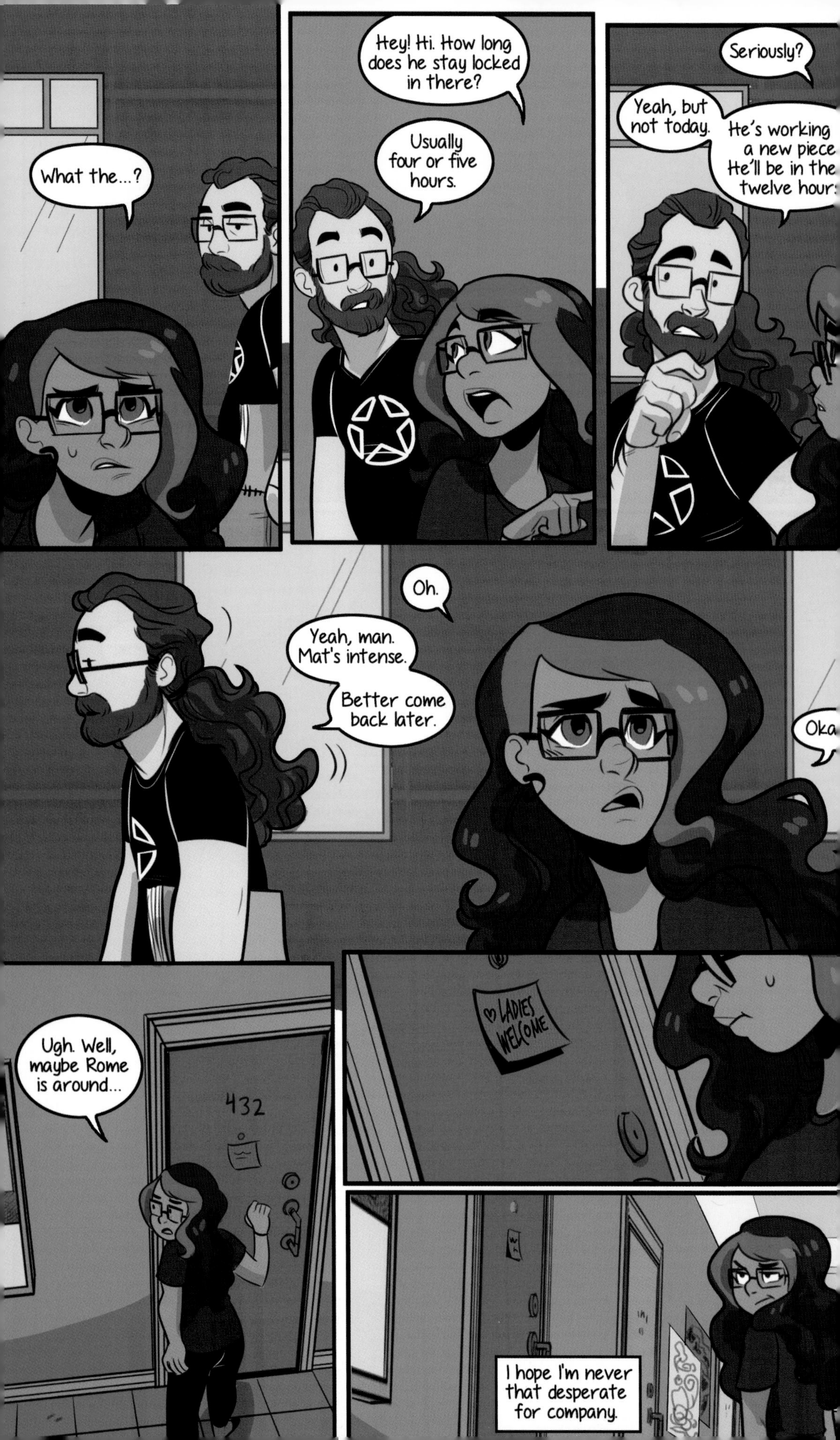
What the...?
Hey! Hi. How long does he stay locked in there?
Usually four or five hours.
Seriously?
Yeah, but not today.
He's working a new piece He'll be in the twelve hours
Oh.
Yeah, man. Mat's intense.
Better come back later.
Oka
Ugh. Well, maybe Rome is around...
432
LADIES WELCOME
I hope I'm never that desperate for company.

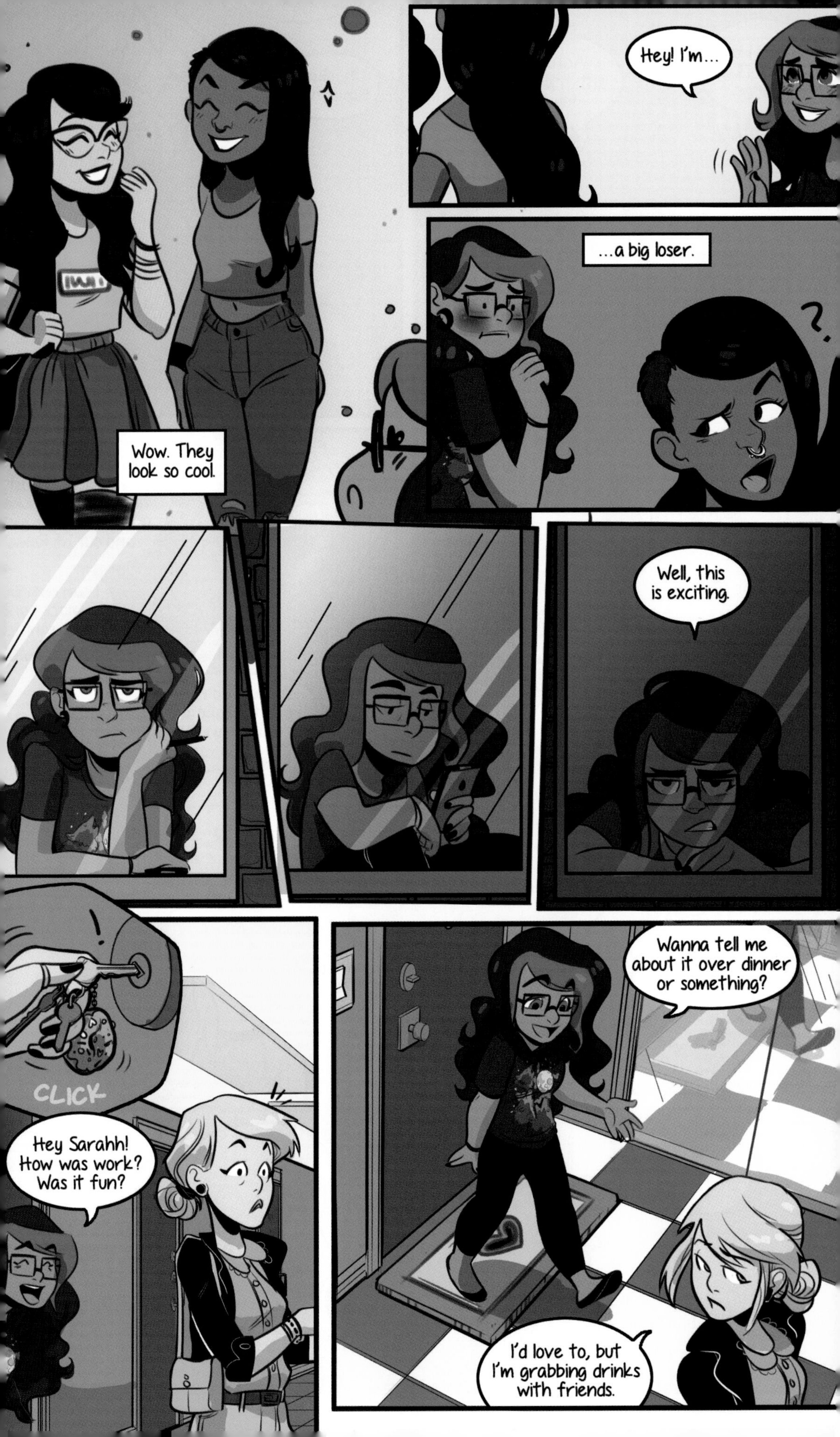
Hey! I'm...
...a big loser.
Wow. They look so cool.
Well, this is exciting.
CLICK
Hey Sarahh! How was work? Was it fun?
Wanna tell me about it over dinner or something?
I'd love to, but I'm grabbing drinks with friends.

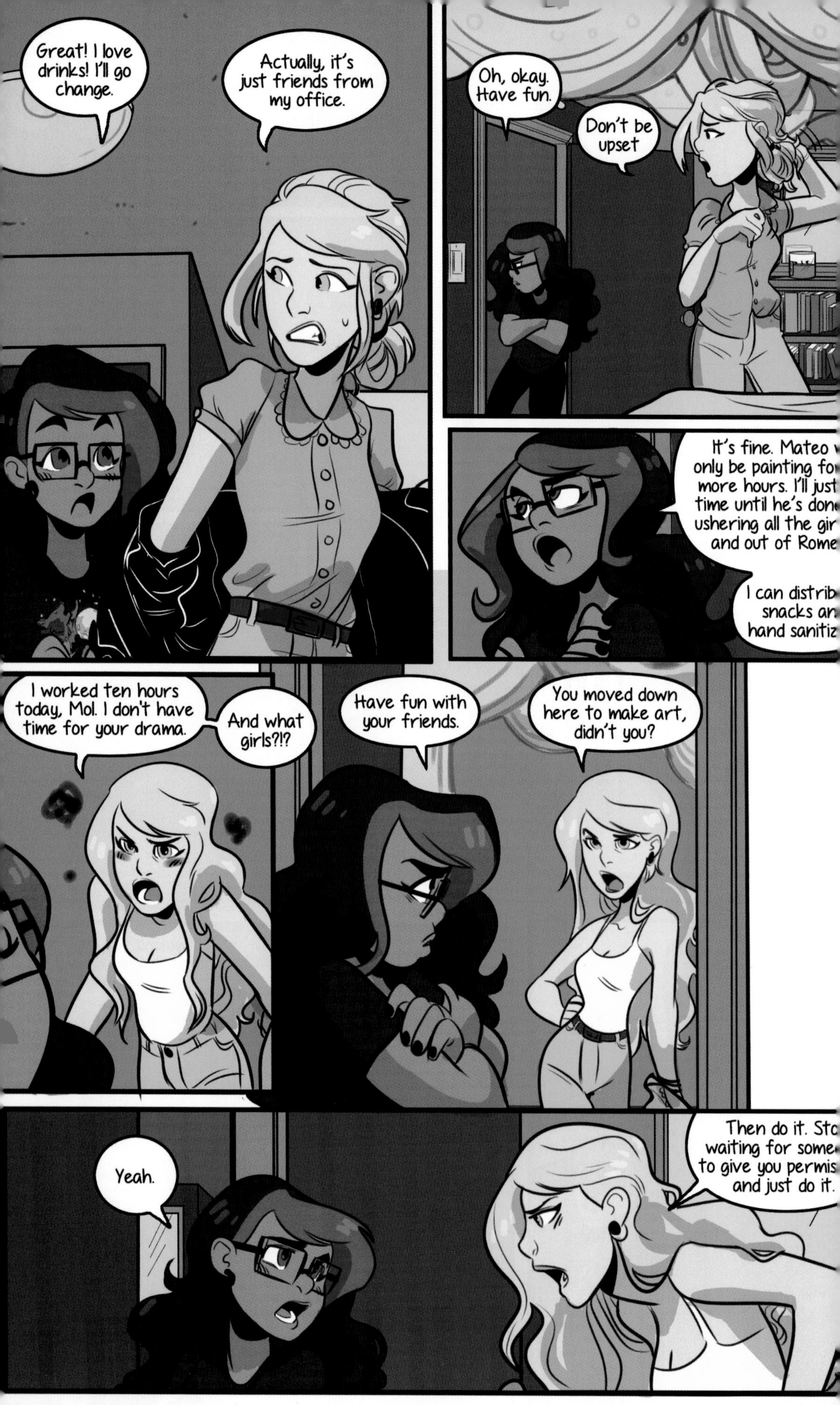
Great! I love drinks! I'll go change.
Actually, it's just friends from my office.
Oh, okay. Have fun.
Don't be upset
It's fine. Mateo
only be painting fo
more hours. I'll just
time until he's don
ushering all the gir
and out of Rome
I can distrib
snacks an
hand sanitiz
I worked ten hours today, Mol. I don't have time for your drama.
And what girls?!?
Have fun with your friends.
You moved down here to make art, didn't you?
Yeah.
Then do it. Sto
waiting for some
to give you permis
and just do it.

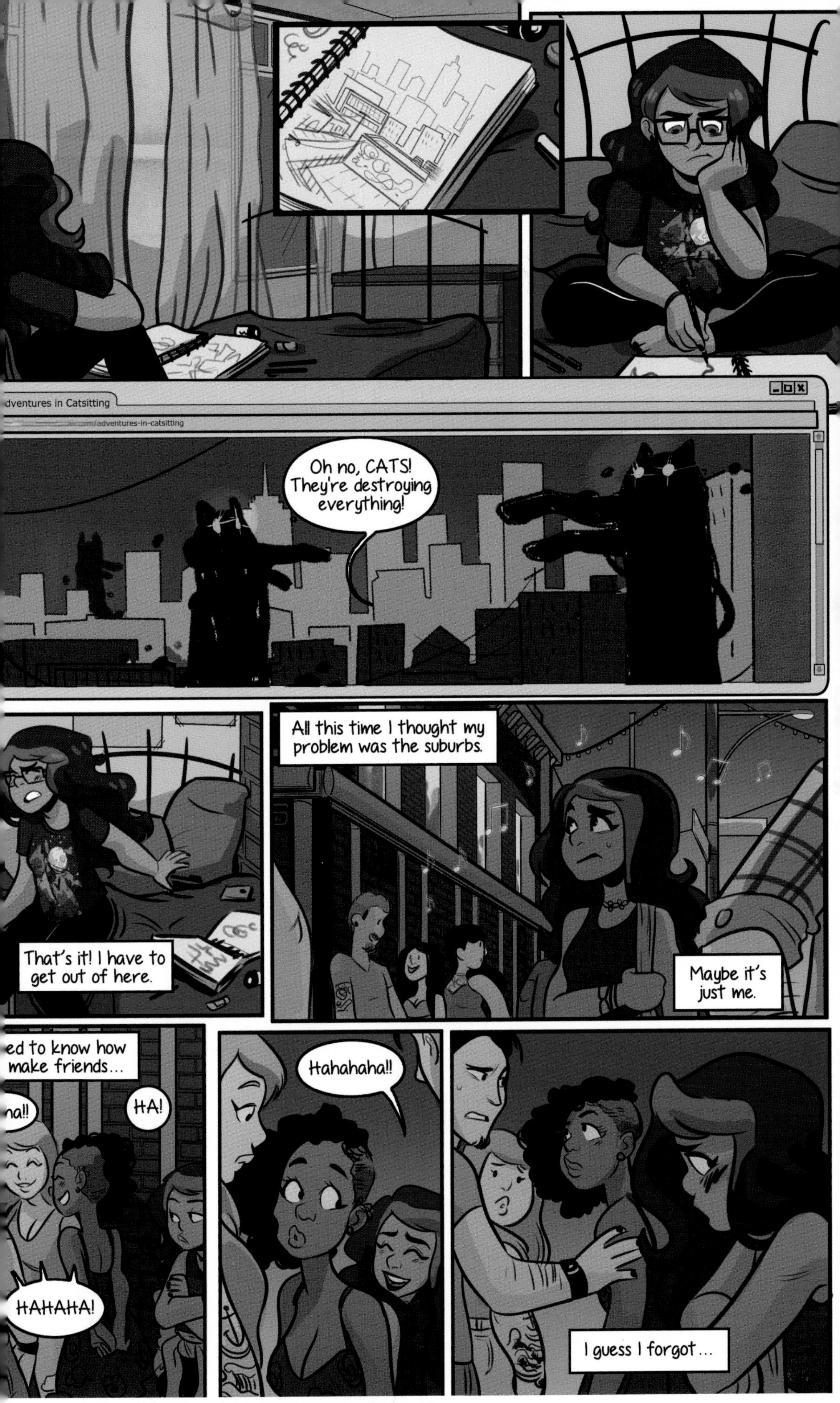

dventures in Catsitting
com/adventures-in-catsitting
Oh no, CATS! They're destroying everything!
That's it! I have to get out of here.
All this time I thought my problem was the suburbs.
Maybe it's just me.
ed to know how make friends...
na!!
HA!
HAHAHA!
Hahahaha!!
I guess I forgot...

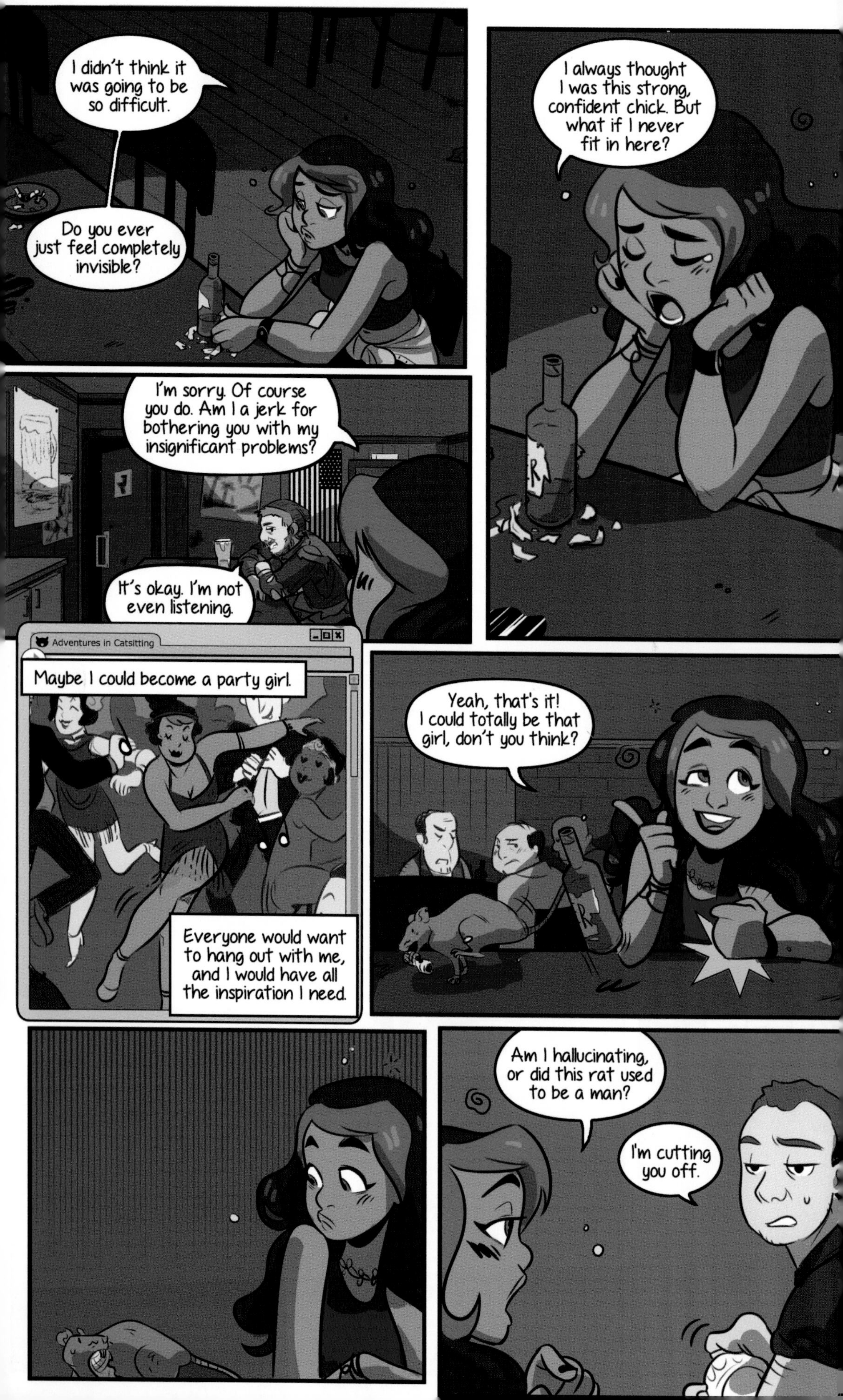
I didn't think it was going to be so difficult.
Do you ever just feel completely invisible?
I always thought I was this strong, confident chick. But what if I never fit in here?
I'm sorry. Of course you do. Am I a jerk for bothering you with my insignificant problems?
It's okay. I'm not even listening.
Adventures in Catsitting
Maybe I could become a party girl.
Everyone would want to hang out with me, and I would have all the inspiration I need.
Yeah, that's it! I could totally be that girl, don't you think?
Am I hallucinating, or did this rat used to be a man?
I'm cutting you off.

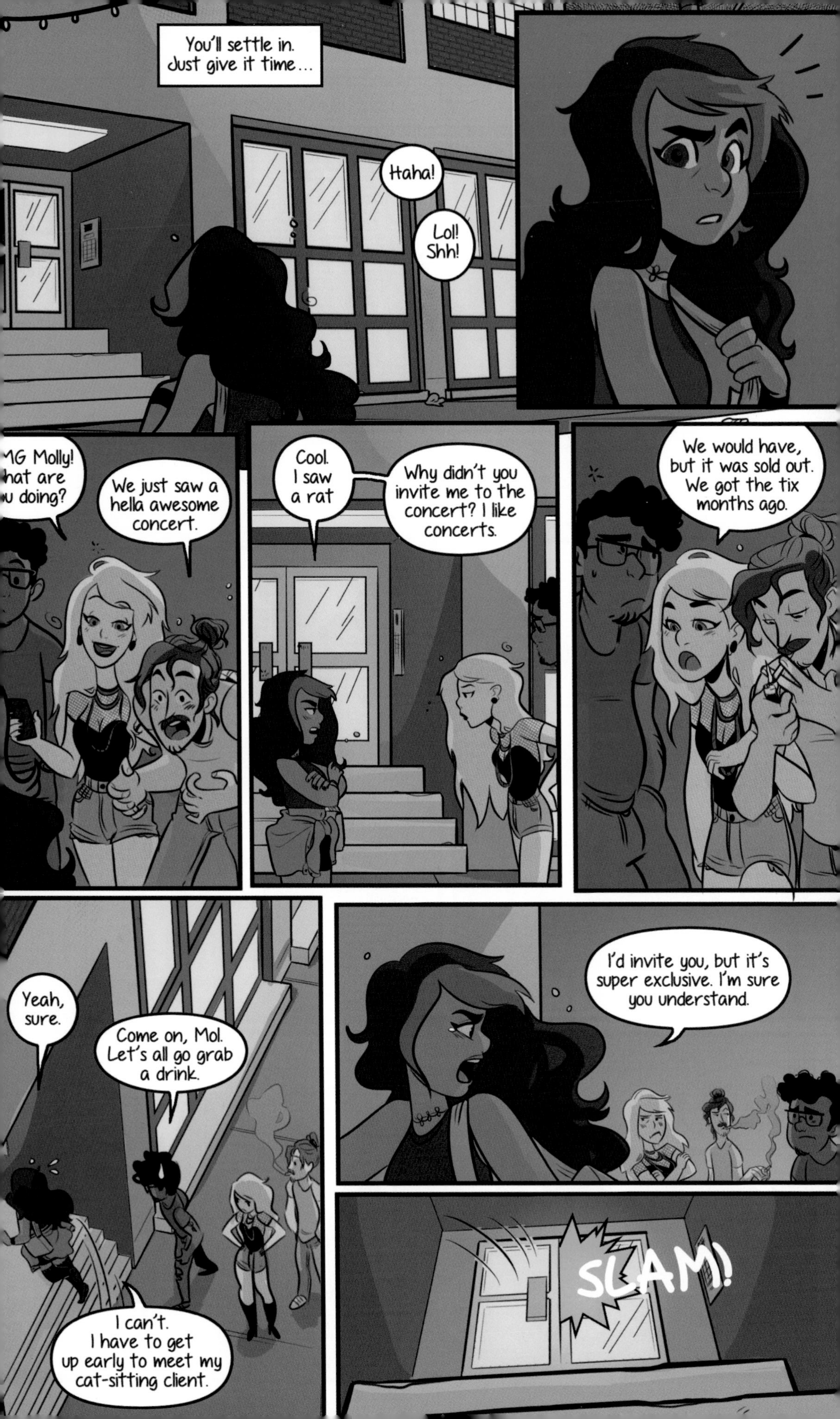

You'll settle in. Just give it time...
Haha!
Lol! Shh!
MG Molly! hat are u doing?
We just saw a hella awesome concert.
Cool. I saw a rat
Why didn't you invite me to the concert? I like concerts.
We would have, but it was sold out. We got the tix months ago.
Yeah, sure.
Come on, Mol. Let's all go grab a drink.
I can't. I have to get up early to meet my cat-sitting client.
I'd invite you, but it's super exclusive. I'm sure you understand.
SLAM!

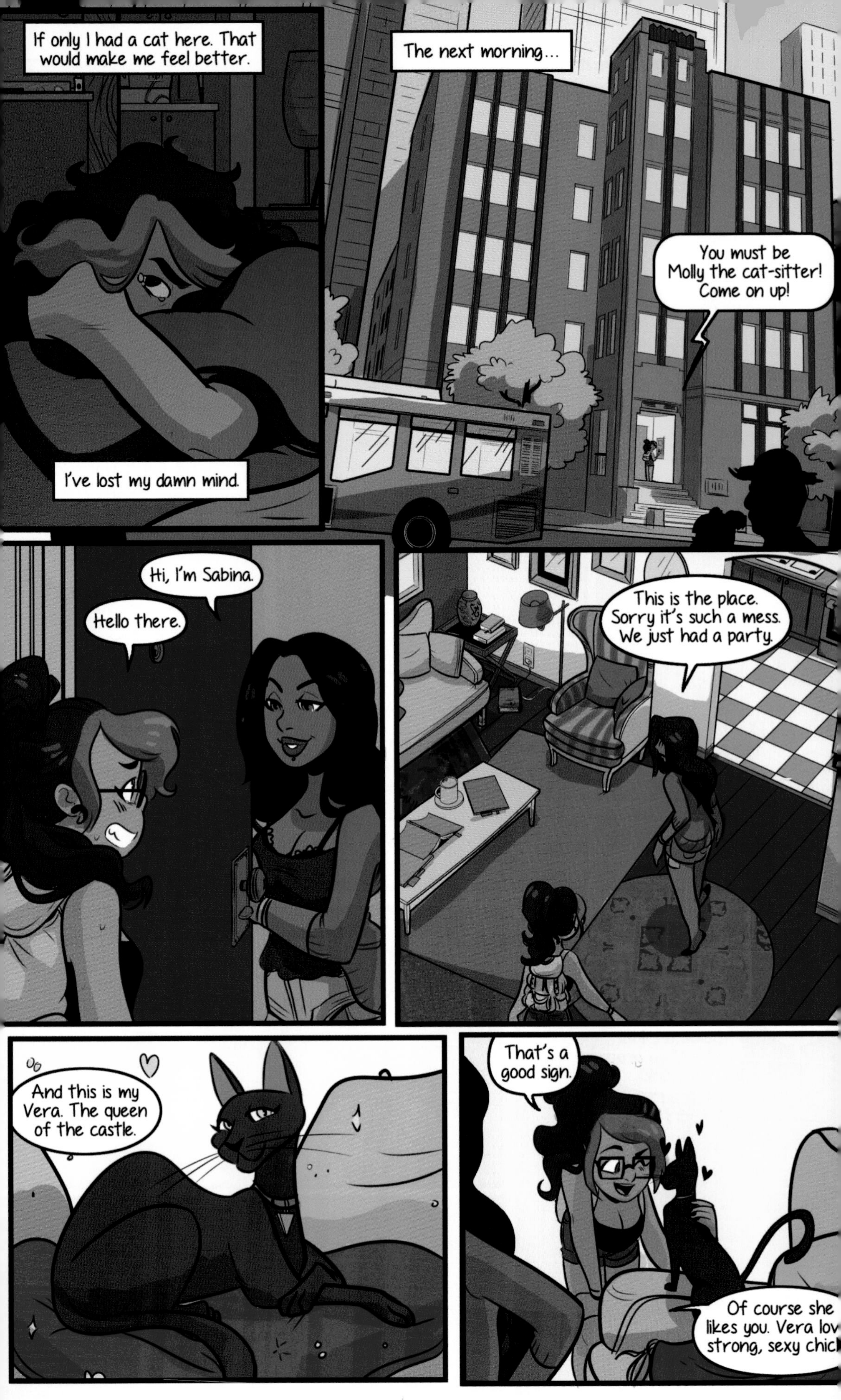
If only I had a cat here. That would make me feel better.
I've lost my damn mind.
The next morning...
You must be Molly the cat-sitter! Come on up!
Hi, I'm Sabina.
Hello there.
This is the place. Sorry it's such a mess. We just had a party.
And this is my Vera. The queen of the castle.
That's a good sign.
Of course she likes you. Vera lov strong, sexy chic

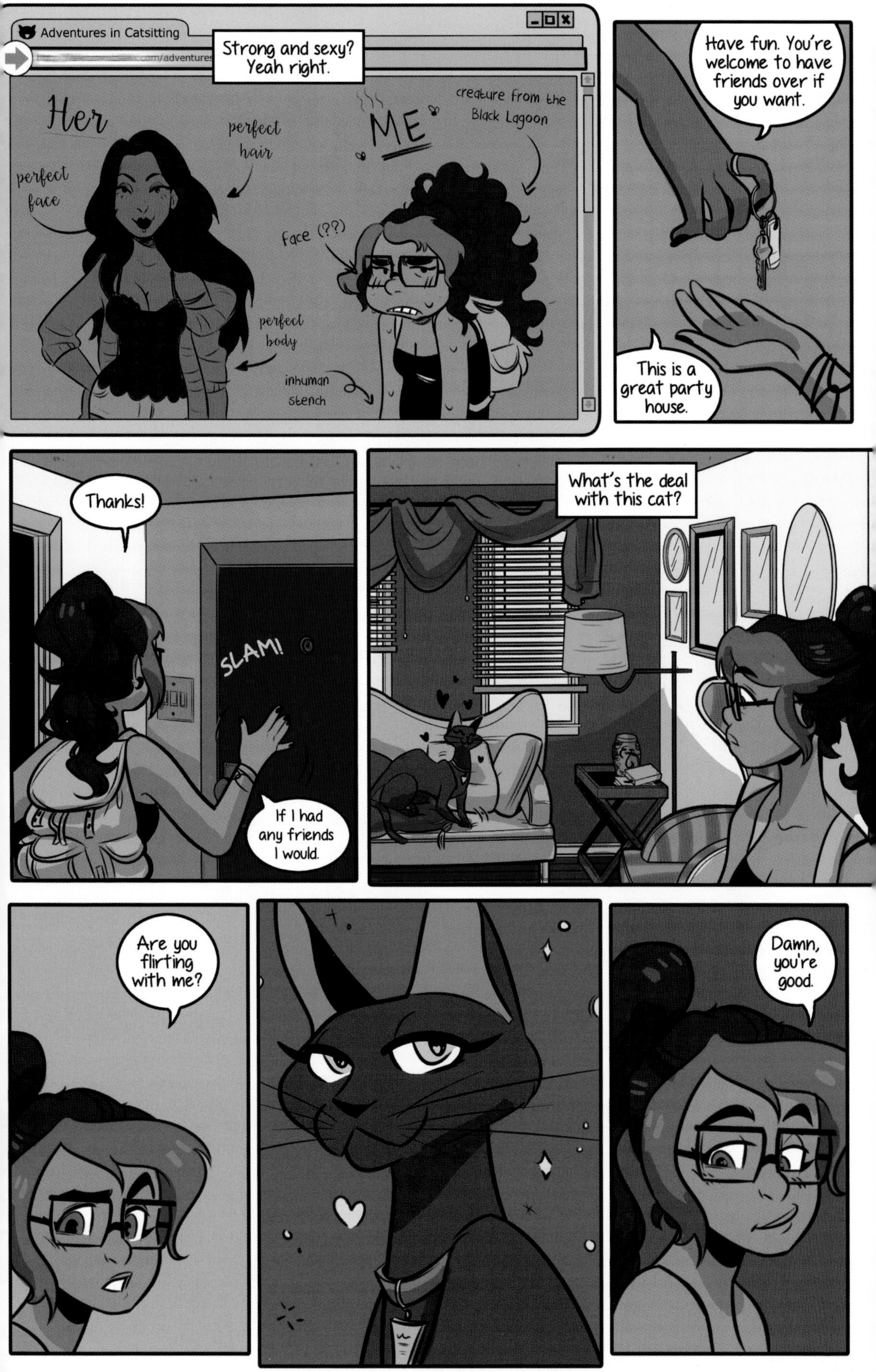
Adventures in Catsitting
Strong and sexy? Yeah right.
Her
perfect hair
perfect face
perfect body
ME
creature from the Black Lagoon
Face (??)
inhuman stench
Have fun. You're welcome to have friends over if you want.
This is a great party house.
Thanks!
SLAM!
If I had any friends I would.
What's the deal with this cat?
Are you flirting with me?
Damn, you're good.

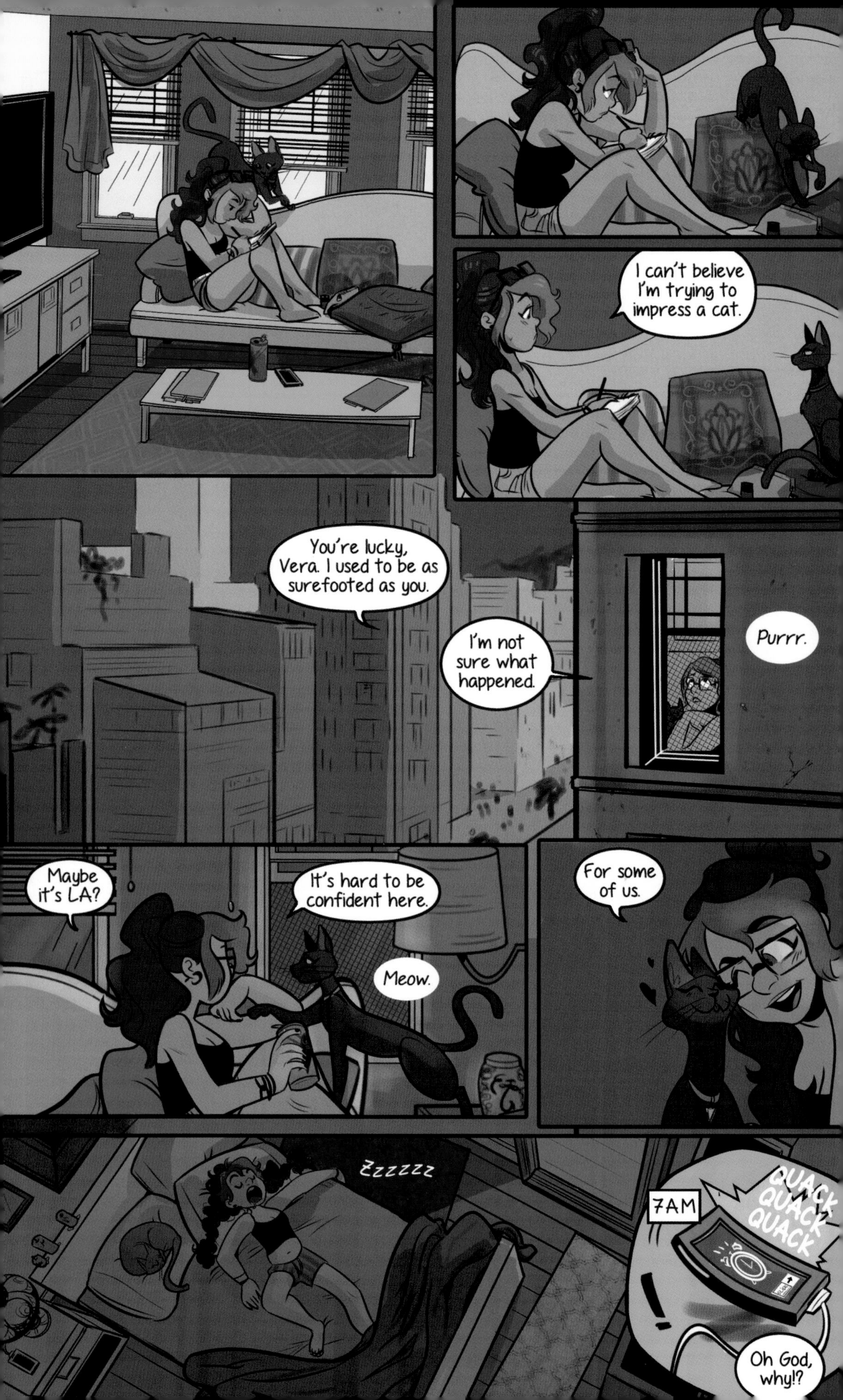
I can't believe I'm trying to impress a cat.
You're lucky, Vera. I used to be as surefooted as you.
I'm not sure what happened.
Purrr.
Maybe it's LA?
It's hard to be confident here.
Meow.
For some of us.
Zzzzzz
7AM
QUACK QUACK QUACK
Oh God, why!?

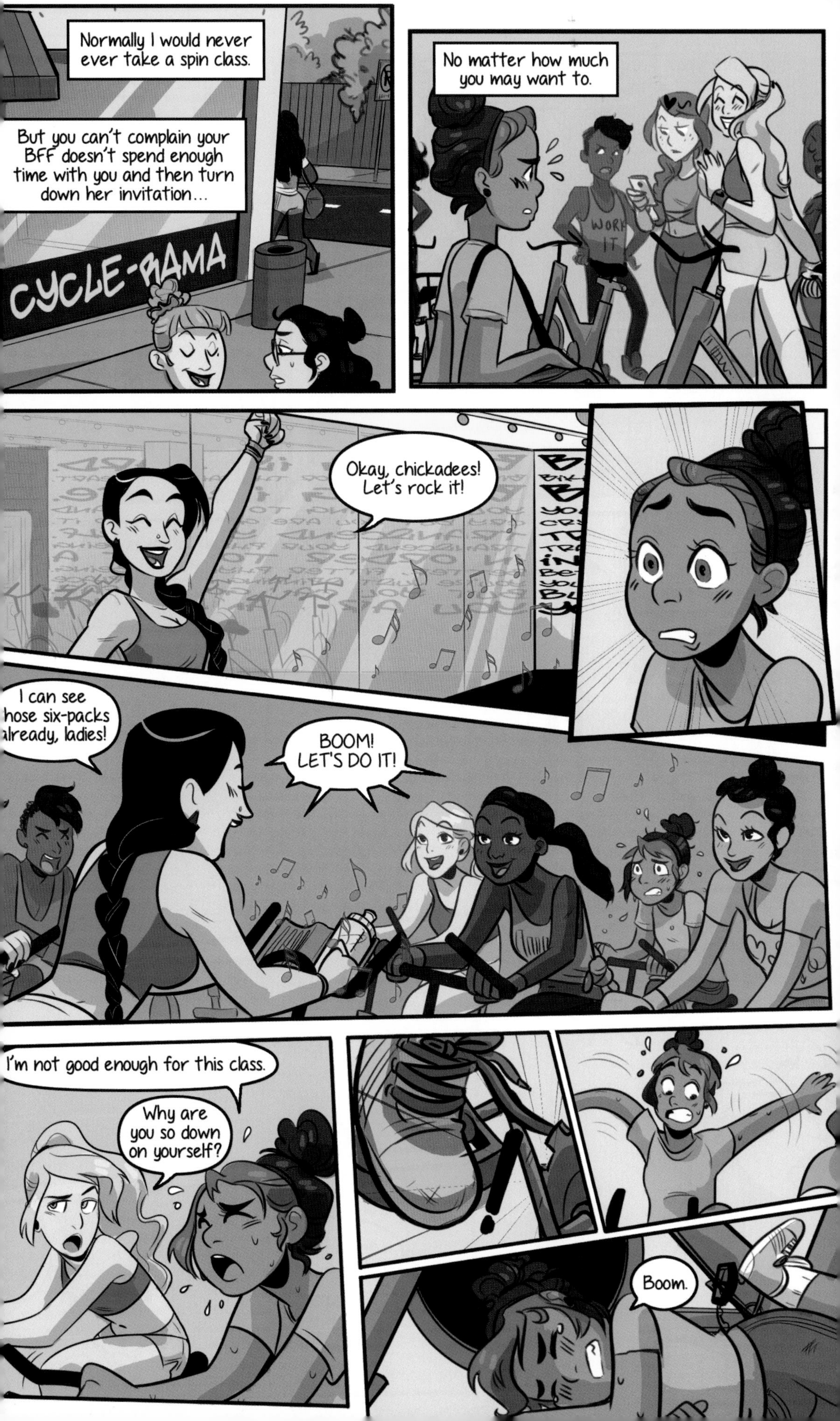
Normally I would never ever take a spin class.
But you can't complain your BFF doesn't spend enough time with you and then turn down her invitation...
CYCLE-RAMA
No matter how much you may want to.
WORK IT
Okay, chickadees! Let's rock it!
I can see hose six-packs already, ladies!
BOOM! LET'S DO IT!
I'm not good enough for this class.
Why are you so down on yourself?
Boom.

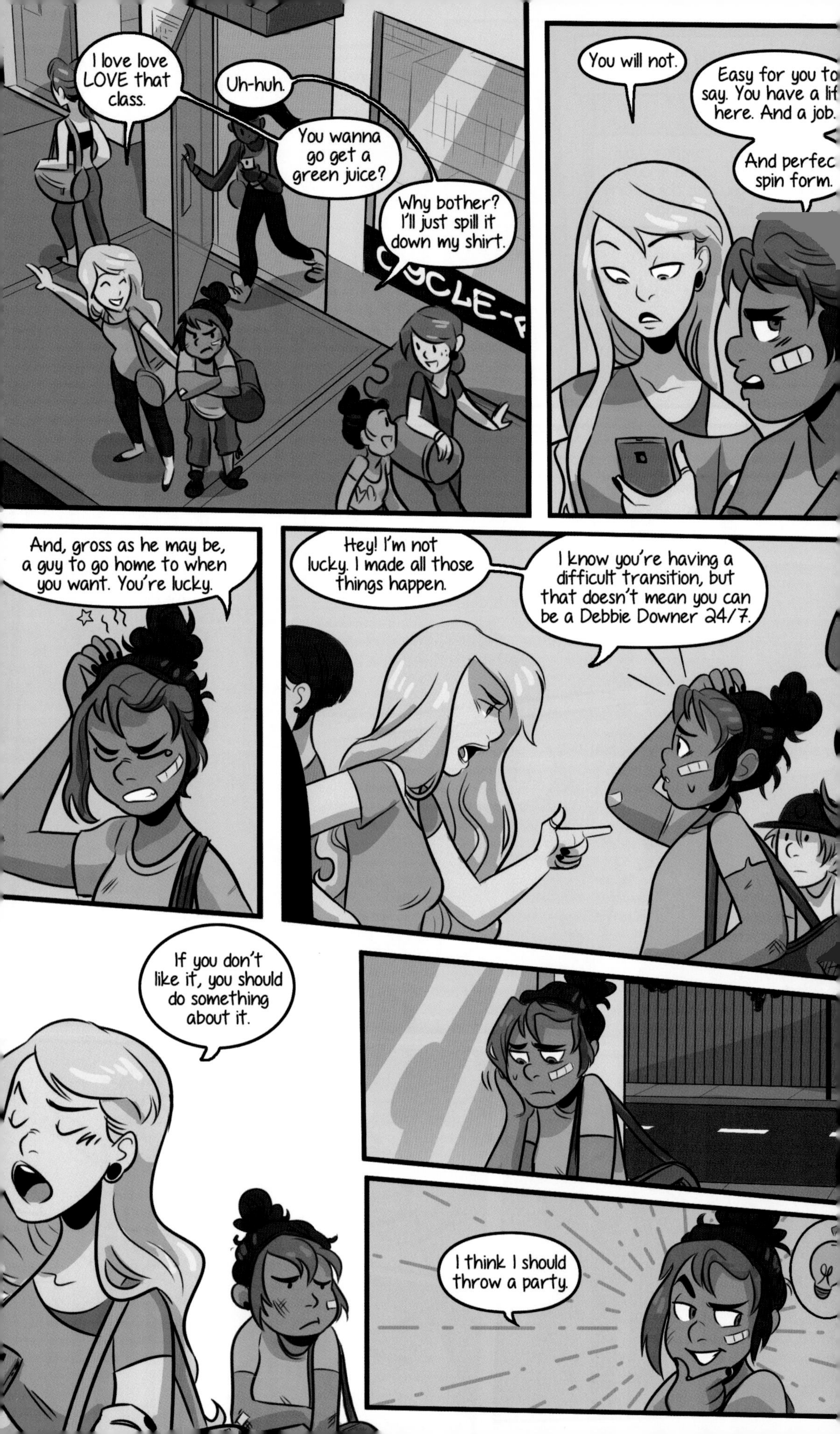
I love love LOVE that class.
Uh-huh.
You wanna go get a green juice?
Why bother? I'll just spill it down my shirt.
CYCLE-
You will not.
Easy for you to say. You have a life here. And a job.
And perfect spin form.
And, gross as he may be, a guy to go home to when you want. You're lucky.
Hey! I'm not lucky. I made all those things happen.
I know you're having a difficult transition, but that doesn't mean you can be a Debbie Downer 24/7.
If you don't like it, you should do something about it.
I think I should throw a party.

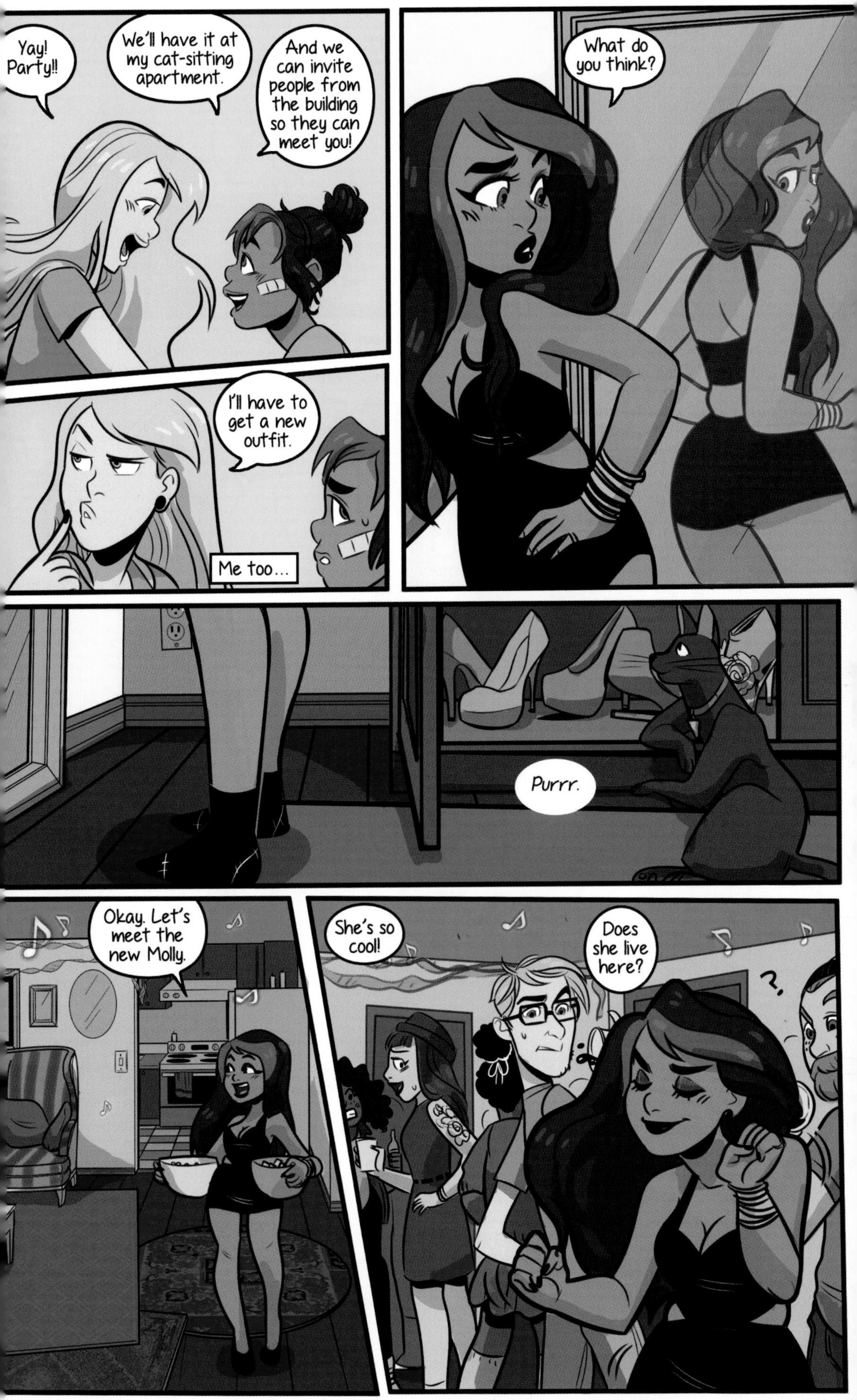
Yay! Party!!
We'll have it at my cat-sitting apartment.
And we can invite people from the building so they can meet you!
I'll have to get a new outfit.
Me too...
What do you think?
Purrr.
Okay. Let's meet the new Molly.
She's so cool!
Does she live here?
?.

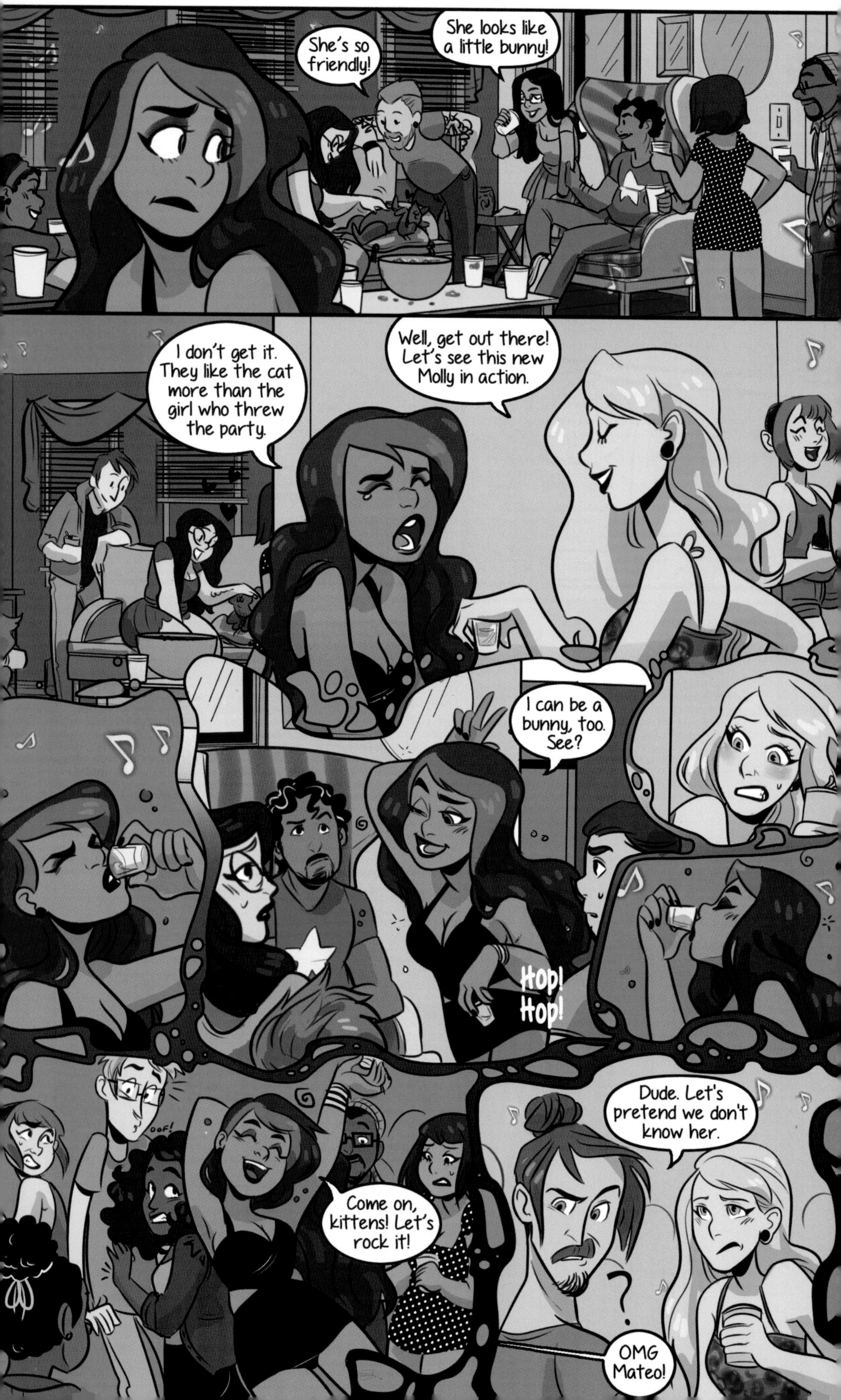
She's so friendly!
She looks like a little bunny!
I don't get it. They like the cat more than the girl who threw the party.
Well, get out there! Let's see this new Molly in action.
I can be a bunny, too. See?
Hop! Hop!
Come on, kittens! Let's rock it!
Dude. Let's pretend we don't know her.
OMG Mateo!

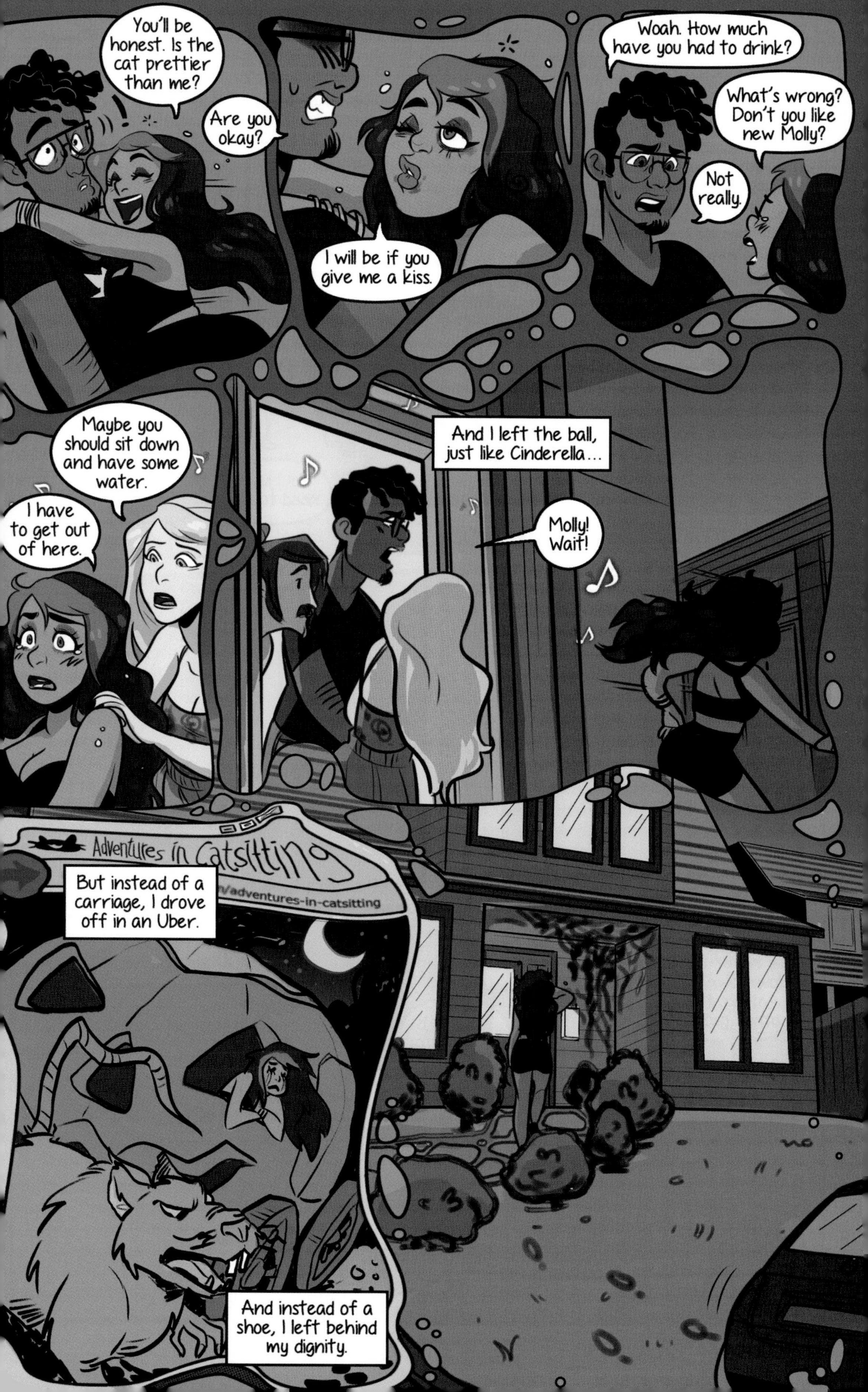
You'll be honest. Is the cat prettier than me?
Are you okay?
I will be if you give me a kiss.
Woah. How much have you had to drink?
What's wrong? Don't you like new Molly?
Not really.
Maybe you should sit down and have some water.
I have to get out of here.
And I left the ball, just like Cinderella...
Molly! Wait!
Adventures in Catsitting
/adventures-in-catsitting
But instead of a carriage, I drove off in an Uber.
And instead of a shoe, I left behind my dignity.

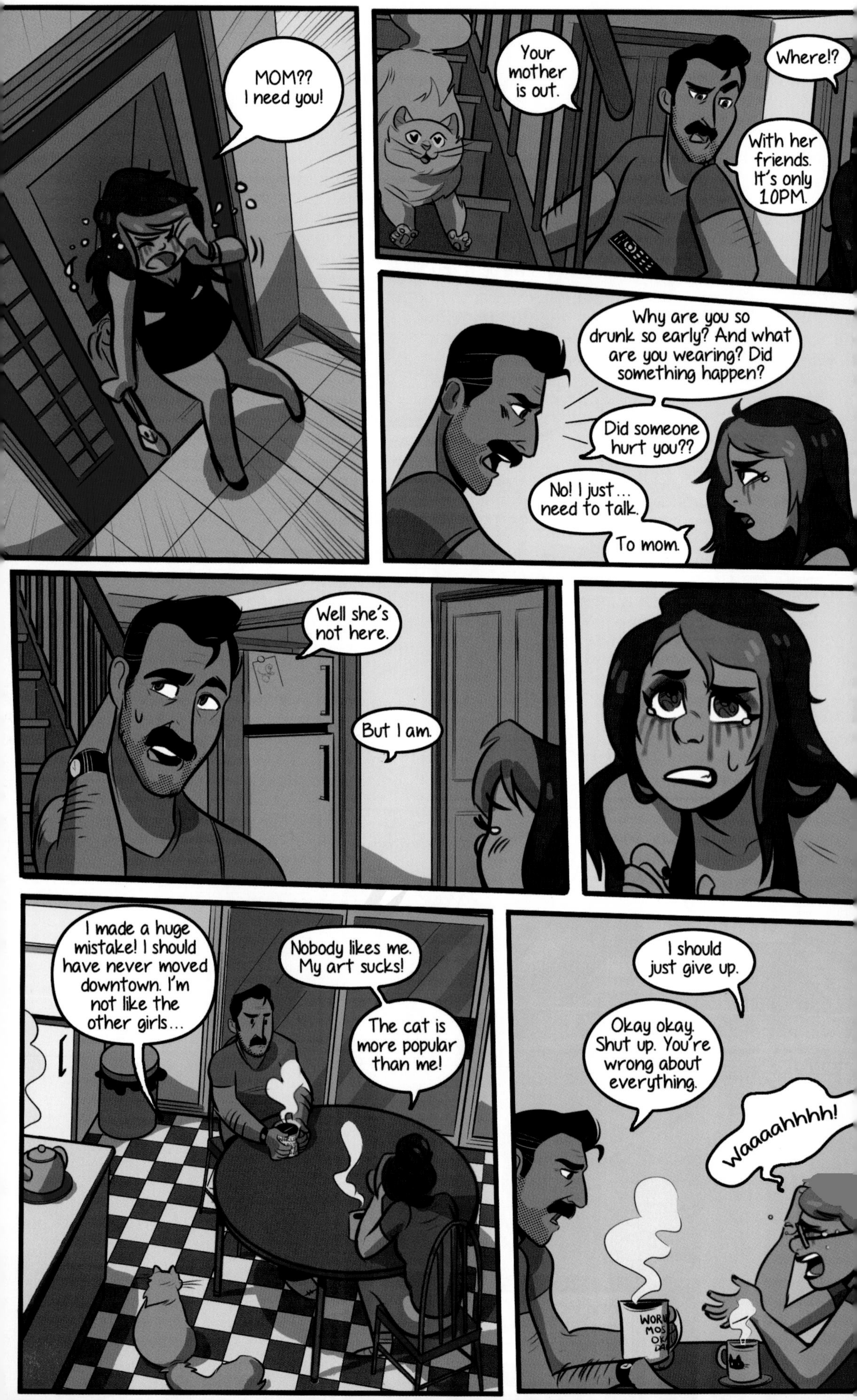
MOM?? I need you!
Your mother is out.
Where!?
With her friends. It's only 10PM.
Why are you so drunk so early? And what are you wearing? Did something happen?
Did someone hurt you??
No! I just... need to talk.
To mom.
Well she's not here.
But I am.
I made a huge mistake! I should have never moved downtown. I'm not like the other girls...
Nobody likes me. My art sucks!
The cat is more popular than me!
I should just give up.
Okay okay. Shut up. You're wrong about everything.
Waaaahhhh!

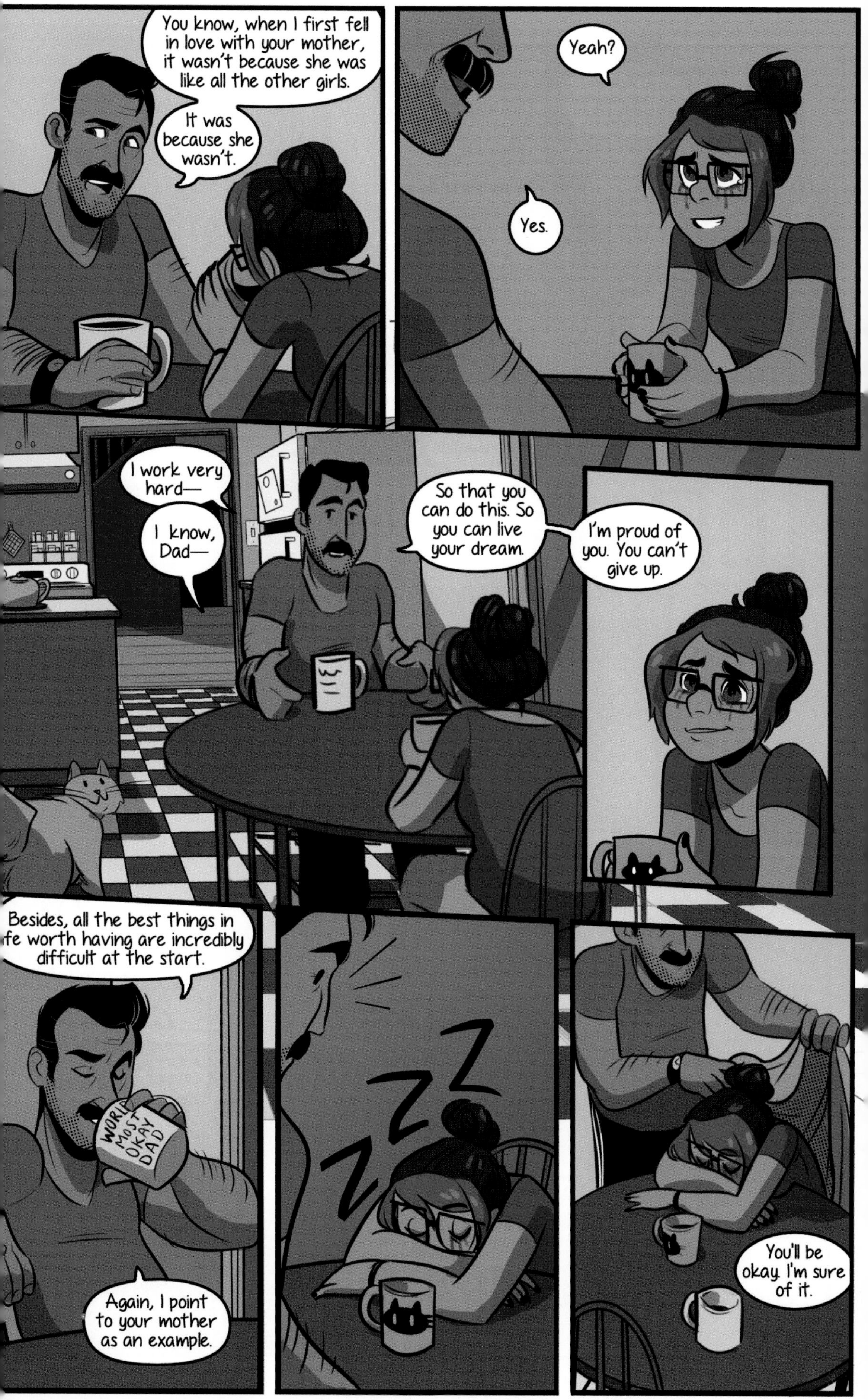

You know, when I first fell in love with your mother, it wasn't because she was like all the other girls.
It was because she wasn't.
Yeah?
Yes.
I work very hard—
I know, Dad—
So that you can do this. So you can live your dream.
I'm proud of you. You can't give up.
Besides, all the best things in life worth having are incredibly difficult at the start.
WORL MOST OKAY DAD
Again, I point to your mother as an example.
Z Z Z
You'll be okay. I'm sure of it.

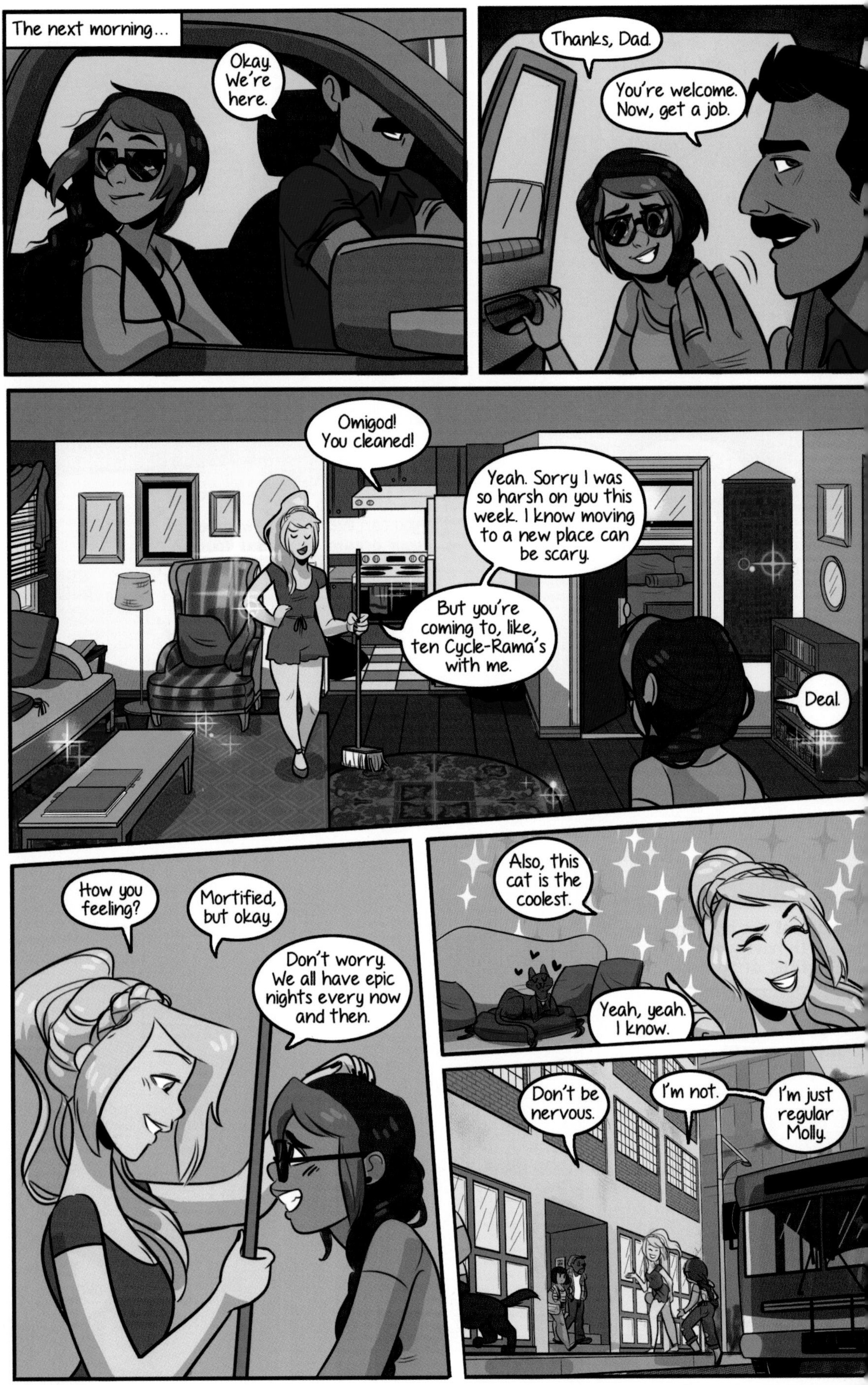
The next morning…
Okay. We're here.
Thanks, Dad.
You're welcome. Now, get a job.
Omigod! You cleaned!
Yeah. Sorry I was so harsh on you this week. I know moving to a new place can be scary.
But you're coming to, like, ten Cycle-Rama's with me.
Deal.
How you feeling?
Mortified, but okay.
Don't worry. We all have epic nights every now and then.
Also, this cat is the coolest.
Yeah, yeah. I know.
Don't be nervous.
I'm not.
I'm just regular Molly.

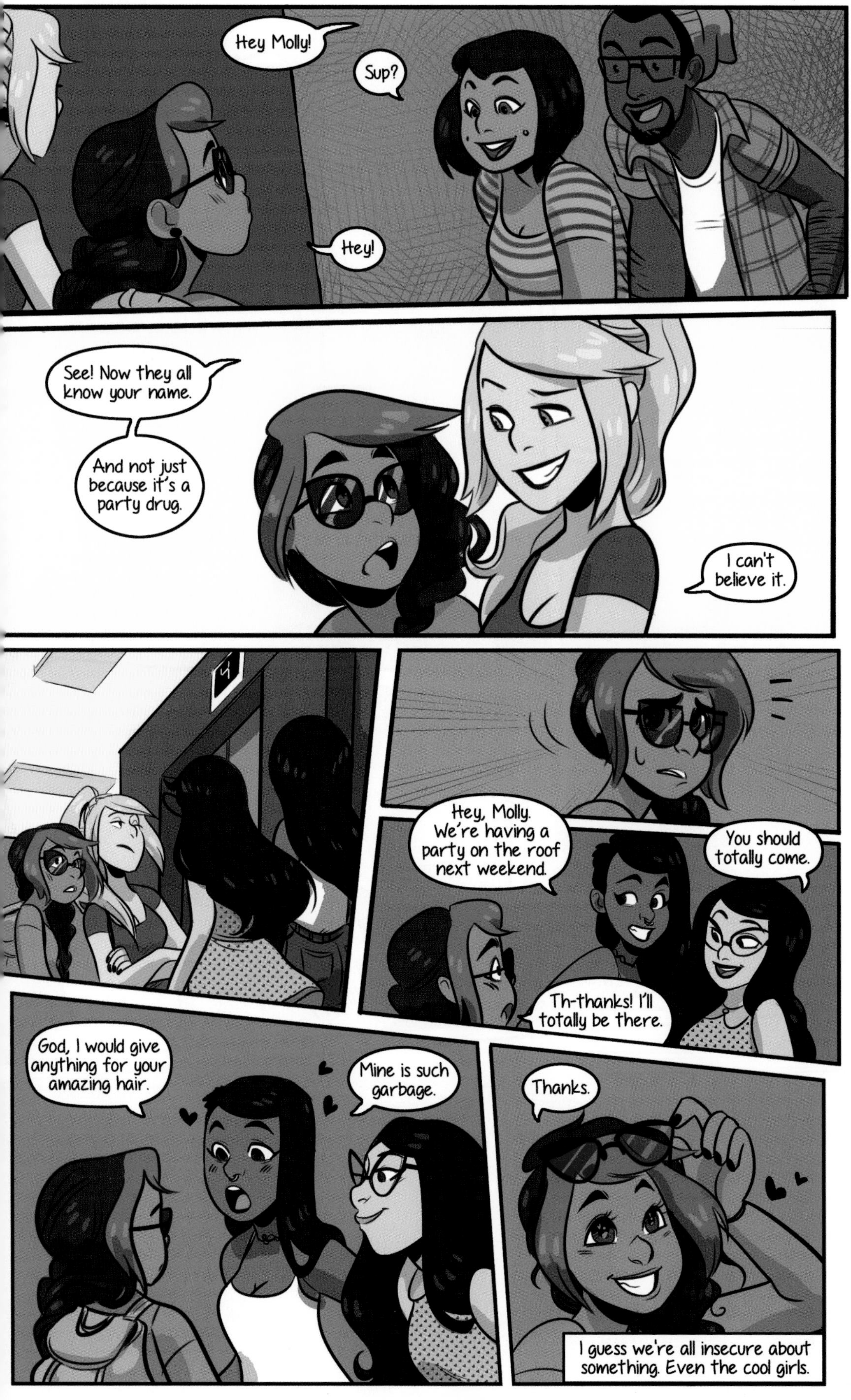
Hey Molly!
Sup?
Hey!
See! Now they all know your name.
And not just because it's a party drug.
I can't believe it.
Hey, Molly. We're having a party on the roof next weekend.
You should totally come.
Th-thanks! I'll totally be there.
God, I would give anything for your amazing hair.
Mine is such garbage.
Thanks.
I guess we're all insecure about something. Even the cool girls.

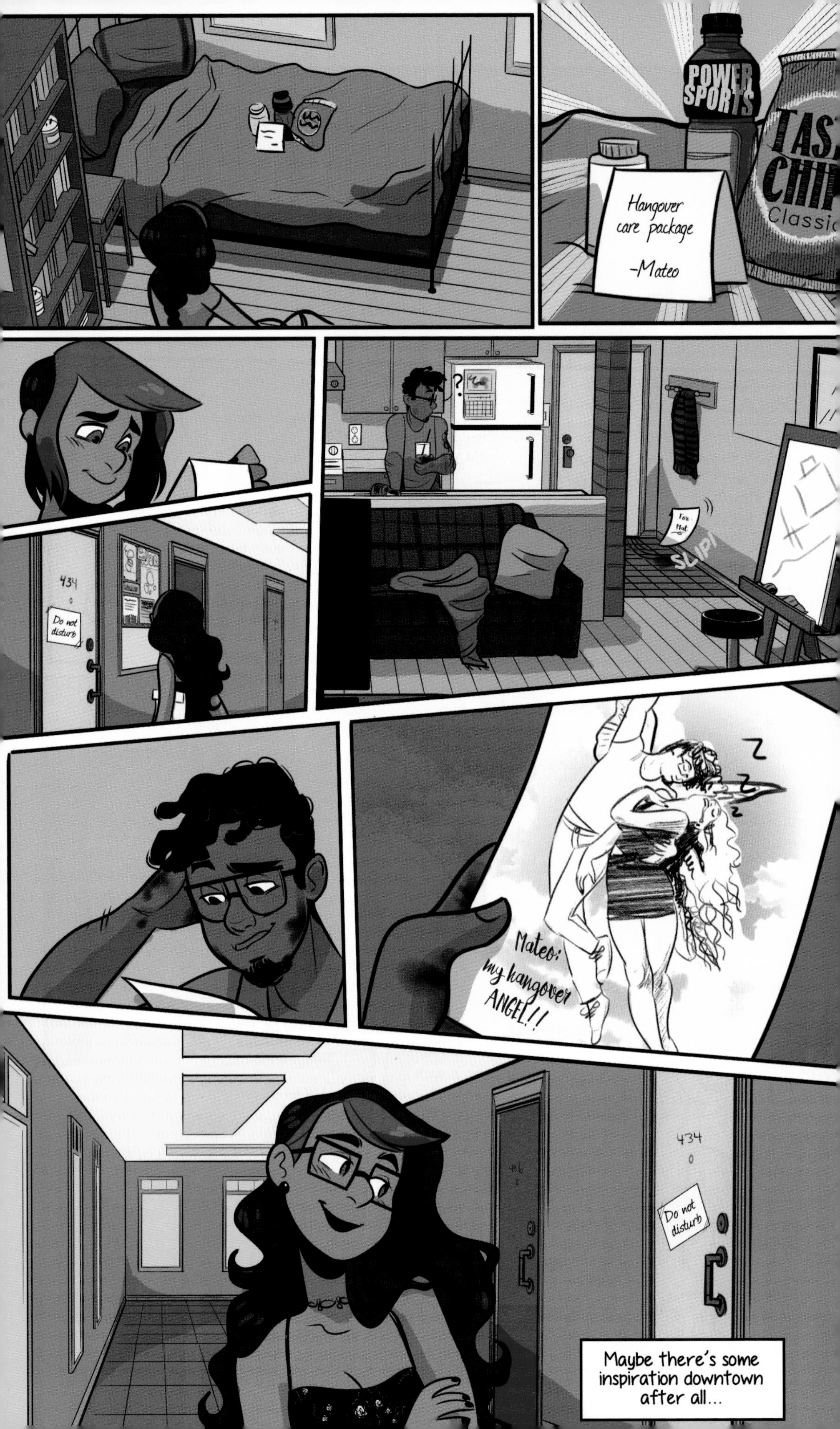
POWER SPORTS
TASTY CHIPS Classic
Hangover care package
-Mateo
434
Do not disturb
?
For Mat
SLIP!
Mateo: my hangover ANGEL!!
434
Do not disturb
Maybe there's some inspiration downtown after all...

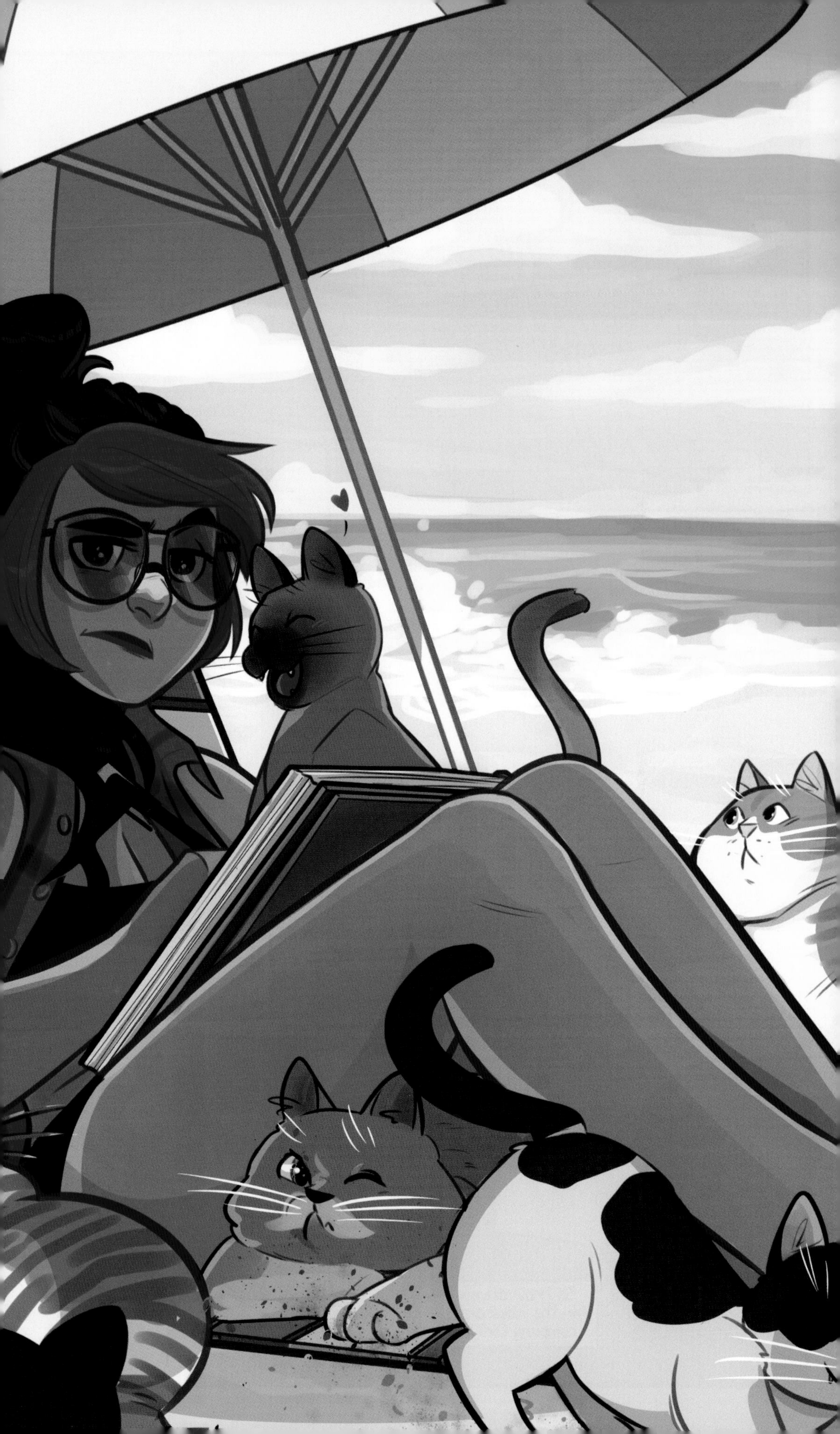

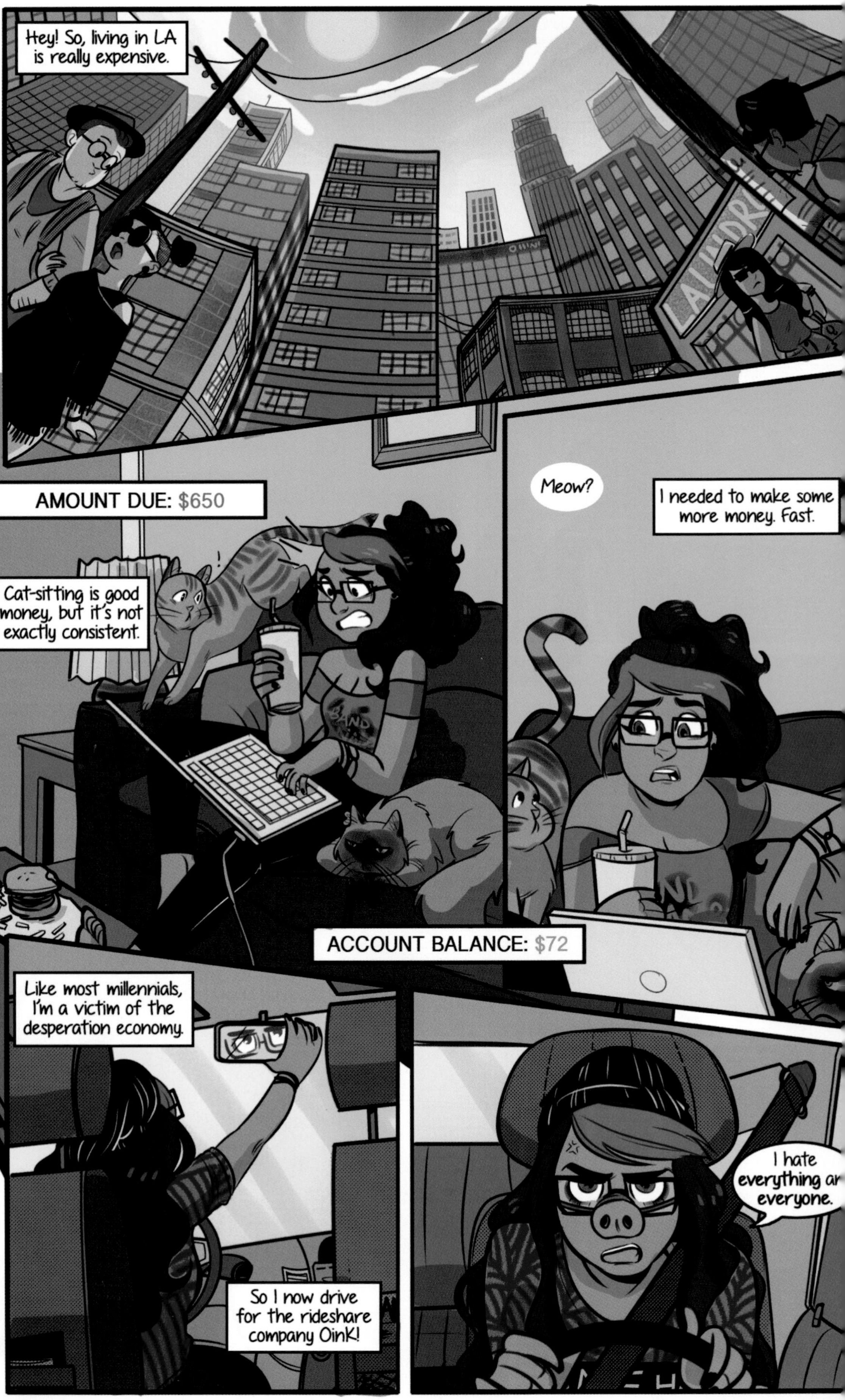
Hey! So, living in LA is really expensive.
AMOUNT DUE: $650
Cat-sitting is good money, but it's not exactly consistent.
Meow?
I needed to make some more money. Fast.
ACCOUNT BALANCE: $72
Like most millennials, I'm a victim of the desperation economy.
So I now drive for the rideshare company Oink!
I hate everything ar everyone.

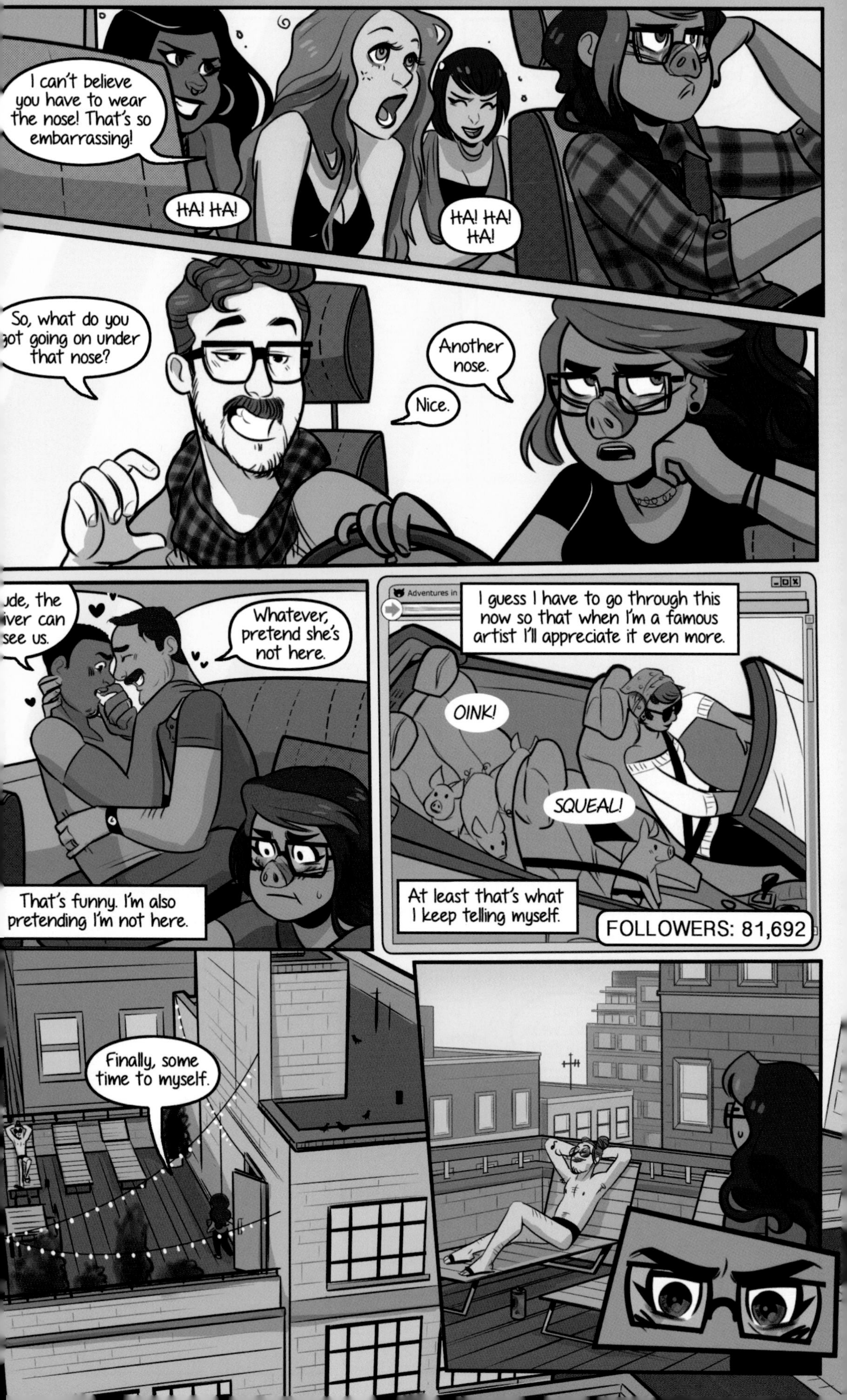
I can't believe you have to wear the nose! That's so embarrassing!
HA! HA!
HA! HA! HA!
So, what do you got going on under that nose?
Another nose.
Nice.
ude, the iver can see us.
Whatever, pretend she's not here.
That's funny. I'm also pretending I'm not here.
I guess I have to go through this now so that when I'm a famous artist I'll appreciate it even more.
OINK!
SQUEAL!
At least that's what I keep telling myself.
FOLLOWERS: 81,692
Finally, some time to myself.

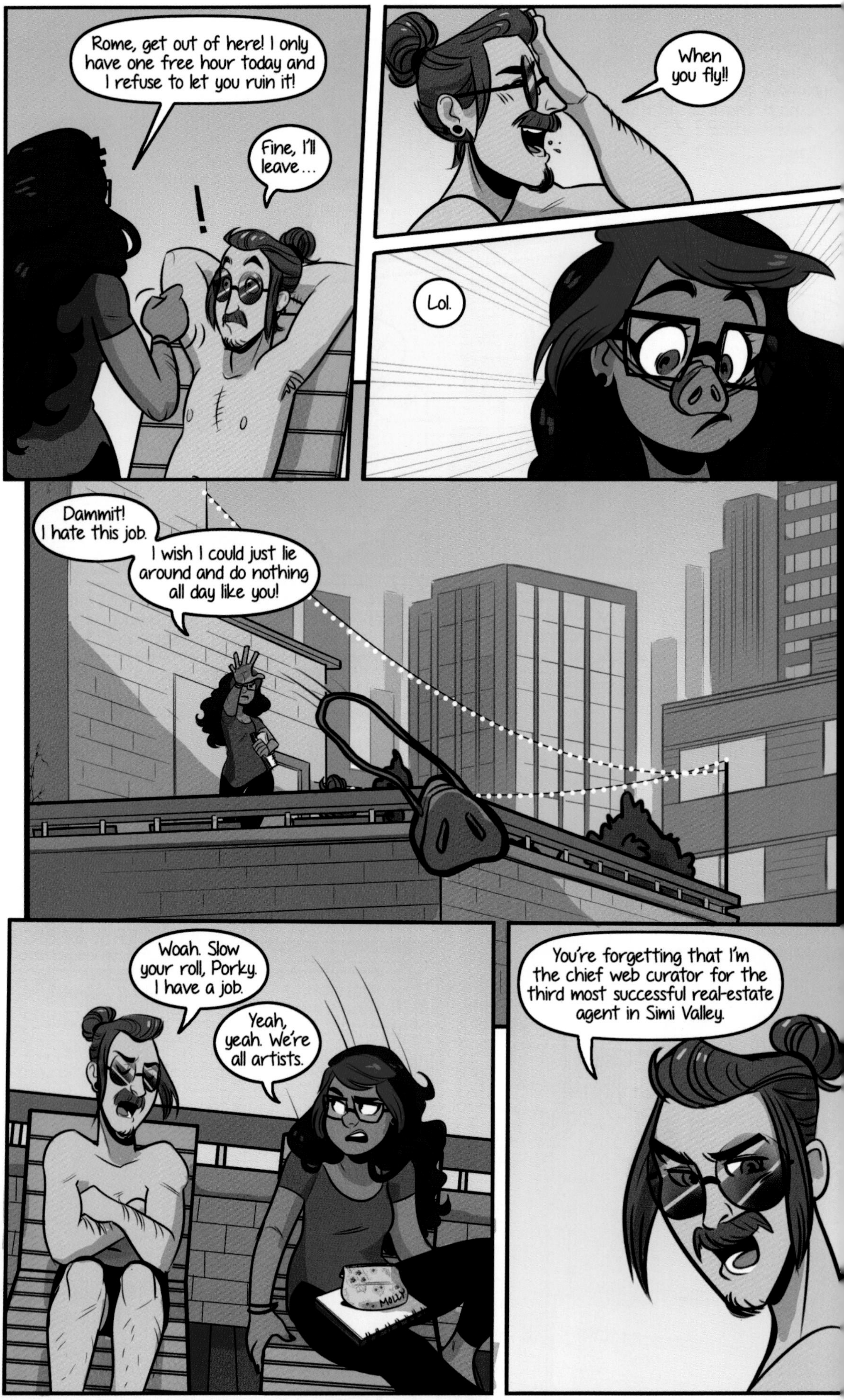
Rome, get out of here! I only have one free hour today and I refuse to let you ruin it!
Fine, I'll leave…
!
When you fly!!
Lol.
Dammit! I hate this job.
I wish I could just lie around and do nothing all day like you!
Woah. Slow your roll, Porky. I have a job.
Yeah, yeah. We're all artists.
MOLLY
You're forgetting that I'm the chief web curator for the third most successful real-estate agent in Simi Valley.

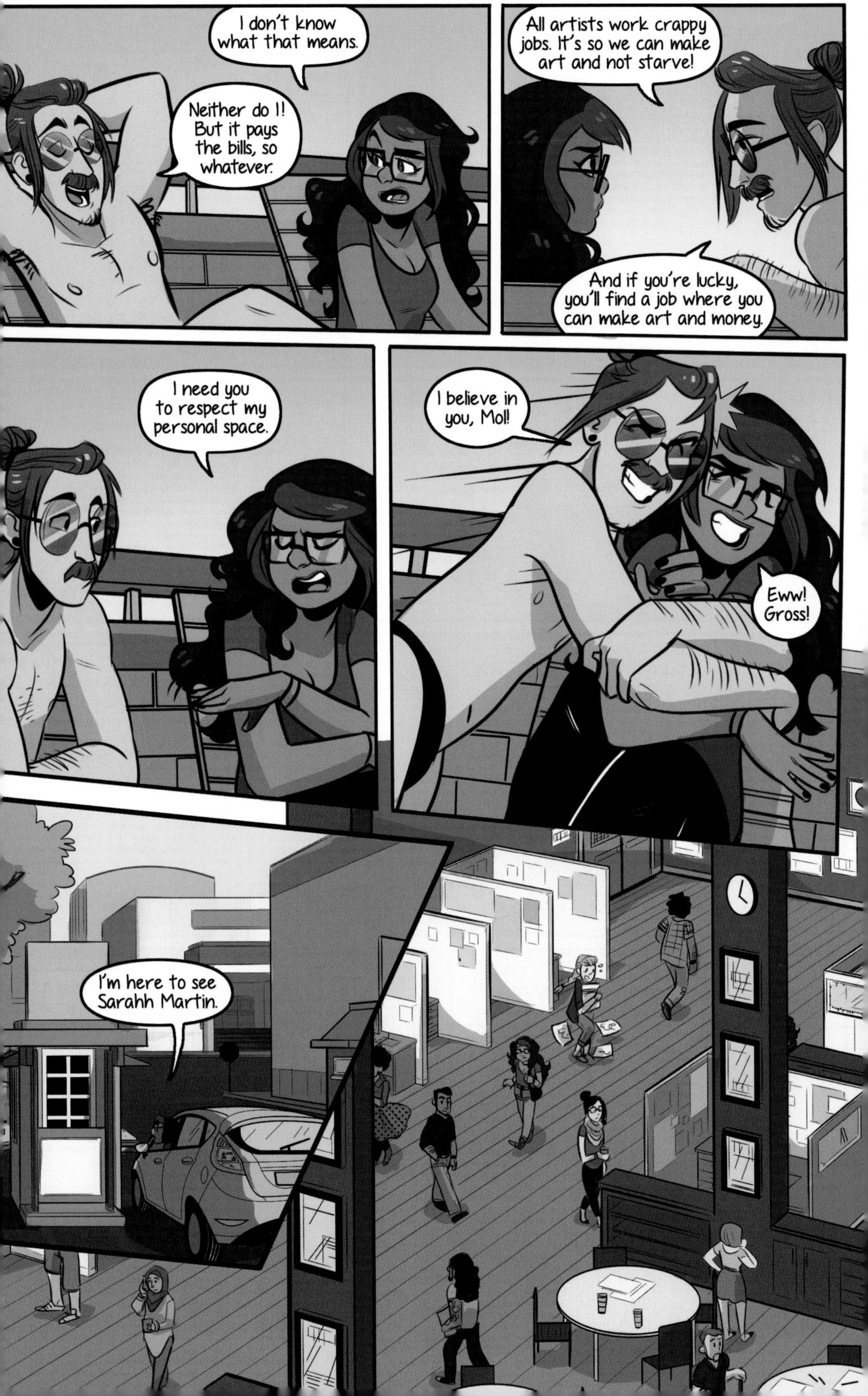
I don't know what that means.
Neither do I! But it pays the bills, so whatever.
All artists work crappy jobs. It's so we can make art and not starve!
And if you're lucky, you'll find a job where you can make art and money.
I need you to respect my personal space.
I believe in you, Mol!
Eww! Gross!
I'm here to see Sarahh Martin.

Wow, girl. I can't believe you work here.

Yay! You made it.

This place is intense.

And they work me to the bone.

Are you ready to eat? I'm starving.

Usually I have to eat at my desk because I have so much work to do.

I couldn't work at a place like this. So corporate. So professional.

I don't know how you do it.

It's not for everyone. But I love it.

Adventures in Catsitting

.com/adventures-in-cats

It's not the job would want, bu damn, my BFF so awesome.

Well, I have BIG news. You know the website TheSauce?

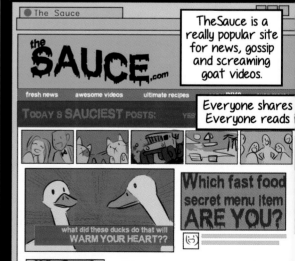

The Sauce

the SAUCE.com

fresh news   awesome videos   ultimate recipes

TODAY'S SAUCIEST POSTS: YES

TheSauce is a really popular site for news, gossip and screaming goat videos.

Everyone shares Everyone reads

Which fast food secret menu item ARE YOU?

what did these ducks do that will WARM YOUR HEART??

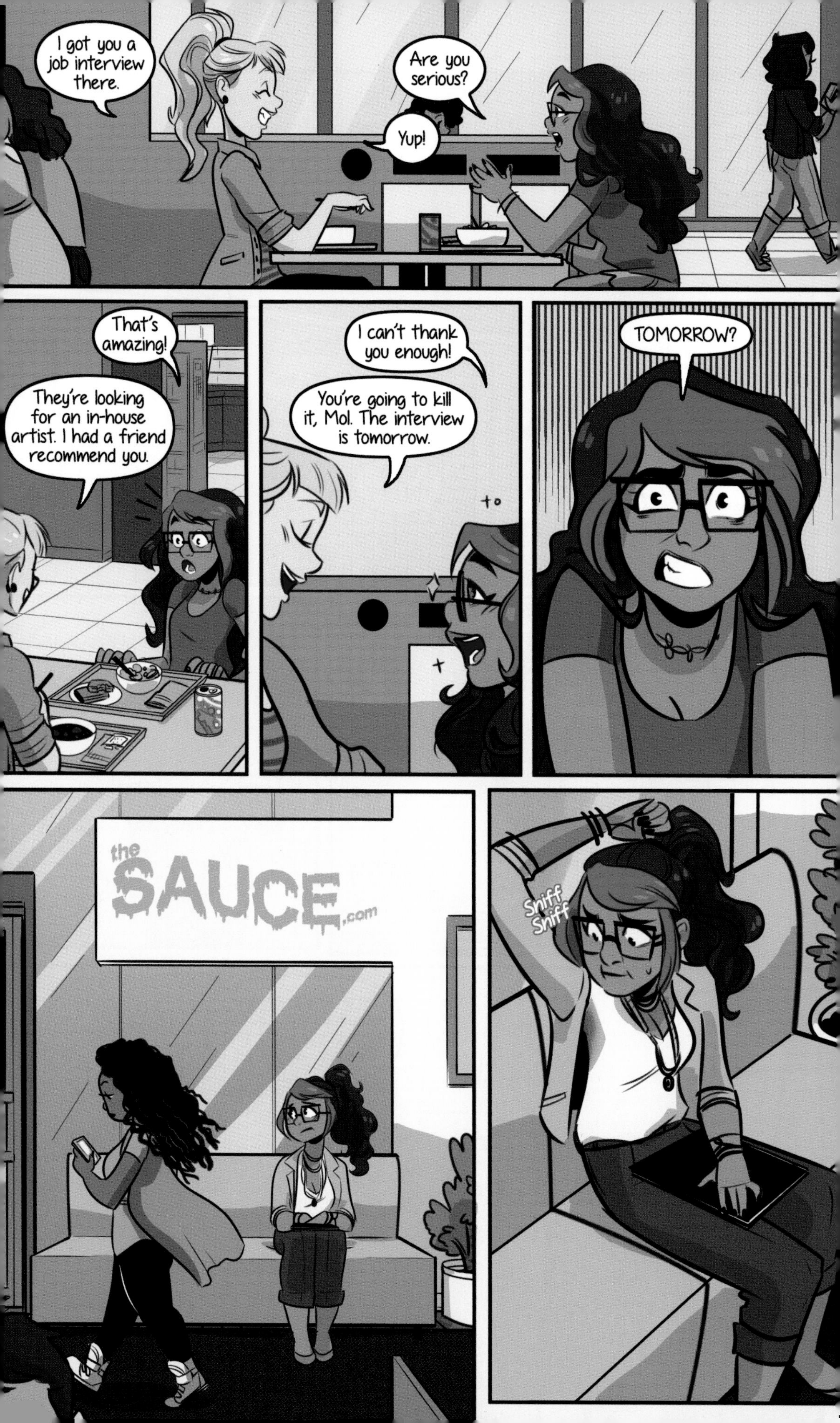
I got you a job interview there.
Are you serious?
Yup!
That's amazing!
They're looking for an in-house artist. I had a friend recommend you.
I can't thank you enough!
You're going to kill it, Mol. The interview is tomorrow.
TOMORROW?
the SAUCE.com
Sniff Sniff

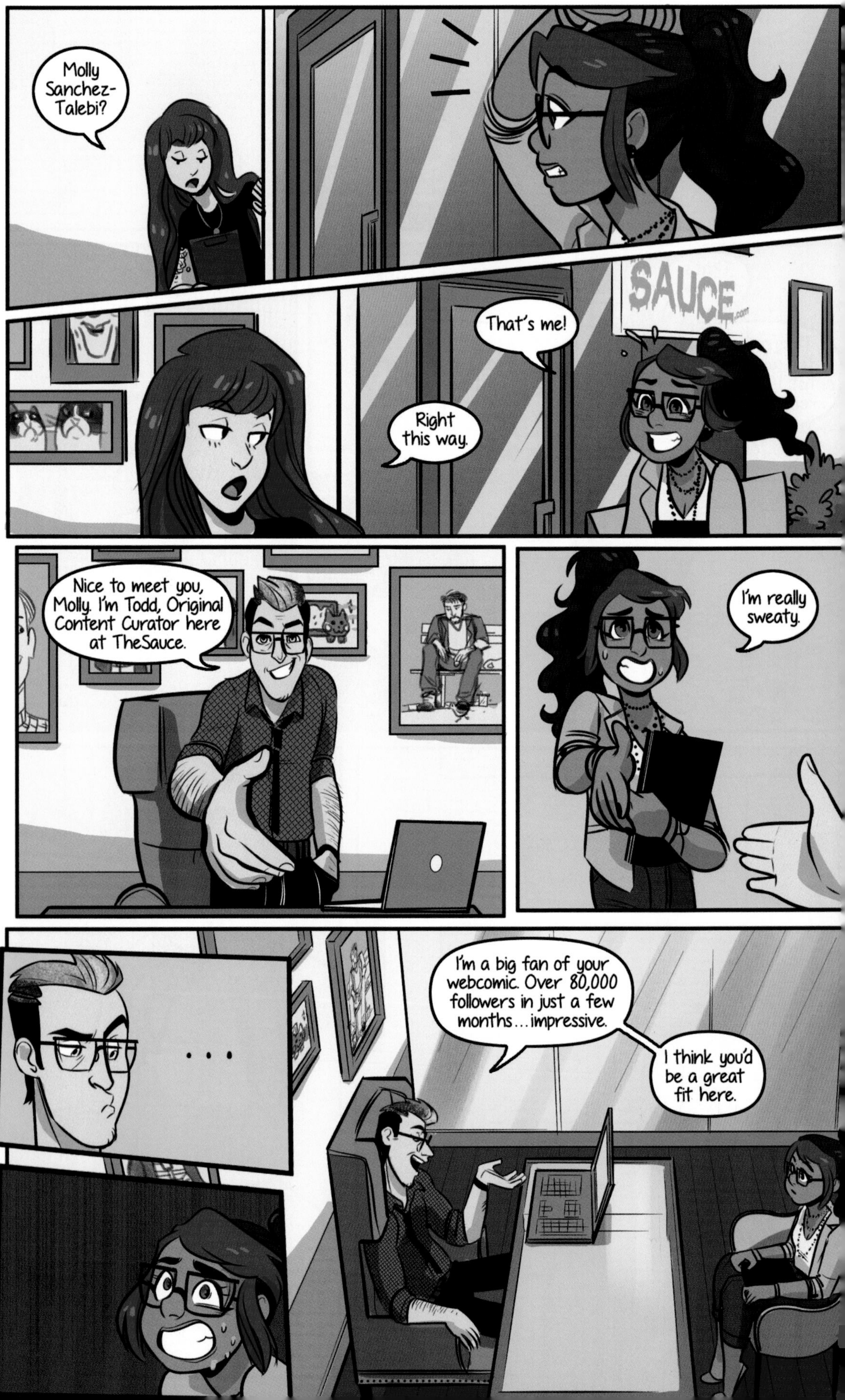
Molly Sanchez-Talebi?
That's me!
Right this way.
SAUCE.com
Nice to meet you, Molly. I'm Todd, Original Content Curator here at TheSauce.
I'm really sweaty.
. . .
I'm a big fan of your webcomic. Over 80,000 followers in just a few months... impressive.
I think you'd be a great fit here.

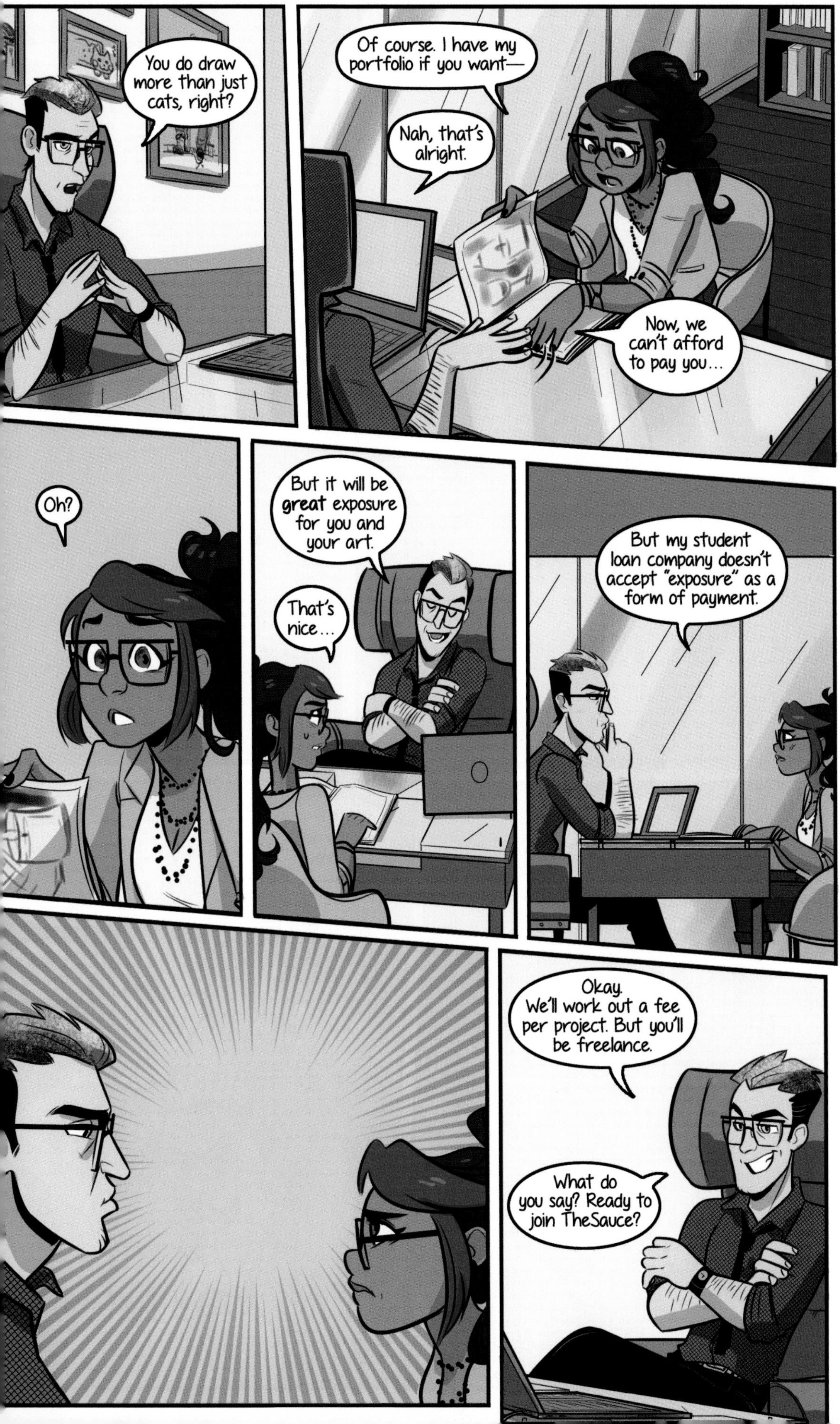
You do draw more than just cats, right?
Of course. I have my portfolio if you want—
Nah, that's alright.
Now, we can't afford to pay you...
Oh?
But it will be **great** exposure for you and your art.
That's nice...
But my student loan company doesn't accept "exposure" as a form of payment.
Okay. We'll work out a fee per project. But you'll be freelance.
What do you say? Ready to join TheSauce?

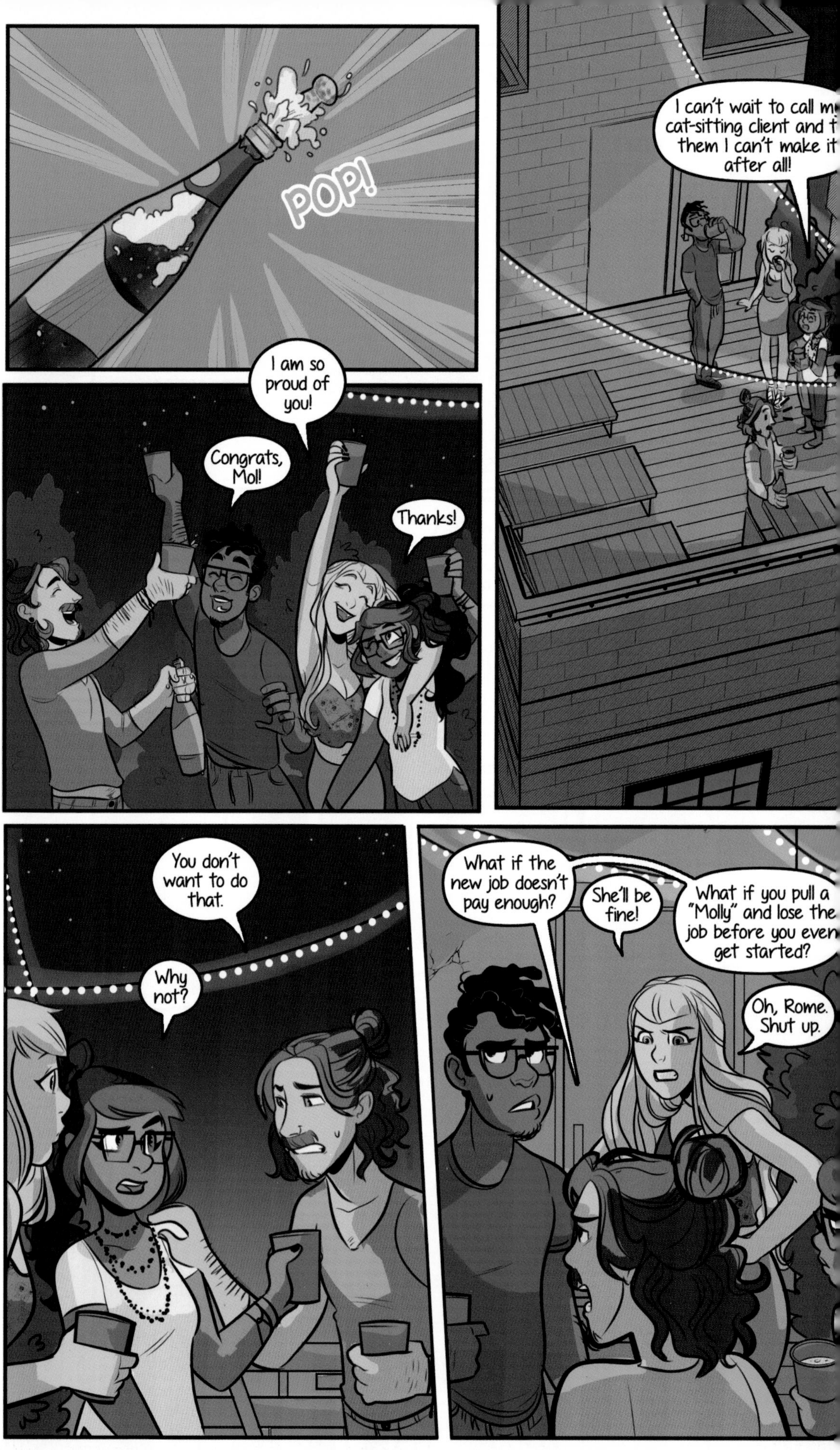
POP!
I am so proud of you!
Congrats, Mol!
Thanks!
I can't wait to call m cat-sitting client and t them I can't make it after all!
You don't want to do that.
Why not?
What if the new job doesn't pay enough?
She'll be fine!
What if you pull a "Molly" and lose the job before you even get started?
Oh, Rome. Shut up.

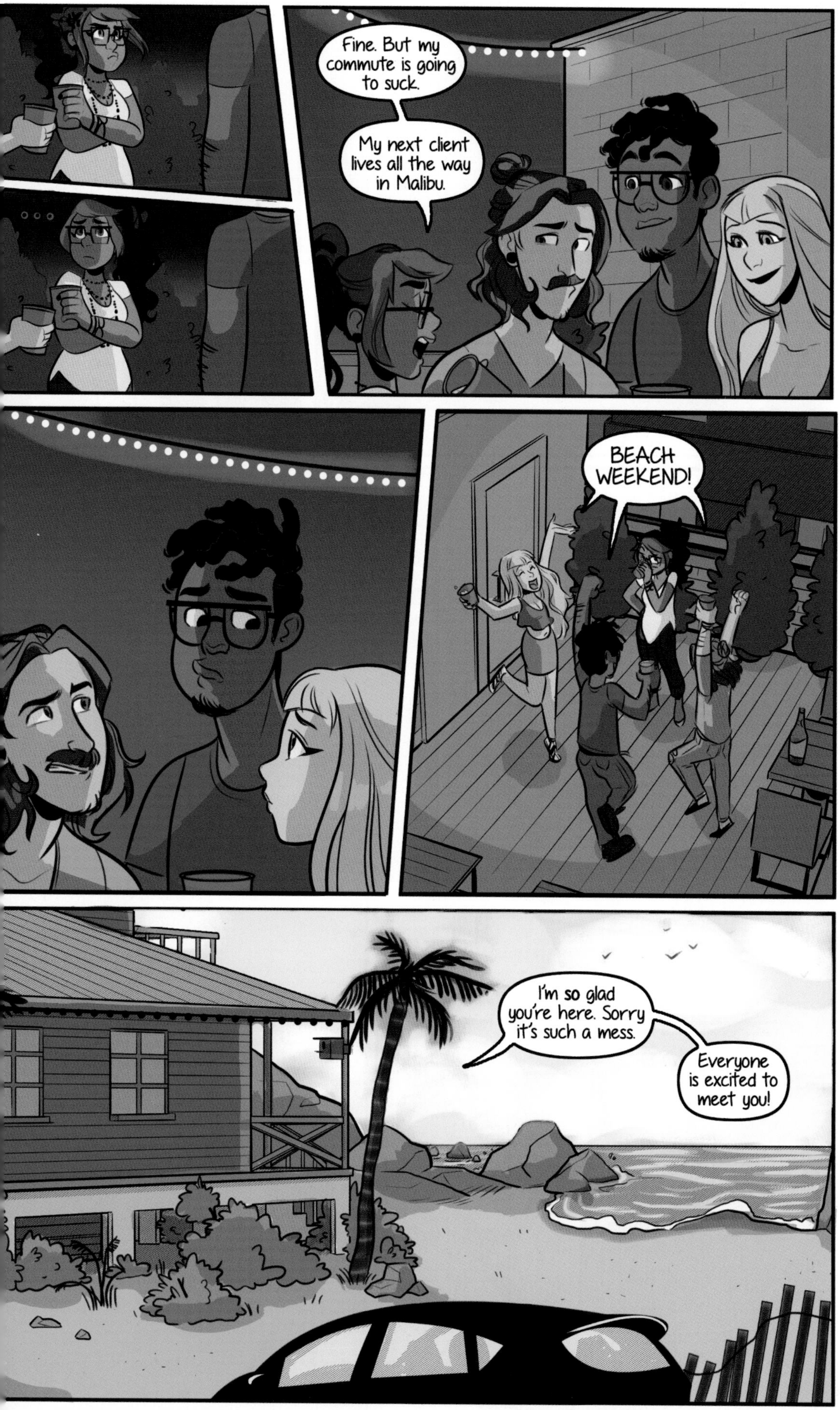
Fine. But my commute is going to suck.
My next client lives all the way in Malibu.
BEACH WEEKEND!
I'm so glad you're here. Sorry it's such a mess.
Everyone is excited to meet you!

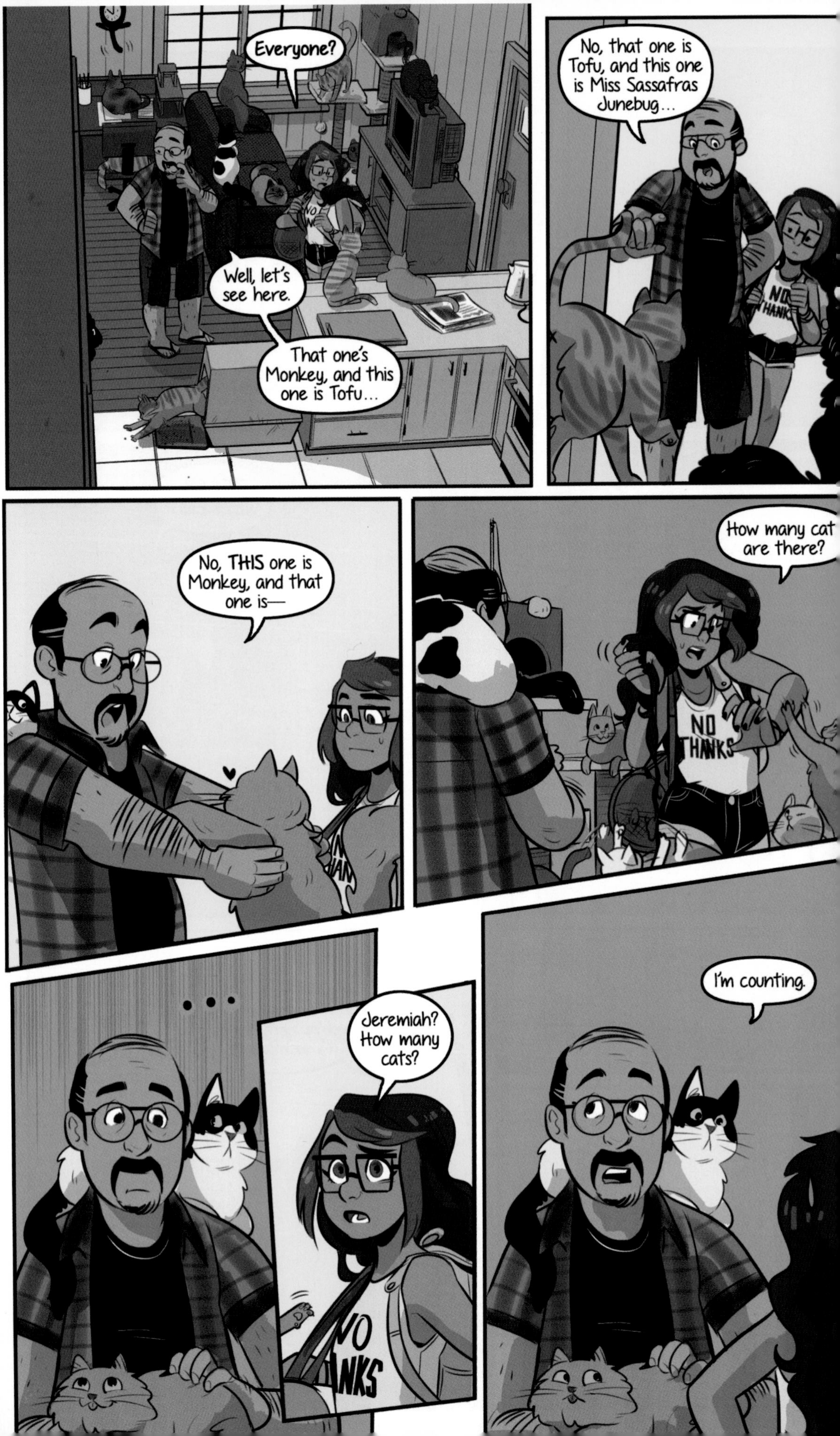
Everyone?
Well, let's see here.
That one's Monkey, and this one is Tofu...
No, that one is Tofu, and this one is Miss Sassafras Junebug...
NO THANKS
No, THIS one is Monkey, and that one is—
How many cat are there?
NO THANKS
. . .
Jeremiah? How many cats?
I'm counting.

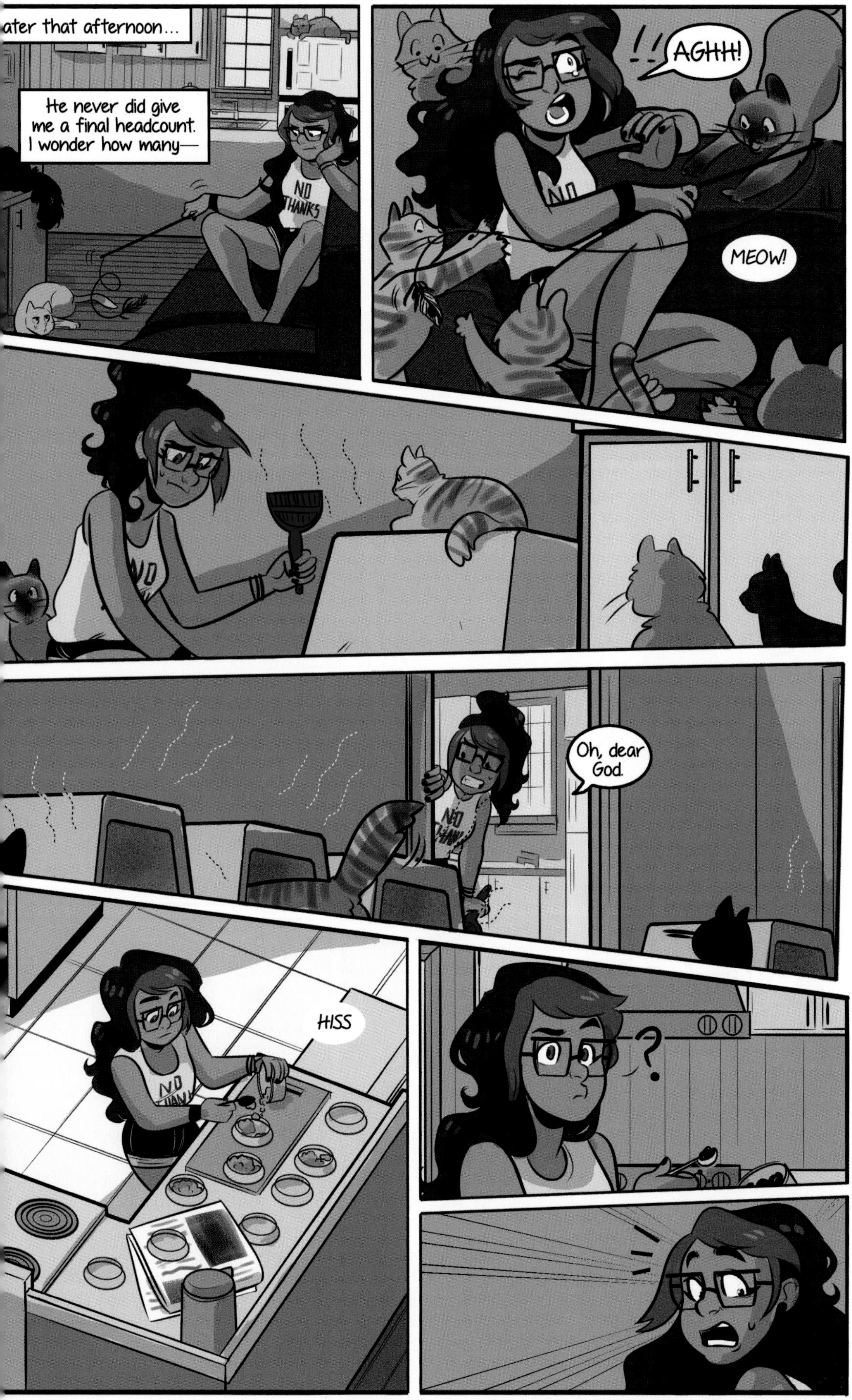
ater that afternoon...
He never did give me a final headcount. I wonder how many—
NO THANKS
AGHH!
MEOW!
Oh, dear God.
HISS
?

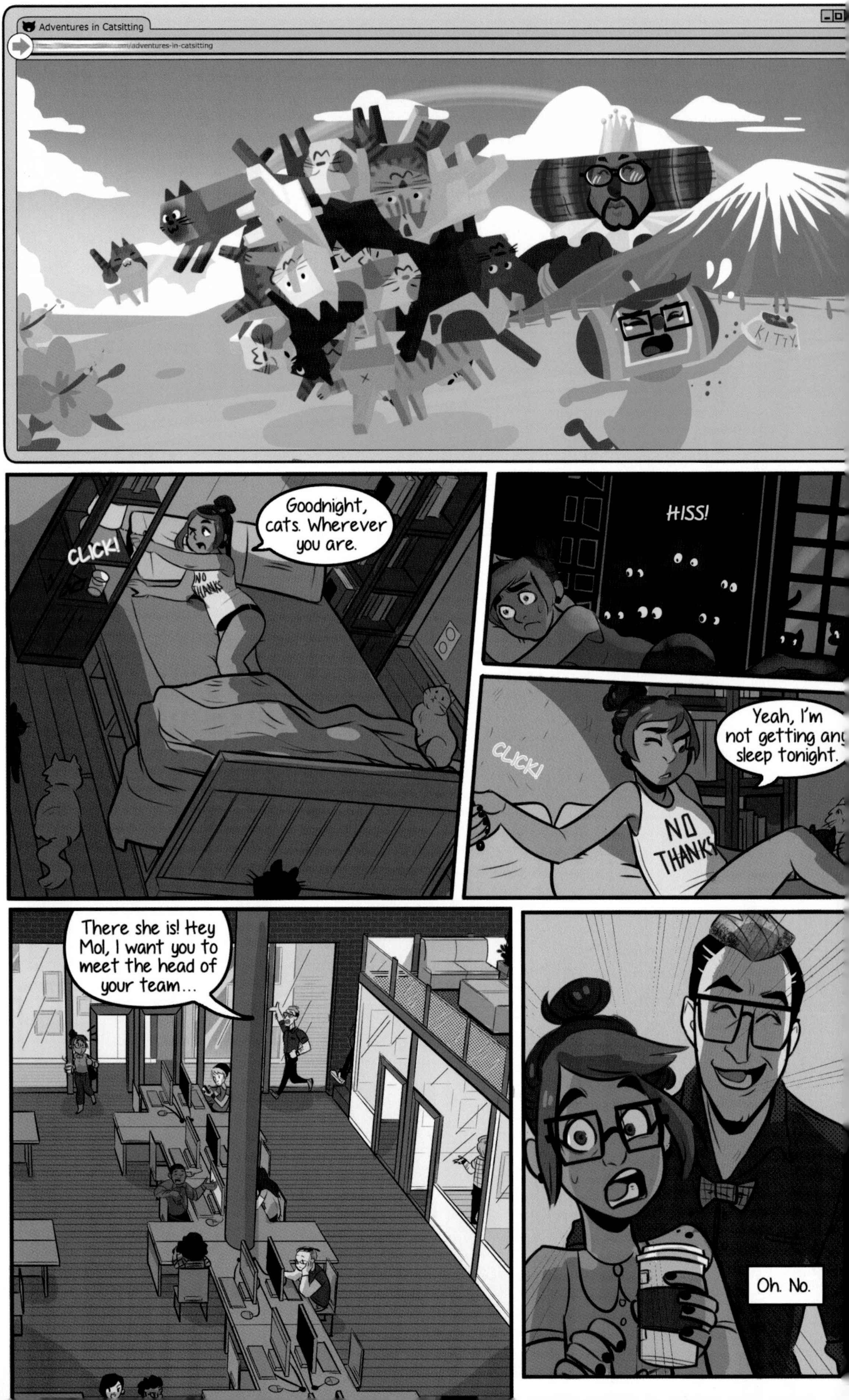

Adventures in Catsitting
m/adventures-in-catsitting
KITTY
CLICK!
Goodnight, cats. Wherever you are.
HISS!
CLICK!
Yeah, I'm not getting an sleep tonight.
There she is! Hey Mol, I want you to meet the head of your team...
Oh. No.

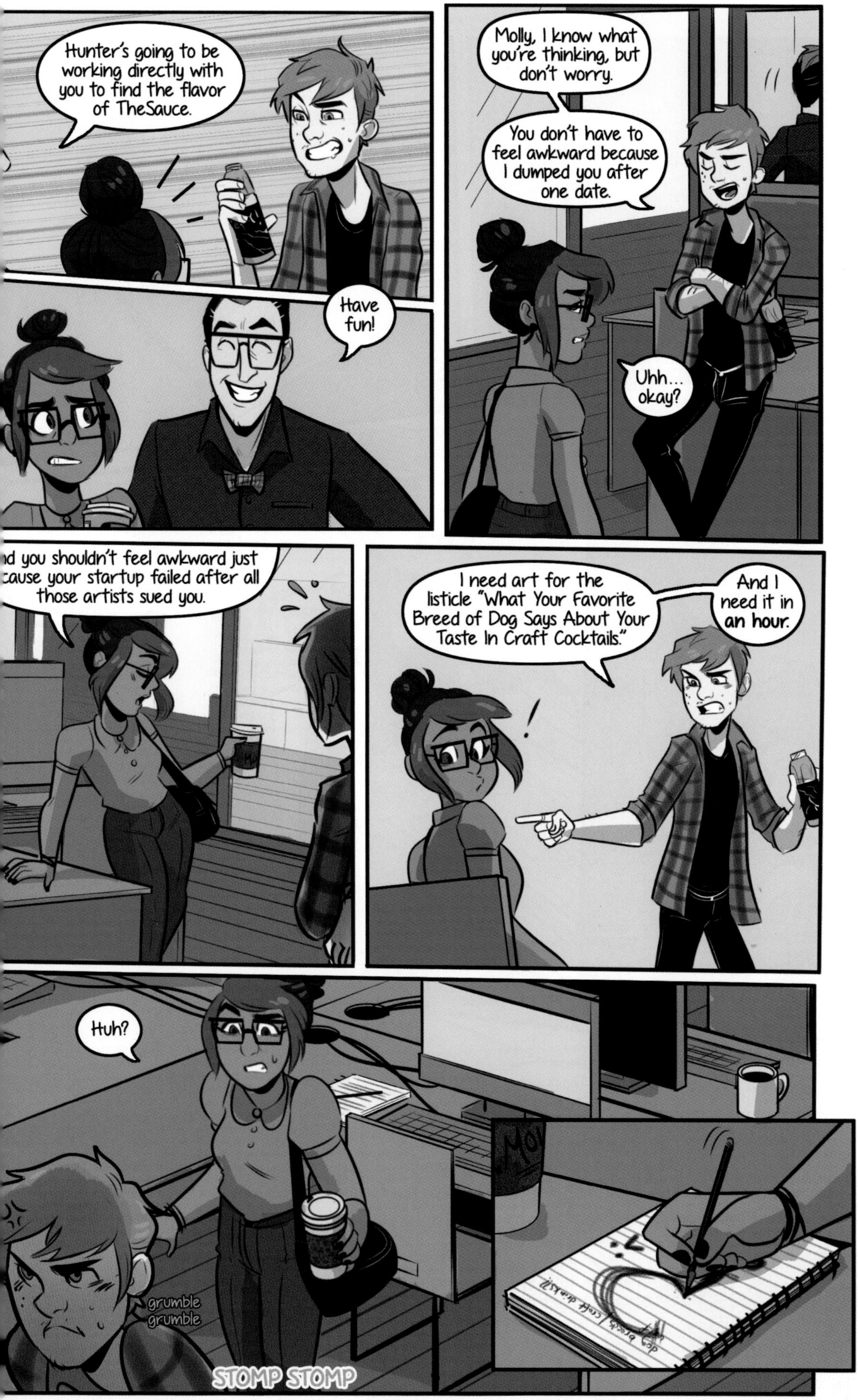

Hunter's going to be working directly with you to find the flavor of TheSauce.
Have fun!
Molly, I know what you're thinking, but don't worry.
You don't have to feel awkward because I dumped you after one date.
Uhh... okay?
nd you shouldn't feel awkward just cause your startup failed after all those artists sued you.
I need art for the listicle "What Your Favorite Breed of Dog Says About Your Taste In Craft Cocktails."
And I need it in **an hour.**
!
Huh?
grumble grumble
STOMP STOMP

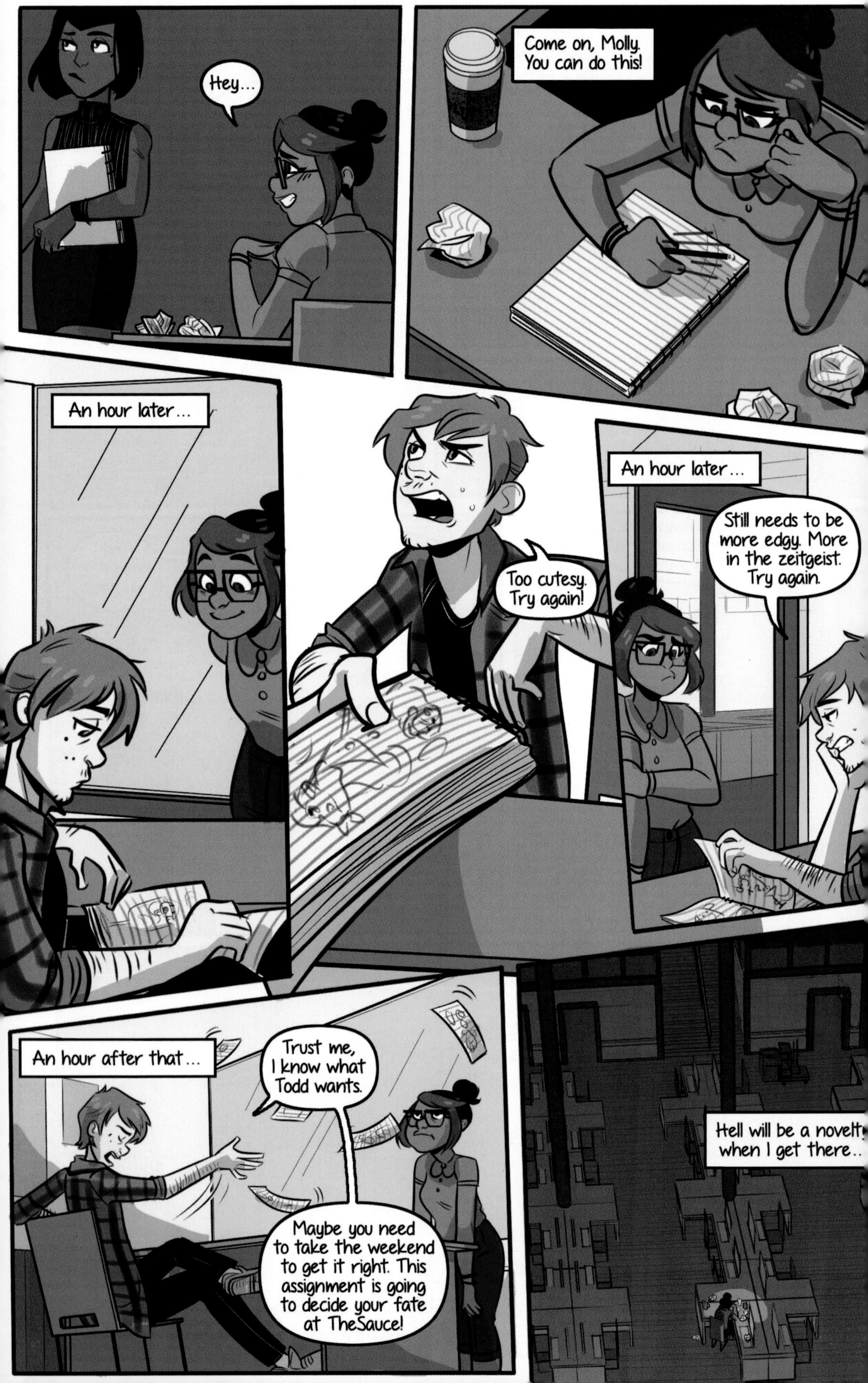
Hey...
Come on, Molly. You can do this!
An hour later...
Too cutesy. Try again!
An hour later...
Still needs to be more edgy. More in the zeitgeist. Try again.
An hour after that...
Trust me, I know what Todd wants.
Maybe you need to take the weekend to get it right. This assignment is going to decide your fate at TheSauce!
Hell will be a novelt
when I get there...

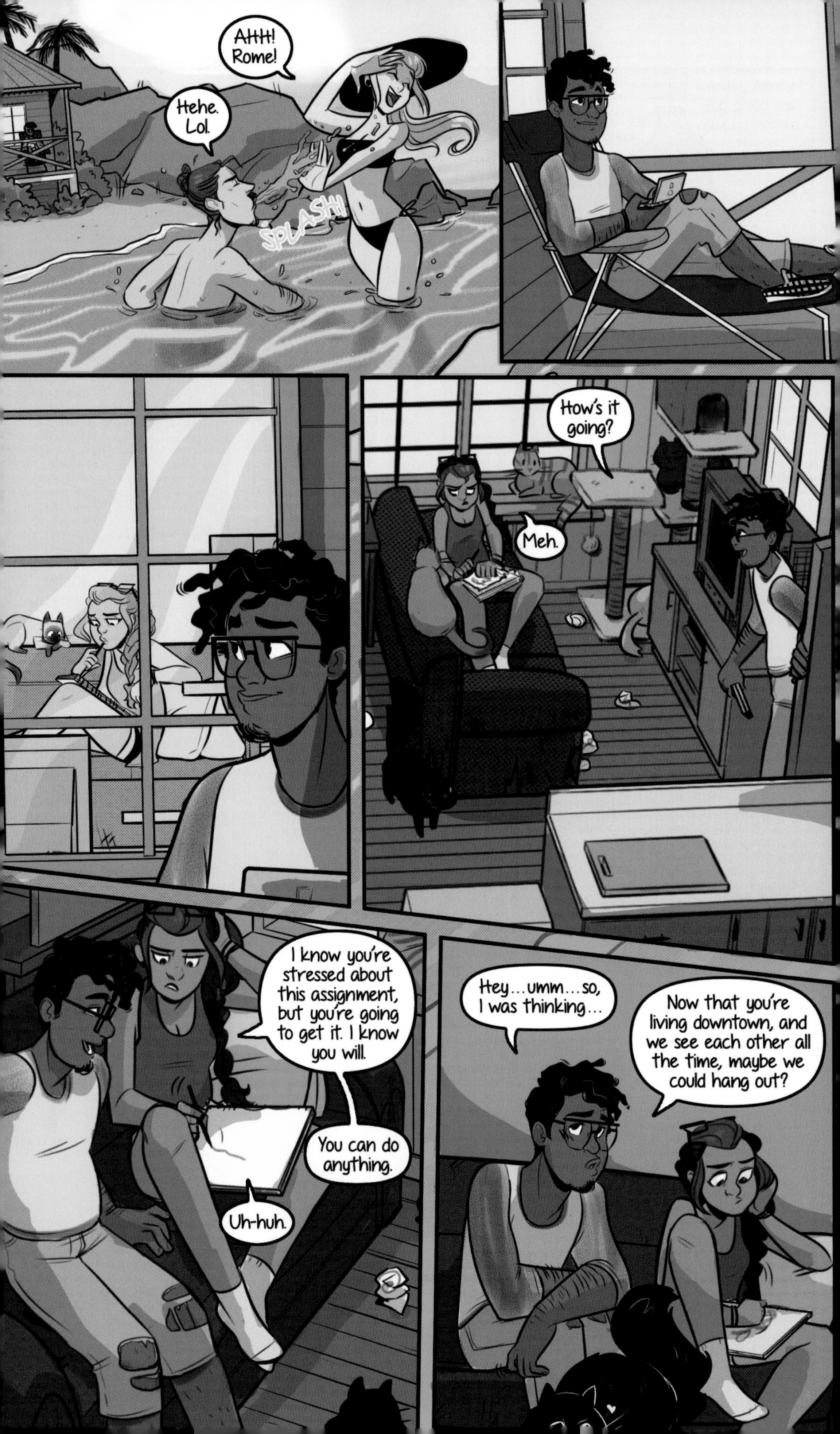
AHH! Rome!
Hehe. Lol.
SPLASH!
How's it going?
Meh.
I know you're stressed about this assignment, but you're going to get it. I know you will.
You can do anything.
Uh-huh.
Hey...umm...so, I was thinking...
Now that you're living downtown, and we see each other all the time, maybe we could hang out?

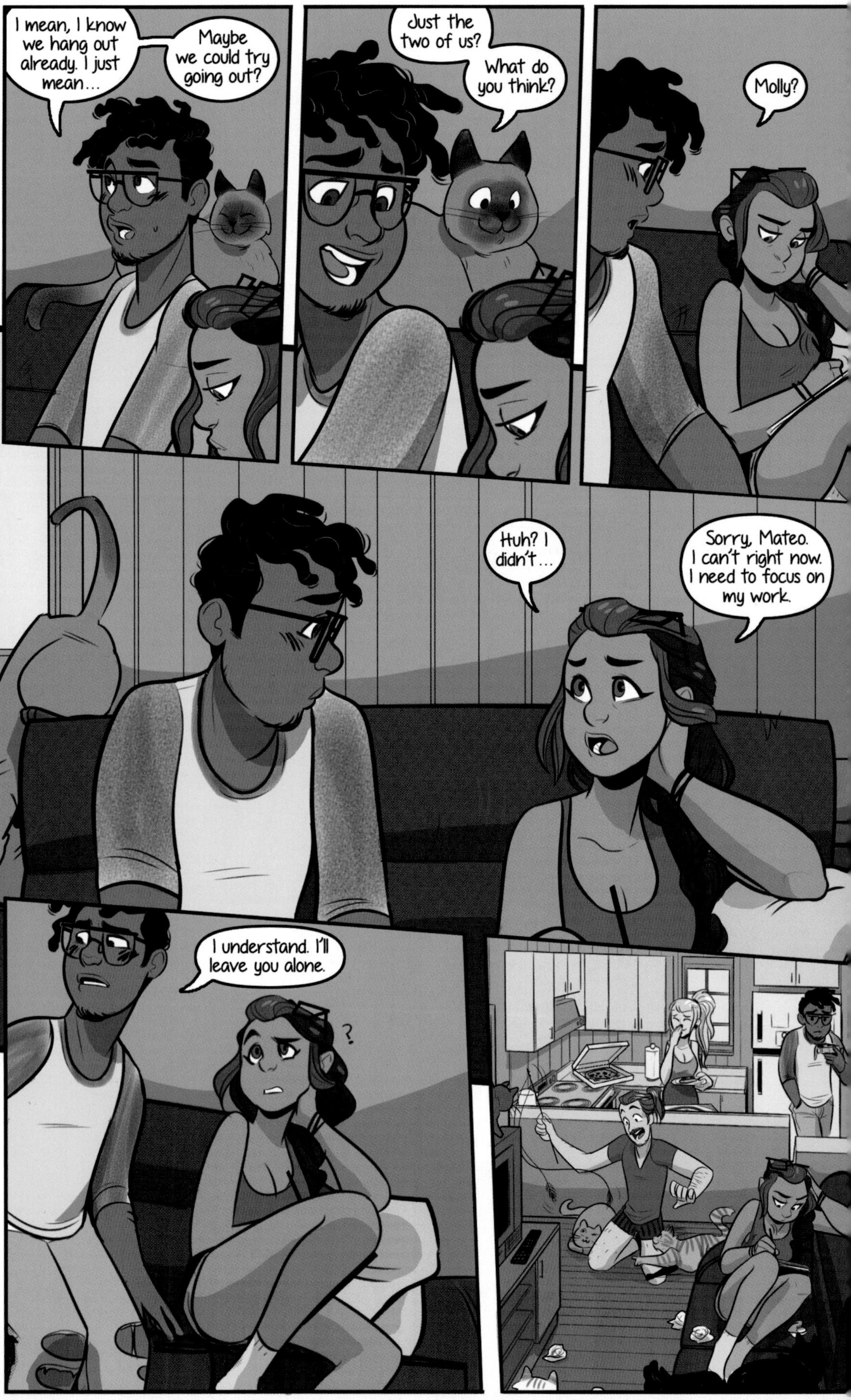
I mean, I know we hang out already. I just mean...
Maybe we could try going out?
Just the two of us?
What do you think?
Molly?
Huh? I didn't...
Sorry, Mateo. I can't right now. I need to focus on my work.
I understand. I'll leave you alone.
?

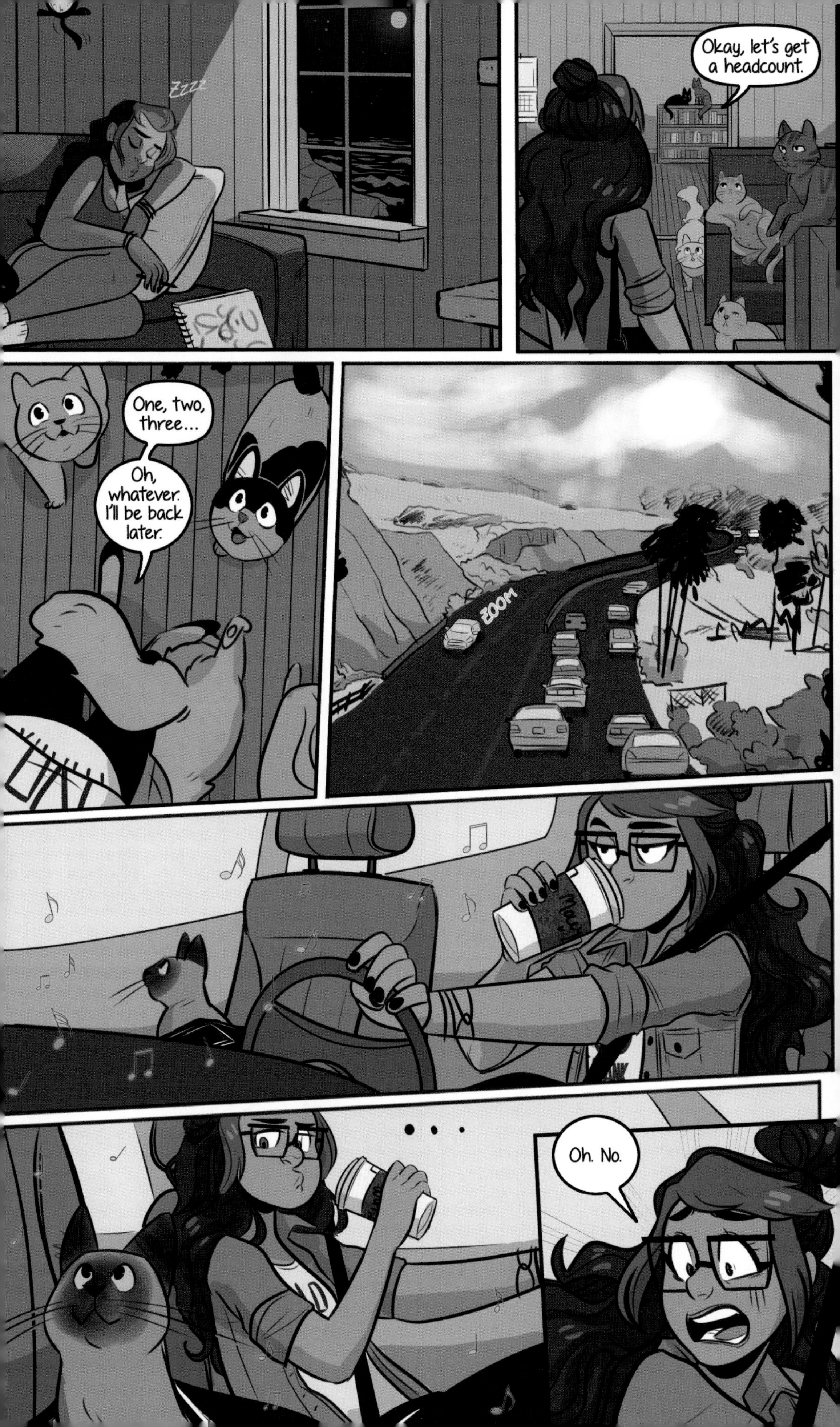

Zzzz
Okay, let's get a headcount.
One, two, three...
Oh, whatever. I'll be back later.
ZOOM
...
Oh. No.

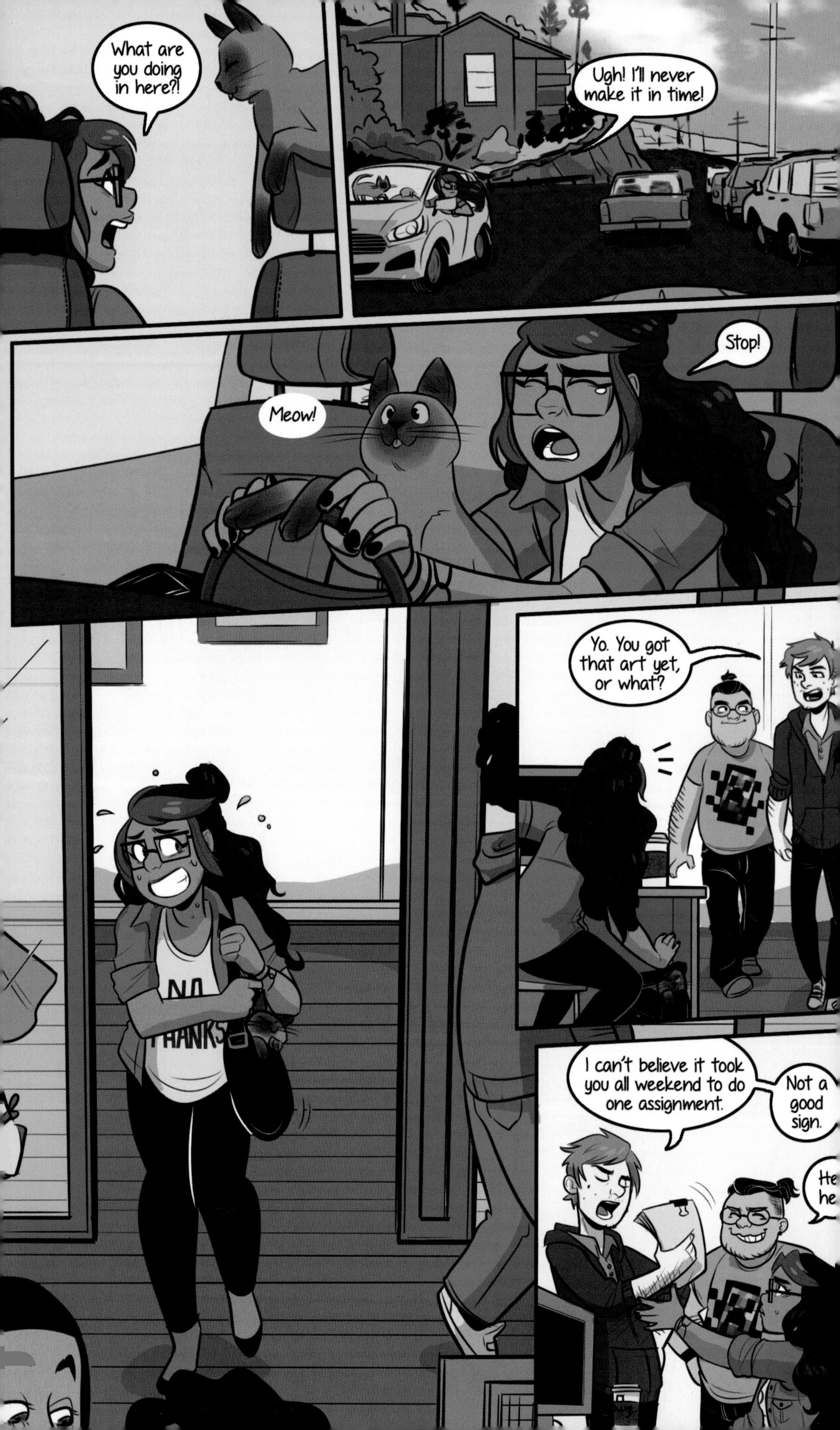
What are you doing in here?!
Ugh! I'll never make it in time!
Meow!
Stop!
NO THANKS
Yo. You got that art yet, or what?
I can't believe it took you all weekend to do one assignment.
Not a good sign.
He he

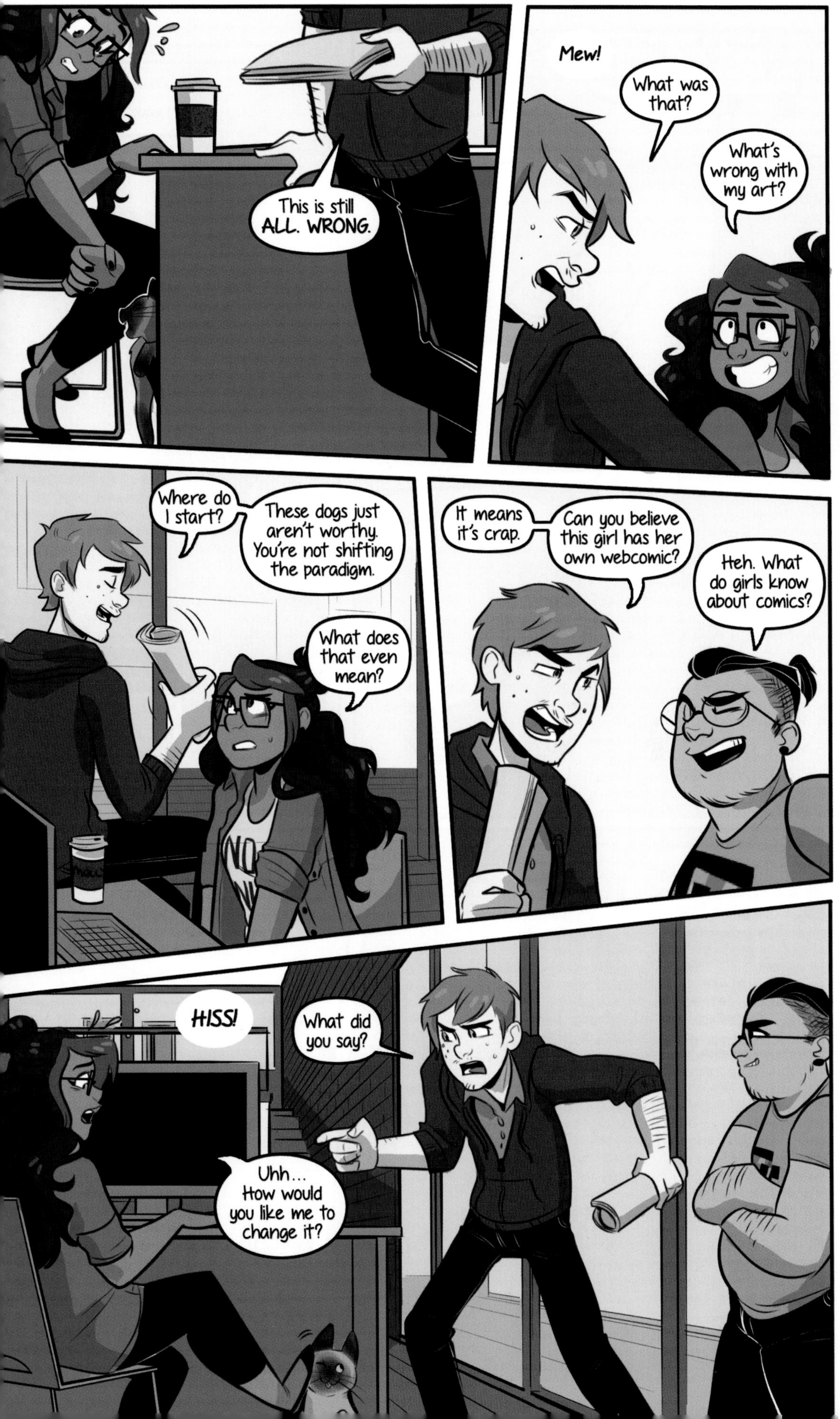
This is still ALL. WRONG.
Mew!
What was that?
What's wrong with my art?
Where do I start?
These dogs just aren't worthy. You're not shifting the paradigm.
What does that even mean?
It means it's crap.
Can you believe this girl has her own webcomic?
Heh. What do girls know about comics?
HISS!
What did you say?
Uhh... How would you like me to change it?

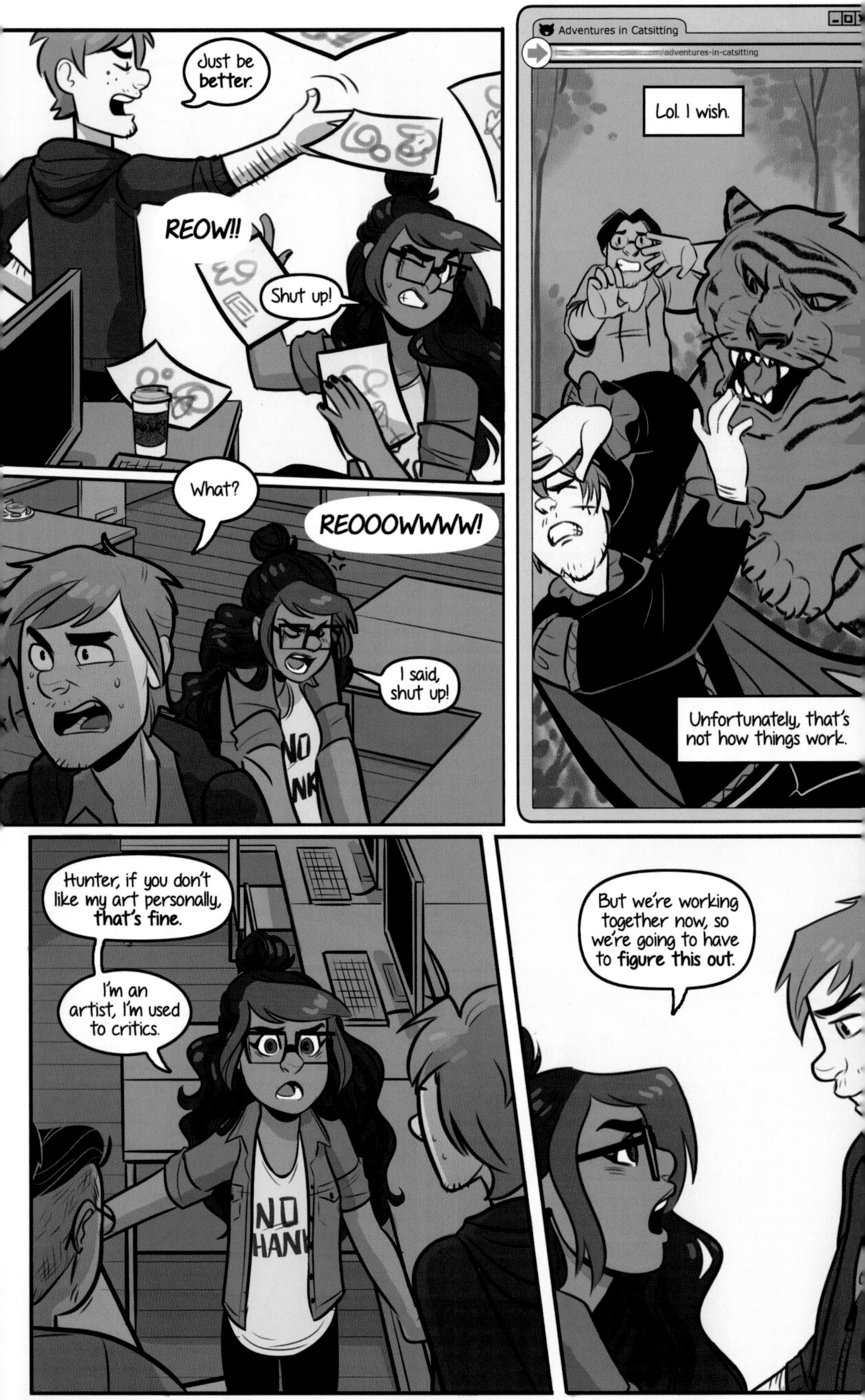
Just be better.
REOW!!
Shut up!
What?
REOOOWWWW!
I said, shut up!
Adventures in Catsitting
/adventures-in-catsitting
Lol. I wish.
Unfortunately, that's not how things work.
Hunter, if you don't like my art personally, that's fine.
I'm an artist, I'm used to critics.
But we're working together now, so we're going to have to figure this out.

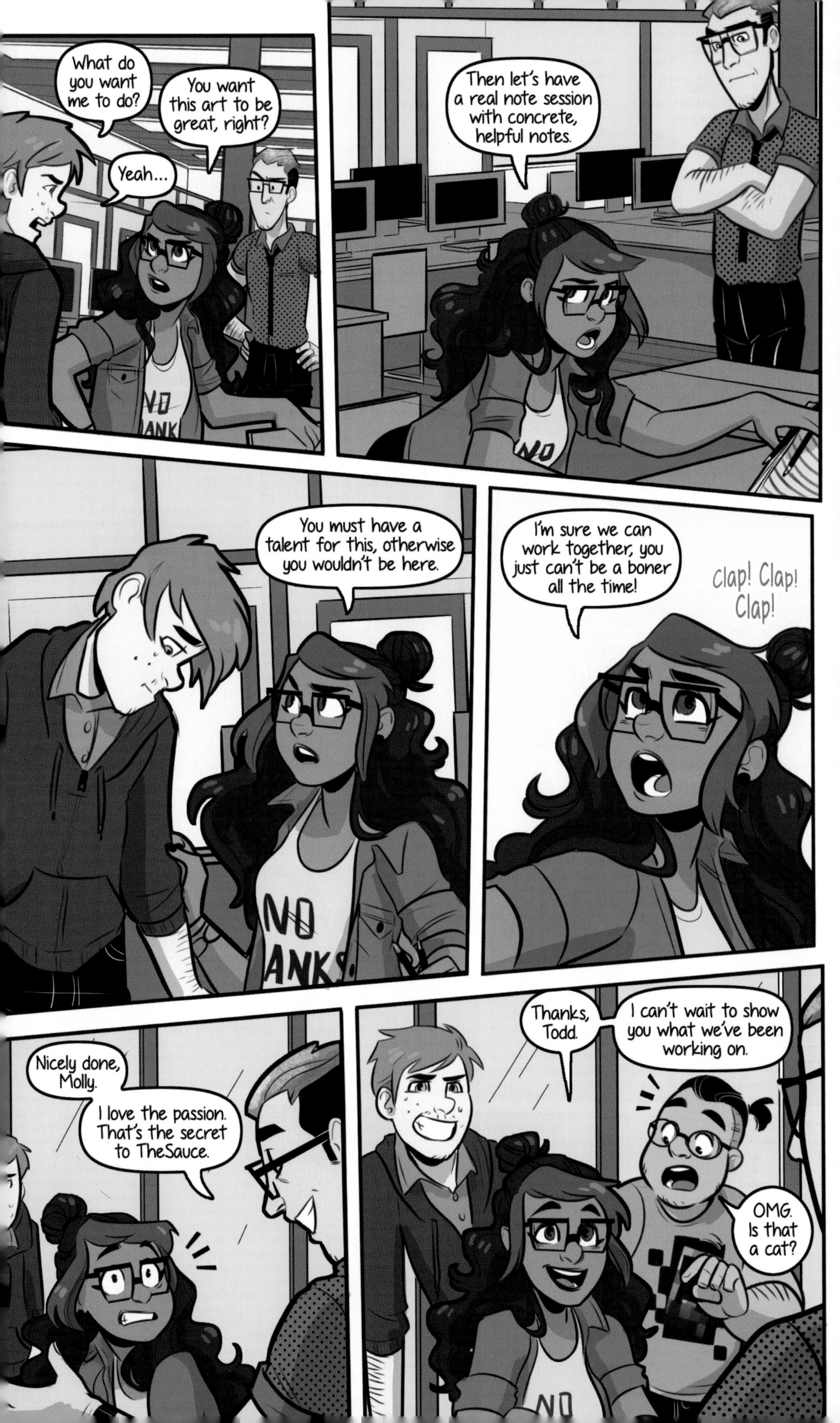
What do you want me to do?
You want this art to be great, right?
Yeah...
Then let's have a real note session with concrete, helpful notes.
NO
ANK
You must have a talent for this, otherwise you wouldn't be here.
NO
ANKS
I'm sure we can work together, you just can't be a boner all the time!
Clap! Clap! Clap!
Nicely done, Molly.
I love the passion. That's the secret to TheSauce.
Thanks, Todd.
I can't wait to show you what we've been working on.
OMG. Is that a cat?
NO

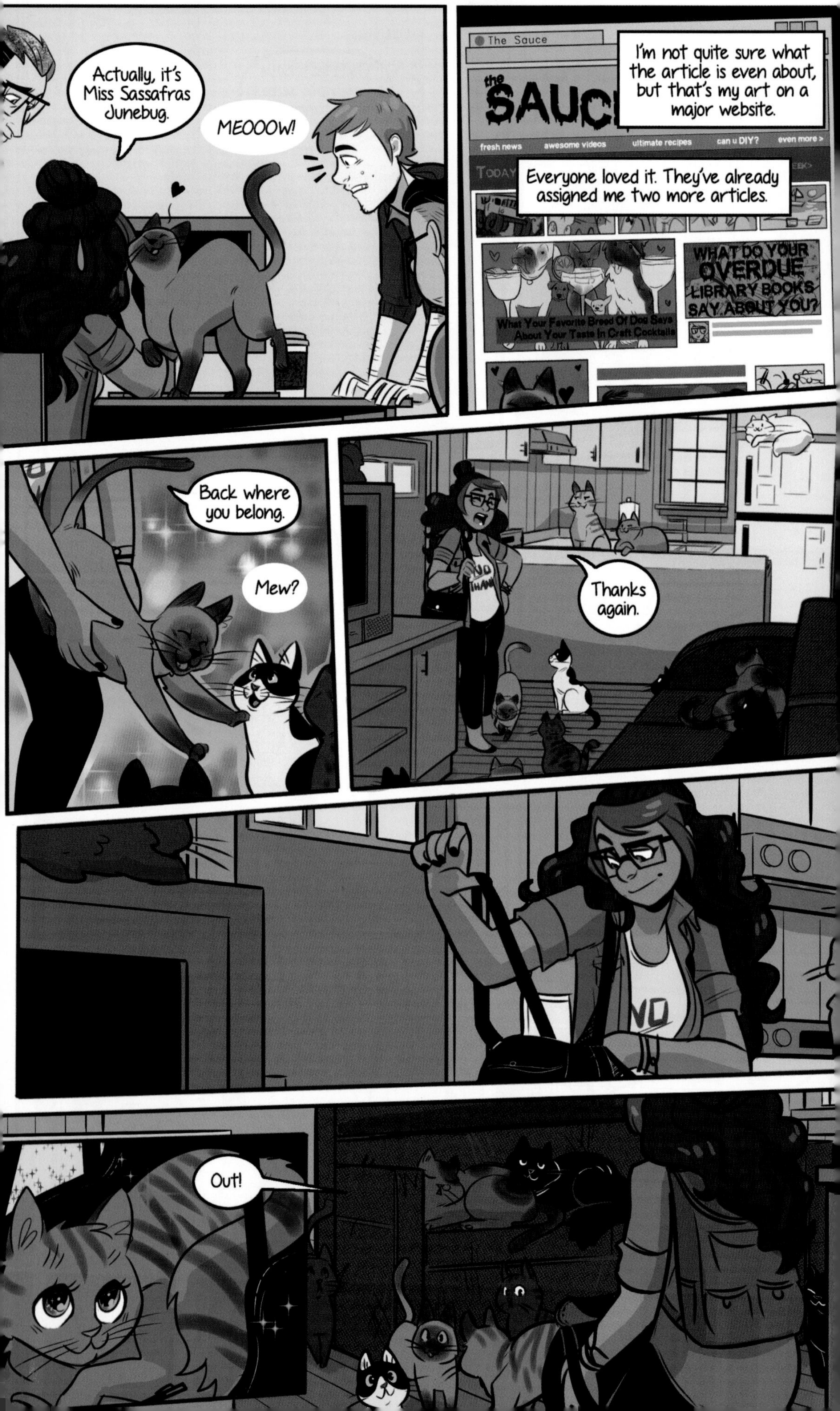

Actually, it's Miss Sassafras Junebug.
MEOOOW!
The Sauce
the SAUC
fresh news
awesome videos
ultimate recipes
can u DIY?
even more >
I'm not quite sure what the article is even about, but that's my art on a major website.
Everyone loved it. They've already assigned me two more articles.
WHAT DO YOUR OVERDUE LIBRARY BOOKS SAY ABOUT YOU?
What Your Favorite Breed Of Dog Says About Your Taste In Craft Cocktails
Back where you belong.
Mew?
Thanks again.
Out!

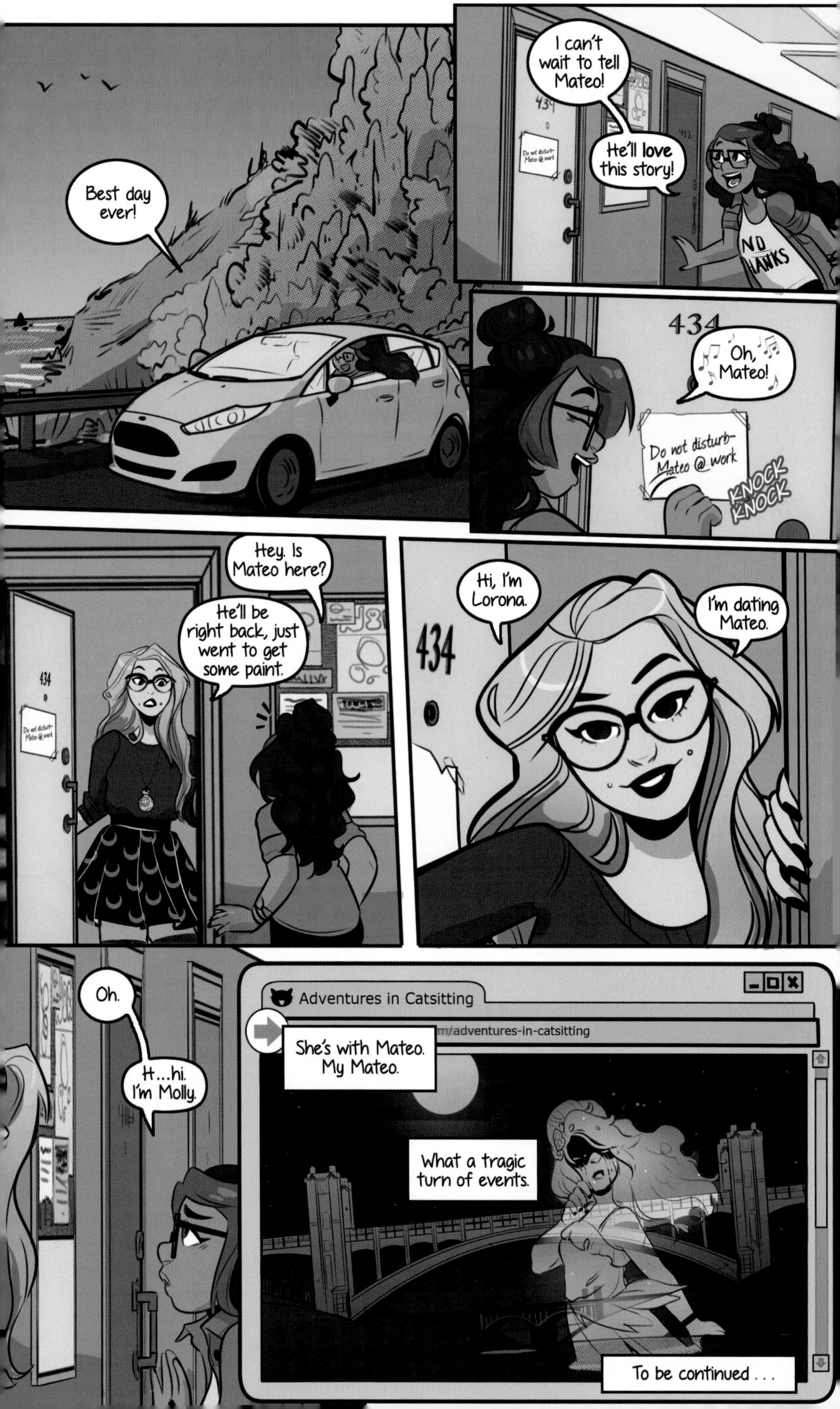
Best day ever!
I can't wait to tell Mateo!
He'll **love** this story!
NO THANKS
434
Do not disturb- Mateo @ work
Oh, Mateo!
KNOCK KNOCK
Hey. Is Mateo here?
He'll be right back, just went to get some paint.
Hi, I'm Lorona.
I'm dating Mateo.
Oh.
H...hi. I'm Molly.
Adventures in Catsitting
m/adventures-in-catsitting
She's with Mateo. My Mateo.
What a tragic turn of events.
To be continued . . .

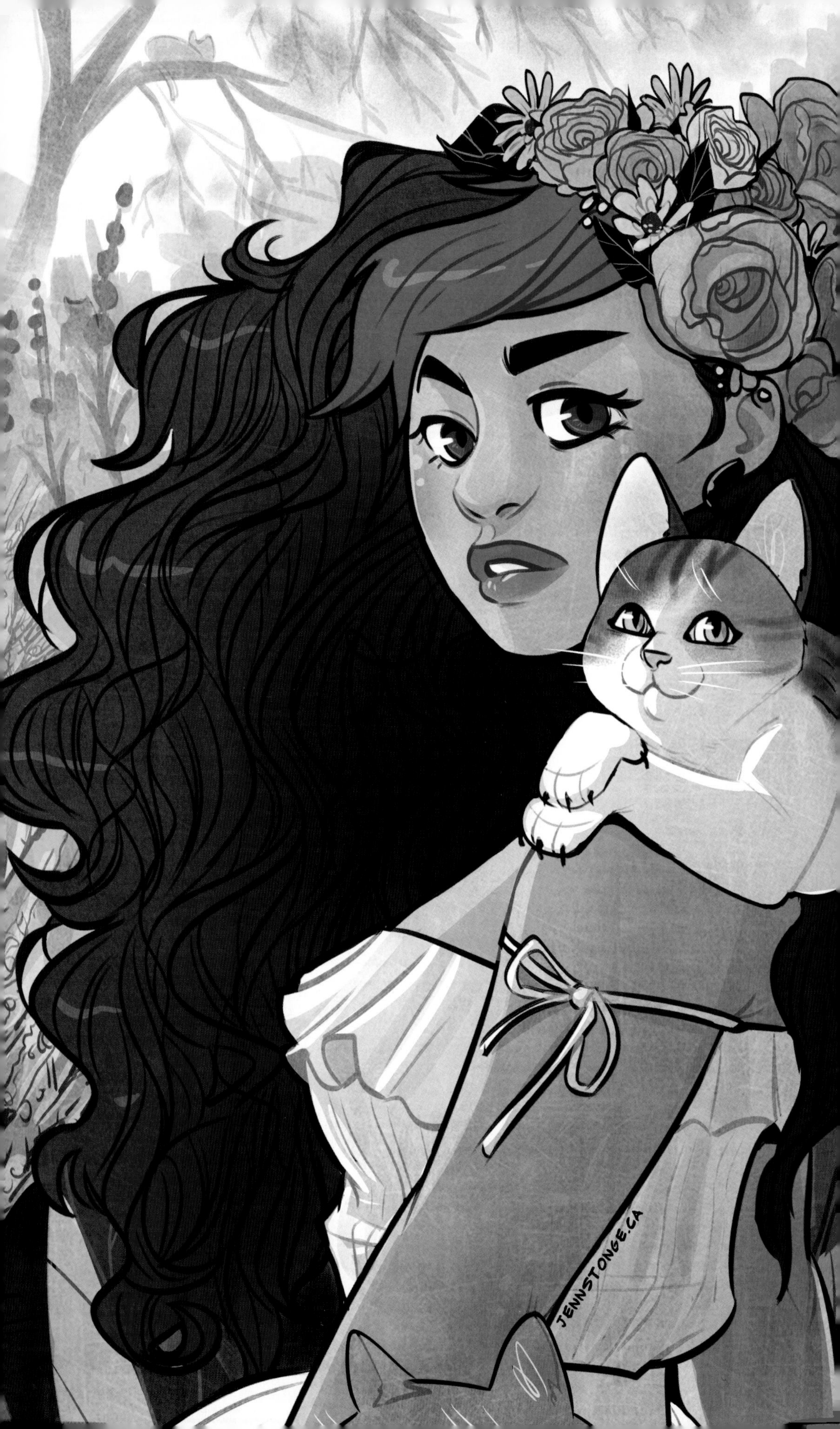
JENNSTONGE.CA

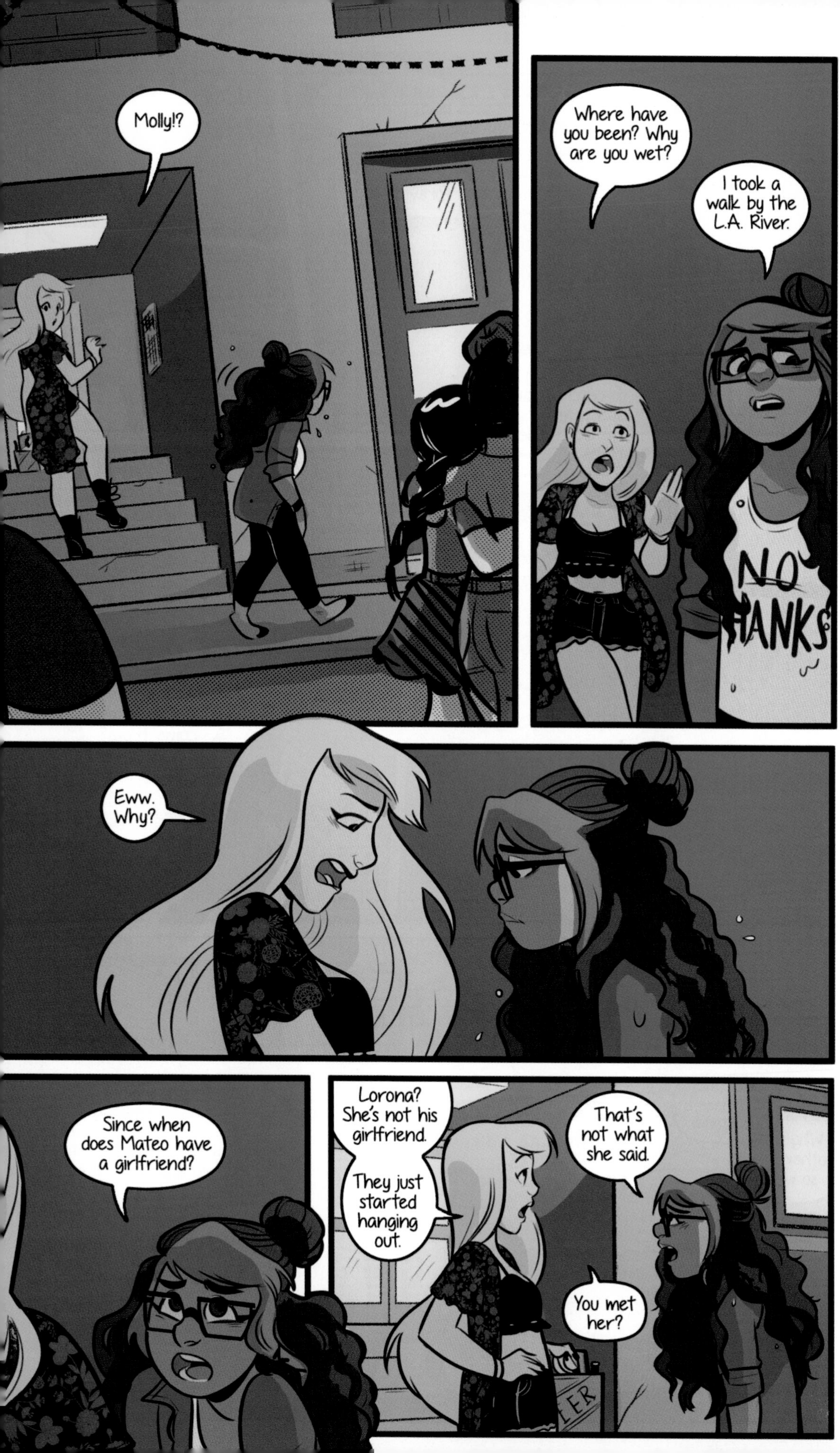
Molly!?
Where have you been? Why are you wet?
I took a walk by the L.A. River.
NO THANKS
Eww. Why?
Since when does Mateo have a girlfriend?
Lorona? She's not his girlfriend.
They just started hanging out.
That's not what she said.
You met her?

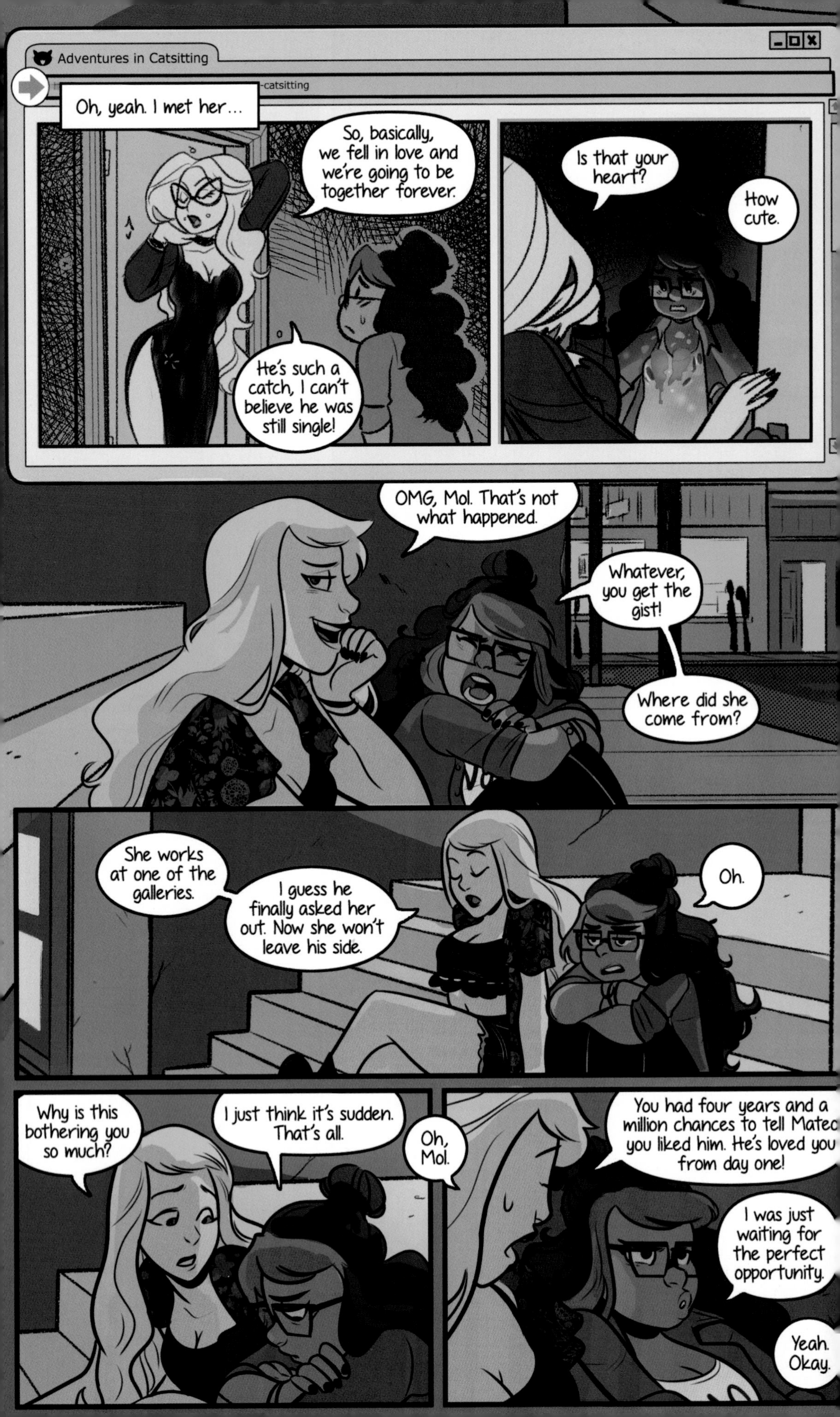
Adventures in Catsitting
-catsitting
Oh, yeah. I met her...
So, basically, we fell in love and we're going to be together forever.
He's such a catch, I can't believe he was still single!
Is that your heart?
How cute.
OMG, Mol. That's not what happened.
Whatever, you get the gist!
Where did she come from?
She works at one of the galleries.
I guess he finally asked her out. Now she won't leave his side.
Oh.
Why is this bothering you so much?
I just think it's sudden. That's all.
Oh, Mol.
You had four years and a million chances to tell Mateo you liked him. He's loved you from day one!
I was just waiting for the perfect opportunity.
Yeah. Okay.

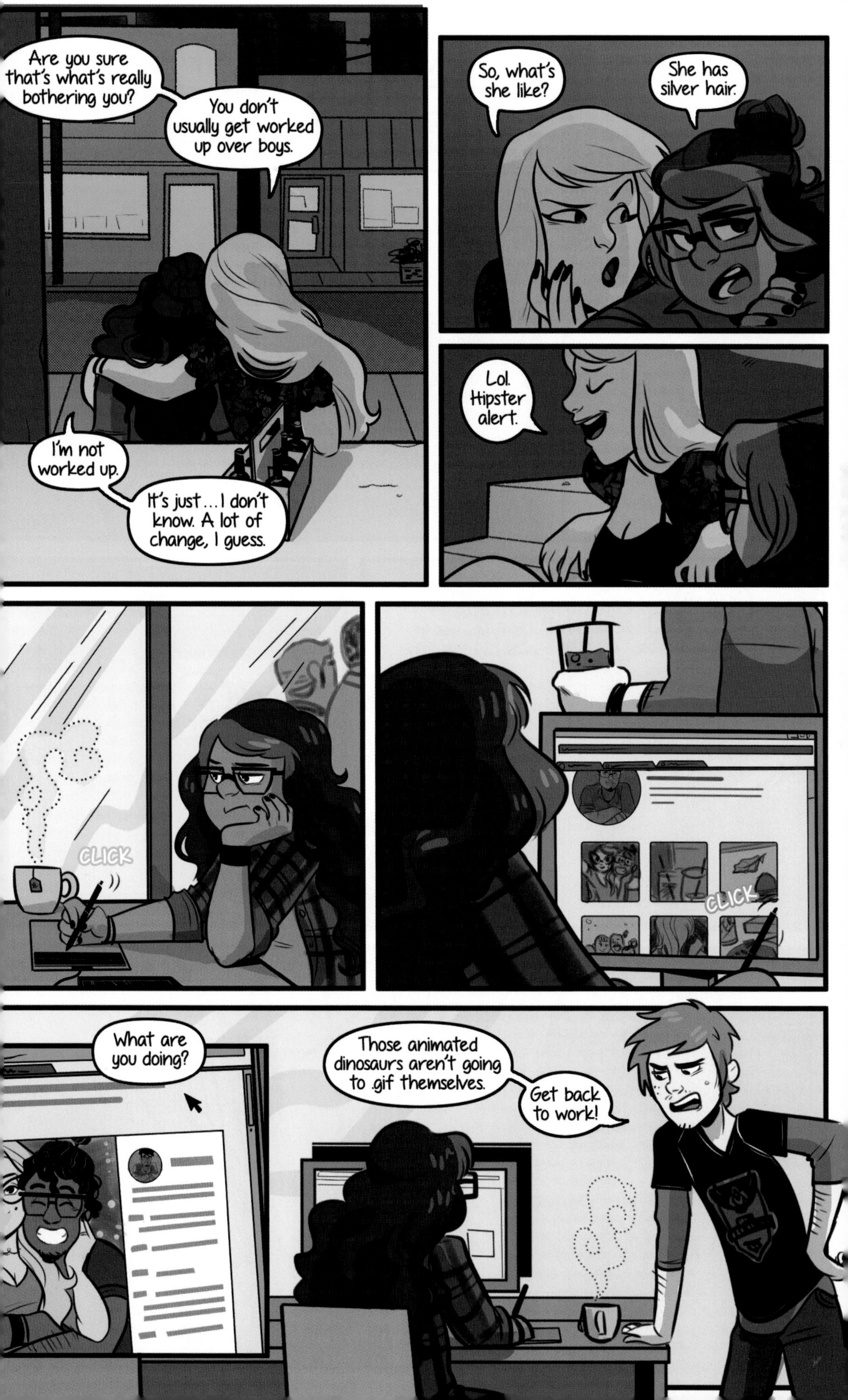
Are you sure that's what's really bothering you?
You don't usually get worked up over boys.
I'm not worked up.
It's just... I don't know. A lot of change, I guess.
So, what's she like?
She has silver hair.
Lol. Hipster alert.
CLICK
CLICK
What are you doing?
Those animated dinosaurs aren't going to .gif themselves.
Get back to work!

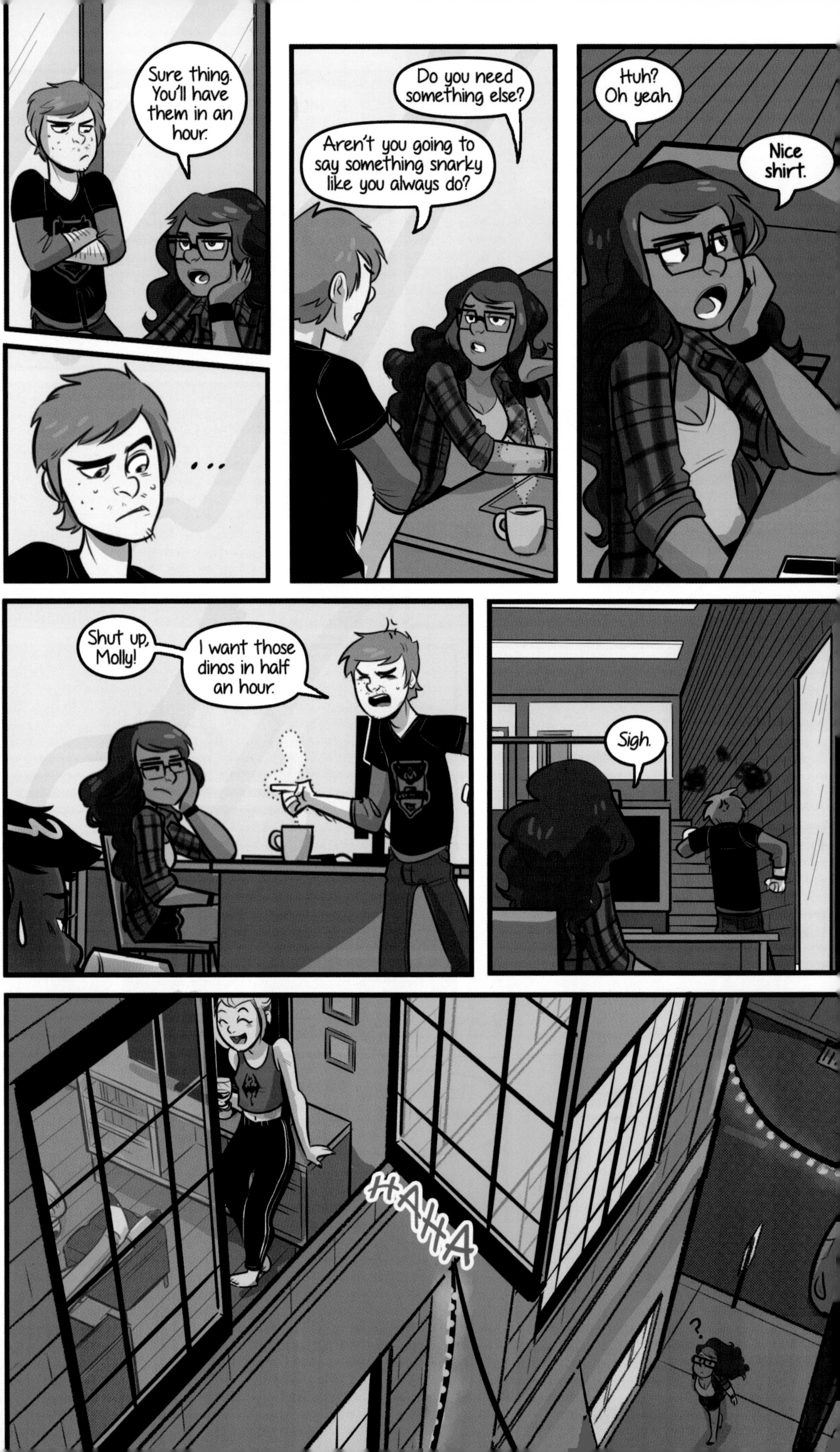
Sure thing. You'll have them in an hour.
...
Do you need something else?
Aren't you going to say something snarky like you always do?
Huh? Oh yeah.
Nice shirt.
Shut up, Molly!
I want those dinos in half an hour.
Sigh.
HAHA
?

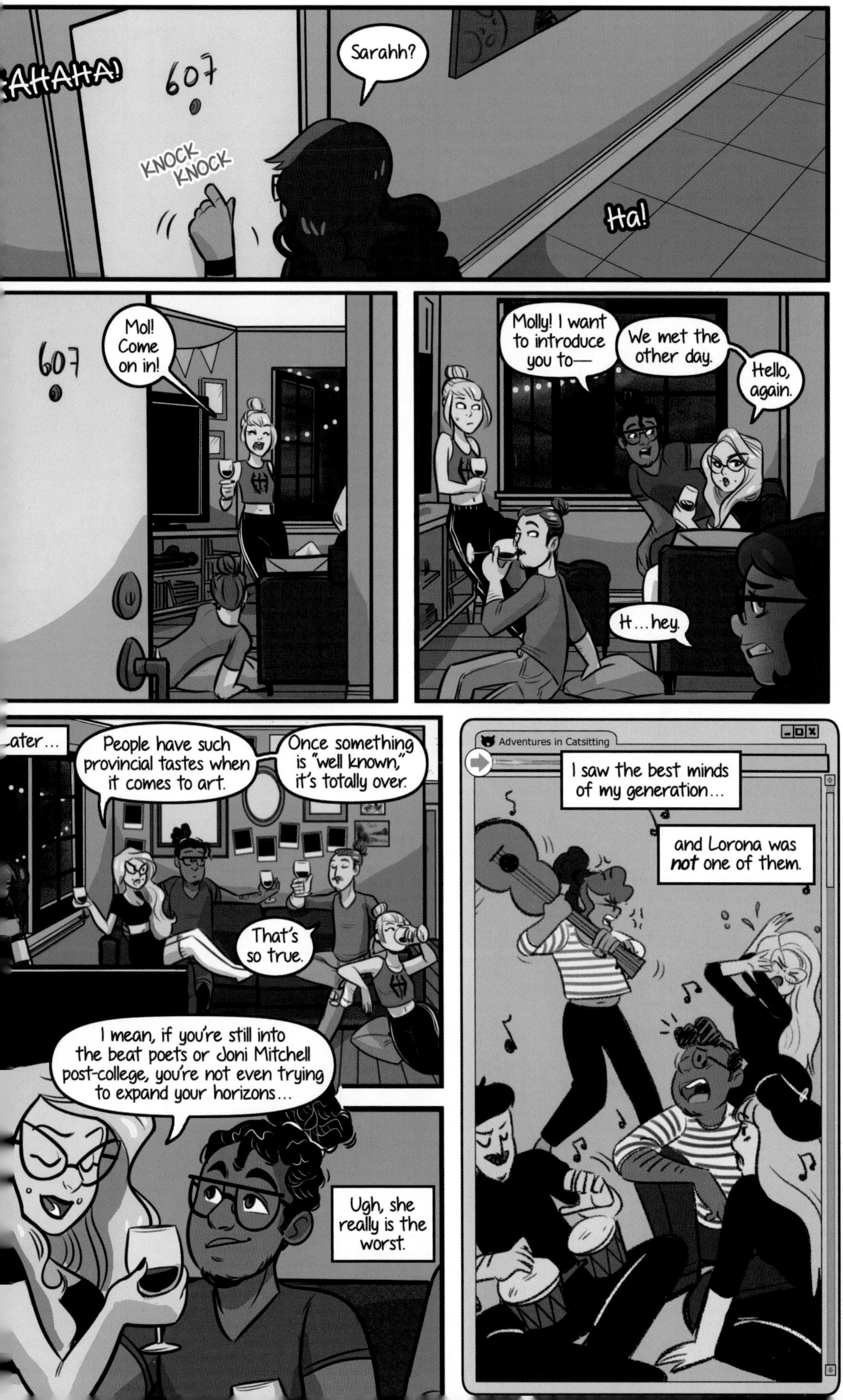

AHAHA!
607
KNOCK KNOCK
Sarahh?
Ha!
607
Mol! Come on in!
Molly! I want to introduce you to—
We met the other day.
Hello, again.
H…hey.
Later…
People have such provincial tastes when it comes to art.
Once something is "well known," it's totally over.
That's so true.
I mean, if you're still into the beat poets or Joni Mitchell post-college, you're not even trying to expand your horizons…
Ugh, she really is the worst.
Adventures in Catsitting
I saw the best minds of my generation…
and Lorona was **not** one of them.

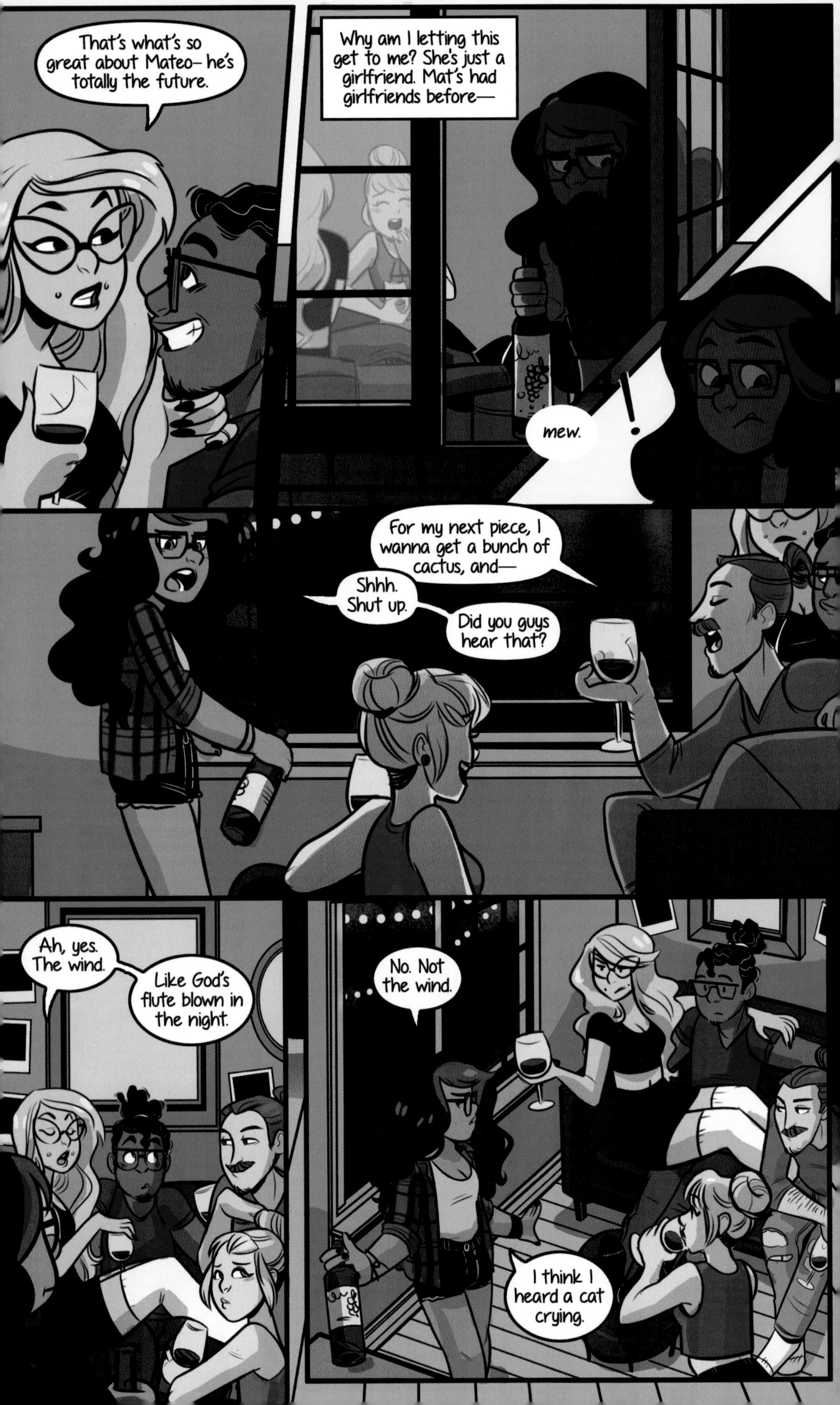
That's what's so great about Mateo– he's totally the future.
Why am I letting this get to me? She's just a girlfriend. Mat's had girlfriends before—
!
mew.
For my next piece, I wanna get a bunch of cactus, and—
Shhh. Shut up.
Did you guys hear that?
Ah, yes. The wind.
Like God's flute blown in the night.
No. Not the wind.
I think I heard a cat crying.

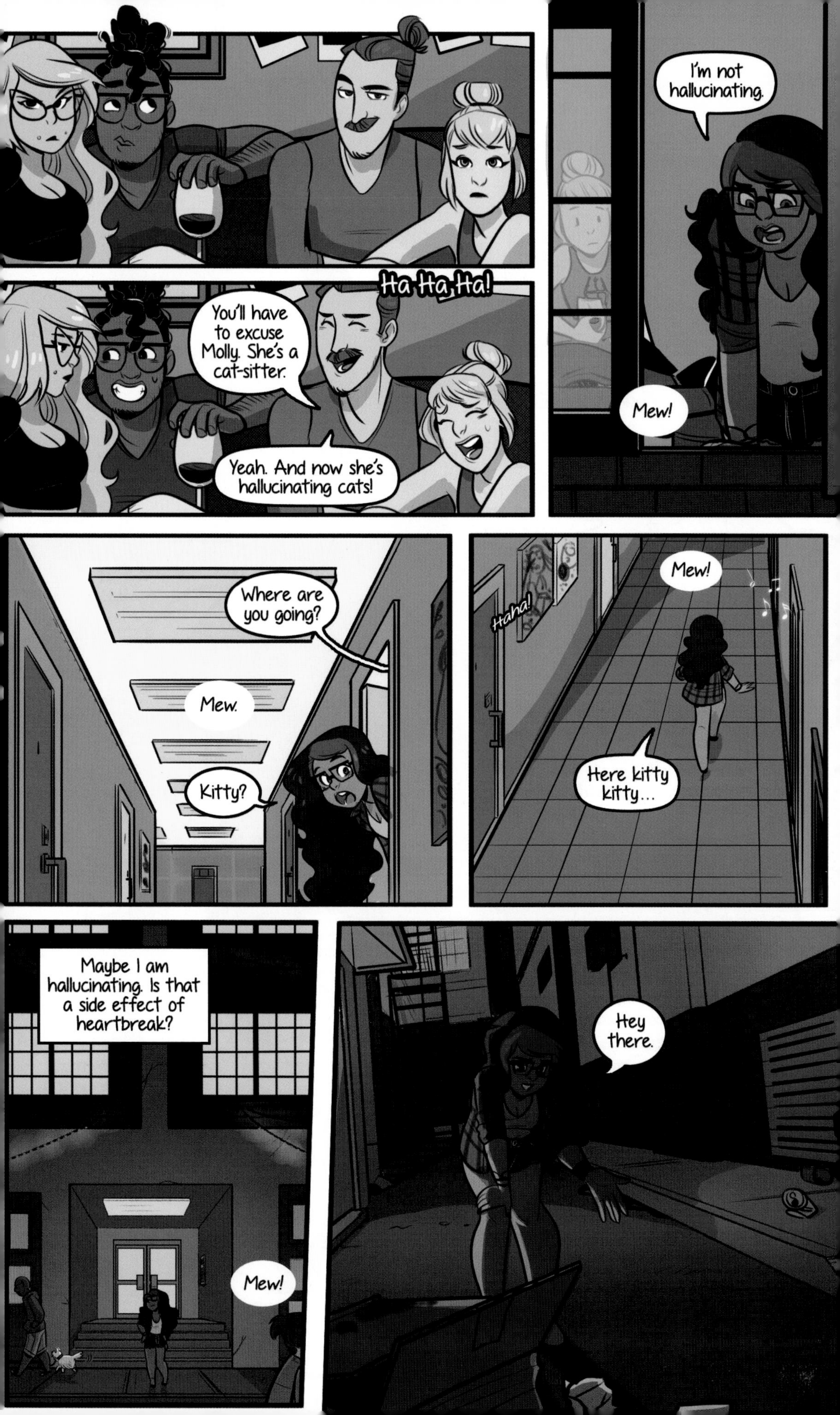
I'm not hallucinating.
Mew!
Ha Ha Ha!
You'll have to excuse Molly. She's a cat-sitter.
Yeah. And now she's hallucinating cats!
Where are you going?
Mew.
Kitty?
Mew!
Haha!
Here kitty kitty...
Maybe I am hallucinating. Is that a side effect of heartbreak?
Mew!
Hey there.

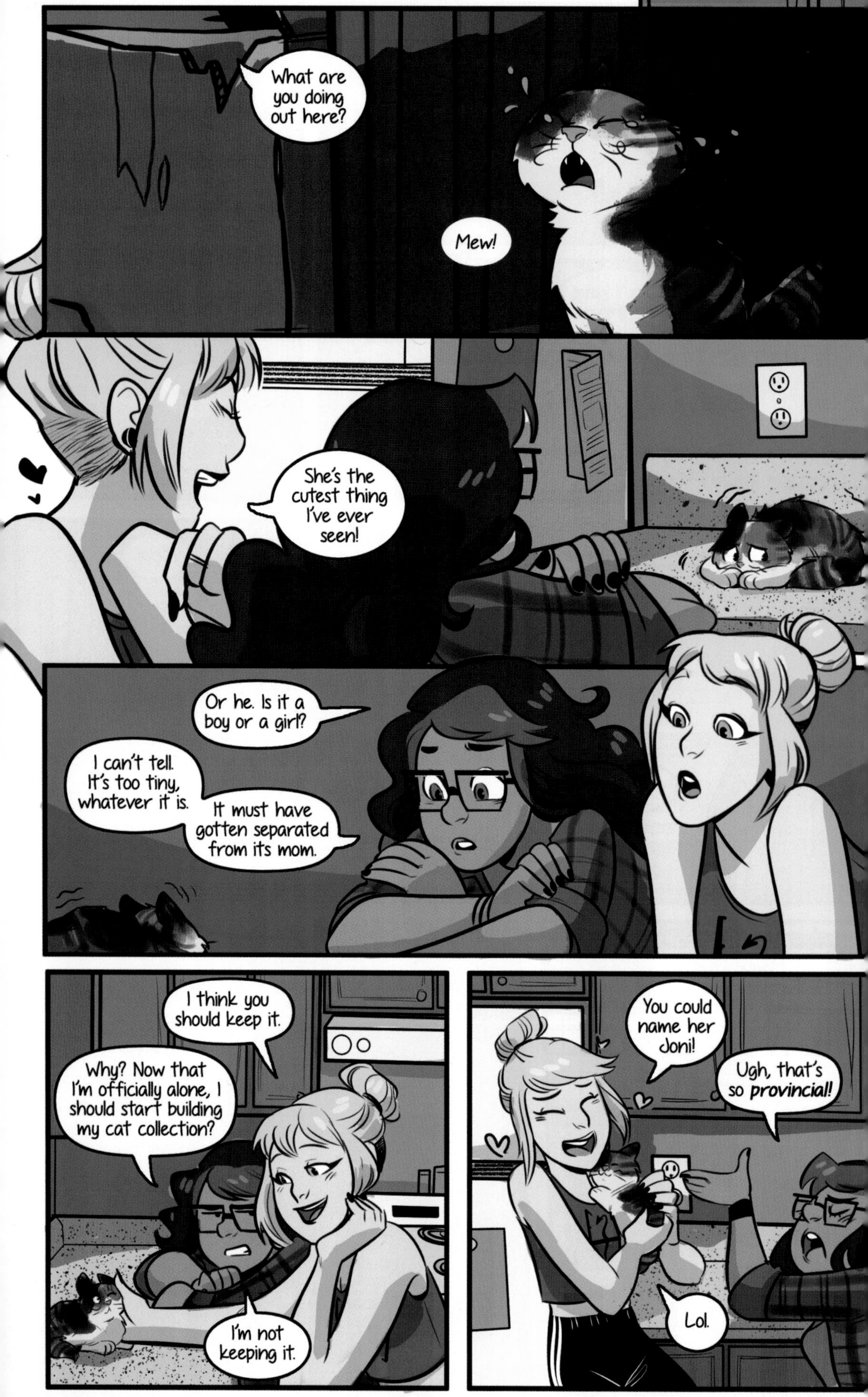
What are you doing out here?
Mew!
She's the cutest thing I've ever seen!
Or he. Is it a boy or a girl?
I can't tell. It's too tiny, whatever it is.
It must have gotten separated from its mom.
I think you should keep it.
Why? Now that I'm officially alone, I should start building my cat collection?
I'm not keeping it.
You could name her Joni!
Ugh, that's so ***provincial!***
Lol.

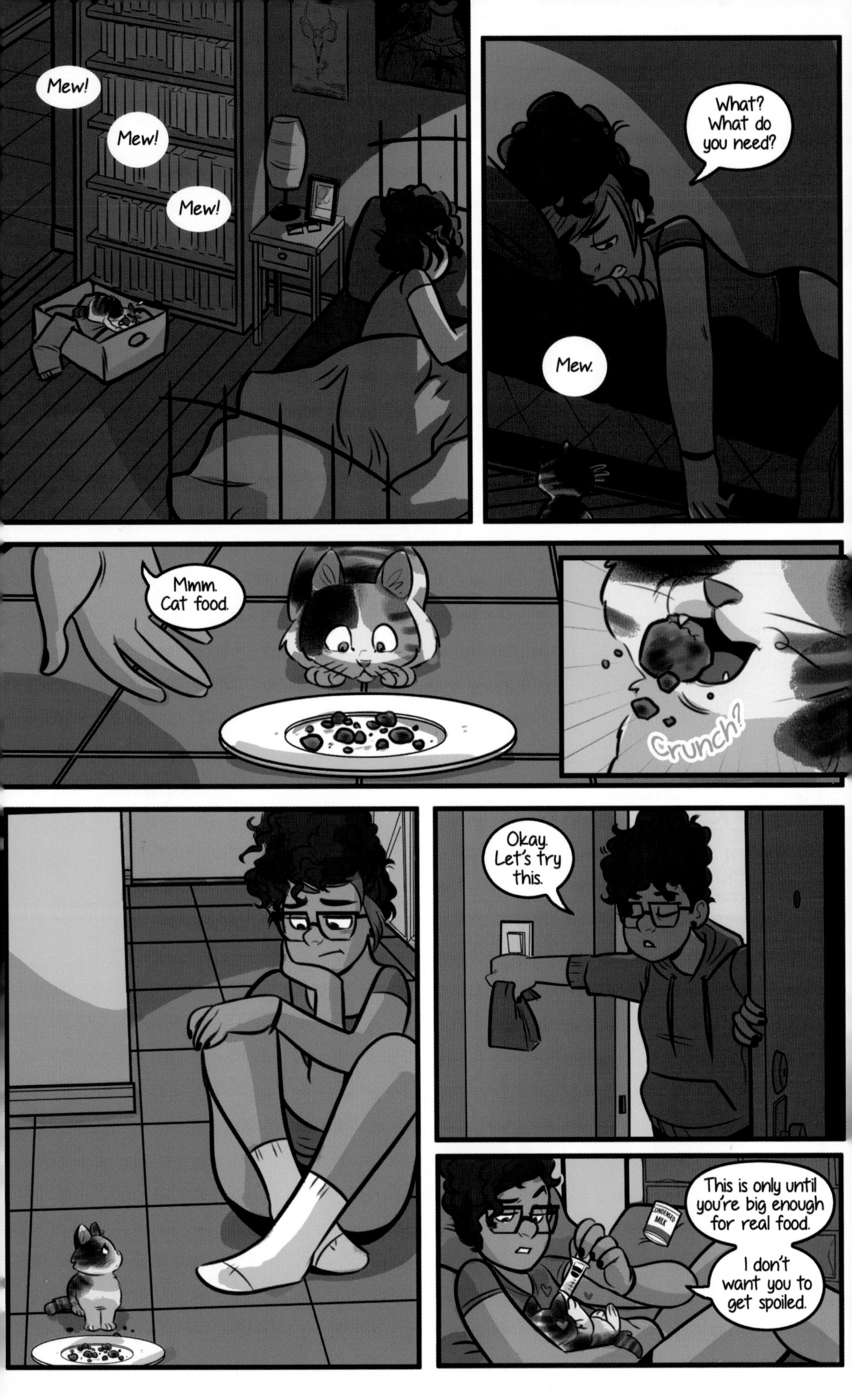
Mew!
Mew!
Mew!
What? What do you need?
Mew.
Mmm. Cat food.
Crunch?
Okay. Let's try this.
CONDENSED MILK
This is only until you're big enough for real food.
I don't want you to get spoiled.

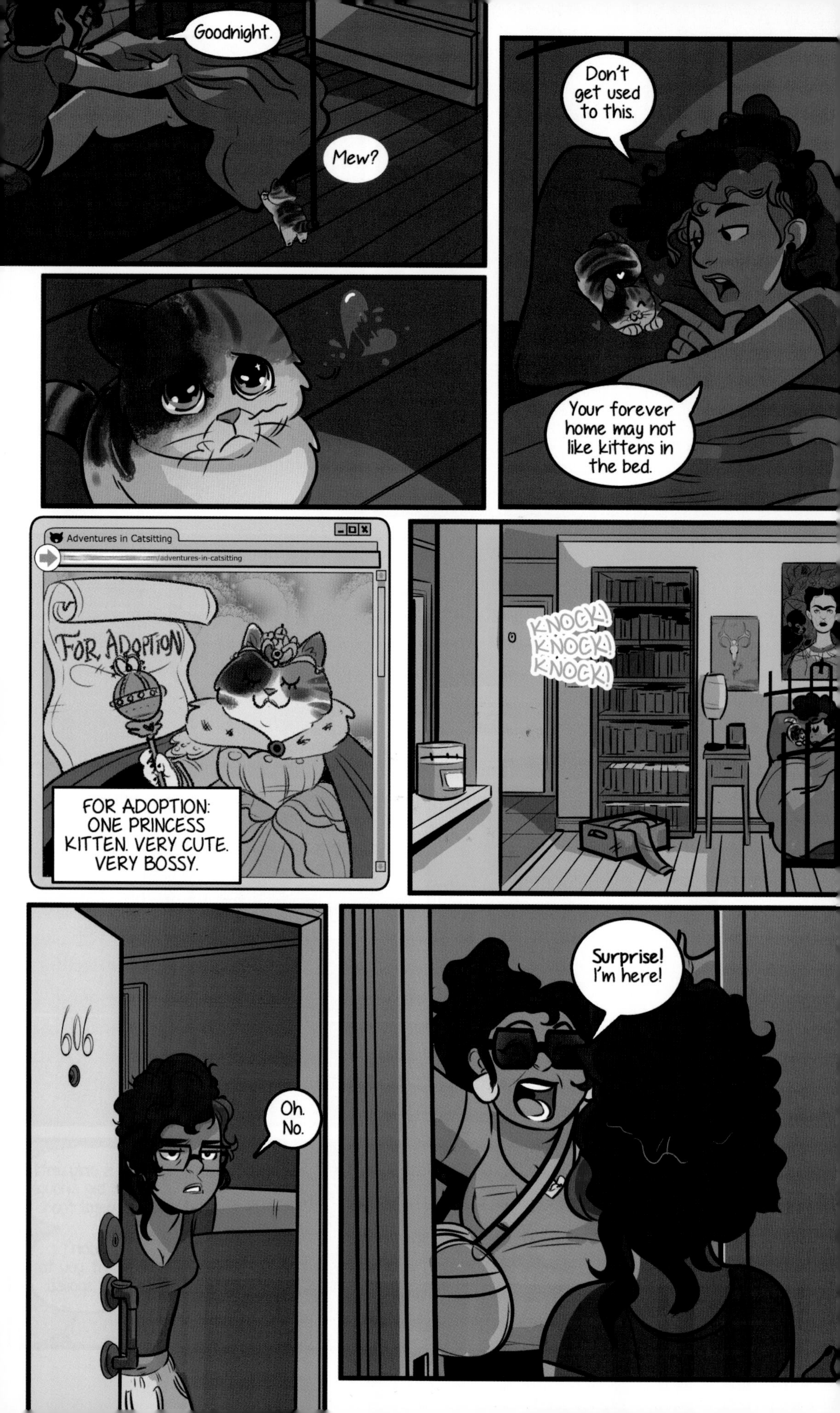
Goodnight.
Mew?
Don't get used to this.
Your forever home may not like kittens in the bed.
Adventures in Catsitting
.com/adventures-in-catsitting
FOR ADOPTION
FOR ADOPTION: ONE PRINCESS KITTEN. VERY CUTE. VERY BOSSY.
KNOCK! KNOCK! KNOCK!
606
Oh. No.
Surprise! I'm here!

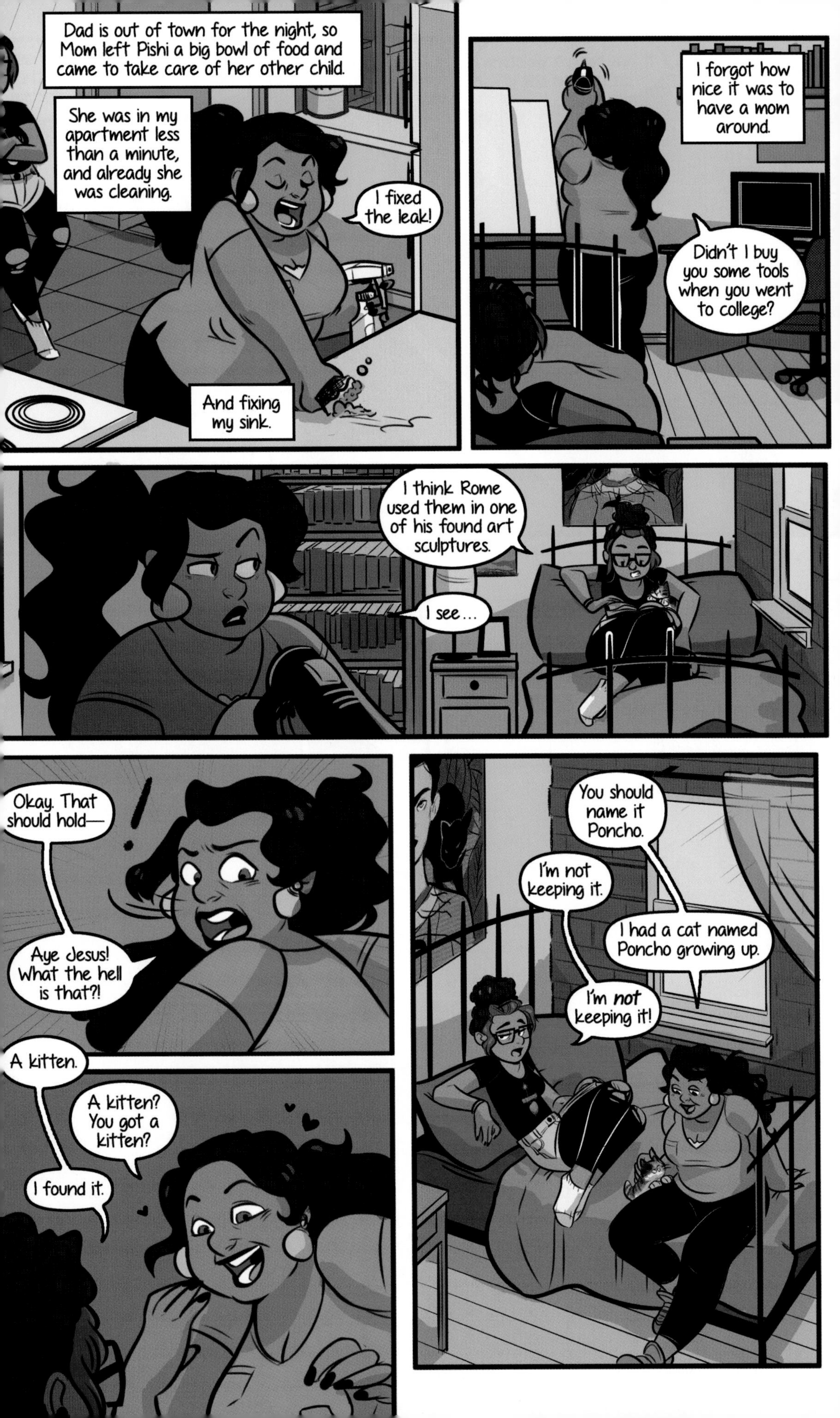
Dad is out of town for the night, so Mom left Pishi a big bowl of food and came to take care of her other child.
She was in my apartment less than a minute, and already she was cleaning.
I fixed the leak!
And fixing my sink.
I forgot how nice it was to have a mom around.
Didn't I buy you some tools when you went to college?
I think Rome used them in one of his found art sculptures.
I see...
Okay. That should hold—
!
Aye Jesus! What the hell is that?!
A kitten.
A kitten? You got a kitten?
I found it.
You should name it Poncho.
I'm not keeping it.
I had a cat named Poncho growing up.
I'm *not* keeping it!

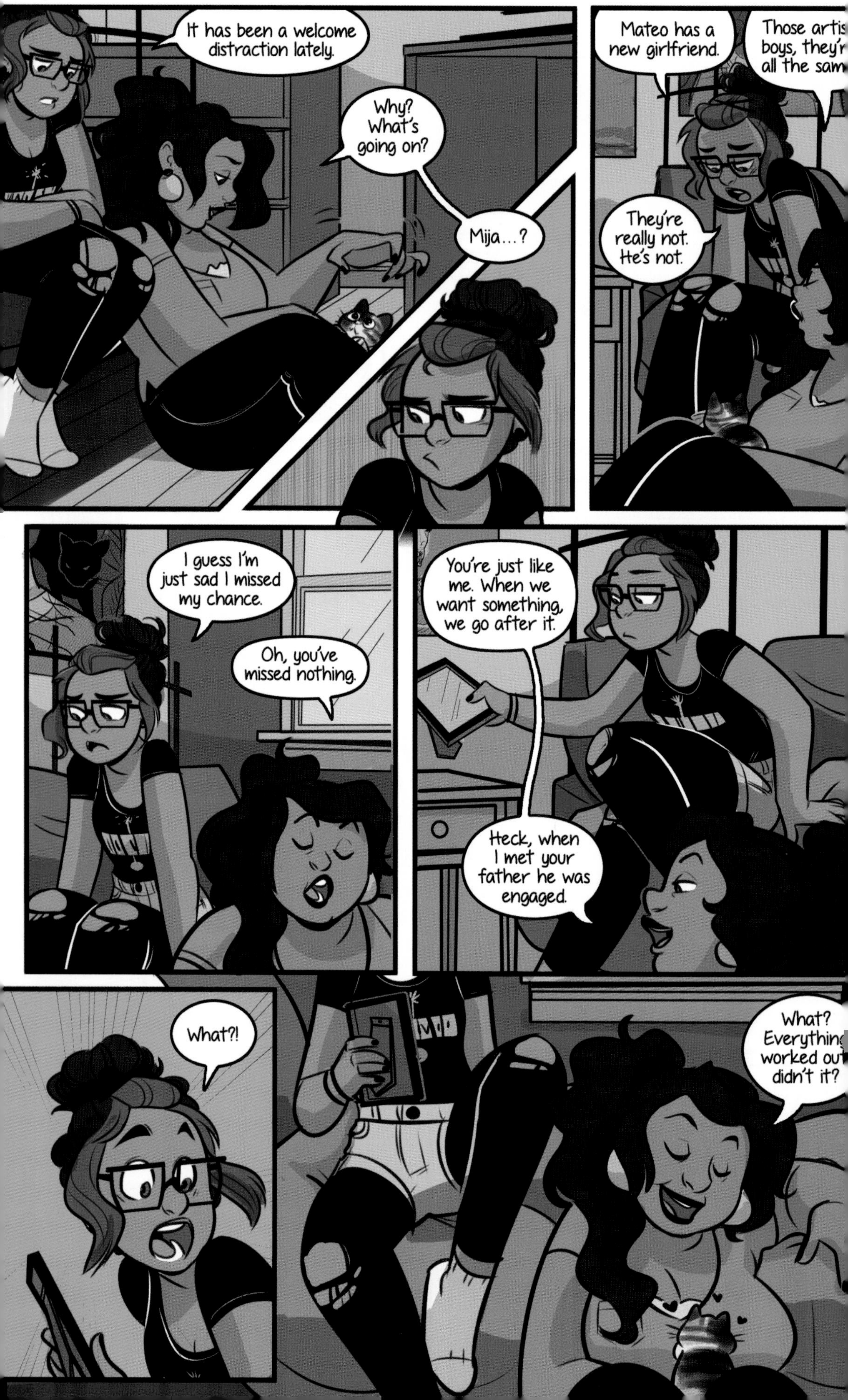
It has been a welcome distraction lately.
Why? What's going on?
Mija...?
Mateo has a new girlfriend.
Those artis
boys, they'r
all the sam
They're really not. He's not.
I guess I'm just sad I missed my chance.
Oh, you've missed nothing.
You're just like me. When we want something, we go after it.
Heck, when I met your father he was engaged.
What?!
What? Everythin
worked ou
didn't it?

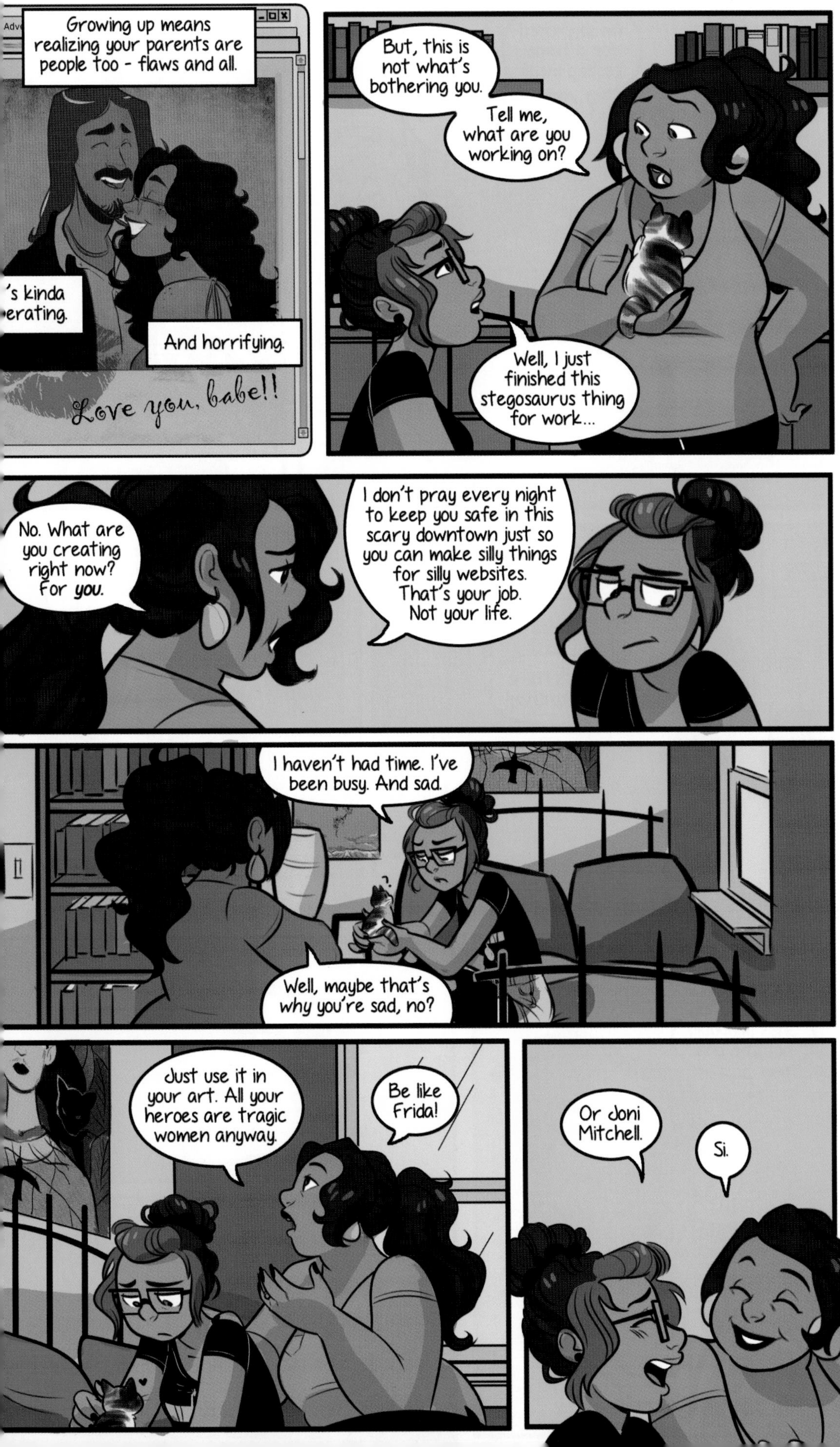

Growing up means realizing your parents are people too - flaws and all.
's kinda erating.
And horrifying.
Love you, babe!!
But, this is not what's bothering you.
Tell me, what are you working on?
Well, I just finished this stegosaurus thing for work...
No. What are you creating right now? For **you**.
I don't pray every night to keep you safe in this scary downtown just so you can make silly things for silly websites. That's your job. Not your life.
I haven't had time. I've been busy. And sad.
Well, maybe that's why you're sad, no?
Just use it in your art. All your heroes are tragic women anyway.
Be like Frida!
Or Joni Mitchell.
Si.

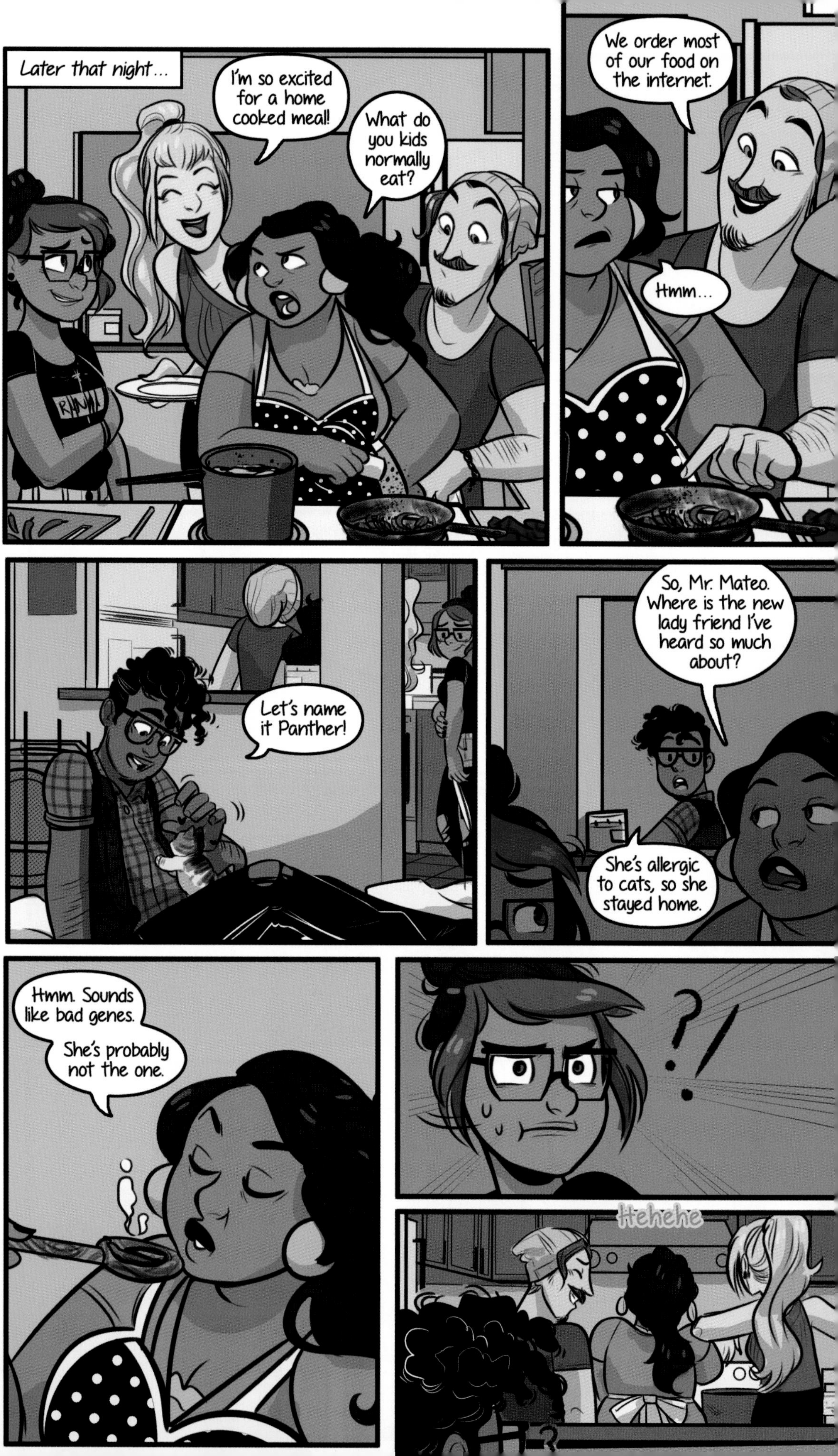

Later that night...
I'm so excited for a home cooked meal!
What do you kids normally eat?
We order most of our food on the internet.
Hmm...
Let's name it Panther!
So, Mr. Mateo. Where is the new lady friend I've heard so much about?
She's allergic to cats, so she stayed home.
Hmm. Sounds like bad genes.
She's probably not the one.
?!
Hehehe

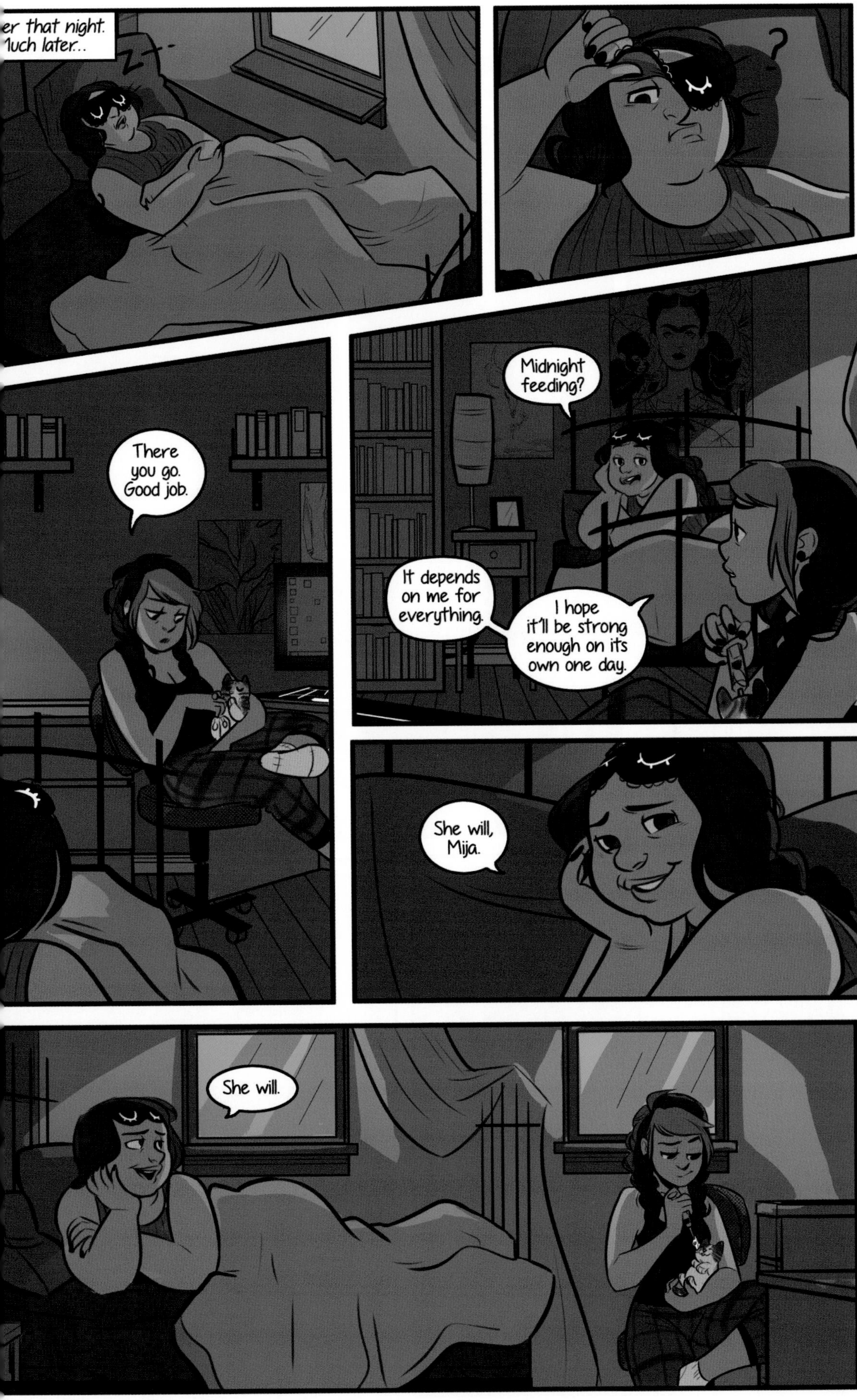
er that night.
Much later...
There you go. Good job.
Midnight feeding?
It depends on me for everything.
I hope it'll be strong enough on its own one day.
She will, Mija.
She will.

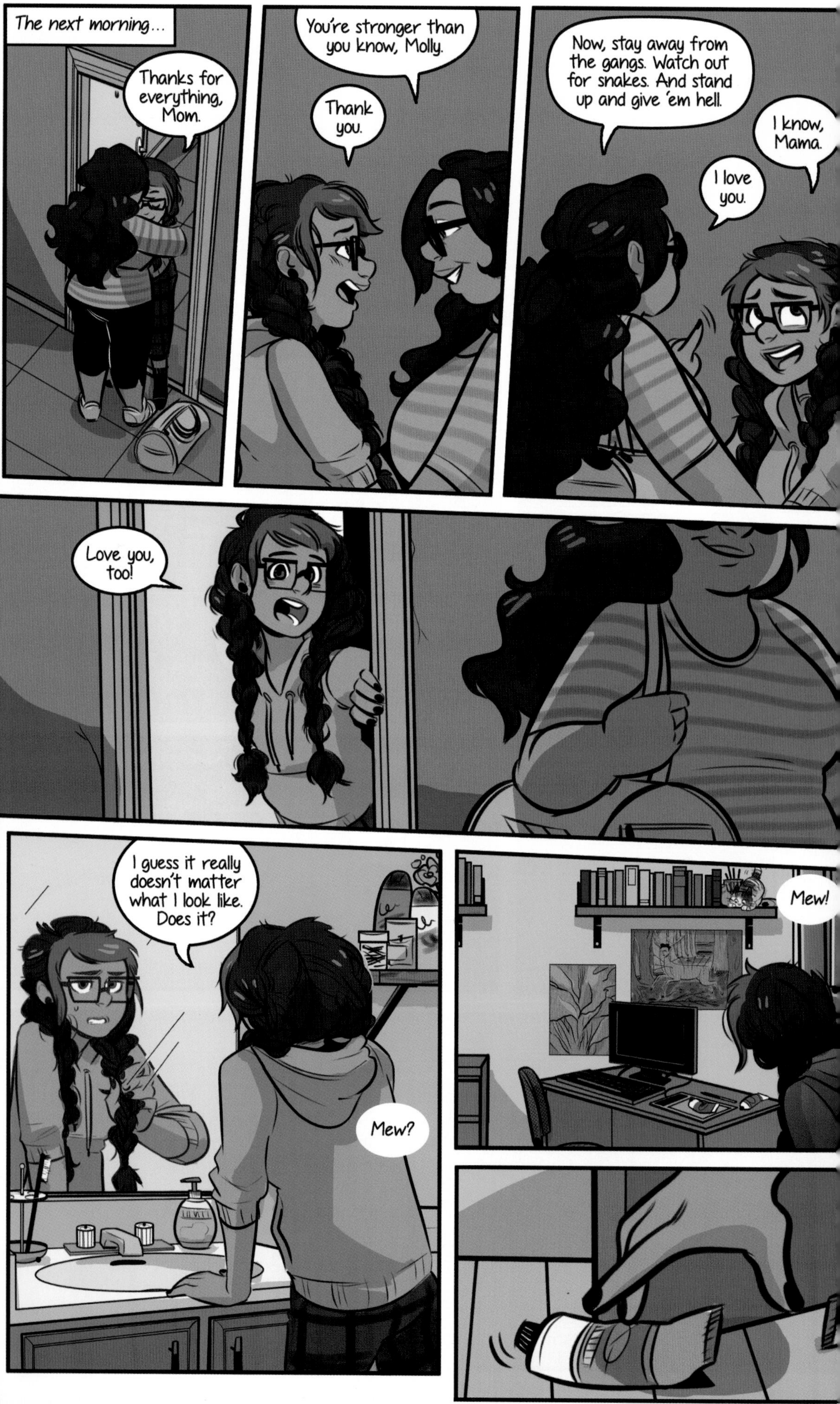
The next morning...
Thanks for everything, Mom.
You're stronger than you know, Molly.
Thank you.
Now, stay away from the gangs. Watch out for snakes. And stand up and give 'em hell.
I know, Mama.
I love you.
Love you, too!
I guess it really doesn't matter what I look like. Does it?
Mew?
Mew!

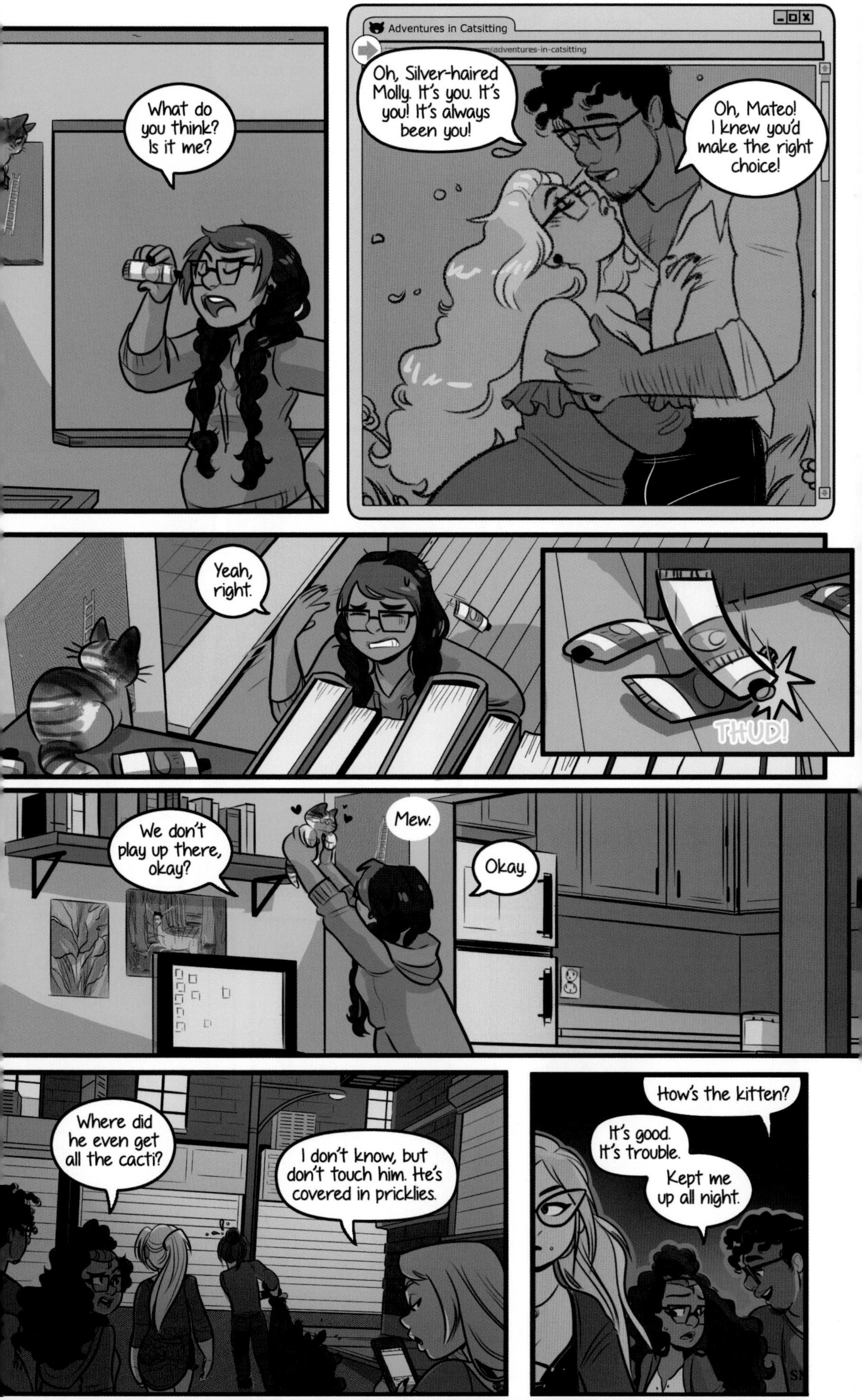
What do you think? Is it me?
Adventures in Catsitting
/adventures-in-catsitting
Oh, Silver-haired Molly. It's you. It's you! It's always been you!
Oh, Mateo! I knew you'd make the right choice!
Yeah, right.
THUD!
We don't play up there, okay?
Mew.
Okay.
Where did he even get all the cacti?
I don't know, but don't touch him. He's covered in pricklies.
How's the kitten?
It's good. It's trouble.
Kept me up all night.

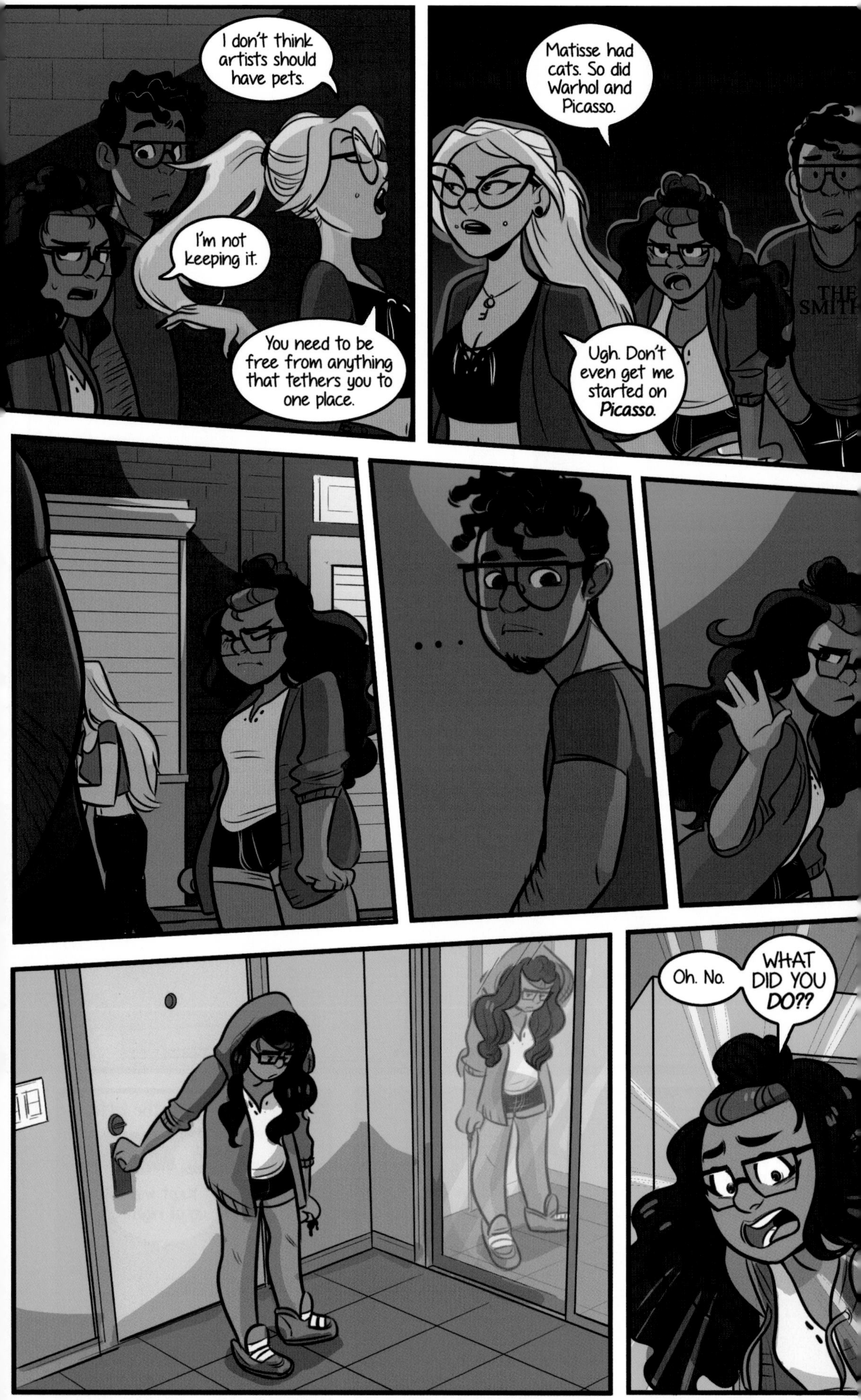
I don't think artists should have pets.
I'm not keeping it.
You need to be free from anything that tethers you to one place.
Matisse had cats. So did Warhol and Picasso.
Ugh. Don't even get me started on *Picasso*.
THE SMITHS
. . .
Oh. No.
WHAT DID YOU *DO??*

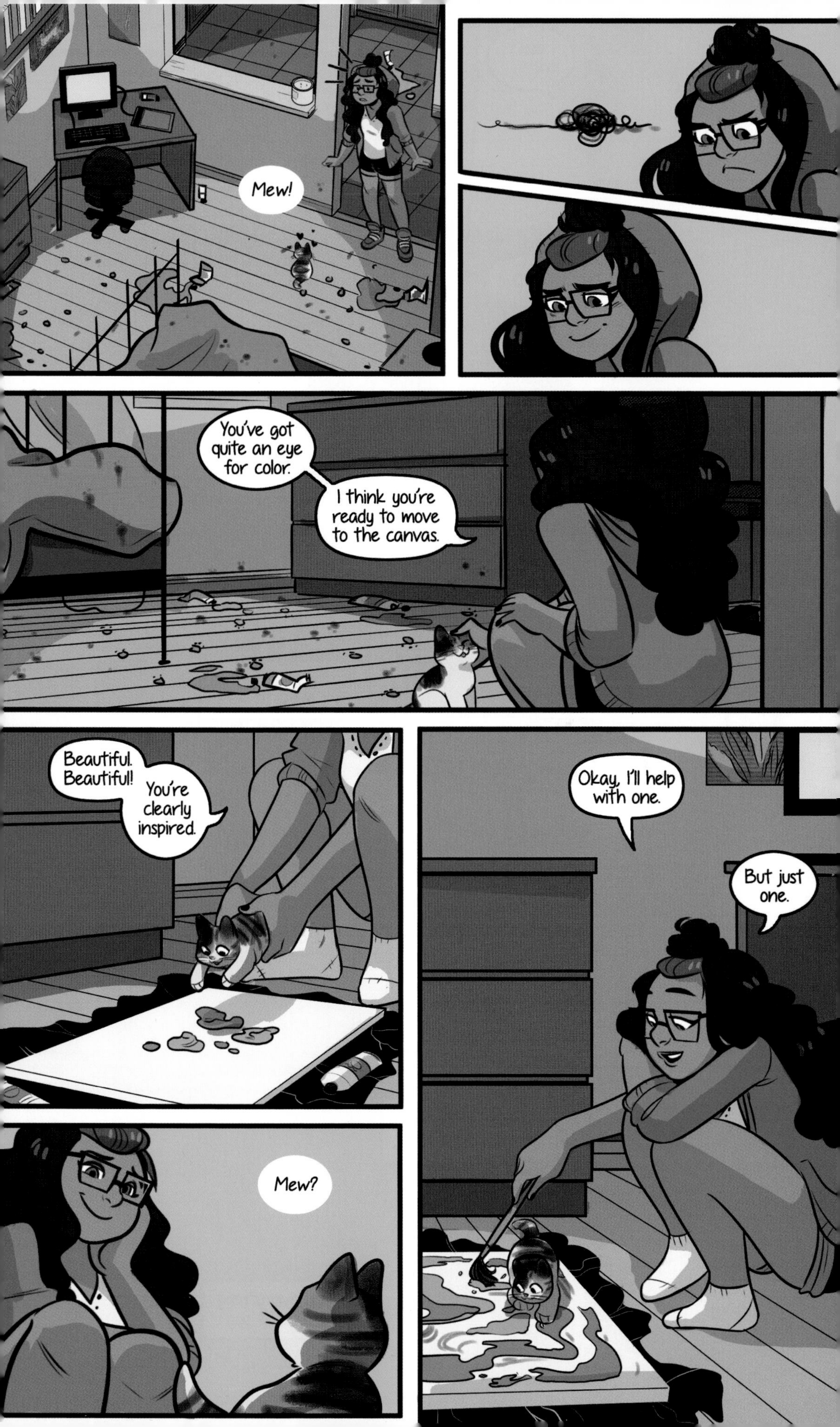
Mew!
You've got quite an eye for color.
I think you're ready to move to the canvas.
Beautiful. Beautiful!
You're clearly inspired.
Okay, I'll help with one.
But just one.
Mew?

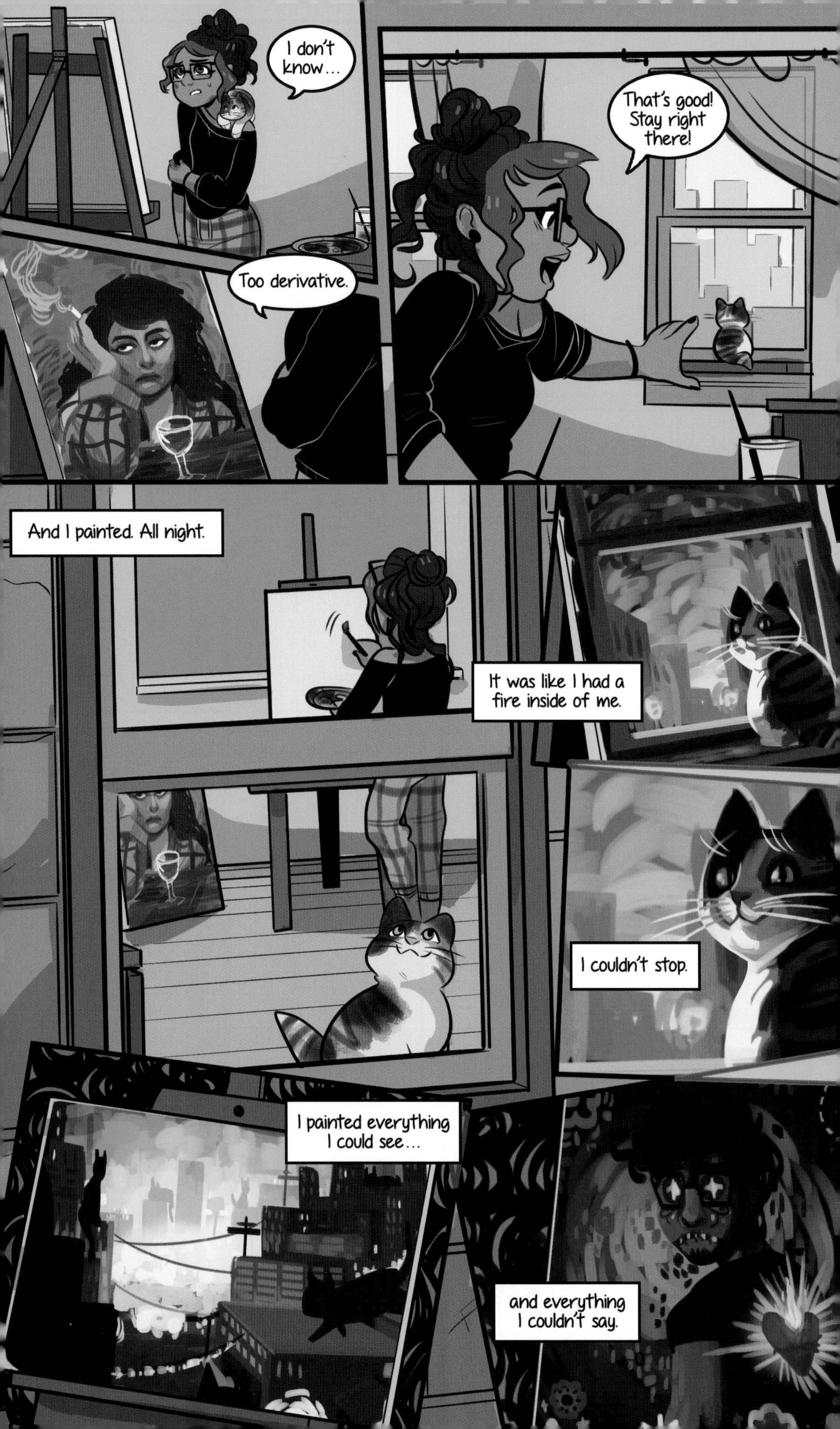
I don't know…
Too derivative.
That's good! Stay right there!
And I painted. All night.
It was like I had a fire inside of me.
I couldn't stop.
I painted everything I could see…
and everything I couldn't say.

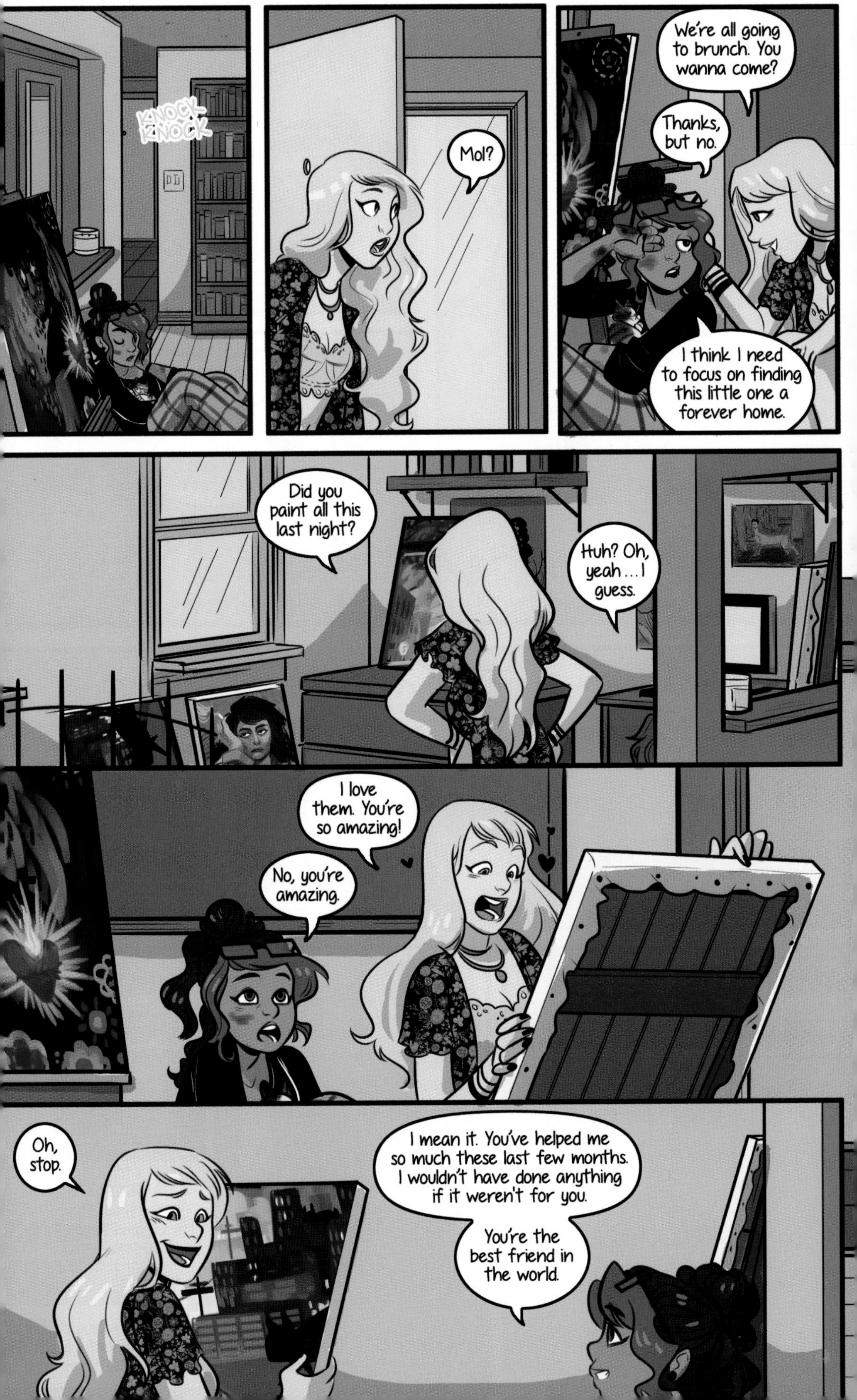
KNOCK KNOCK
Mol?
We're all going to brunch. You wanna come?
Thanks, but no.
I think I need to focus on finding this little one a forever home.
Did you paint all this last night?
Huh? Oh, yeah... I guess.
I love them. You're so amazing!
No, you're amazing.
Oh, stop.
I mean it. You've helped me so much these last few months. I wouldn't have done anything if it weren't for you.
You're the best friend in the world.

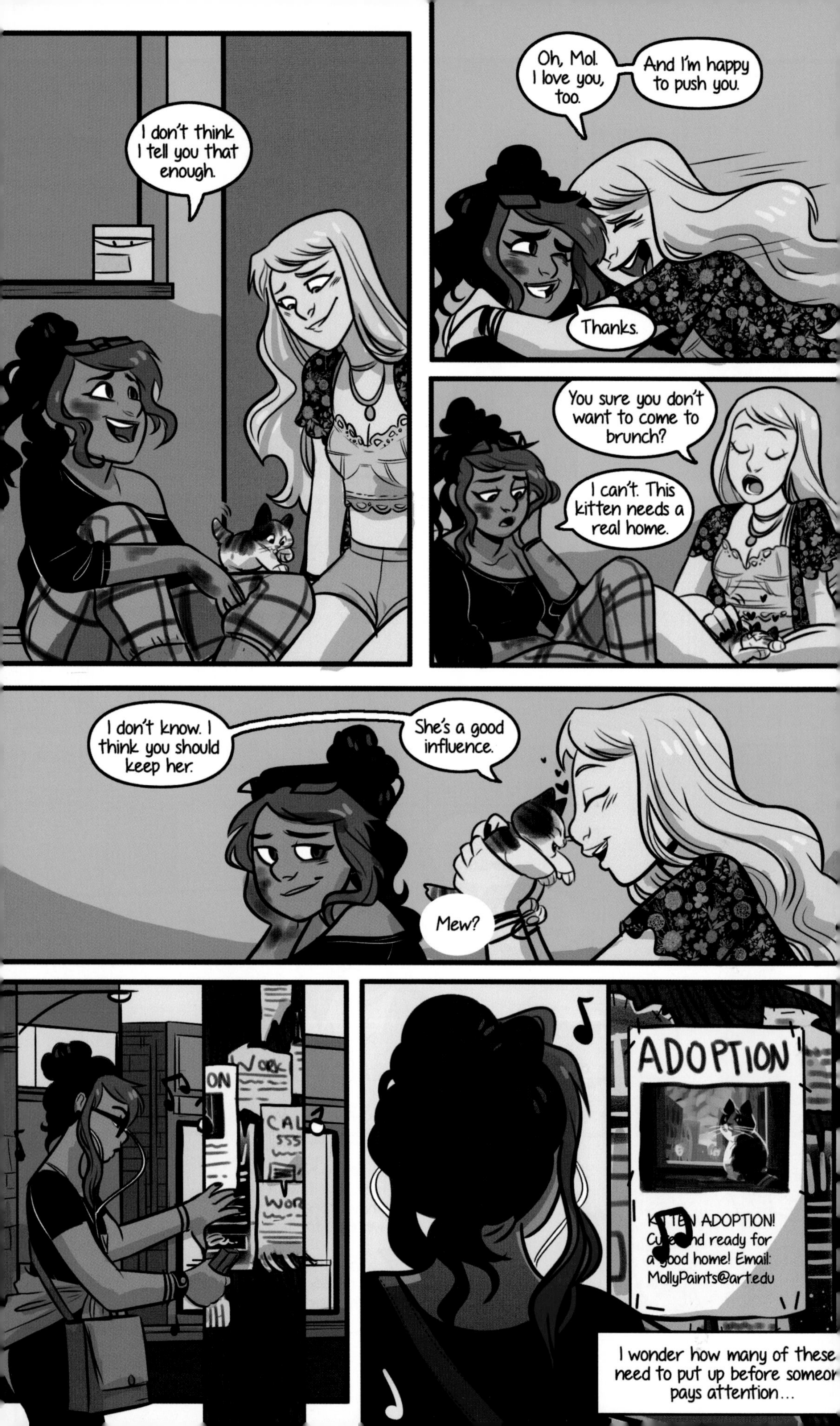
I don't think I tell you that enough.
Oh, Mol. I love you, too.
And I'm happy to push you.
Thanks.
You sure you don't want to come to brunch?
I can't. This kitten needs a real home.
I don't know. I think you should keep her.
She's a good influence.
Mew?
ADOPTION
MollyPaints@art.edu
I wonder how many of these need to put up before someo pays attention...

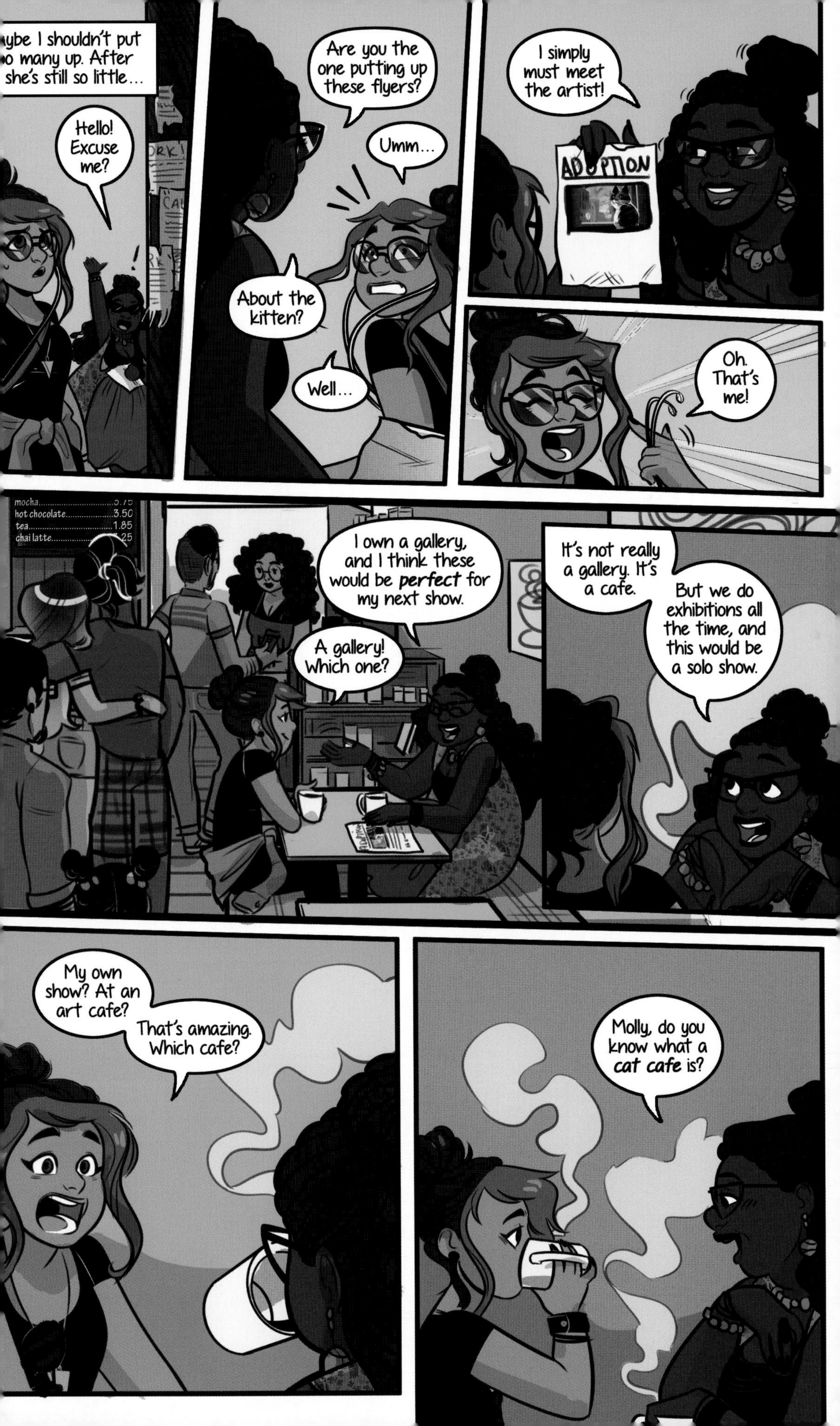

ybe I shouldn't put
o many up. After
she's still so little...
Hello! Excuse me?
Are you the one putting up these flyers?
Umm...
About the kitten?
Well...
I simply must meet the artist!
ADOPTION
Oh. That's me!
mocha
hot chocolate 3.50
tea 1.85
chai latte
I own a gallery, and I think these would be *perfect* for my next show.
A gallery! Which one?
It's not really a gallery. It's a cafe.
But we do exhibitions all the time, and this would be a solo show.
My own show? At an art cafe?
That's amazing. Which cafe?
Molly, do you know what a ***cat cafe*** is?

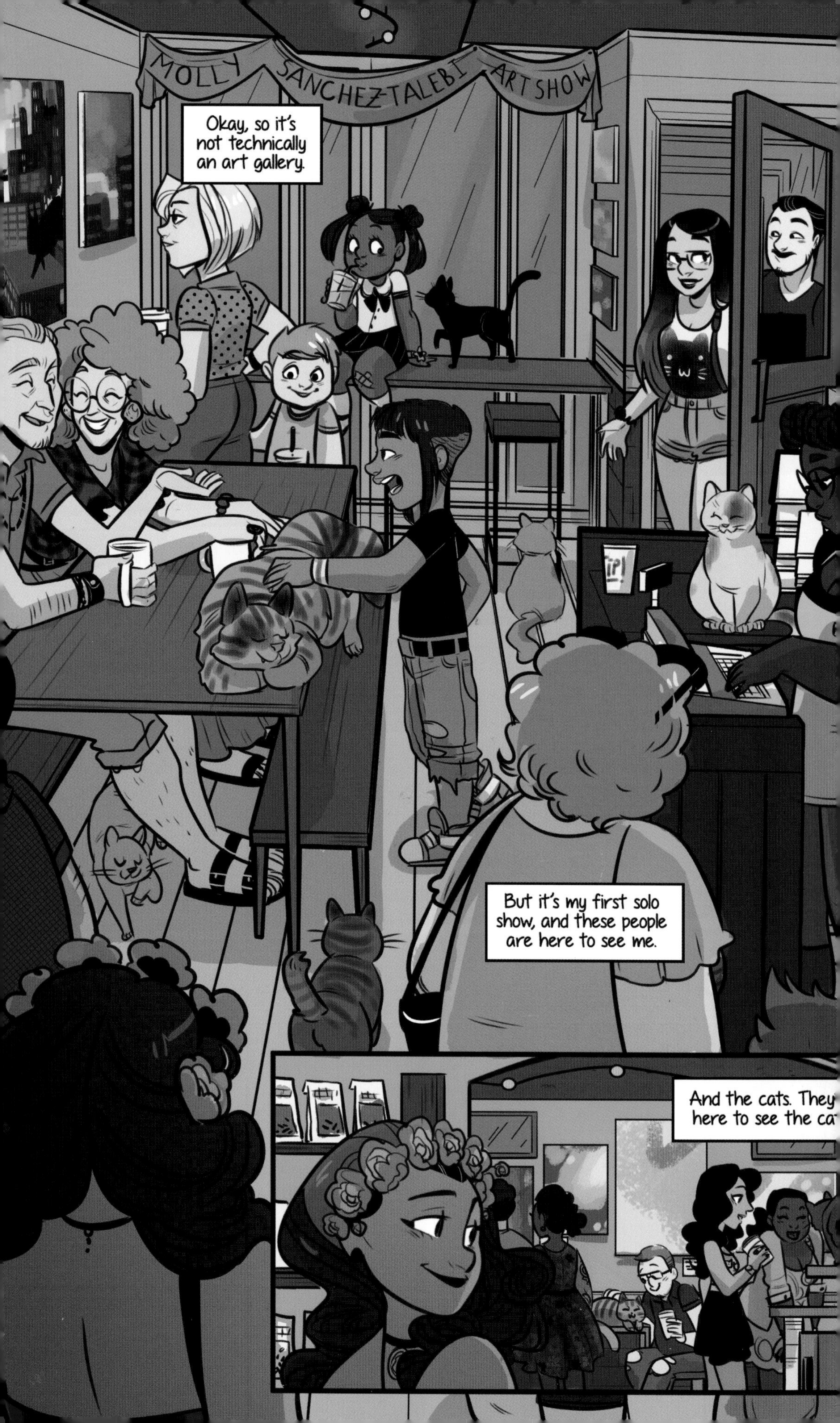
MOLLY SANCHEZ-TALEBI ART SHOW
Okay, so it's not technically an art gallery.
TIP!
But it's my first solo show, and these people are here to see me.
And the cats. They
here to see the ca

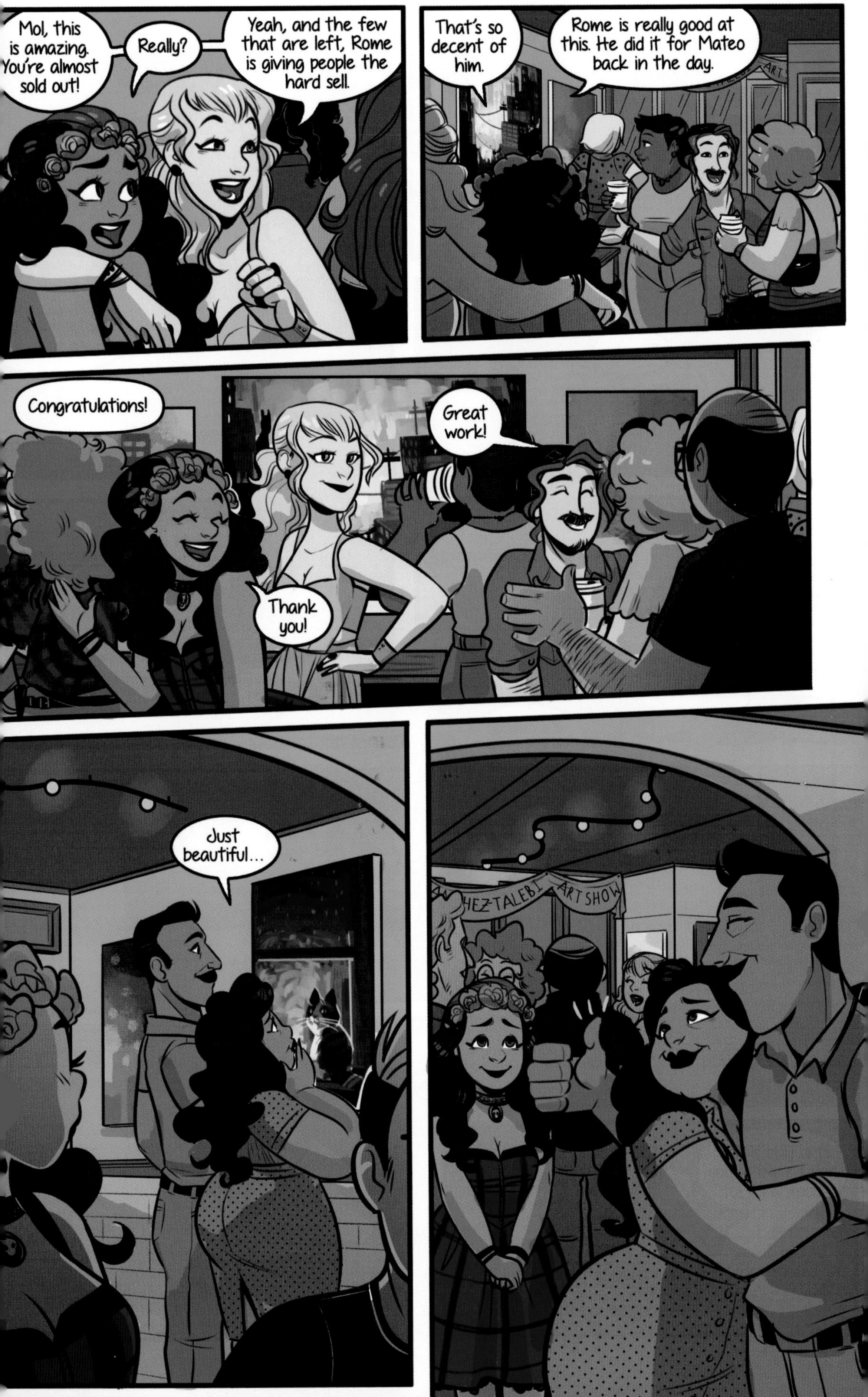

Mol, this is amazing. You're almost sold out!
Really?
Yeah, and the few that are left, Rome is giving people the hard sell.
That's so decent of him.
Rome is really good at this. He did it for Mateo back in the day.
Congratulations!
Great work!
Thank you!
Just beautiful...
HEZ-TALEBI
ART SHOW

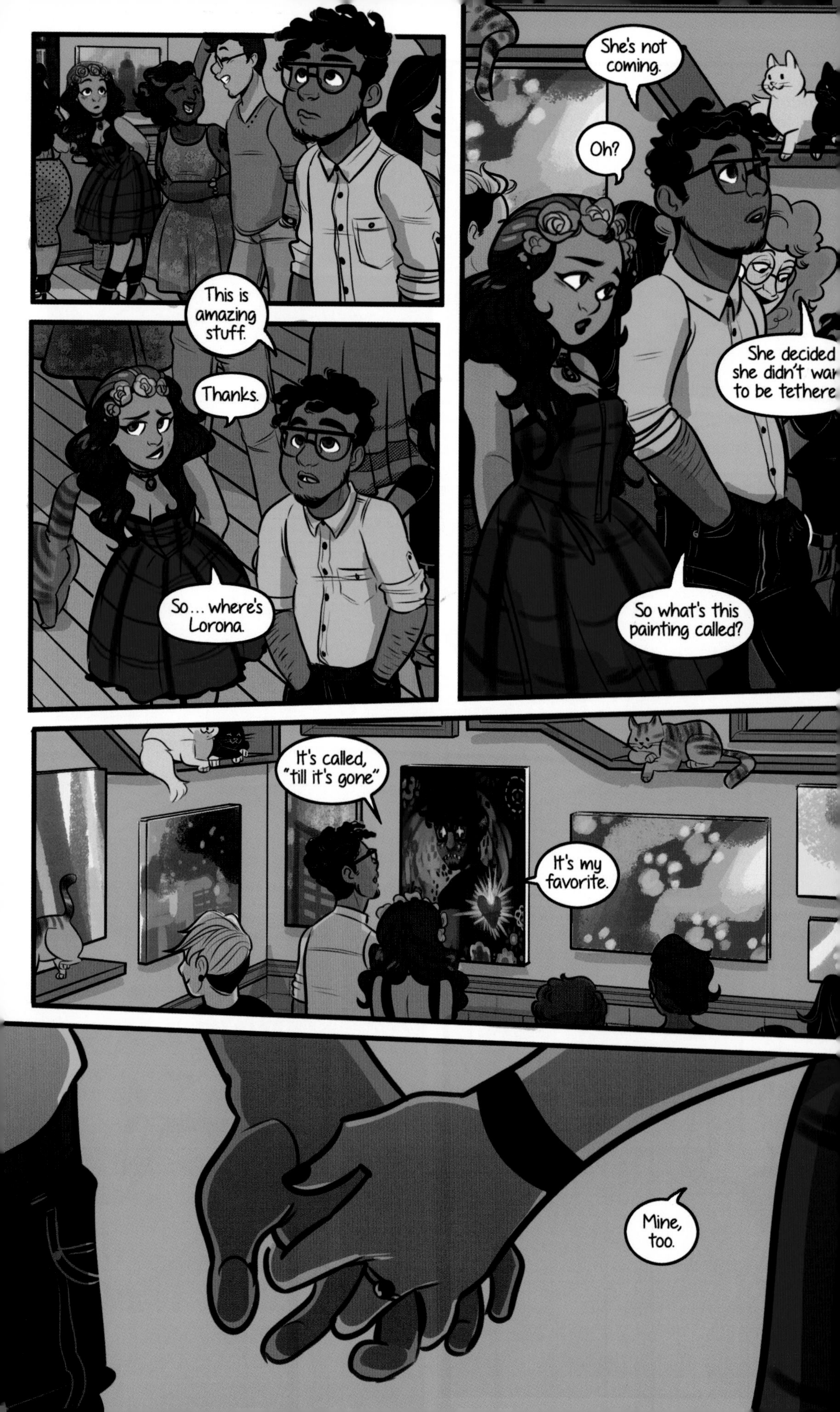
This is amazing stuff.
Thanks.
So... where's Lorona.
She's not coming.
Oh?
She decided she didn't wa
to be tethere
So what's this painting called?
It's called, "till it's gone"
It's my favorite.
Mine, too.

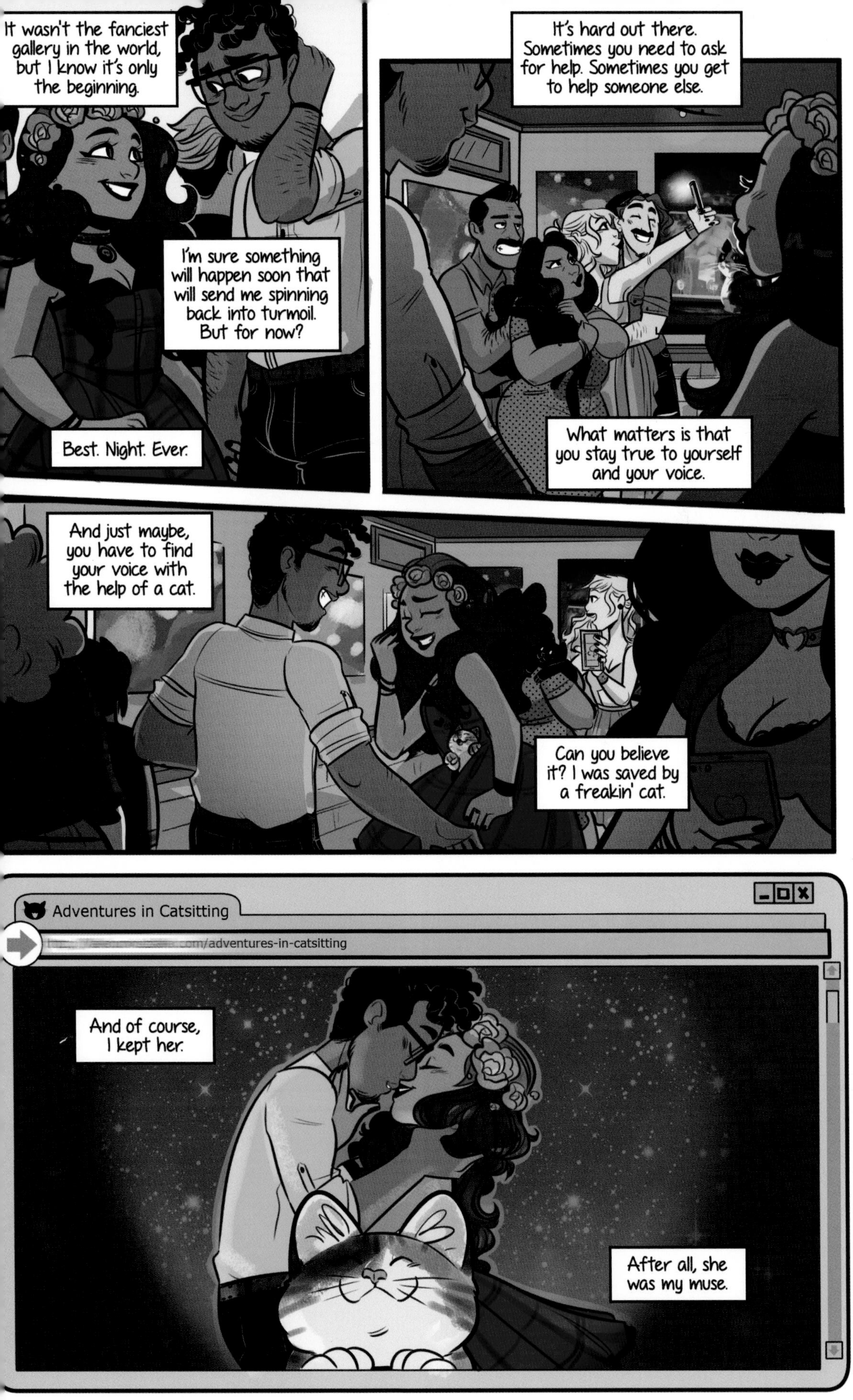
It wasn't the fanciest gallery in the world, but I know it's only the beginning.
I'm sure something will happen soon that will send me spinning back into turmoil. But for now?
Best. Night. Ever.
It's hard out there. Sometimes you need to ask for help. Sometimes you get to help someone else.
What matters is that you stay true to yourself and your voice.
And just maybe, you have to find your voice with the help of a cat.
Can you believe it? I was saved by a freakin' cat.
Adventures in Catsitting
com/adventures-in-catsitting
And of course, I kept her.
After all, she was my muse.

BEHIND the SCENES

molly (23) Flashback Profile

Jenn's early character designs

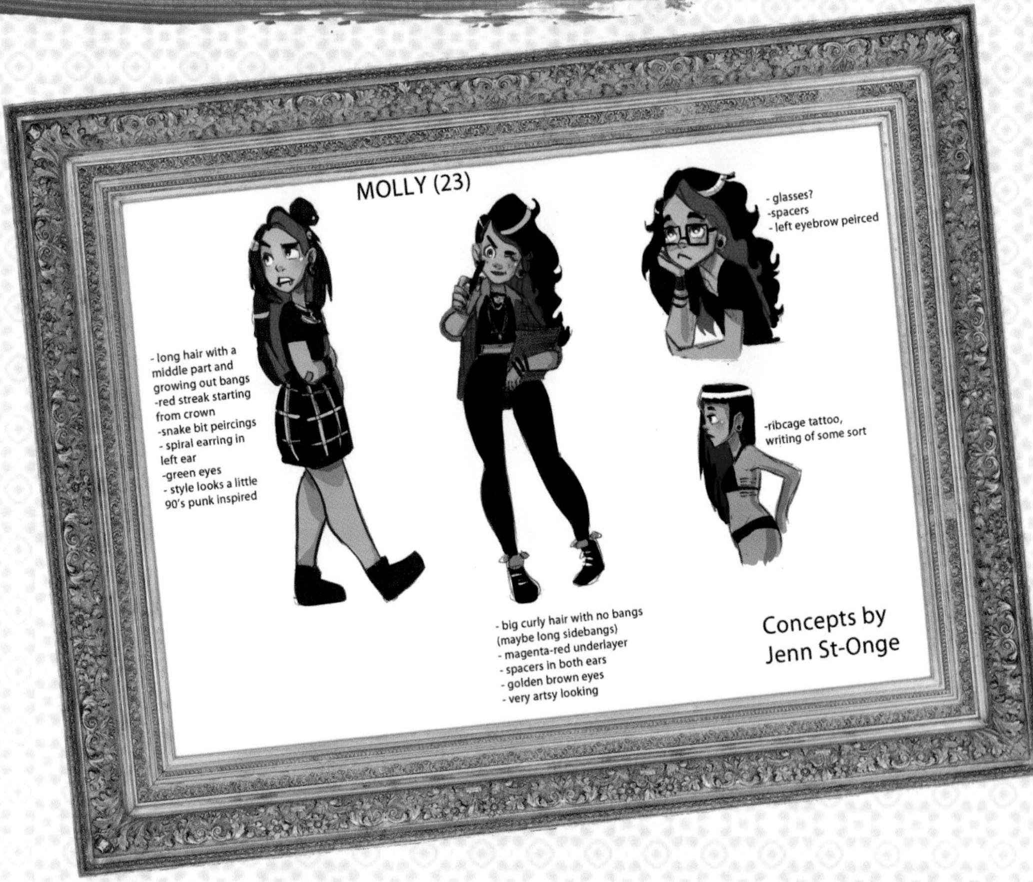
MOLLY (23)
- long hair with a middle part and growing out bangs
-red streak starting from crown
-snake bit peircings
- spiral earring in left ear
-green eyes
- style looks a little 90's punk inspired
- big curly hair with no bangs (maybe long sidebangs)
- magenta-red underlayer
- spacers in both ears
- golden brown eyes
- very artsy looking
- glasses?
-spacers
- left eyebrow peirced
-ribcage tattoo, writing of some sort
Concepts by Jenn St-Onge

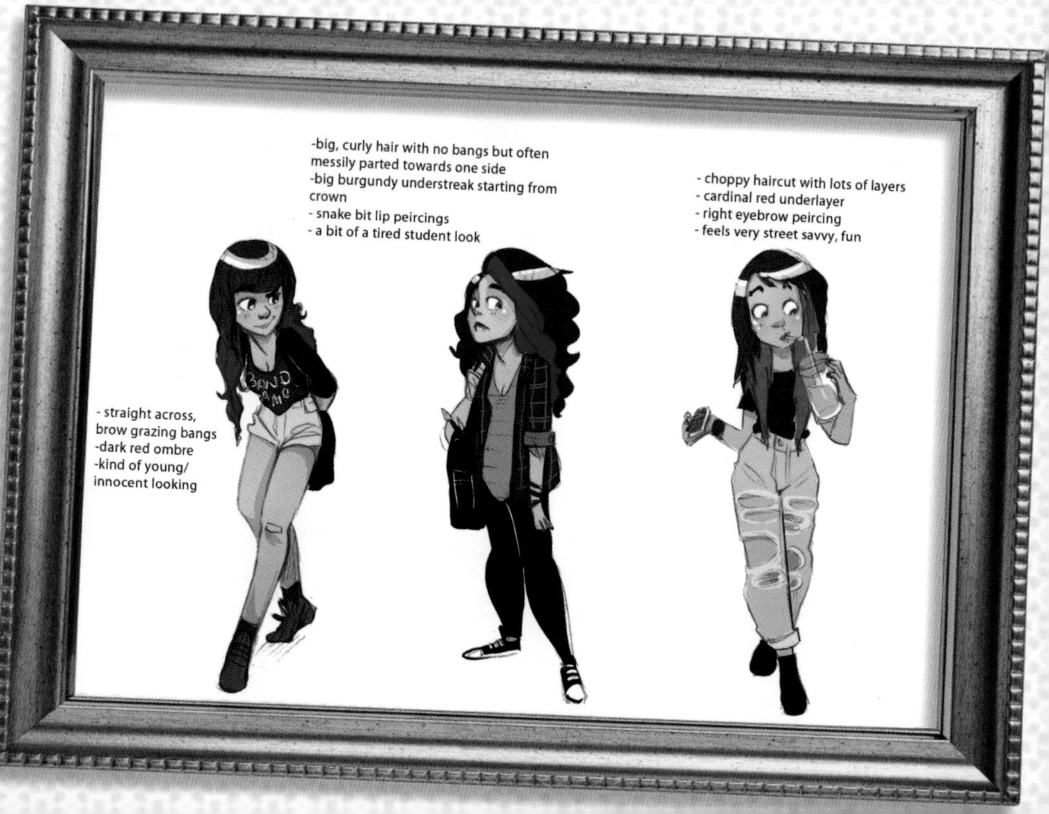
- straight across, brow grazing bangs
-dark red ombre
-kind of young/ innocent looking
-big, curly hair with no bangs but often messily parted towards one side
-big burgundy understreak starting from crown
- snake bit lip peircings
- a bit of a tired student look
- choppy haircut with lots of layers
- cardinal red underlayer
- right eyebrow peircing
- feels very street savvy, fun

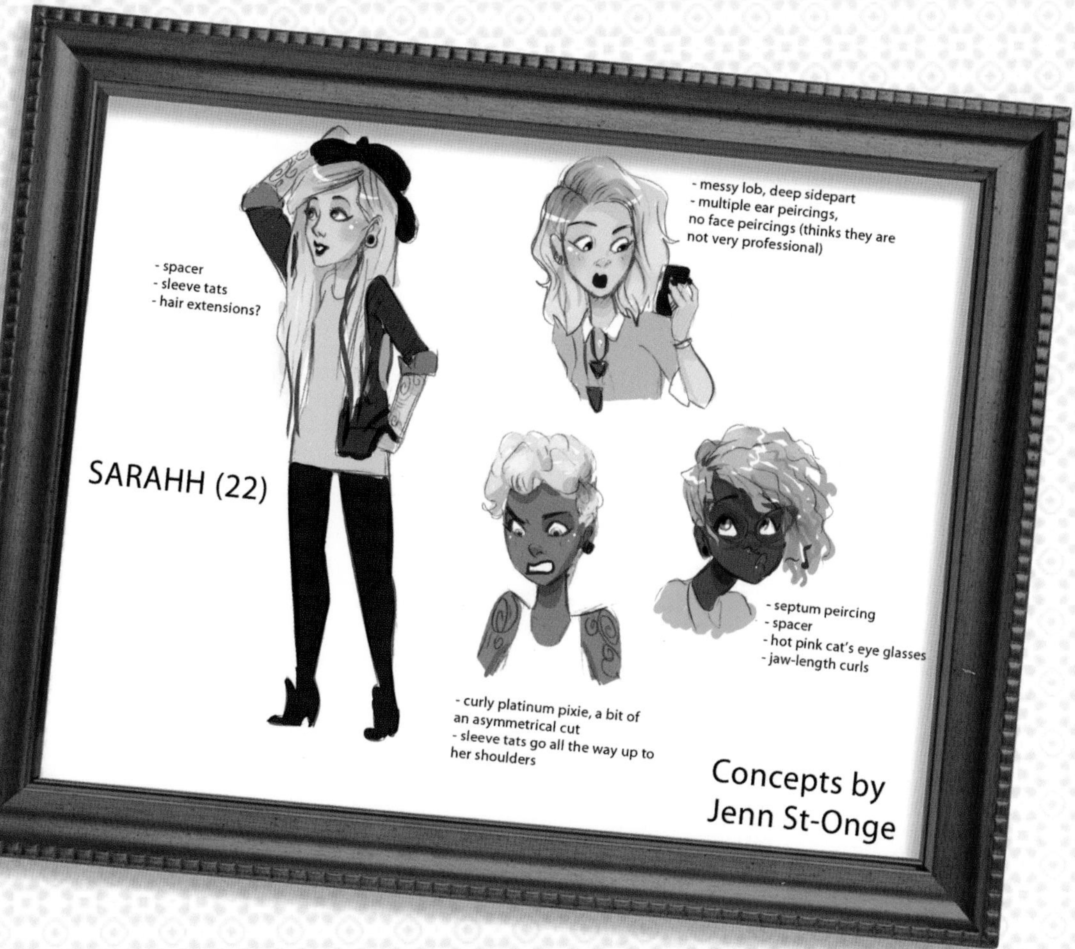

- spacer
- sleeve tats
- hair extensions?
SARAHH (22)
- messy lob, deep sidepart
- multiple ear peircings,
no face peircings (thinks they are not very professional)
- septum peircing
- spacer
- hot pink cat's eye glasses
- jaw-length curls
- curly platinum pixie, a bit of an asymmetrical cut
- sleeve tats go all the way up to her shoulders
Concepts by Jenn St-Onge

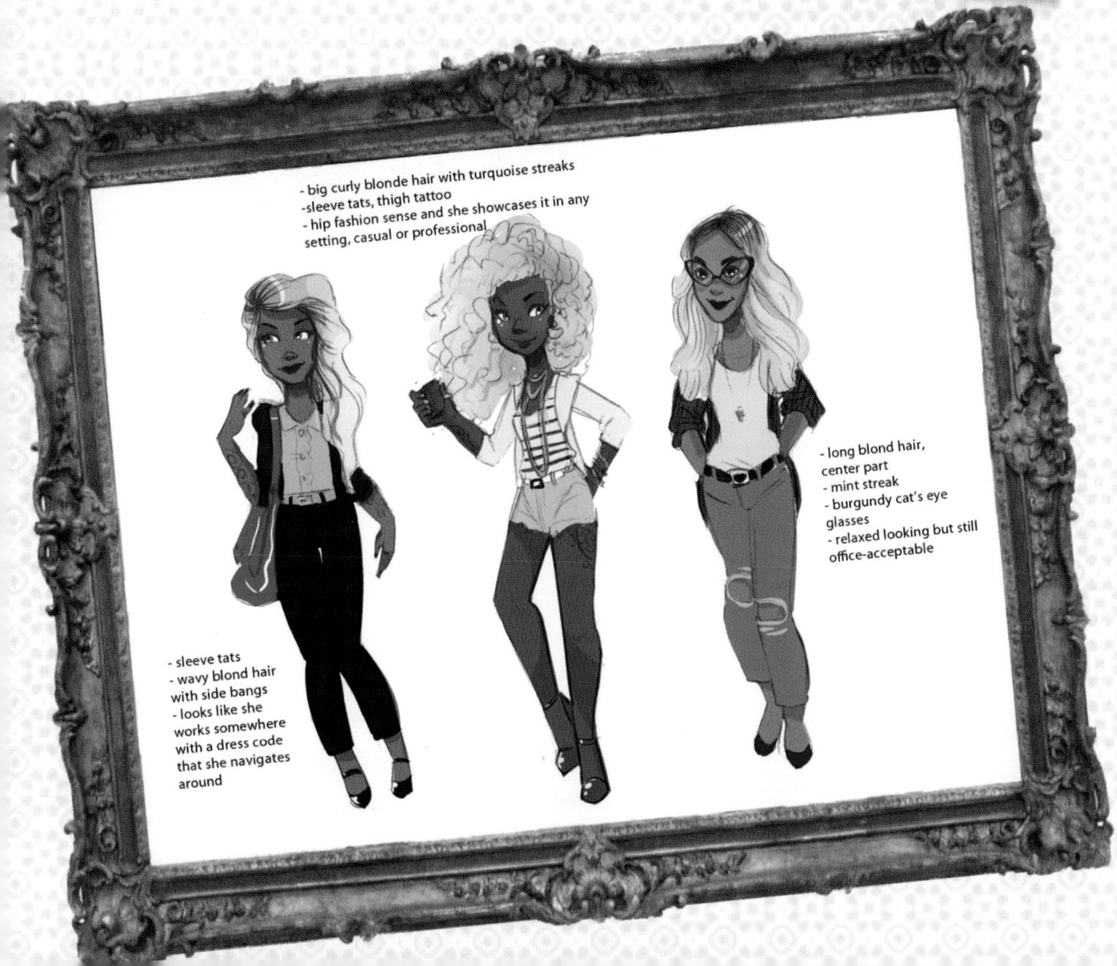

- big curly blonde hair with turquoise streaks
-sleeve tats, thigh tattoo
- hip fashion sense and she showcases it in any setting, casual or professional
- long blond hair, center part
- mint streak
- burgundy cat's eye glasses
- relaxed looking but still office-acceptable
- sleeve tats
- wavy blond hair with side bangs
- looks like she works somewhere with a dress code that she navigates around

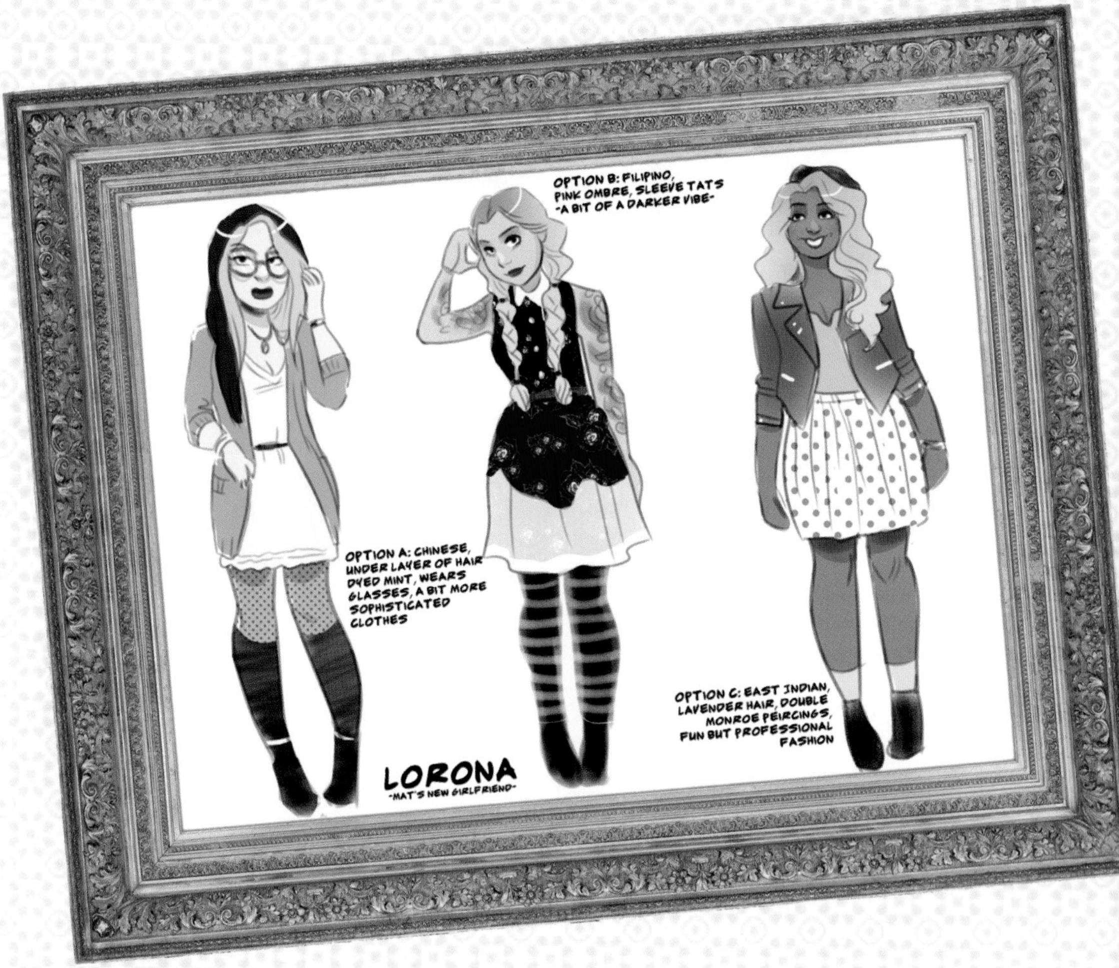
OPTION A: CHINESE, UNDER LAYER OF HAIR DYED MINT, WEARS GLASSES, A BIT MORE SOPHISTICATED CLOTHES
OPTION B: FILIPINO, PINK OMBRE, SLEEVE TATS -A BIT OF A DARKER VIBE-
OPTION C: EAST INDIAN, LAVENDER HAIR, DOUBLE MONROE PEIRCINGS, FUN BUT PROFESSIONAL FASHION
LORONA
-MAT'S NEW GIRLFRIEND-

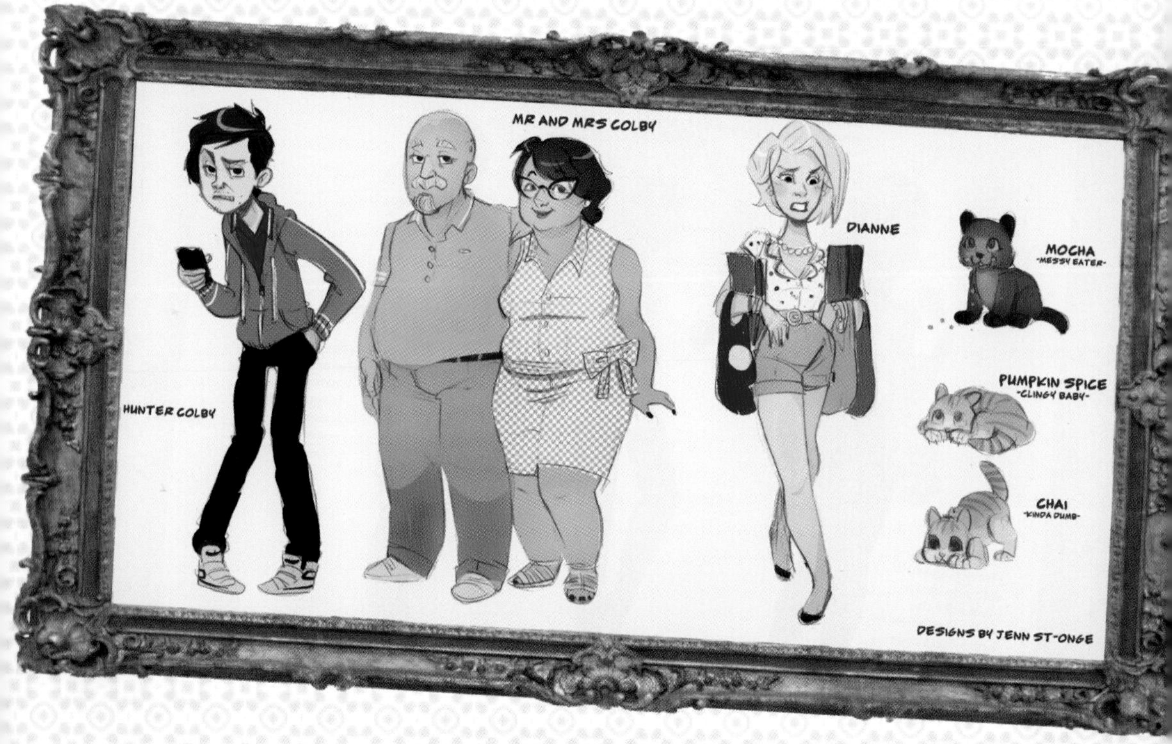
HUNTER COLBY
MR AND MRS COLBY
DIANNE
MOCHA
-MESSY EATER-
PUMPKIN SPICE
-CLINGY BABY-
CHAI
-KINDA DUMB-
DESIGNS BY JENN ST-ONGE

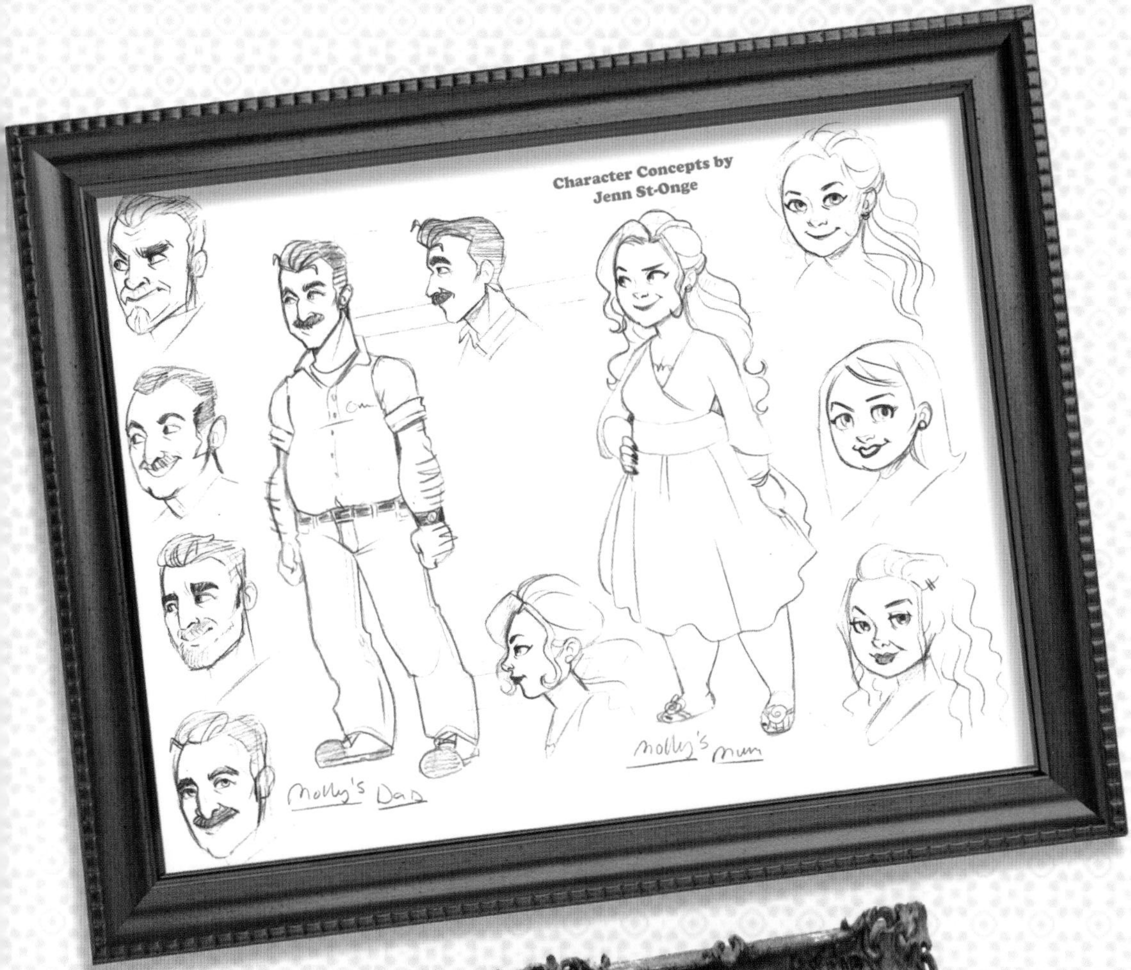
Character Concepts by
Jenn St-Onge
Molly's Dad
Molly's Mum

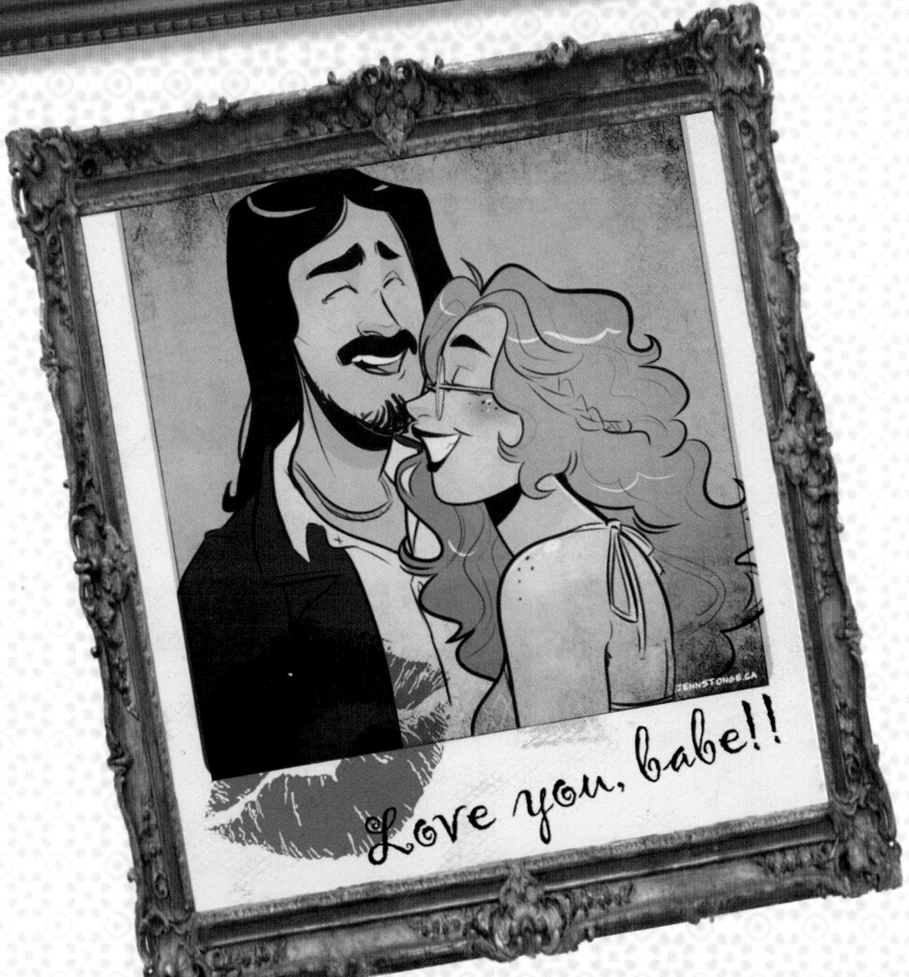
JENNSTONGE.CA
Love you, babe!!

Jenn's layouts

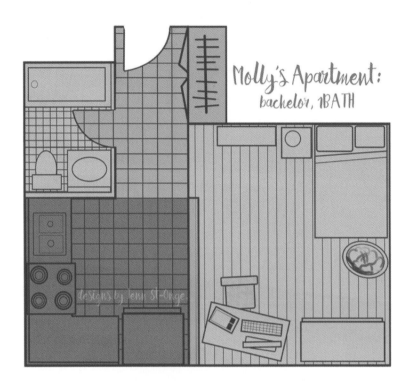

Molly's Apartment:
bachelor, 1BATH
designs by Jenn St-Onge.

Sarah's Apartment:
1BDRM+DEN, 1BATH

designs by Jenn St-Onge.

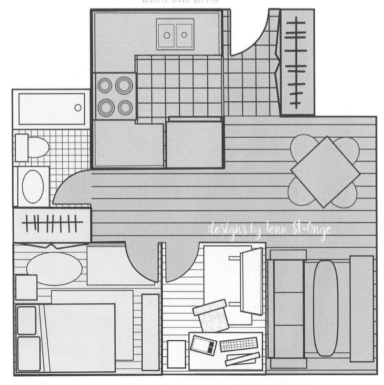

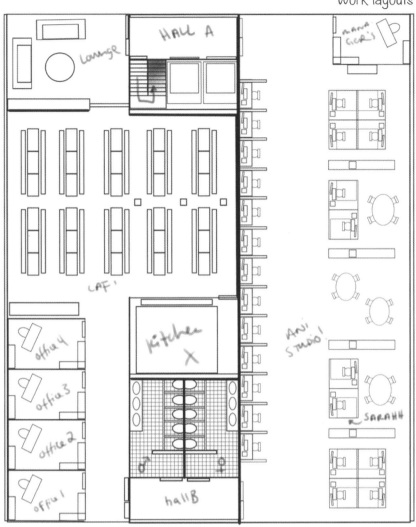

Lounge

HALL A

MAMA GIGI's

CAF!

ANI STUDIO!

Kitchen
X

office 4

office 3

office 2

office 1

R SARAHH

hall B

Sabina's Apartment:
1BDRM, 1BATH

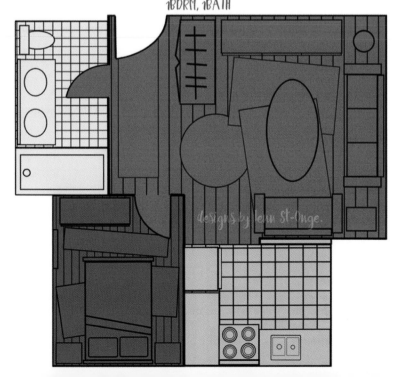

designs by Jenn St-Onge.

Page Twelve - Eight Panels

12.1 - Downtown LA. The street is practically empty this late at night. A beat-up blue pick-up truck is parked under a street light. Molly, Sarahh and Mateo walk toward it. Rome stands at the back of the truck bed.
NARRATION (MOLLY): Rome designs real estate websites by day. But by night, he's Banksy.

12.2 - CU of Rome's smug but handsome face.
NARRATION (MOLLY): Well, not *actually* Banksy - but he thinks he is. Or, the next Banksy. He's a street artist and he's getting a lot of attention. He's known as "WhenIN"
ROME: Get it? Like, WhenIN Rome?
NARRATION (MOLLY): Yeah, we got it.

12.3 - Molly, Sarahh and Mateo sidle up to the truck bed. Rome is rigging up paint cans, spray paint, rope and brushes to the back.
ROME: Sup?
SARAHH: Hey, Rome.
ROME: Hey babe. You ready to do this?
MOLLY: Wait. What exactly are we doing?

12.4 - WIDE of truck from side. Mateo drives. Molly and Sarahh in truck bed. Rome is hanging off the back, spray painting the street below him.
ROME: K, BACK!
SARAHH: Back up, Mateo!
MOLLY: The great WhenIN at work.

12.5 - Just the girls in the back of the truck.
SARAHH: Yeah. Hope he makes a cat pic this time! Or would you consider that plagiarism?
MOLLY: Shut up.
SARAHH: Seriously though…

12.6 - CU of Sarah, she's being genuine now.
SARAHH: What's up with the cat drawings? You're so talented. You should seriously get your portfolio together.
ROME (OS): FORWARD!

12.7 - CU of Molly
SARAHH (OS): Mateo! Forward!
MOLLY: I have a portfolio. No one wants it. And there is absolutely no inspiration for anything new in the suburbs.
ROME (OS): Back!

12.8 - CU of Sarahh again.
MOLLY (OS): Back, Mateo!
SARAHH: Well you better find some. The cats make me sad. That's not your real voice, and you know it.
ROME (OS): K, DONE!

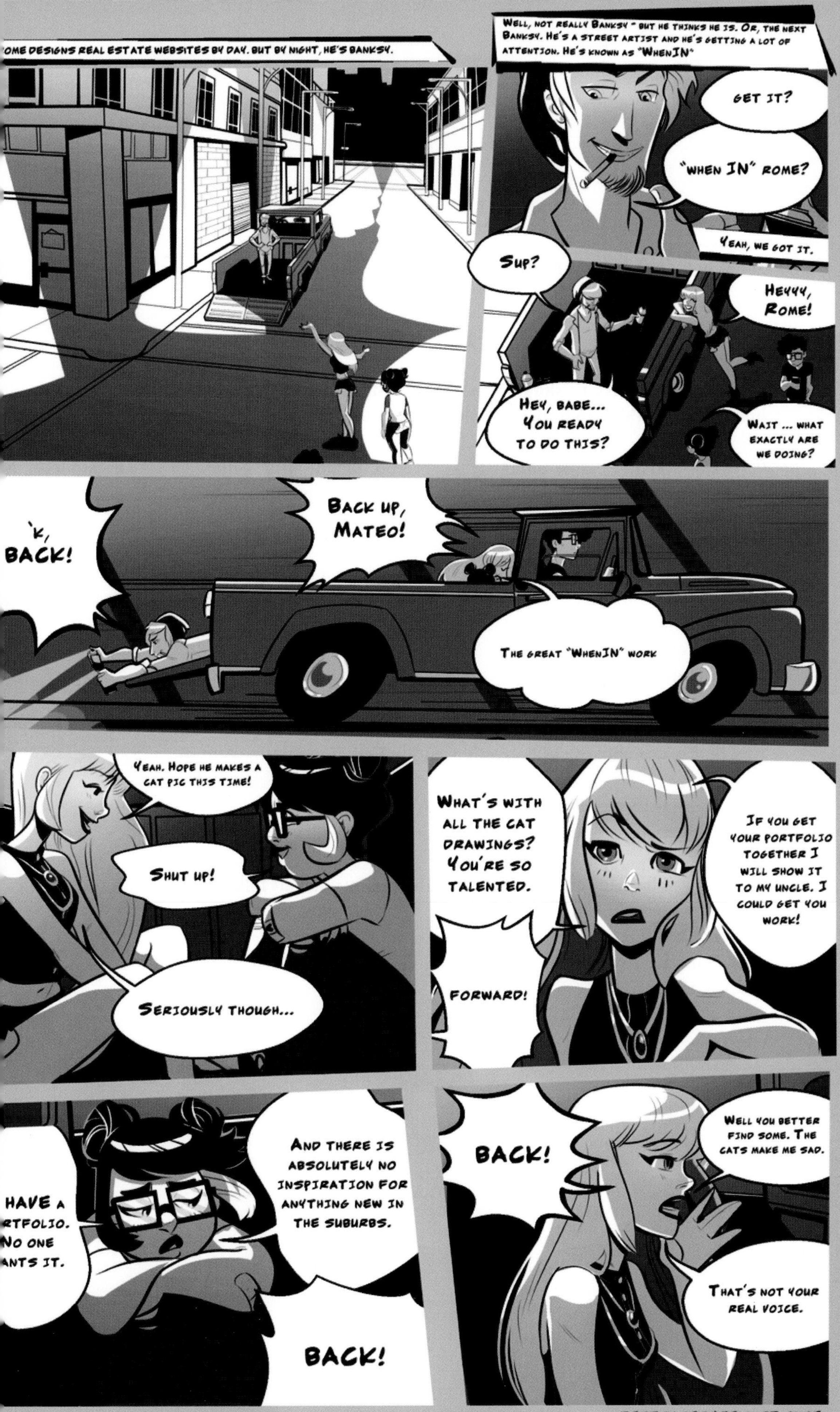
OME DESIGNS REAL ESTATE WEBSITES BY DAY. BUT BY NIGHT, HE'S BANKSY.
WELL, NOT REALLY BANKSY - BUT HE THINKS HE IS. OR, THE NEXT BANKSY. HE'S A STREET ARTIST AND HE'S GETTING A LOT OF ATTENTION. HE'S KNOWN AS "WHENIN"
GET IT?
"WHEN IN" ROME?
YEAH, WE GOT IT.
SUP?
HEYYY, ROME!
HEY, BABE... YOU READY TO DO THIS?
WAIT ... WHAT EXACTLY ARE WE DOING?
'K, BACK!
BACK UP, MATEO!
THE GREAT "WHENIN" WORK
YEAH. HOPE HE MAKES A CAT PIC THIS TIME!
SHUT UP!
SERIOUSLY THOUGH...
WHAT'S WITH ALL THE CAT DRAWINGS? YOU'RE SO TALENTED.
IF YOU GET YOUR PORTFOLIO TOGETHER I WILL SHOW IT TO MY UNCLE. I COULD GET YOU WORK!
FORWARD!
HAVE A RTFOLIO. NO ONE ANTS IT.
AND THERE IS ABSOLUTELY NO INSPIRATION FOR ANYTHING NEW IN THE SUBURBS.
BACK!
BACK!
WELL YOU BETTER FIND SOME. THE CATS MAKE ME SAD.
THAT'S NOT YOUR REAL VOICE.

TEST PAGE BY JENN ST-ONGE

We thought you'd like to see how comics are made! From script...

Page Zero - Five Panels

DREAM SEQUENCE: should have a dream-like quality to the color and edging of the borders. Something that distinguishes it from the real world.

0:1 - BIG PANEL - Establishing night shot from outside an art gallery looking in through window. Inside is an art show (paintings) lots of artsy types milling around. People drink champagne - it's a very classy and artistic event.

0.2 - Molly (looking done up and beautiful) stands near one of her paintings (still life) and a small crowd fawns over her work. The lead impressed art guy, ARTIE, gestures to the painting He's handsome with a beard and holds a flute of champagne. Molly beams with pride.
ARTIE: Your work is magnificent, Molly!
Molly: Thank you.

0.3 - Artie as seen over Molly's shoulder. He looks sincere.
ARTIE: This painting is easily worth twenty MEOWS.

0.4 - Molly as seen over Artie's shoulder. She looks confused.
MOLLY: I'm sorry, what did you say?

0.5 - Molly's back to camera. Artie is surrounded by other art folks who smile and agree with him.
ARTIE: MEOW gallery in the MEOW and MEOW MEOW!
ART FOLKS (scattered throughout group): Meow. Meow! Meow.
THOUGHT BUBBLE OVER MOLLY'S HEAD: **???**

to pencils...

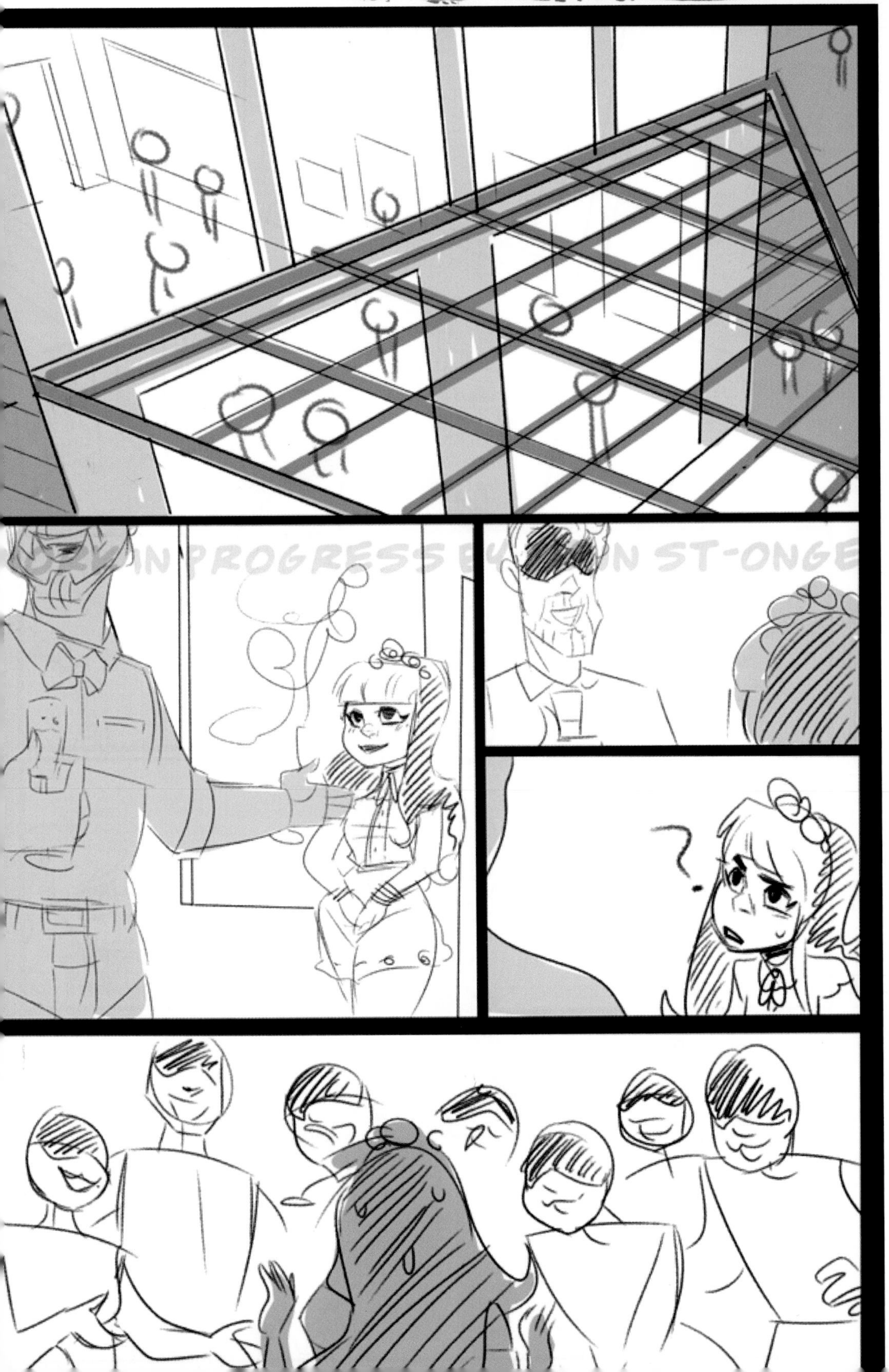
?

to inks...

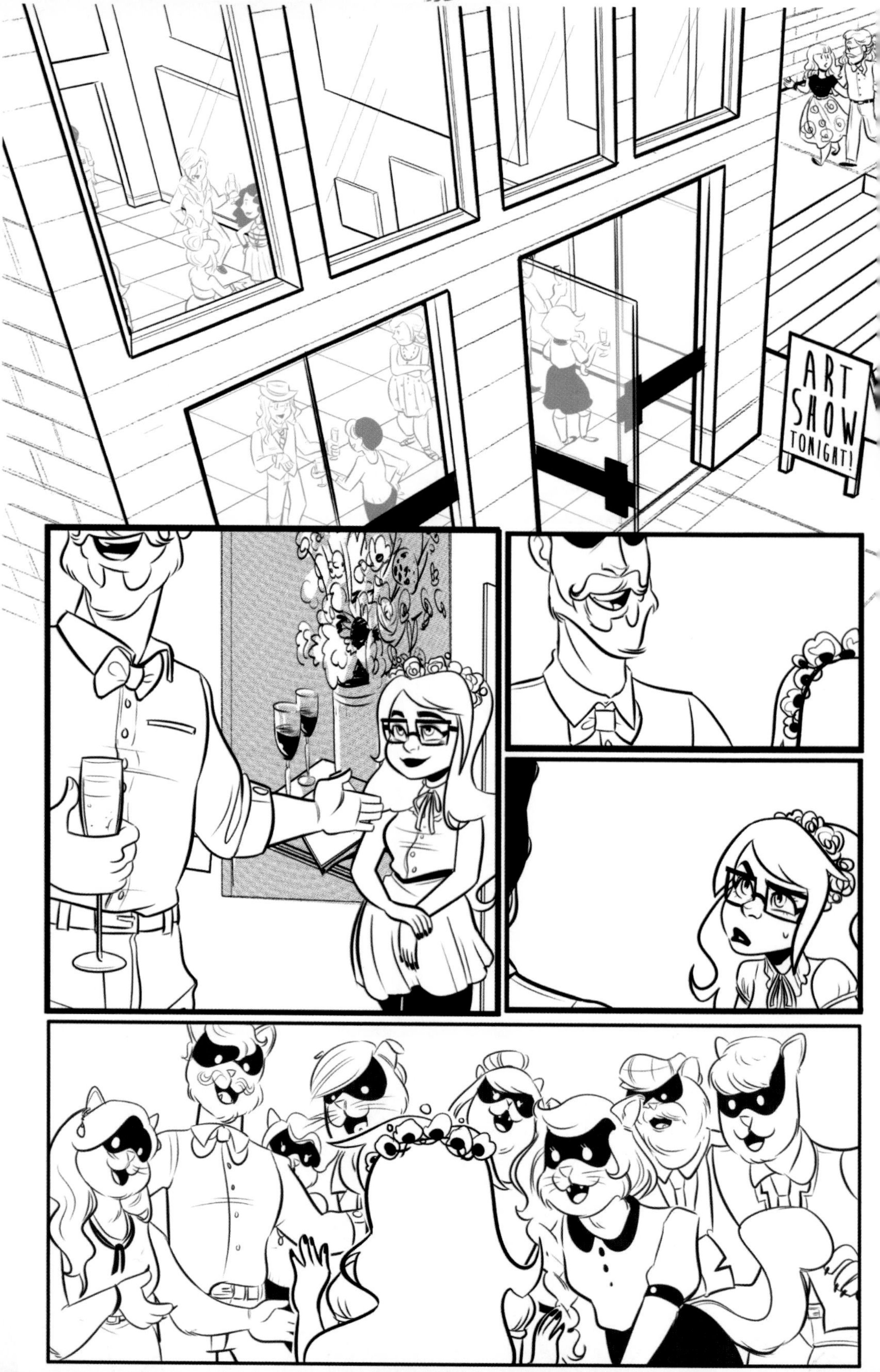

to colors...

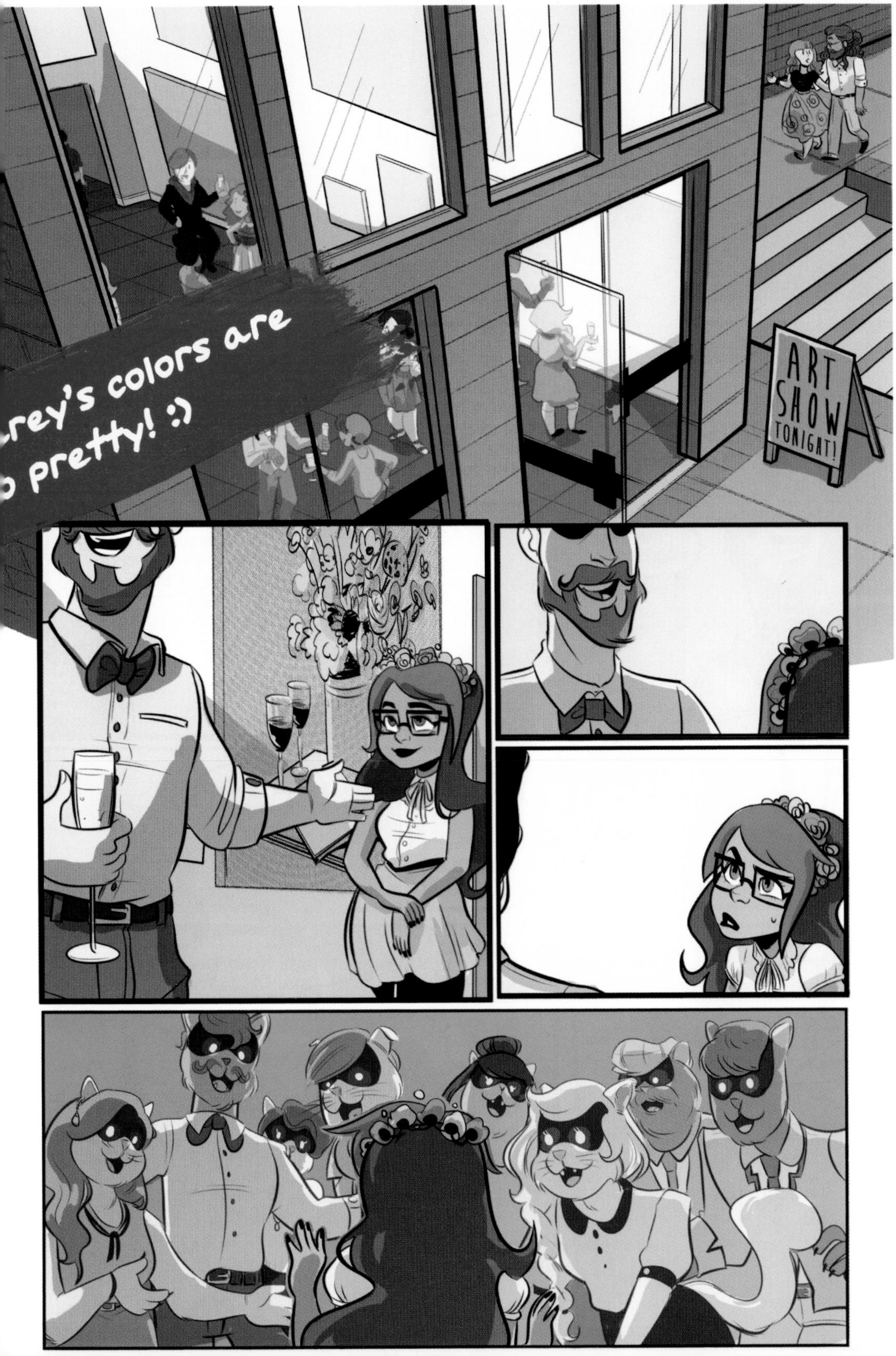
ART SHOW TONIGHT!

rey's colors are
o pretty! :)

to lettering...

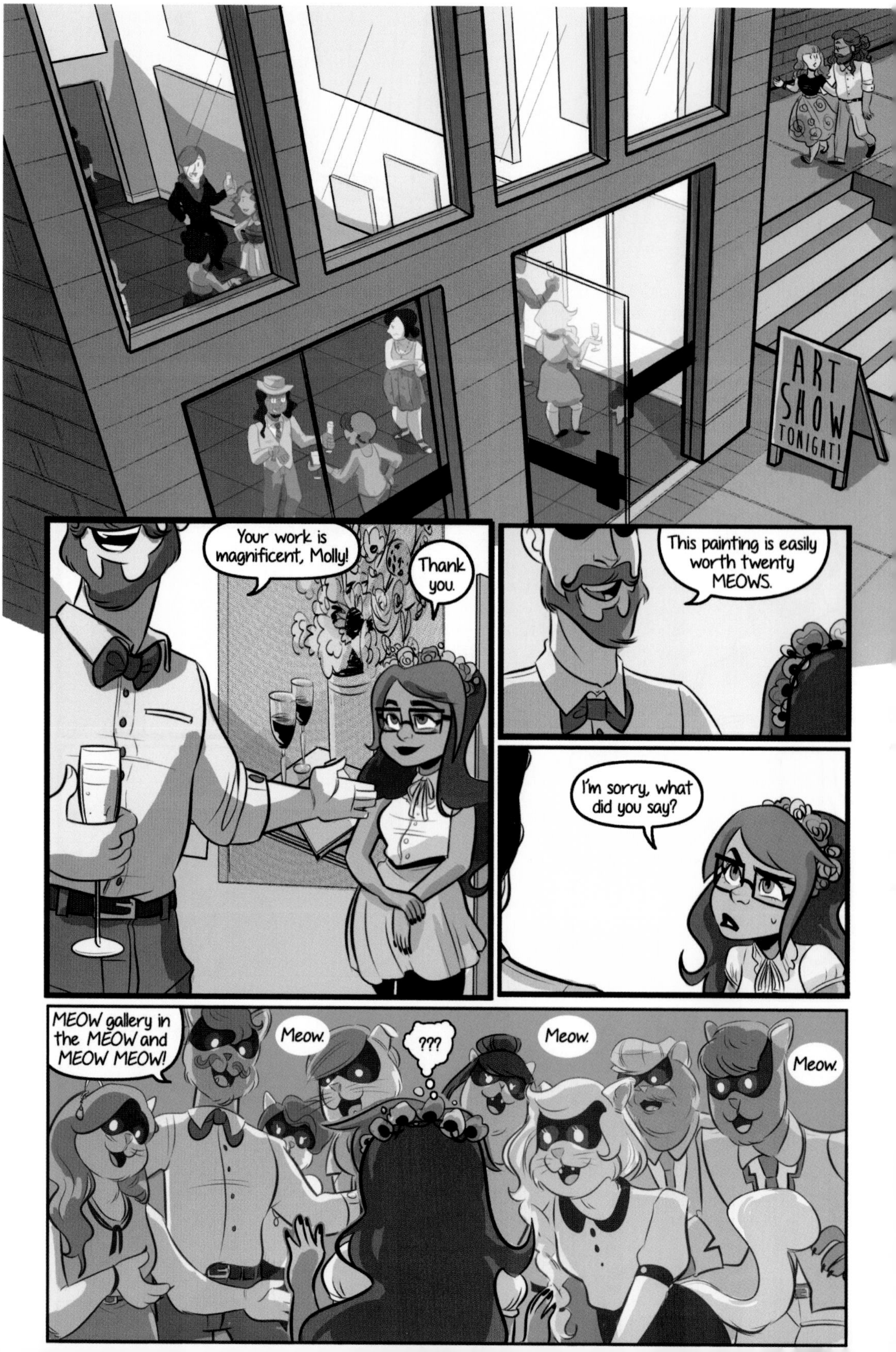
ART SHOW TONIGHT!
Your work is magnificent, Molly!
Thank you.
This painting is easily worth twenty MEOWS.
I'm sorry, what did you say?
MEOW gallery in the MEOW and MEOW MEOW!
Meow.
???
Meow.
Meow.

ustine Prado - March 25 - Final Draft   Finding Molly - Issue 3   14 of 25

Page Twelve - Five Panels

2.1 - **WEBCOMIC PANEL** - Molly and Sabina as they were next to the couch - Sabina ooking ravishing and perfectly wind-blown and Molly looks like garbage. Literal garbage - ither in a trash can à la Oscar the grouch, or just made of garbage wearing tattered rags of lothing and looking like a hot mess.
NARRATION (MOLLY): Strong and sexy? Yeah right.

2.2 - CU of Sabina handing Molly the house keys.
SABINA (OS): Have fun. You're welcome to have friends over if you want.
SABINA (OS): This is a great party house.

2.3 - Molly waves goodbye at the front door as is shuts.
MOLLY: Thanks!
SFX: SLAM!
MOLLY (Smaller font, quieter): If I had any, I would.

2.4 - Molly turns back to the beautiful apartment. She sees Vera perched on a chair nearby. Vera s making bedroom eyes at Molly.

INSERT: Molly scrunches up her face - confused.
MOLLY: Are you flirting with me?

2.5 - Close on Vera's face - even more flirtatious.

INSERT: Molly smiles, blushes. She's helpless to Vera's charm.
MOLLY: Damn, you're good.

pencils...

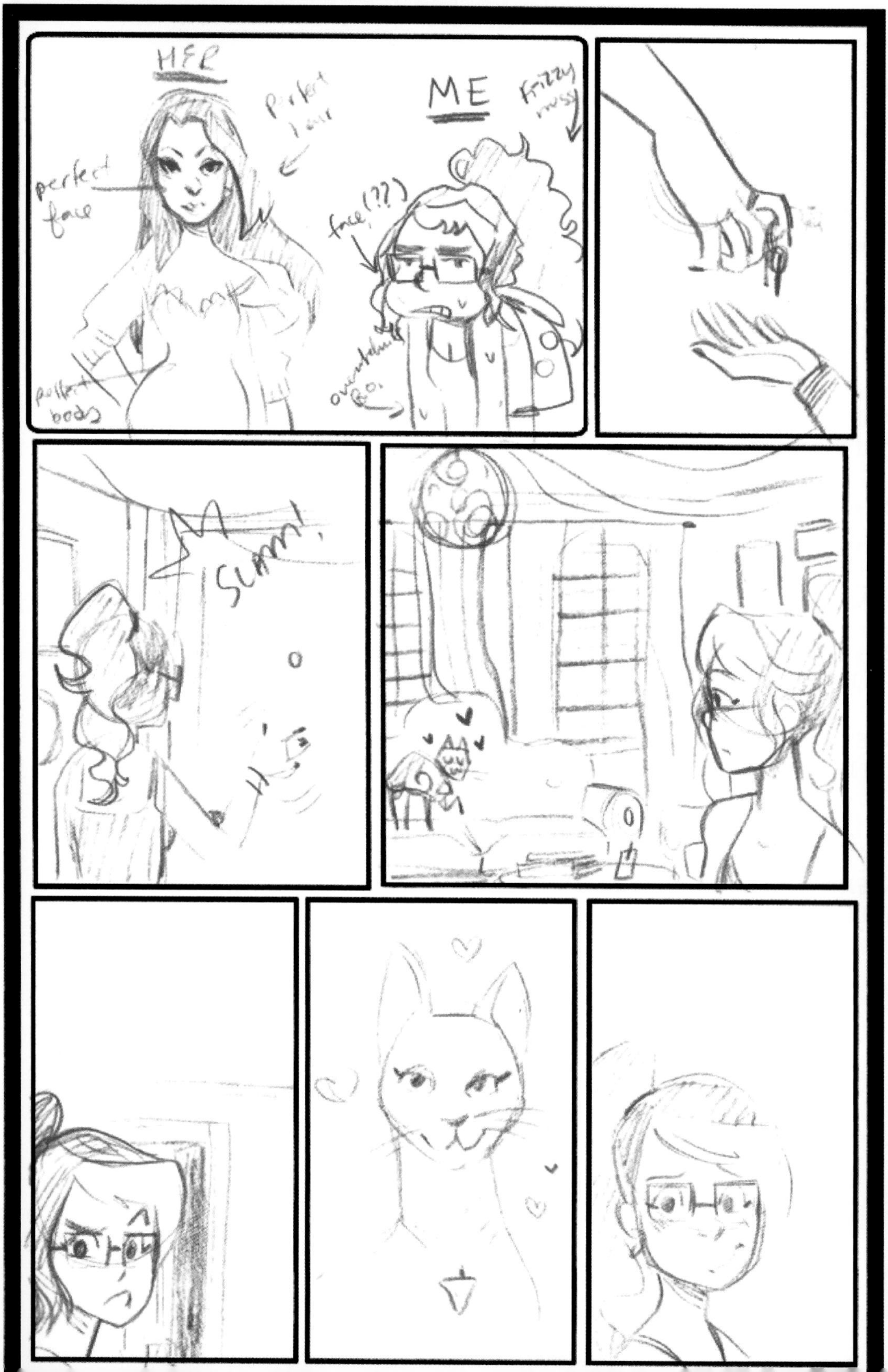
HER
perfect hair
perfect face
perfect bods
ME
frizzy mess
face(??)
SLAM!

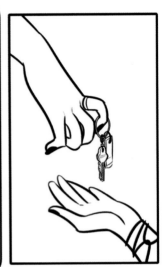

colors...

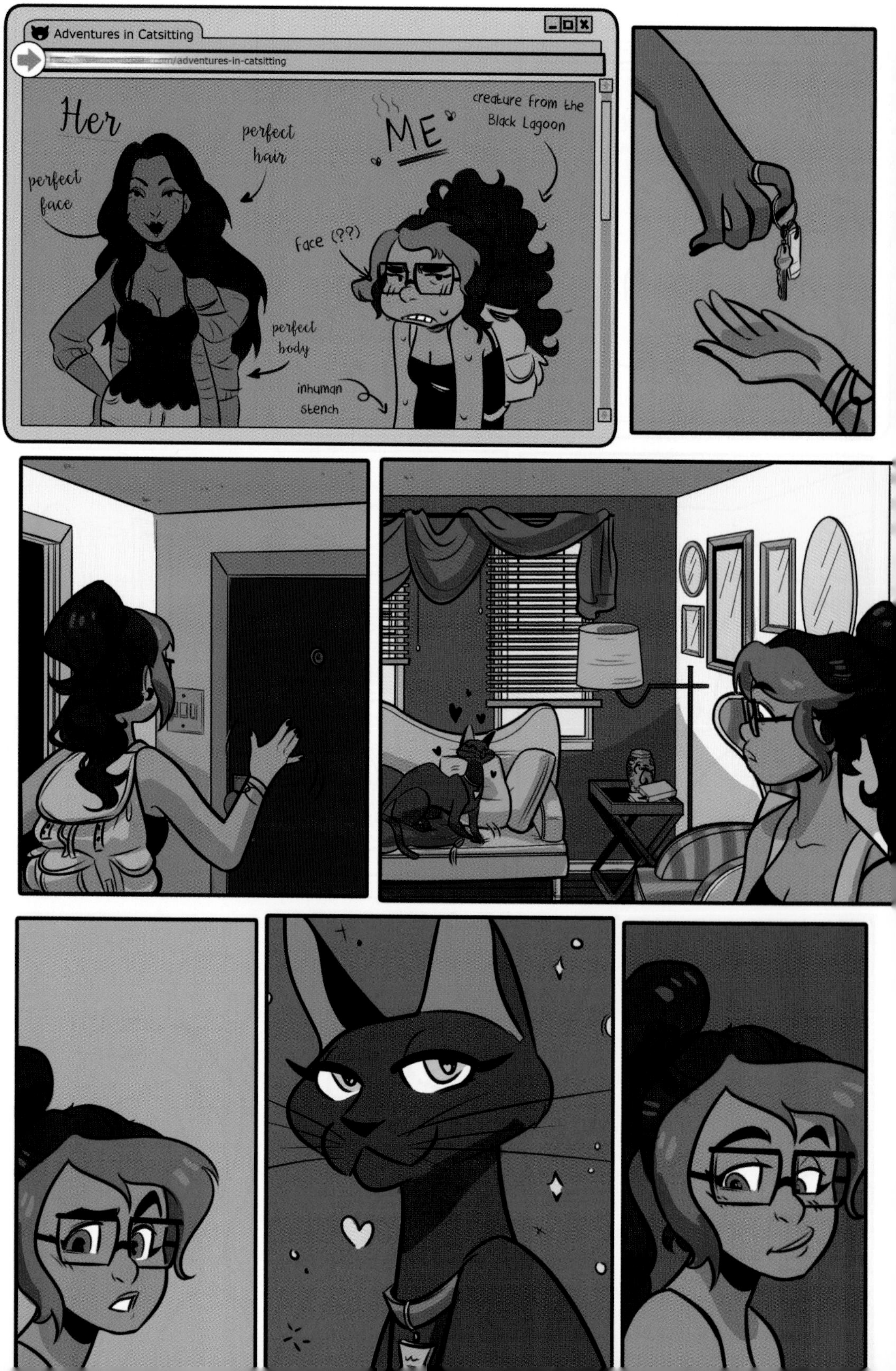
Adventures in Catsitting
/adventures-in-catsitting
Her
perfect face
perfect hair
perfect body
ME
creature from the Black Lagoon
Face (??)
inhuman stench

...and words!

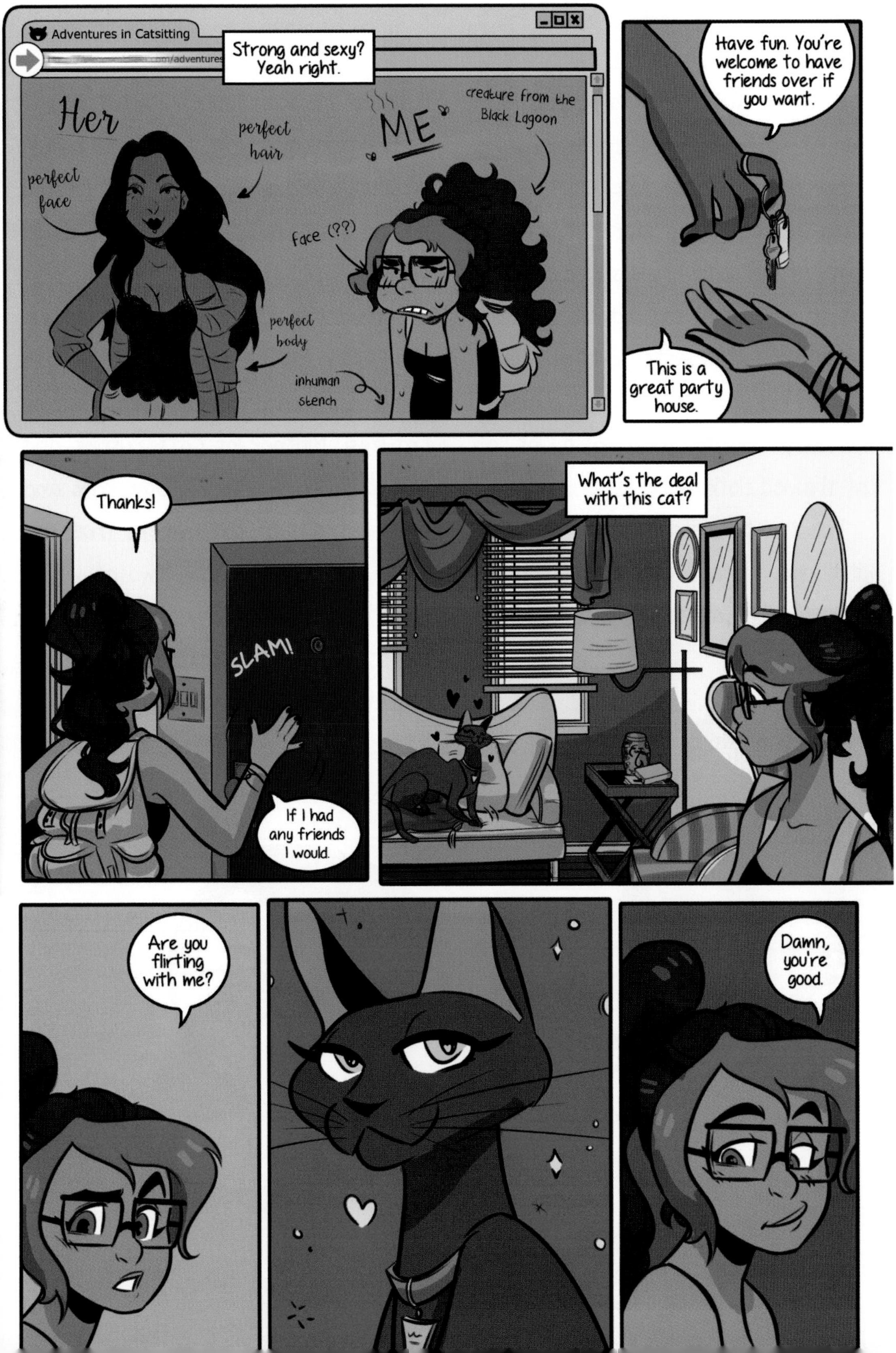

Adventures in Catsitting
.com/adventures
Strong and sexy? Yeah right.
Her
perfect face
perfect hair
ME
creature from the Black Lagoon
Face (??)
perfect body
inhuman stench
Have fun. You're welcome to have friends over if you want.
This is a great party house.
Thanks!
SLAM!
If I had any friends I would.
What's the deal with this cat?
Are you flirting with me?
Damn, you're good.

CREATING FINDING MOLLY

In early 2015, Maytal Gilboa, the founder of Emet Comics, was listening to her friend Lauren talk about all her crazy L.A. catsitting stories. They had plenty of evil cats, clueless rich owners, and even some cat-induced injuries. Maytal then met writer Justine Prado, who has her own adorable cat, Thriller, and is prone to wearing a lot of cat-themed clothing.

The two brainstormed and came up with the idea for Finding Molly: Adventure in Catsitting—a comic about a young Mexican/Persian artist trying to find her voice while taking on a bunch of crappy and amusing catsitting jobs. After that, it was time to find an artist!

Jenn St-Onge is the queen cat lady on the Finding Molly team. She has five cats and may or may not refer to herself as Cat-leesi, Mother of Cats. Justine and Maytal loved Jenn's adorable style and her portraits of cat owners that she drew for an art show, two of which you'll find below. After that, Carey Pietsch joined the team to do coloring, and Joyana McDiarmid came on to do lettering. And with that, a catsitting comic was born.

oh hey gurl

MEET JENN ST-ONGE

Finding Molly artist Jenn St-Onge is a Canadian illustrator/comic artist who graduated from Seneca College's Independent Illustration program in 2012 and has since worked with companies like IDW Publishing, Archie Comics, BOOM! Studios, and Valiant Entertainment. She is the princess of coffee-loving cat ladies and currently lives just outside Toronto, Ontario, with her husband and their five kitties."

Thanks to Major Spoilers for providing this interview with Jenn!

MAJOR SPOILERS: LET'S START RIGHT OFF BY TALKING ABOUT HOW YOU CAME TO BE A PART OF FINDING MOLLY.

JENN ST-ONGE: I'm sure this is something that a lot of young artists will be happy to hear. I found a job announcement from Emet Comics on Tumblr. It was basically a post saying that they were looking for female writers and comic artists, so I sent off my portfolio to my now editor. She actually really liked this series I did for a gallery show I was in two summers ago that featured a lot of people with their cats and that was partly how I got hired.

MS: HOW DID YOU END UP TEAMED WITH JUSTINE PRADO? HOW MUCH INPUT DO YOU HAVE ON THE SCRIPTS THAT YOU WORK ON?

JENN ST-ONGE: For me, I know that between my editor and Justine they're like, "Yeah, tell us what you think. We're open to feedback if you want things changed." But I'm a super big control freak, and I feel like as soon as I start suggesting things I don't want to over-step too much. Unless there's something that I feel is maybe a little thing in the script that isn't going to take a lot of revision and needs changing, I try to not step on anybody's toes in that department.

MS: ARE THERE A LOT OF STORY BEATS IN FINDING MOLLY THAT ARE ACCIDENTALLY OR PURPOSEFULLY AUTOBIOGRAPHICAL?

JENN ST-ONGE: I find that Finding Molly has been a very interesting project because, in some ways, I don't feel like I connect with who Molly is at all because I'm a super big cat person – I love cats – Molly is a little bit less into cats than I am, but then, some of the other ways in her artist's journey of not knowing where she was going to go with her work and not really having a plan and then having something just fall into her lap and it's like, "Alright, this is what I'm doing now." And it actually could be a very big opportunity for her, I can definitely relate to that. I've been very lucky in the last year with my work.

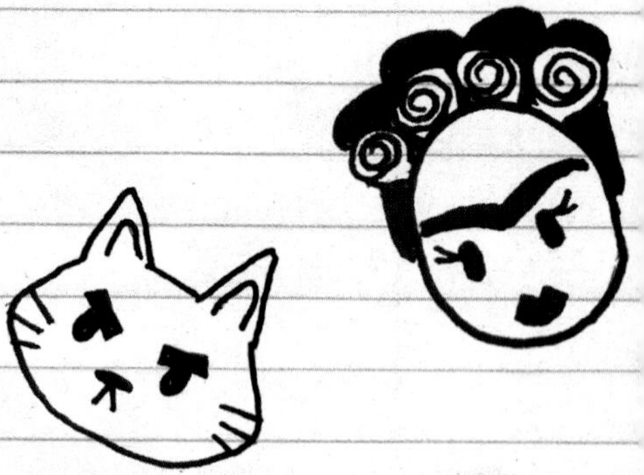

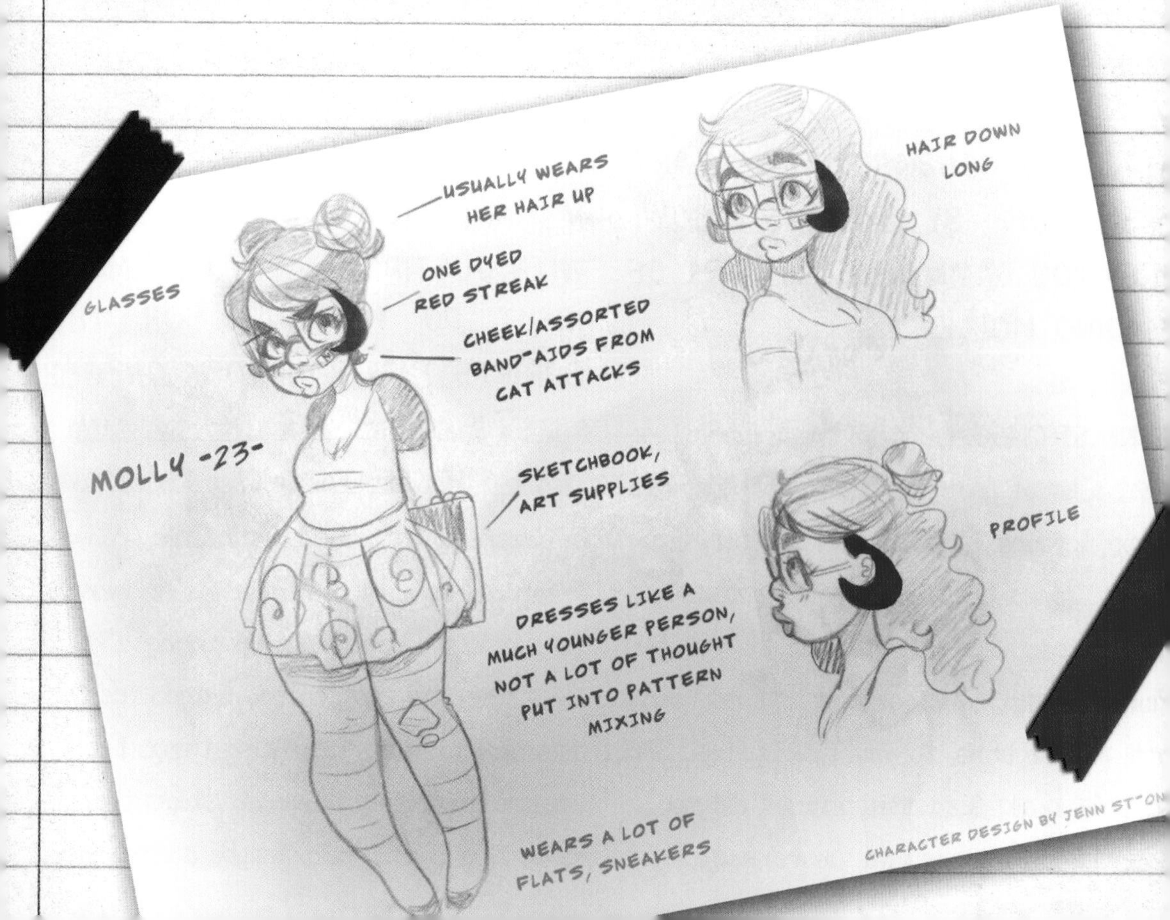

USUALLY WEARS HER HAIR UP
ONE DYED RED STREAK
GLASSES
CHEEK/ASSORTED BAND-AIDS FROM CAT ATTACKS
MOLLY -23-
SKETCHBOOK, ART SUPPLIES
DRESSES LIKE A MUCH YOUNGER PERSON, NOT A LOT OF THOUGHT PUT INTO PATTERN MIXING
WEARS A LOT OF FLATS, SNEAKERS
HAIR DOWN LONG
PROFILE
CHARACTER DESIGN BY JENN ST-ON

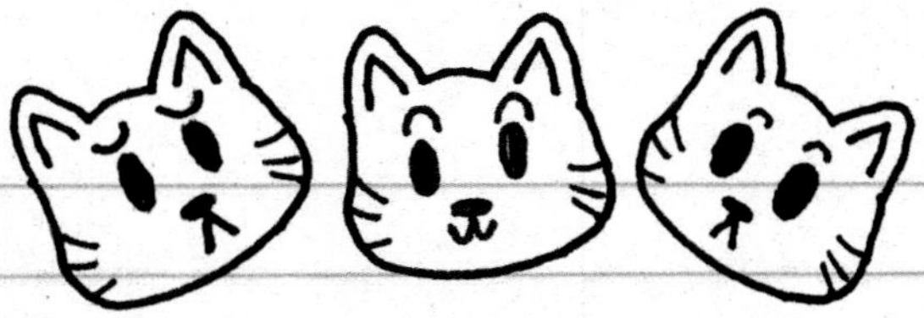

1S: HOW DO YOU FEEL ABOUT 'RAWING CATS YOURSELF?

ENN ST-ONGE: I've liked them a lot longer nan I've been able to draw them, that's efinitely one thing I'll say. Drawing animals sed to be a very big gap in my portfolio. I dn't used to be very good at them at all nd I feel like I got better at them even nce I left college a couple years ago, but nce about the last year when I've been oing full-time with my art there's been a uge learning curve and it's funny because ve also started getting a lot more private ommission traffic and verybody wants to be rawn with their pets.

1S: ARE THERE NY SECONDARY CHARACTERS THAT 'OU ARE LOOKING ORWARD TO EX-'LORING MORE IN PCOMING ISSUES)F FINDING MOLLY?

ENN ST-ONGE: I have o say that it would be 1olly's friend Sarahh. I eel like, right now, arahh's getting the hort end of the stick in the story because she's supposed to be presented as being, kind of, her hot friend who gets everything very easily. I see Sarahh as somebody who's worked really hard. Even though she's maybe had a few doors opened for her she still works really hard to get what she wants and she's actually a very responsible, good adult compared to Molly (laughs).

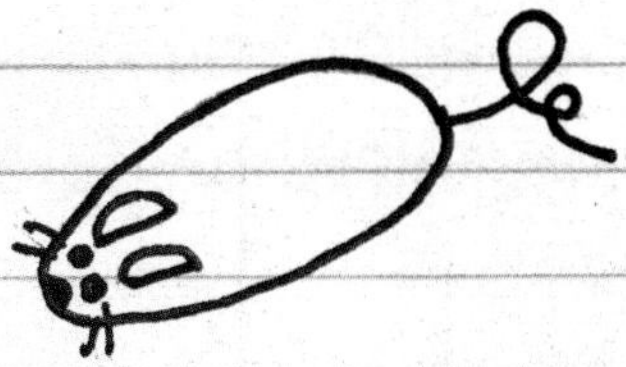

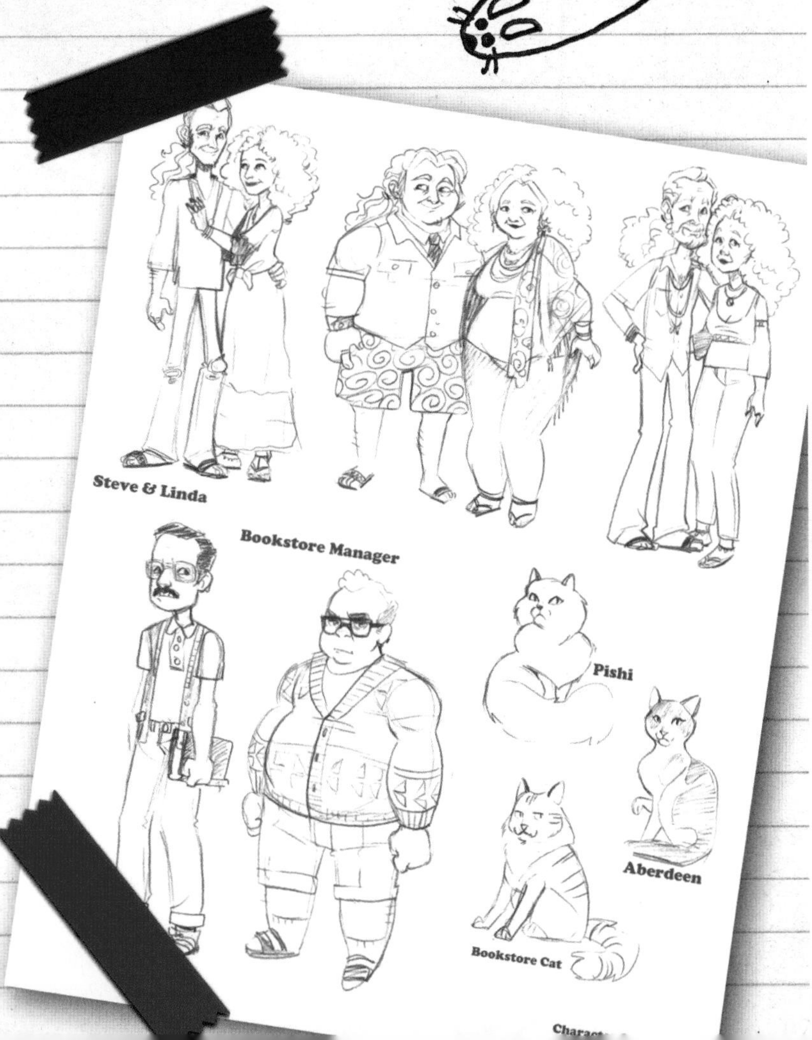
Steve & Linda
Bookstore Manager
Pishi
Aberdeen
Bookstore Cat

MS: WHO OR WHAT IS THE MOST FUN TO DRAW IN FINDING MOLLY?

JENN ST-ONGE: I do like drawing the cats because I have a lot of cats at home that are a lot of inspiration for me. Basically every cat that I've drawn so far has a little bit of inspiration from one of the cats that me and my husband own. We have five cats, so. There's a lot. (laughs)

MS: FLIPSIDE, WHO OR WHAT IS THE MOST CHALLENGING TO DRAW FOR FINDING MOLLY?

JENN ST-ONGE: I would definitely have to say that it is a very background heavy comic and I know that when my editor had first approached me she said, "You know, this is based in Los Angeles ... the backgrounds are going to be really important. Do you think you could do that?" and I was like, "Yeah, yeah, that's something I can do." and, then I got into and I was like, "Wow! There are so many backgrounds!" and it's all urban setting, so it's intense, but again, I feel like I've learned so much since I've been doing it.

MS: DO YOU HAVE A SPECIFIC LOCATION WHERE YOU DO YOU ARTWORK?

JENN ST-ONGE: Actually, because I'm doin my art full-time I have a home office that work out of, which can be a blessing and curse because I'm sure that, like any perso who works from home, on one hand I'll jus be locked in my room all day working, bu then I come out and I have to do dishes, s it's, kind of, hard balancing the time 'caus

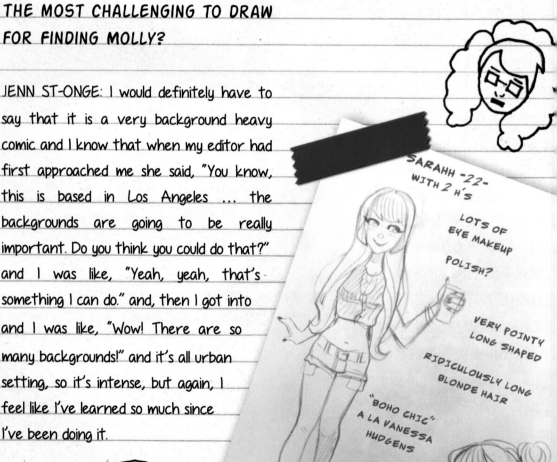

SARAHH -22-
WITH 2 H's

LOTS OF EYE MAKEUP

POLISH?

VERY POINTY LONG SHAPED

RIDICULOUSLY LONG BLONDE HAIR

"BOHO CHIC" A LA VANESSA HUDGENS

PRO

UNDERCU
USU

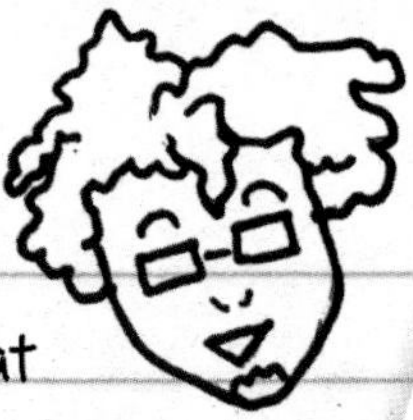

I'm always at home I'm always at work. There is no, "Oh, it's five o'clock. I'm done now." I can be working any time of the day.

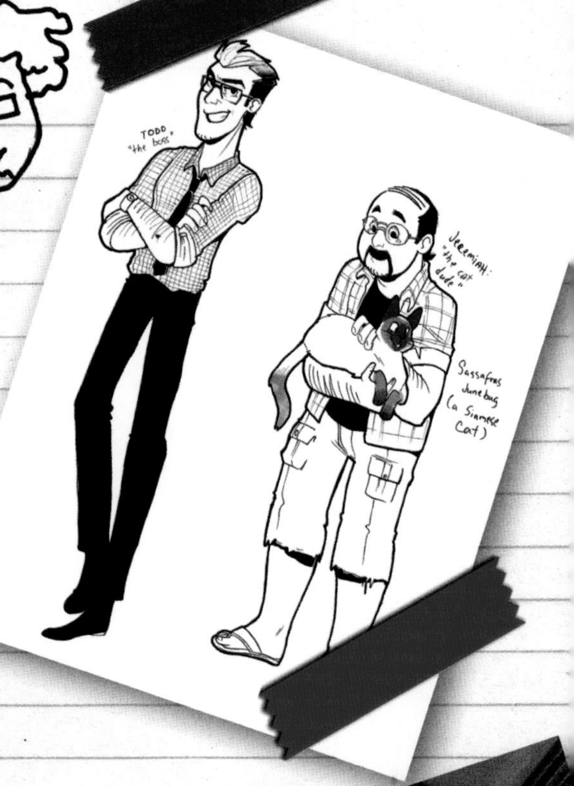
TODD, "the boss"
Jeremiah: "the cat dude"
Sassafras June bug (a Siamese Cat)

MS: FINAL QUESTION, WHAT ADVICE DO YOU HAVE FOR ASPIRING ARTISTS?

JENN ST-ONGE: I think the most important thing for you when you're getting started is to produce a lot of work. (laughs) I realize that that can be a little bit vague, but for me, something that I feel has really benefitted me over the years is that I have a pretty quick turnaround time. If you're clocking the hours, you're getting the practice and you're, hopefully, getting a lot of different material that you're putting out because it's funny nowadays how many people I talk to and they're like, "Yeah, I did this comic or this show and somebody saw it and now I have a job."

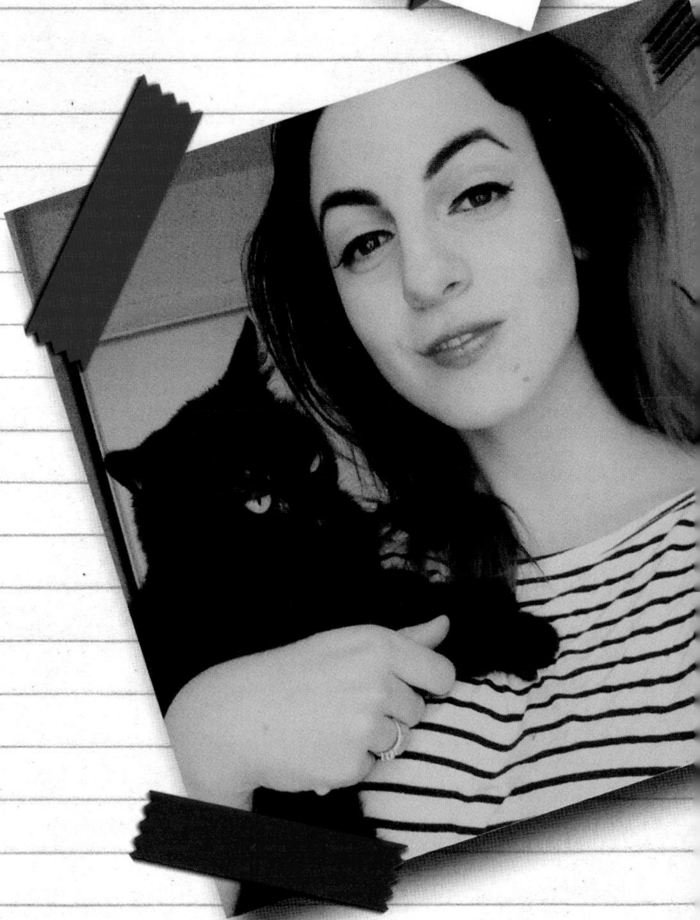

Be prolific. Have lots of work to show people. Update your portfolio a lot and keep making new stuff because you want to stay relevant.

MEET JUSTINE PRADO

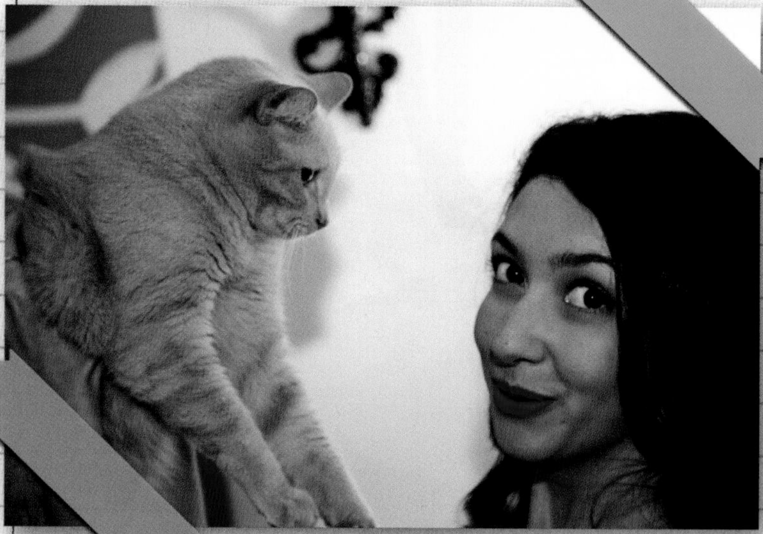

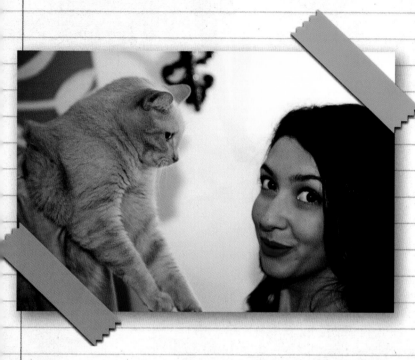

EMET COMICS: WHAT INSPIRED YOU TO WRITE FINDING MOLLY?

JUSTINE PRADO: I guess it all started with my cat, Thriller. He is a monster and he always brings the drama/conflict/hilarity. So when I was given the opportunity to write this series, I knew I wanted cat disasters to be a big part of it. I also really wanted to tell a fun story about the struggles of the modern, millennial girl trying to make it in a world that is constantly telling her to give up. You don't have to be an artist to relate to her story. That feeling of watching your peers sail past you and wondering, "when's my turn?" is almost universal. I was really interested in showing that journey from a young woman's perspective.

Justine is a Los Angeles-based feature and television screenwriter, playwright, and cat lady. She holds a BFA from the Academy of Art University and an MFA from UCLA. Justine has worked as a writer for many major studios, networks and indie production companies. Before her Hollywood career, Justine was a theatre geek, an adequate musician, and a subversive political activist. When she's not writing, she's spending time with her cat, Thriller, who enjoys eating shoelaces.

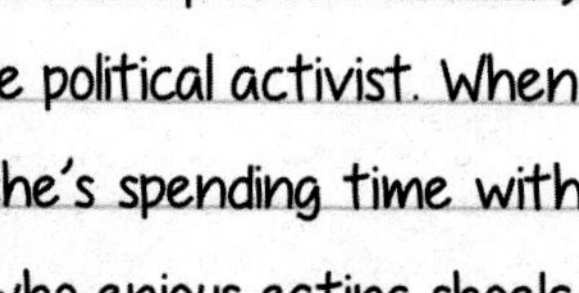

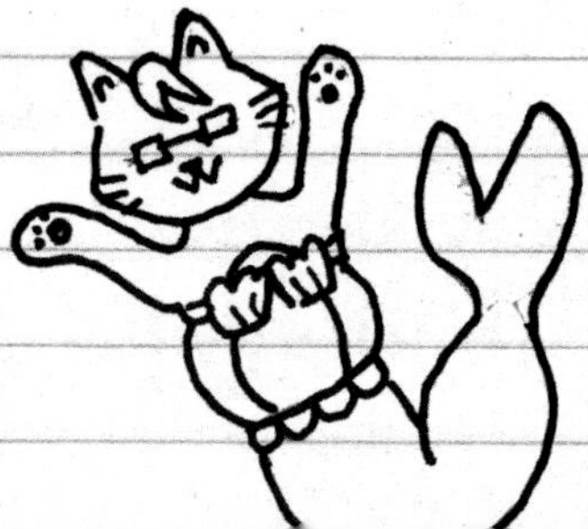

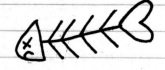

EC: DO YOU RELATE TO MOLLY AS A STRUGGLING ARTIST? DID YOU STRUGGLE FINDING YOUR VOICE AS A WRITER?

JUSTINE PRADO: Molly and I both took out a lot of student loans. So I can definitely relate to that. I think early in my writing career I struggled with a crisis of confidence. I think most artists do. You're afraid to really put yourself out there, because if no one reads or sees your work, no one can tell you it's not good enough. You can't fail if you never try. But you'll also never succeed. I think Molly is in that place, she doesn't believe when people tell her she's good, and when others have success, she chalks it up to some other reason or that they have it easier than her. That's a big part of her arc, not expecting things to just happen to you, you have to go out and make them happen.

EC: IN A WAY, MOLLY IS BEING SUBVERSIVE BY REFUSING TO "GET A REAL JOB OR GET MARRIED". HAVE YOU HAD TO STRUGGLE WITH GOING A TRADITIONAL ROUTE VS. FOLLOWING A DREAM?

FASHIONABLE HAIR BUT NOT VERY WELL KEPT

GLASSES

MATEO -21-

CAN'T GROW A GOOD BEARD YET

NERDY HARRY POTTER TAT

VERY CASUAL OUTFITS

PROFILE

BIG BAG OF ART SUPPLIES

CHARACTER DESIGN BY JENN ST

JUSTINE PRADO: Molly comes from a more traditional household than I did. My parents are so supportive of my art, and always have been. I'm pretty sure they'd rather me end up a crazy artist cat-lady than something more traditional. But there are societal and financial pressures of choosing the life you really want. Molly deals with that constantly, number one being her becoming a cat-sitter when, let's face it, she's not all that crazy about cats. It can be difficult choosing a life route that other people don't understand, but Molly, like me, is never envious of the people who did things exactly as they were supposed to, or did what was expected of them. She and her friends are these awesome, modern bohemians and they're figuring it out as they go. They don't have a blueprint for their lives, they have a blank canvas, which is much more fun.

EC: WHAT'S IT LIKE WORKING ON YOUR FIRST COMIC? AND WHAT HAS IT BEEN LIKE TO WORK WITH JENN?

JUSTINE PRADO: I have a screenwriting background, so learning comic writing took some getting used to. This is definitely the most fun I've had writing anything, ever. And most of that is the team I get to work with—Jenn and everyone at Emet Comics. First of all, working with all women is amazing. These girls are bad ass and s good at everything they do. And Jen blows me away every time she sends page I can't get over how talented she is, and want her to draw everything I writ forever. One thing I learned quickly wo how much I could trust my artist to tell th story with me. Once I saw the art wit the words, I realized how many of thos words I didn't need, and how many joke were so much better because of the art

Character Concepts by Jenn St-Onge

Profile

Flashback

CORAM

EC: WHICH IS YOUR FAVORITE CAT IN THE COMIC?

JUSTINE PRADO: It's so hard to choose! Pishi pulls focus in every frame she's in, and I just love her dumb little face. The bookstore cat Thriller is, clearly, named after my own cat and chews shoelaces just like him. But some of my favorite cats are coming up in future issues. I don't want to spoil anything, but there's a Miss Sassafras Junebug in issue 4 who just steals the show.

EC: WHAT ADVICE DO YOU HAVE FOR ASPIRING ARTISTS AND WRITERS? AND WHAT DO YOU HOPE PEOPLE TAKE AWAY FROM THE COMIC?

JUSTINE PRADO: It sounds cliche, but you really just have to put yourself out there. Tell people what you're working on, and have people read/look at it and give you their thoughts. It's the only way to get better, and it's the best way to build a community around you of fellow writers/artist that you can work with. Don't be shy—don't be annoying—but it's okay to consider yourself a real writer/artist, because if you take yourself seriously then other people will, too. And also, get a cat. They really just make everything better. Get a couple.

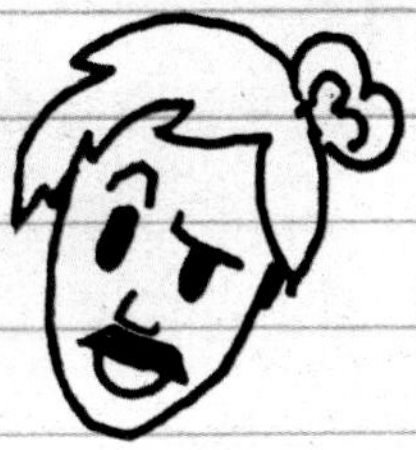

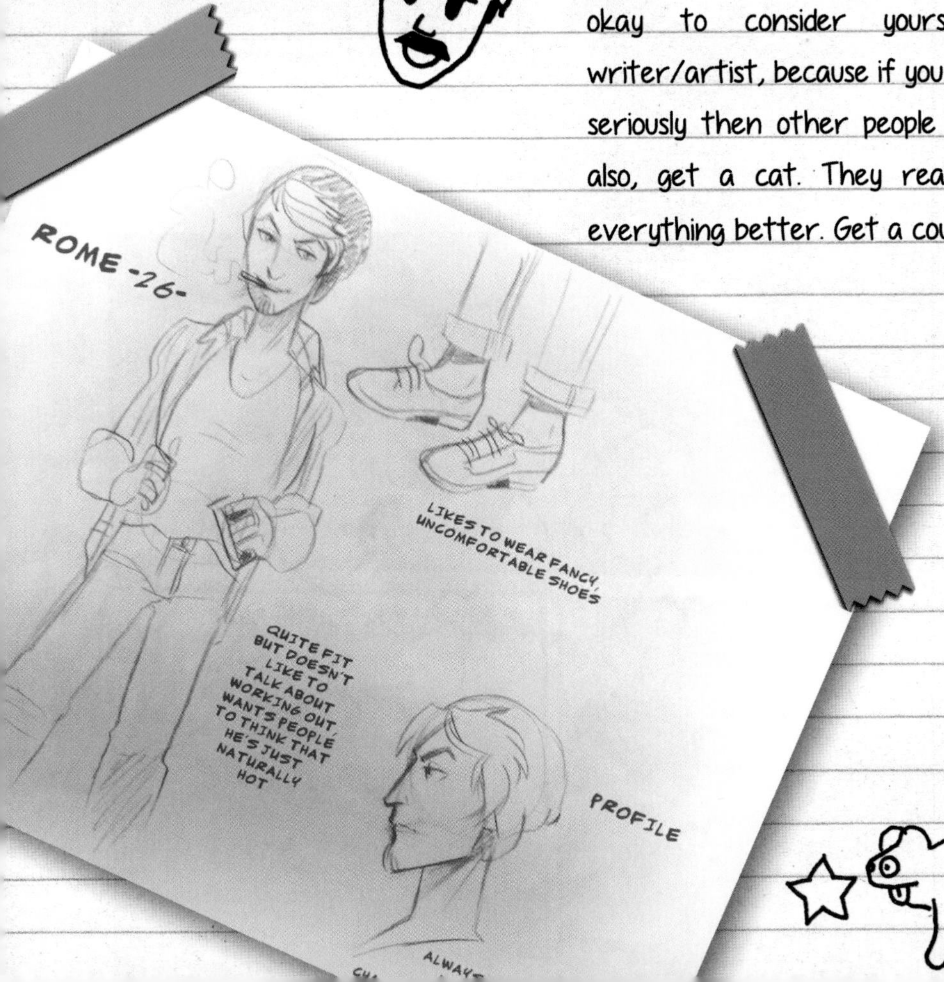
ROME -26-
LIKES TO WEAR FANCY, UNCOMFORTABLE SHOES
QUITE FIT BUT DOESN'T LIKE TO TALK ABOUT WORKING OUT, WANTS PEOPLE TO THINK THAT HE'S JUST NATURALLY HOT
PROFILE

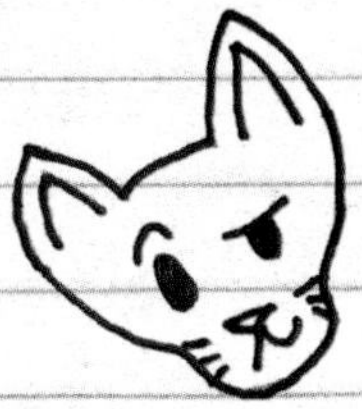

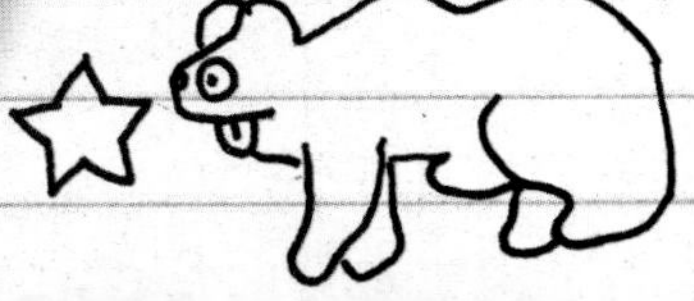

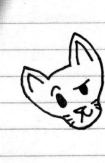

Joyana's lettering test

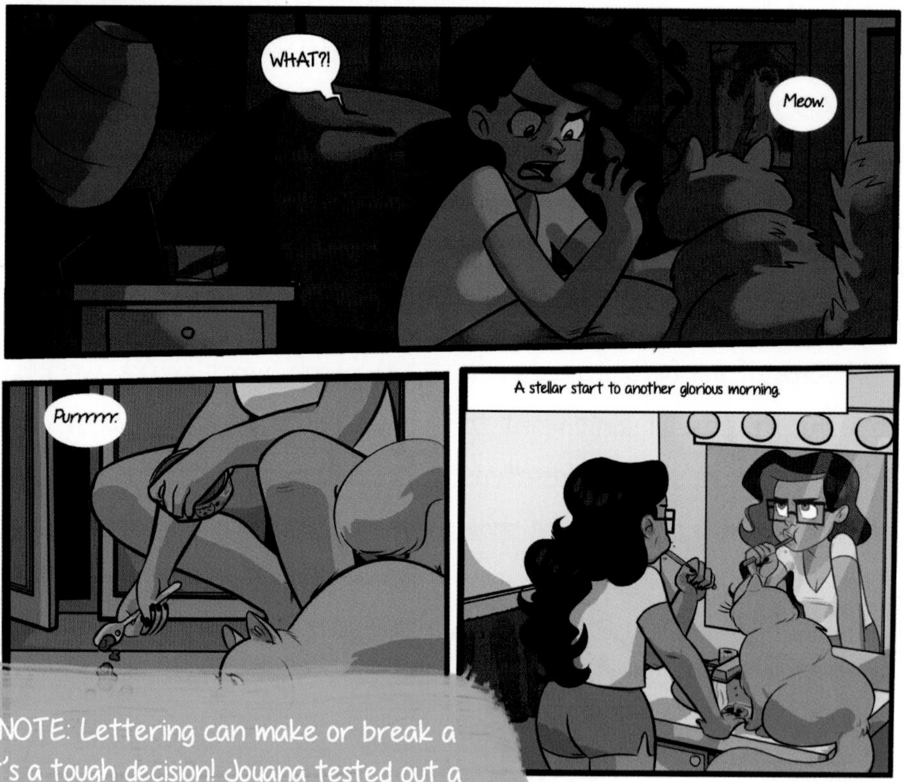
WHAT?!
Meow.
Purrrrrr.
A stellar start to another glorious morning.

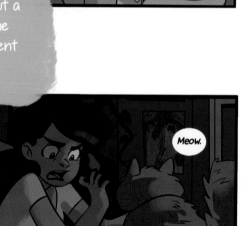

EDITOR'S NOTE: Lettering can make or break a comic, so it's a tough decision! Joyana tested out a few different styles until we settled on the one you see above. The example below has a different and slightly bolder typeface.

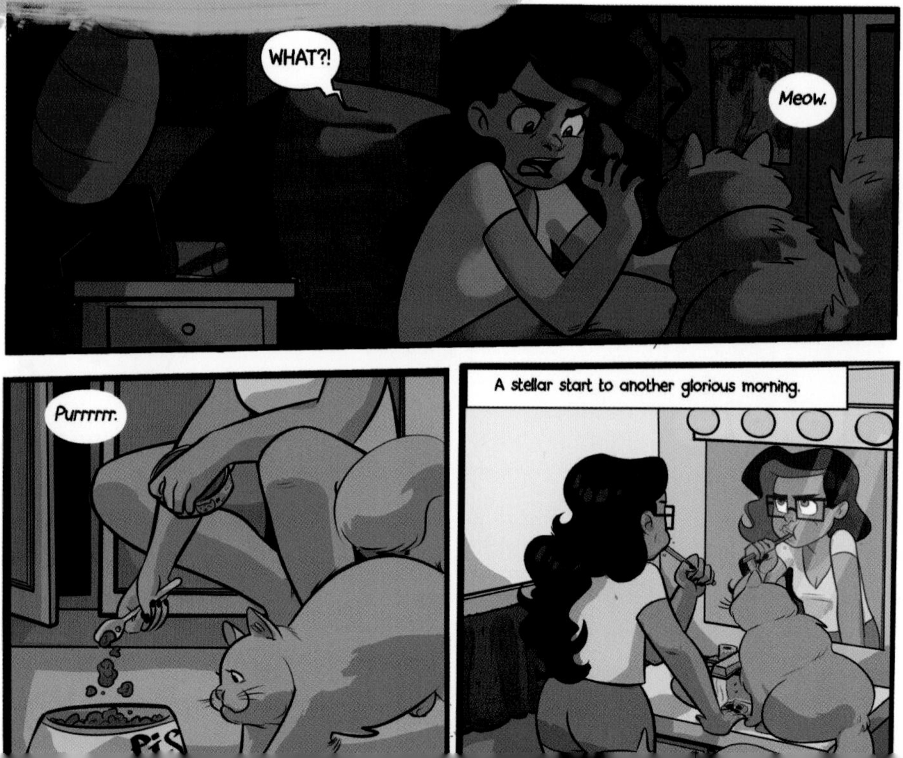
WHAT?!
Meow.
Purrrrrr.
A stellar start to another glorious morning.

Molly's webcomic & room decor

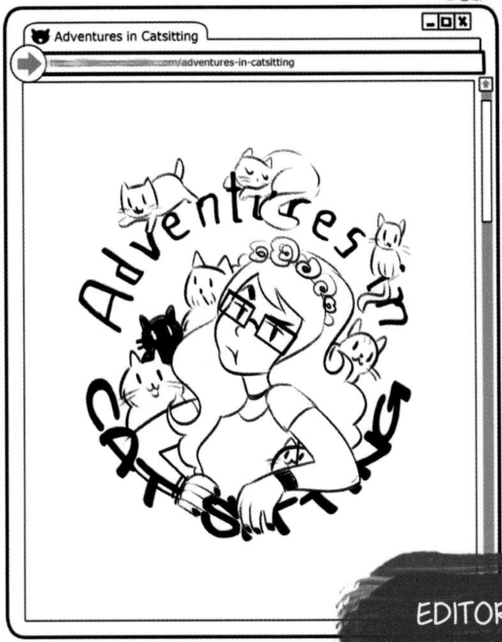
Adventures in Catsitting
Adventures in Catsitting

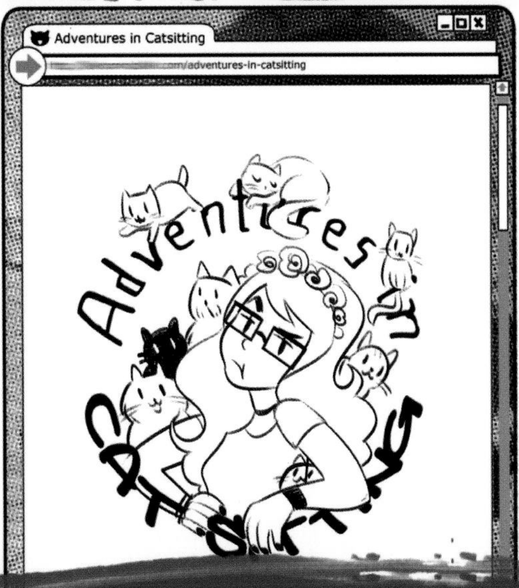
Adventures in Catsitting
Adventures in Catsitting

EDITOR'S NOTE: It was important to us that the visuals of Molly's world reflected her personality. One challenge was figuring out the look of her webcomic--it had to be distinct from the interior artwork while not feeling out of place. Jenn also created lots of extra art that made the environments, like Molly's room, feel lived in.

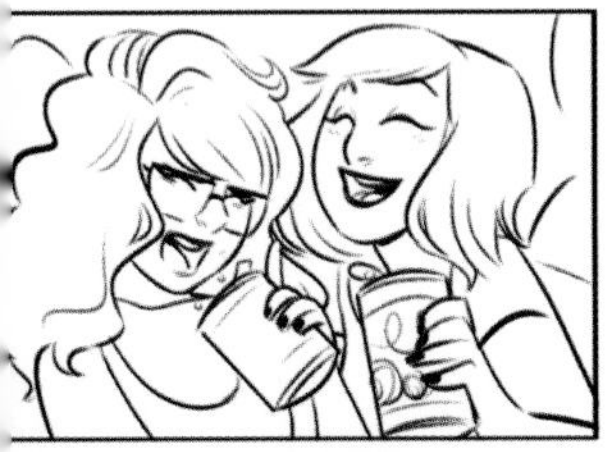

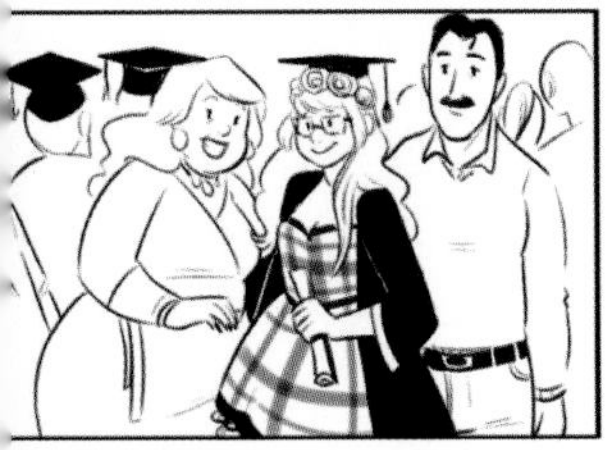

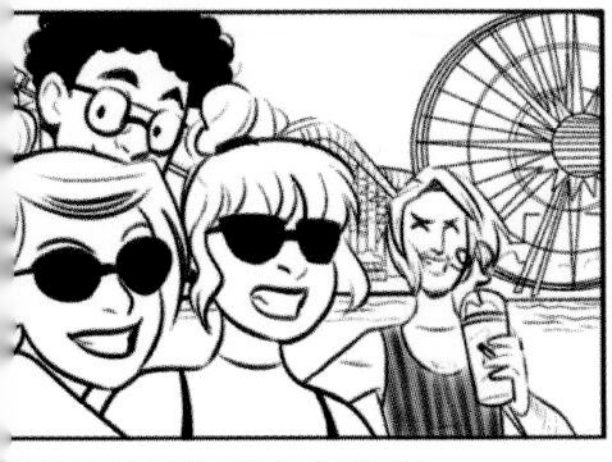

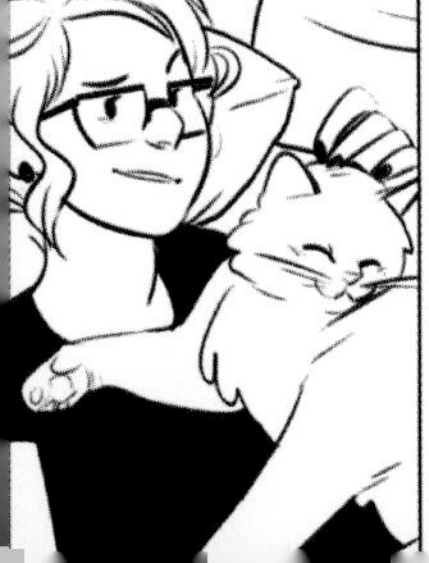

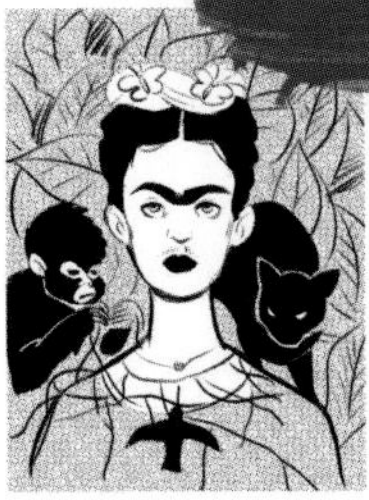

FRIDA KAHLO

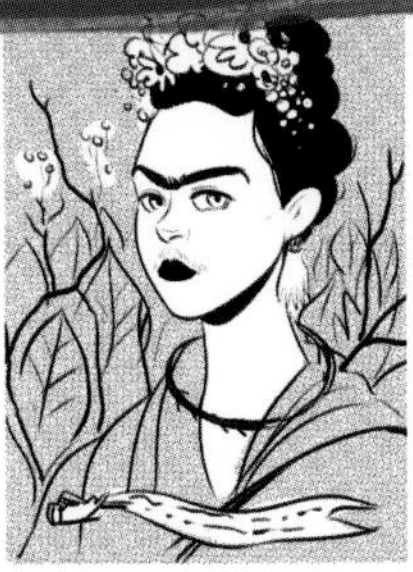

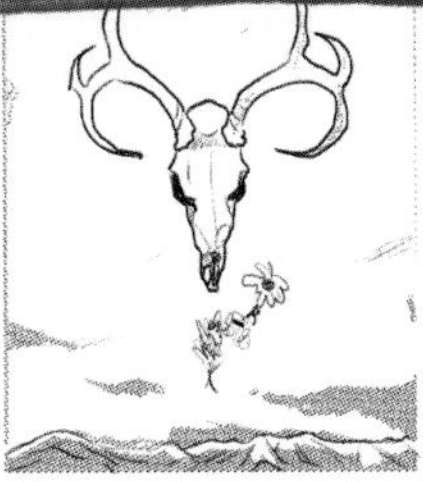

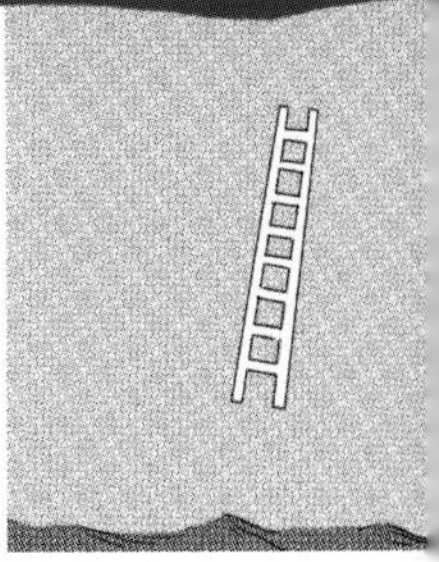

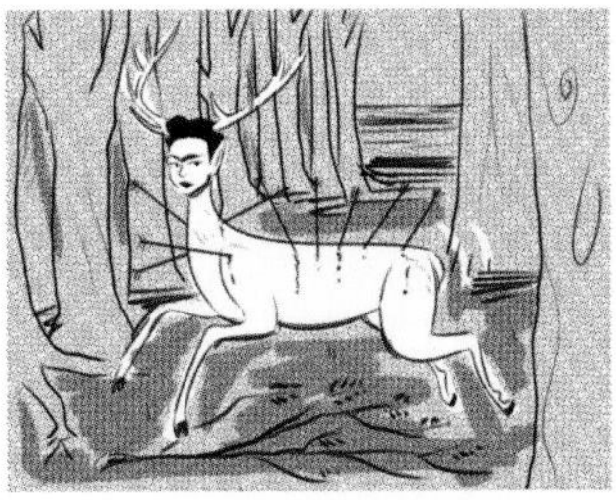

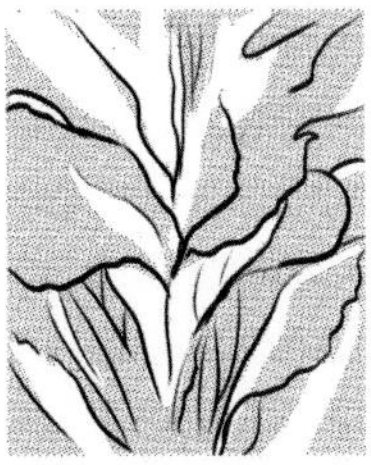

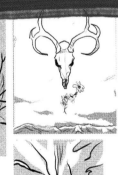

GEORGIA O'KEEFFE

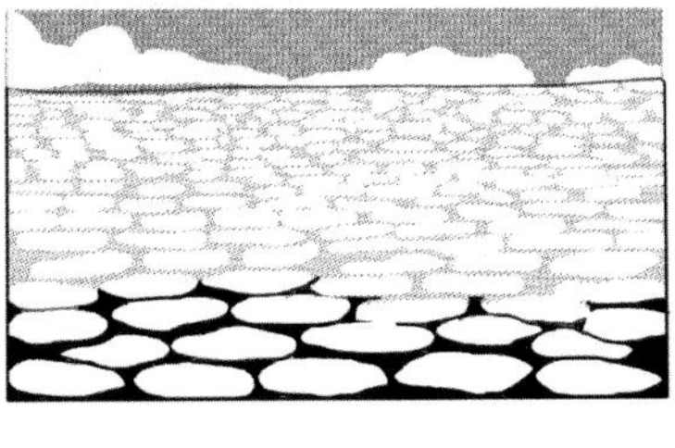

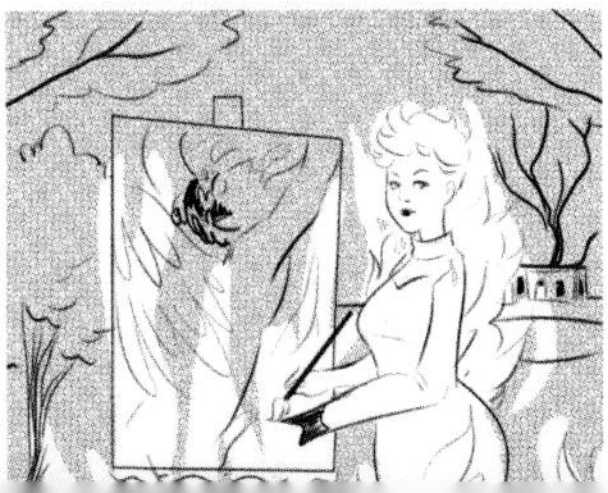

-RECREATED BY JENN ST-ONGE-

Jenn's cover concepts

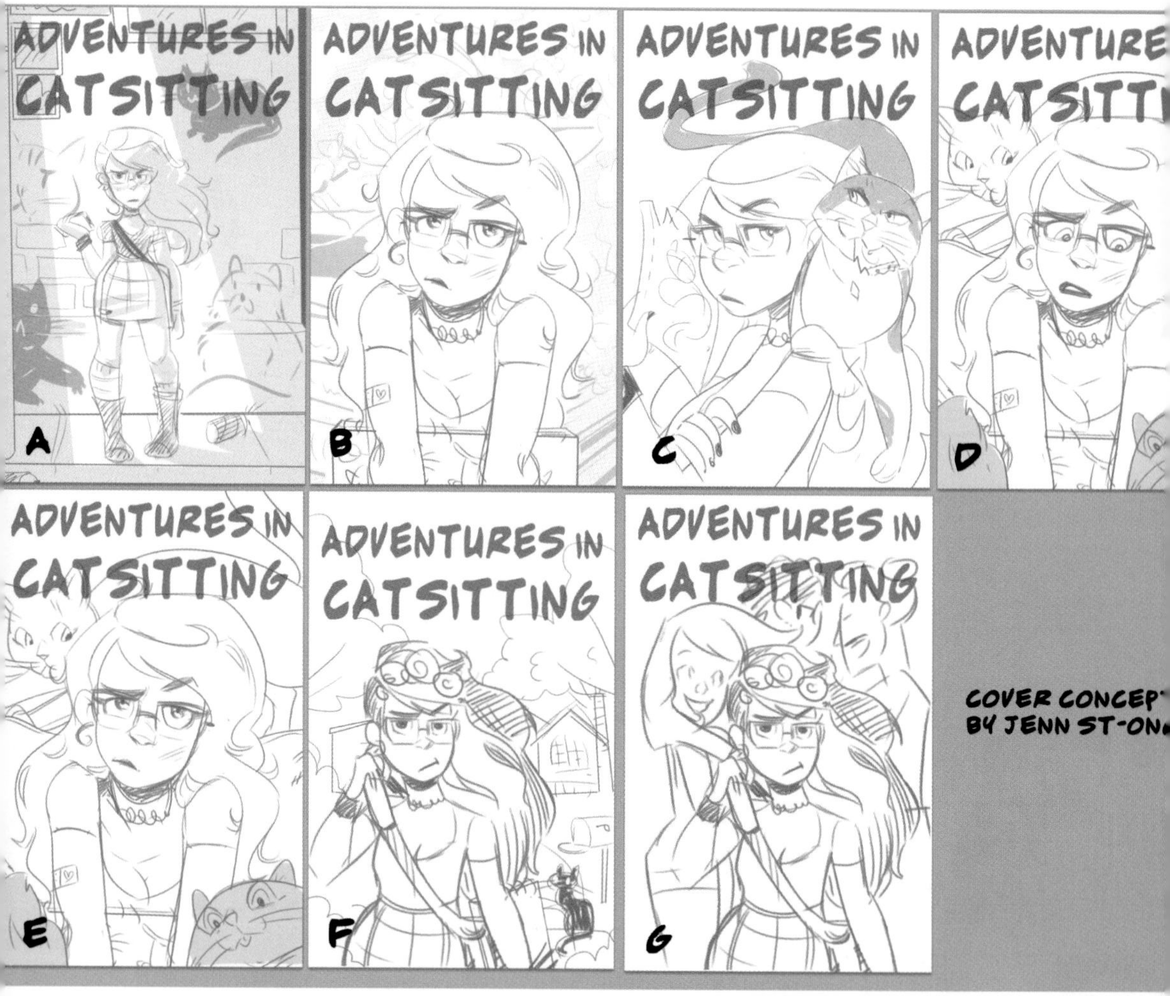

ADVENTURES IN CATSITTING
A
ADVENTURES IN CATSITTING
B
ADVENTURES IN CATSITTING
C
ADVENTURE CATSITT
D
ADVENTURES IN CATSITTING
E
ADVENTURES IN CATSITTING
F
ADVENTURES IN CATSITTING
G
COVER CONCEP
BY JENN ST-ON

Issue 1

Issue 2

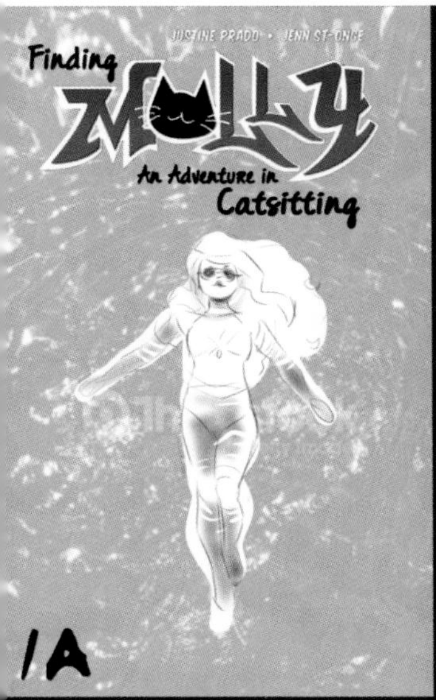
JUSTINE PRADO • JENN ST-ONGE
Finding MOLLY
An Adventure in Catsitting
1A

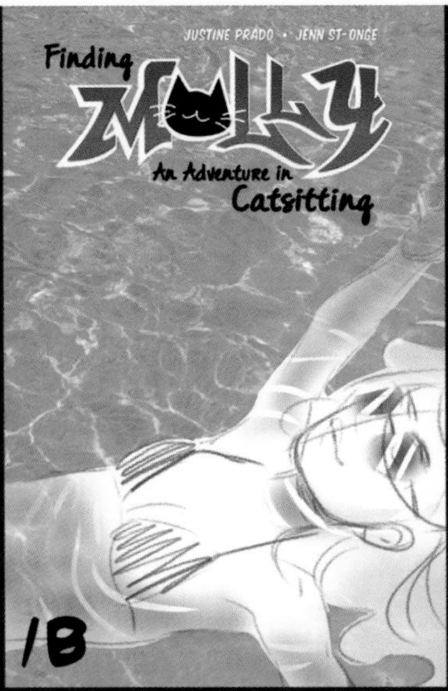
JUSTINE PRADO • JENN ST-ONGE
Finding MOLLY
An Adventure in Catsitting
1B

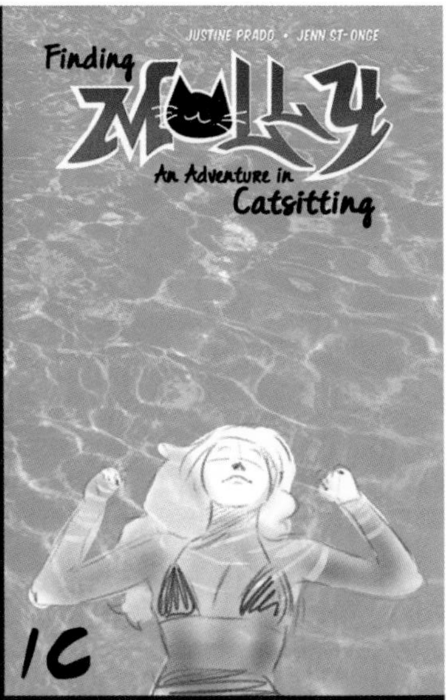
JUSTINE PRADO • JENN ST-ONGE
Finding MOLLY
An Adventure in Catsitting
1C

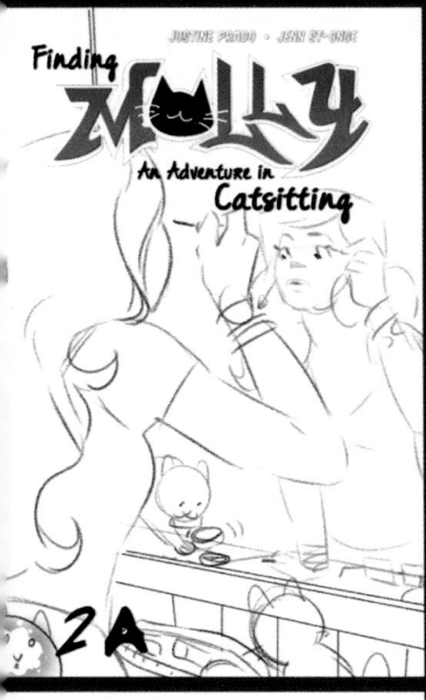
JUSTINE PRADO • JENN ST-ONGE
Finding MOLLY
An Adventure in Catsitting
2A

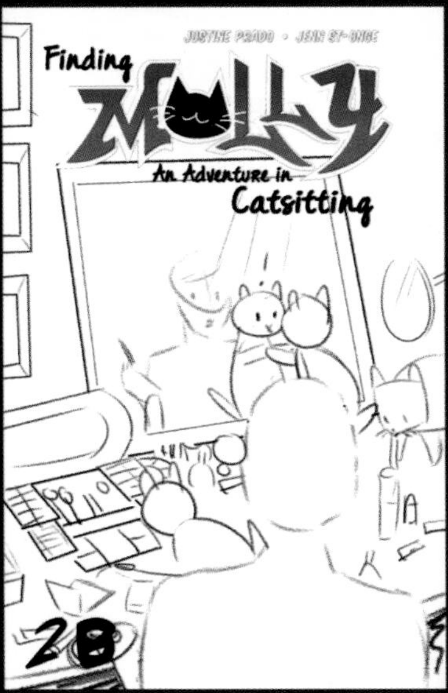
JUSTINE PRADO • JENN ST-ONGE
Finding MOLLY
An Adventure in Catsitting
2B

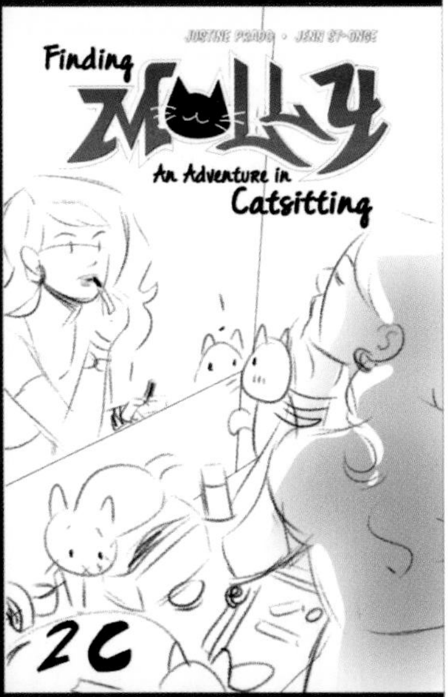
JUSTINE PRADO • JENN ST-ONGE
Finding MOLLY
An Adventure in Catsitting
2C

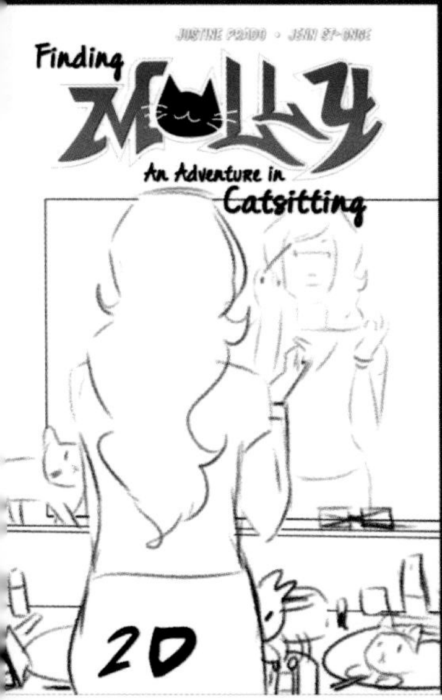
JUSTINE PRADO • JENN ST-ONGE
Finding MOLLY
An Adventure in Catsitting
2D

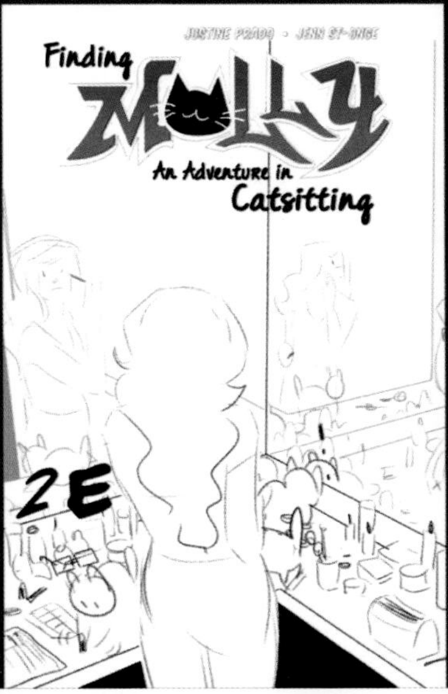
JUSTINE PRADO • JENN ST-ONGE
Finding MOLLY
An Adventure in Catsitting
2E

Issue 3

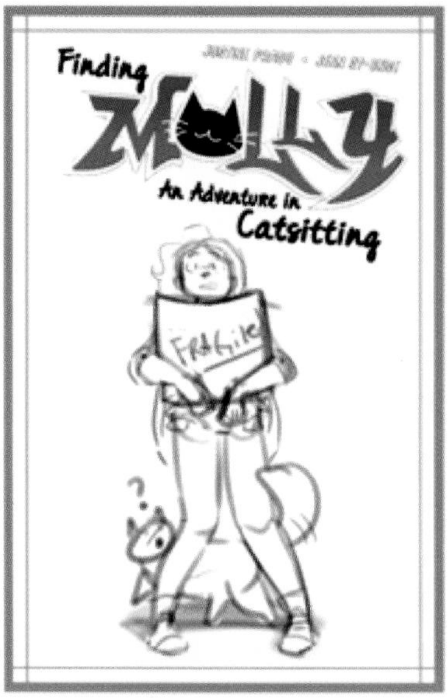
Finding
MOLLY
An Adventure in Catsitting
FRAGILE

A- MOLLY STANDS HOLDING A BOX MARKED "FRAGILE" IN FRONT OF A EMPTY BG -COULD BE COLOUR SWATCH- WITH PISHI AROUND HER ANKLES LOOKING CONCERNED

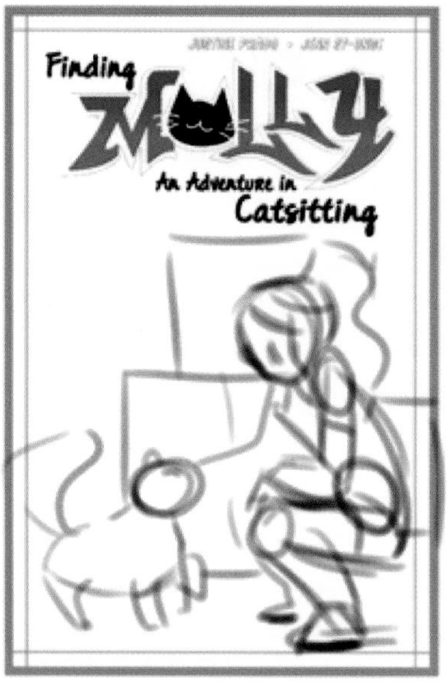
Finding
MOLLY
An Adventure in Catsitting

B- MOLLY IS CROUCHING DOWN IN FRONT OF A STACK OF MOVING BOXES TO PET PISHI, BLANK BG

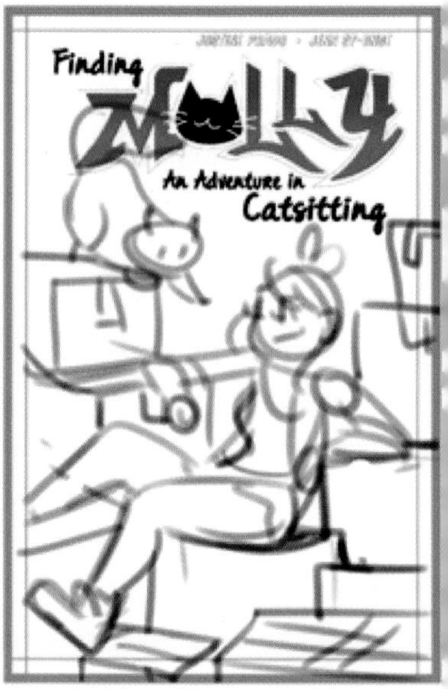
Finding
MOLLY
An Adventure in Catsitting

C- MOLLY IS RECLINING ON A LARGE ASSORTMENT OF MOVING BOXES, LOOKING TIRED LIKE SHE JUST FINISHED PACKING; PISHI LOOKS ON FROM A HIGHER BOX

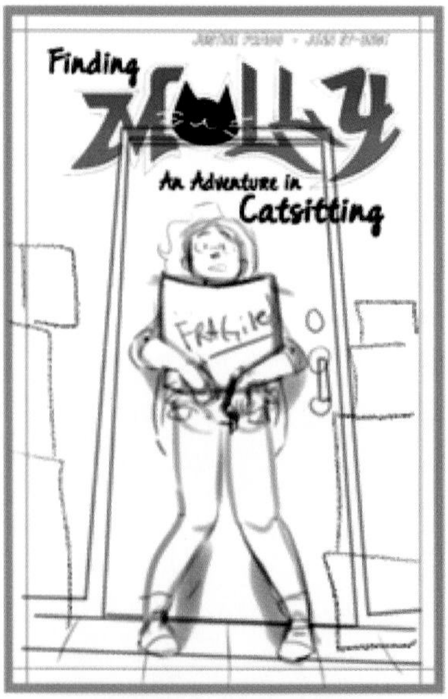
Finding
MOLLY
An Adventure in Catsitting
FRAGILE

D- SIMILAR TO "A", BUT THIS OPTION HAS MOLLY LEANING UP AGAINST HER NEW APARTMENT DOOR

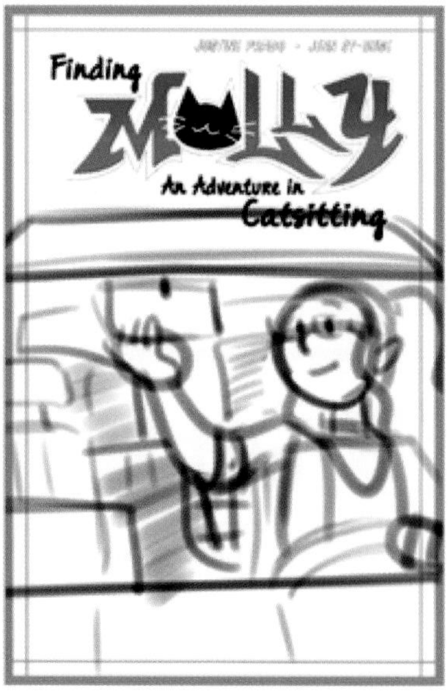
Finding
MOLLY
An Adventure in Catsitting

E- MOLLY IS ADJUSTING THE REARVIEW MIRROR IN HER CAR, THE SEATS ALL ARE FILLED WITH MOVING BOXES, ETC

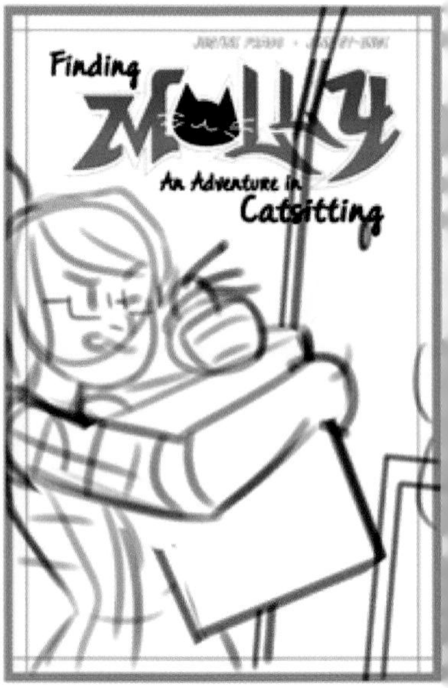
Finding
MOLLY
An Adventure in Catsitting

F- MOLLY IS JUGGLING A MOVING BOX AND A SET OF KEYS AT HER NEW APARTMENT DOOR

Issue 4

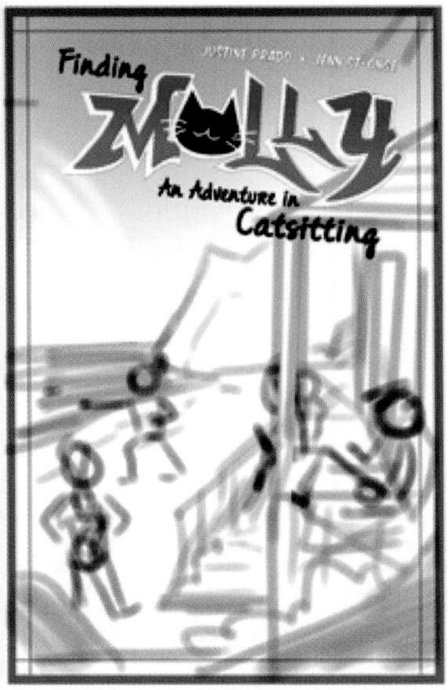
Finding
MOLLY
An Adventure in
Catsitting

D- THE GANG IS OUT ON THE BEACH HOUSE PORCH AT SUNSET. MAT IS ON A CHAIR, MOLLY SITS ON THE STEPS, ROME SKIPS ROCKS, AND SARAHH OBSERVES

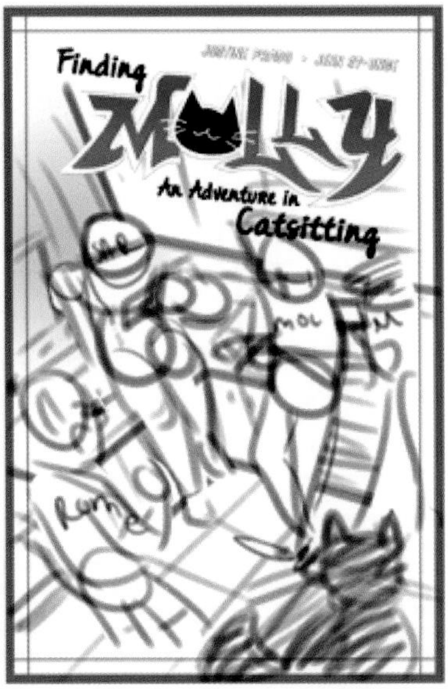
Finding
MOLLY
An Adventure in
Catsitting

E- THE GANG HANGS OUT IN JEREMIAH'S KITCHEN, EATING PIZZA AND LEANING ON COUNTERS, HAVING A GENERALLY GOOD TIME. CATS ARE HIDDEN AROUND THE SCENE

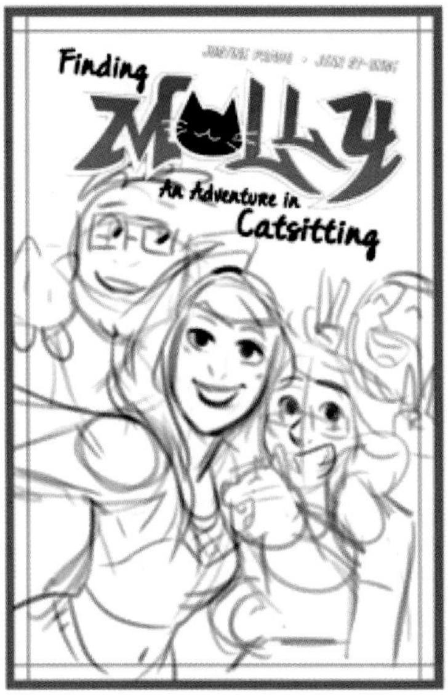
Finding
MOLLY
An Adventure in
Catsitting

F- THE GANG TAKES A SELFIE FROM THE P.O.V OF THE ACTUAL PHOTO. EVERYONE IS HAVING FUN AND BEING GOOFY

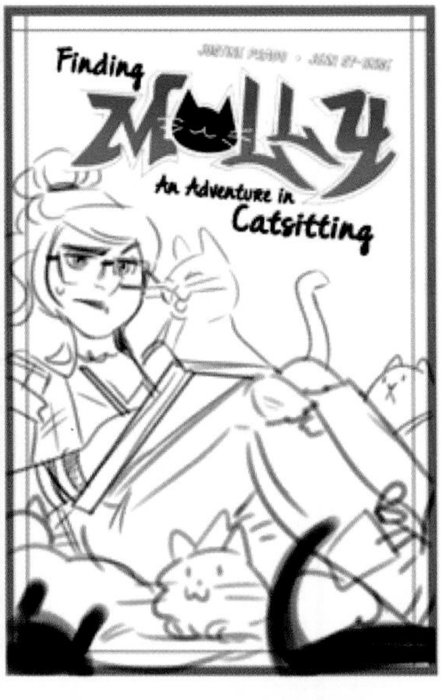
Finding
MOLLY
An Adventure in
Catsitting

G- MOLLY SITS ON THE FLOOR WITH HER FEET PROPPED UP SLIGHTLY, WORKING IN HER SKETCHBOOK BUT THWARTED BY A LARGE NUMBER OF CATS

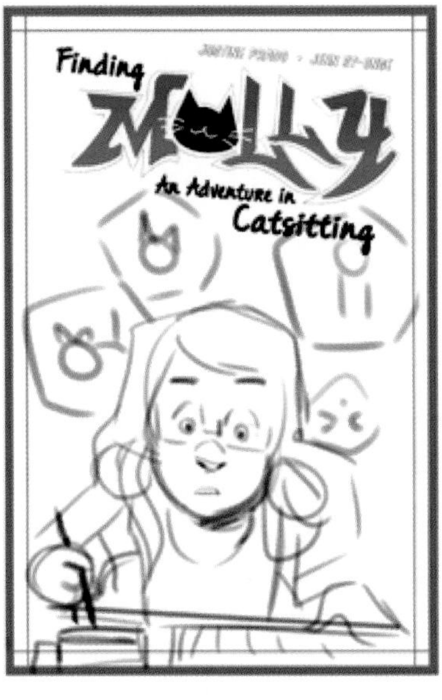
Finding
MOLLY
An Adventure in
Catsitting

H - SHOT AS THOUGH THE VIEWER IS IN THE COMPUTER SCREEN LOOKING OUT, MOLLY IS WORKING ON HER TABLET, A MUG OF TEA OR COFFEE IN THE FOREGROUND. LITTLE COMIC BLURBS FLOAT IN THE AIR BEHIND HER HEAD

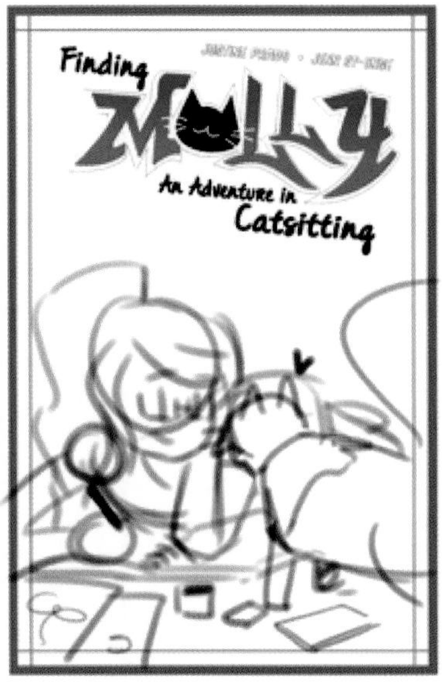
Finding
MOLLY
An Adventure in
Catsitting

I - MOLLY LAYS ON THE GROUND, WORKING IN HER SKETCHBOOK. THERE ARE EXTRA PAPERS AND DRAWING MATERIALS AROUND HER, AND PISHI IS APPROACHING HER AFFECTIONATELY

Issue 5

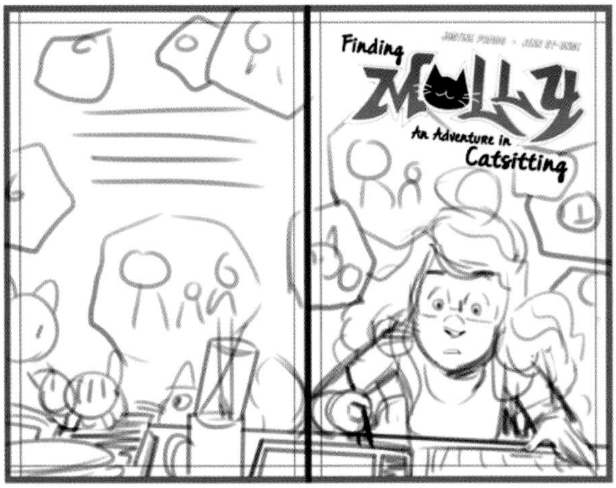

Finding
MOLLY
An Adventure in
Catsitting

IDEA 1: MOLLY IS WORKING ON HER TABLET, LOOKING TOWARDS THE VIEWER AS THOUGH THEY ARE IN HER COMPUTER SCREEN. THE BACK PAGE SHOWS STACKS OF BOOKS AND DISHES, AS WELL AS A KITTIES. GEOMETRIC SHAPES SURROUND EVERYTHING IN THE FOREGROUNG, CONTAINING REFERENCES TO MOLLY'S VARIOUS WEBCOMICS -CAN WE USE THE LINEART FROM THE ACTUAL WEBCOMICS FROM THROUGHOUT THE SERIES FOR THIS ELEMENT?-

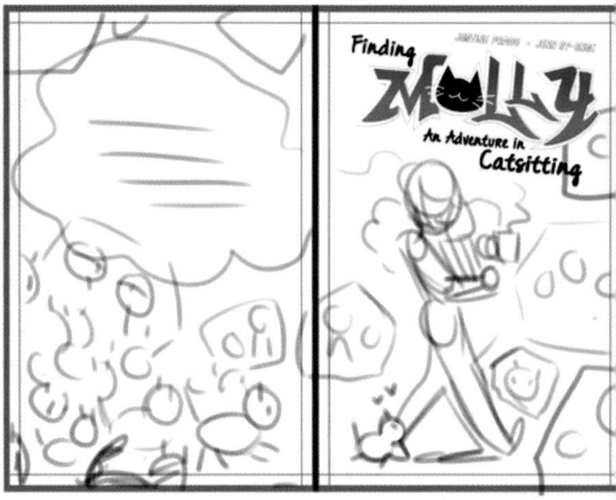

Finding
MOLLY
An Adventure in
Catsitting

IDEA 2: MOLLY IS WALKING ALONG A BLANK BG WITH AN ARMFUL OF SKETCHBOOKS, ART SUPPLIES, COFFEE, THE KITTEN TROTTING ALONGSIDE HER; SHE IS GLANCING OVER HER SHOULDER WITH A SURPRISED OR CONCERNED LOOKING EXPRESSION, AS THE BACK COVER IS FILLED WITH MORE CATS BEHIND HER. THEY ARE ALL SURROUNDED BY WEBCOMIC REFERENCES FLOATING AROUND.

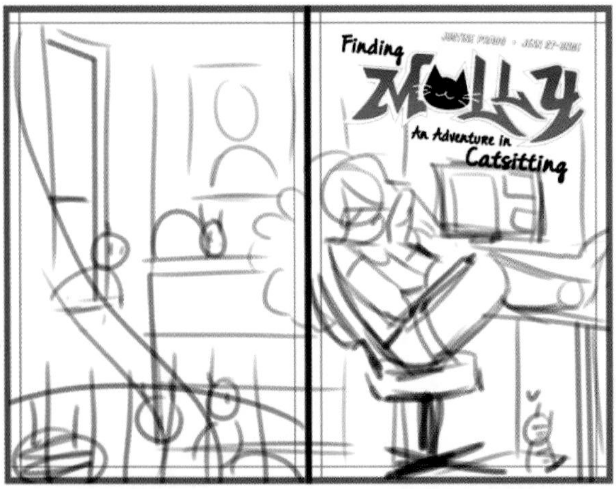

Finding
MOLLY
An Adventure in
Catsitting

IDEA 3: MOLLY SITS AT HER DESK WITH HER FEET PROPPED UP, REFERENCES -WEBCOMIC MAYBE?- UP ON HER COMPUTER SCREEN WHILE SHE DRAWS IN A SKETCHBOOK. THE KITTEN SITS ON THE FLOOR AND THE BACK COVER HAS MORE CATS SITTING AROUND THE ONE SIDE OF HER APARTMENT.

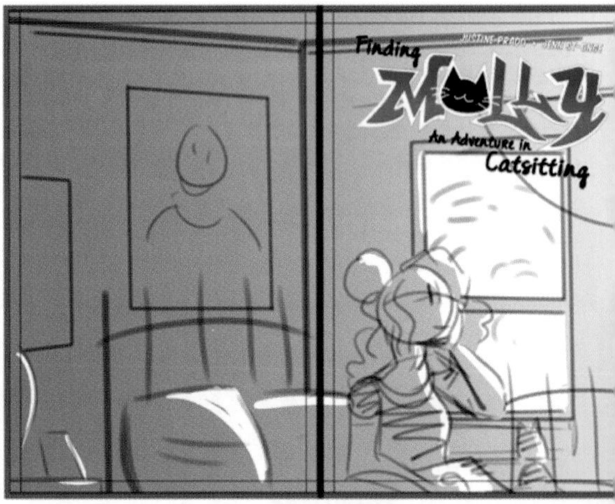

Finding
MOLLY
An Adventure in
Catsitting

IDEA 4: MOLLY AND KITTEN SIT LOOKING OUT THE WINDOW AT URBAN SKYLINE. EXTERIOR IS DONE IN THE STYLE OF MOLLY'S LATER PAINTINGS? ROOM THAT THERE COULD BE THE WEBCOMIC BUBBLES AROUND THEM

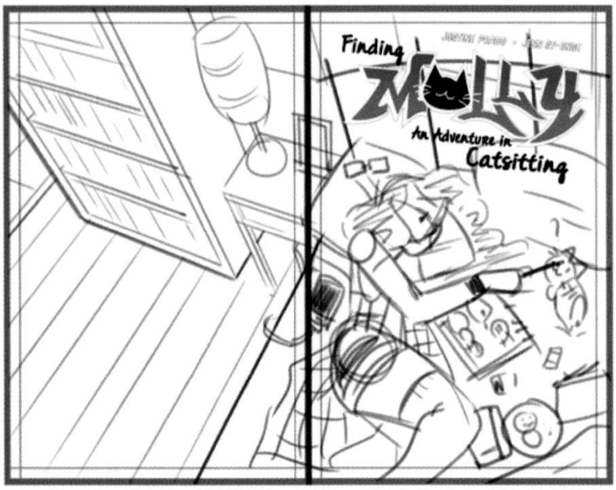

Finding
MOLLY
An Adventure in
Catsitting

IDEA 5: MOLLY LAYS ON HER BED SURROUNDED BY ART SUPPLIES AND OTHER ITEMS LIKE HER PHONE AND SNACKS. SHE'S USING A PENCIL TO PLAY WITH THE KITTEN.

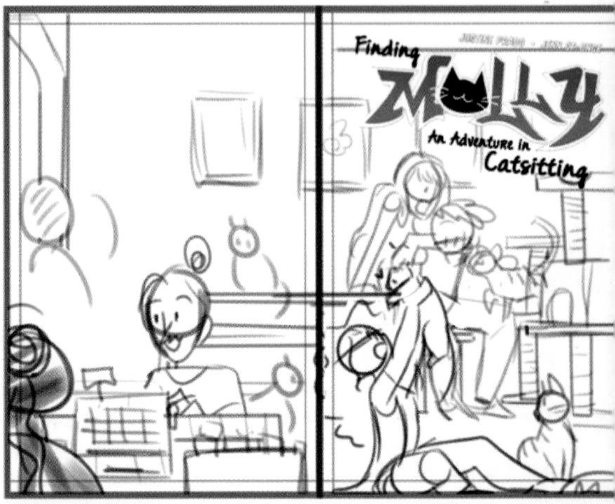

Finding
MOLLY
An Adventure in
Catsitting

IDEA 6: THE GANG ARE AT THE CAT CAFE. ON THE FRONT, MOLLY SITS ON THE GROUND, HOLDING A CAT UP, WHILE MAT AND SARAH INTERACT WITH A CAT STANDING ON A CAT TOWER. THE BACK HALF SHOWS ROME GETTING COFFEE FROM A BARISTA WHILE THERE ARE OTHER CATS AND CUSTOMERS BEHIND HIM.

ore from

EMETCOMICS

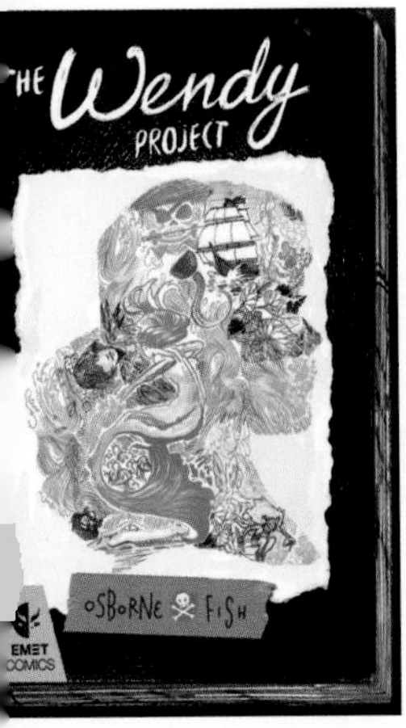

HE Wendy PROJECT
OSBORNE FISH
EMET COMICS

ie Wendy Project #1

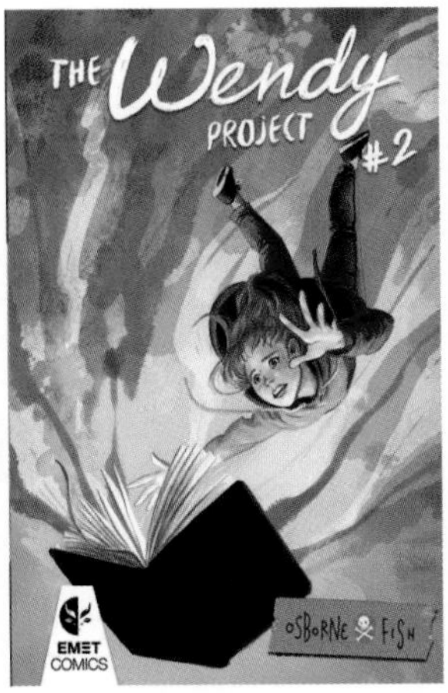

THE Wendy PROJECT #2
OSBORNE FISH
EMET COMICS

The Wendy Project #2

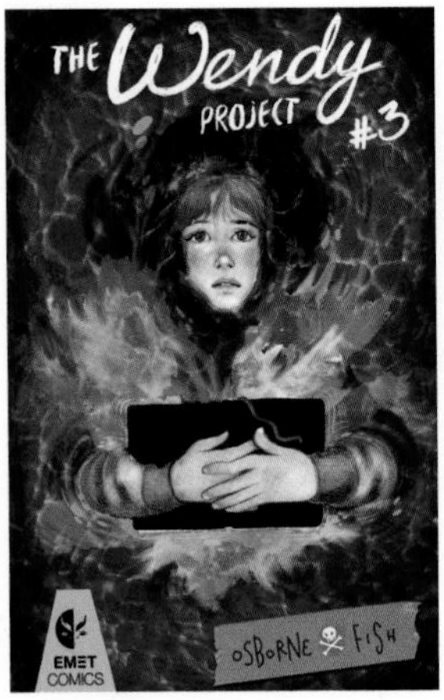

THE Wendy PROJECT #3
OSBORNE FISH
EMET COMICS

The Wendy Project #3

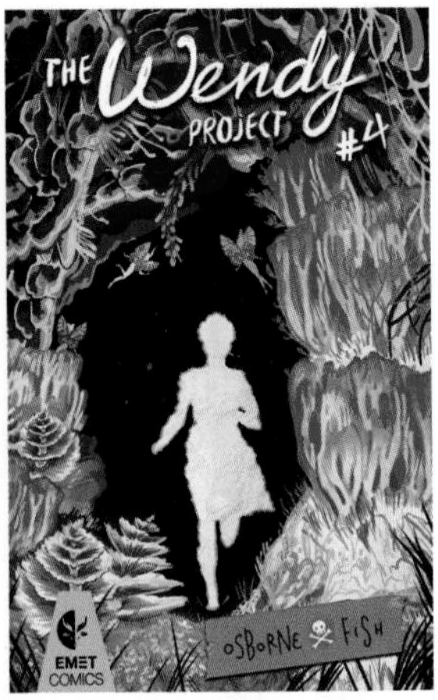

THE Wendy PROJECT #4
OSBORNE FISH
EMET COMICS

The Wendy Project #4

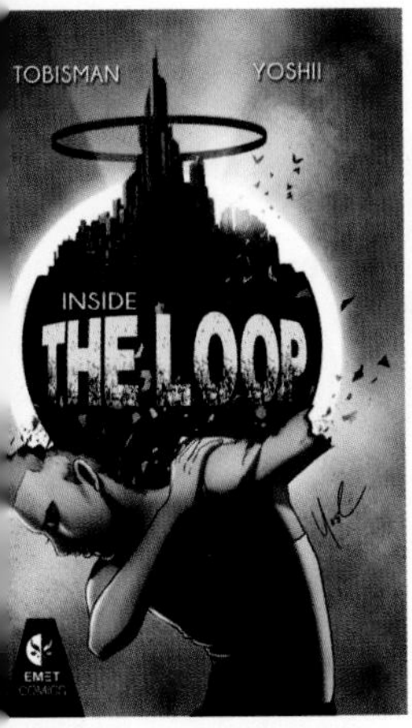

TOBISMAN
YOSHII
INSIDE
THE LOOP
EMET COMICS

side the Loop #1

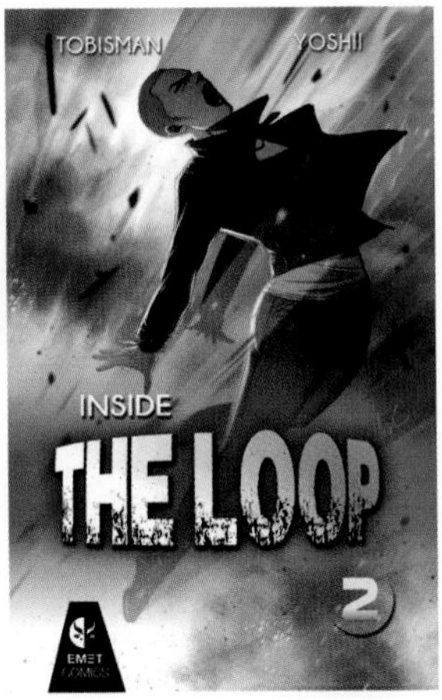

TOBISMAN
YOSHII
INSIDE
THE LOOP
2
EMET COMICS

Inside the Loop #2

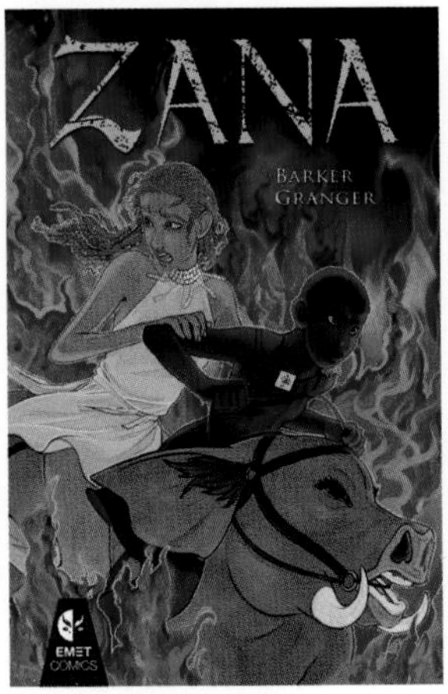

ZANA
BARKER
GRANGER
EMET COMICS

Zana #1

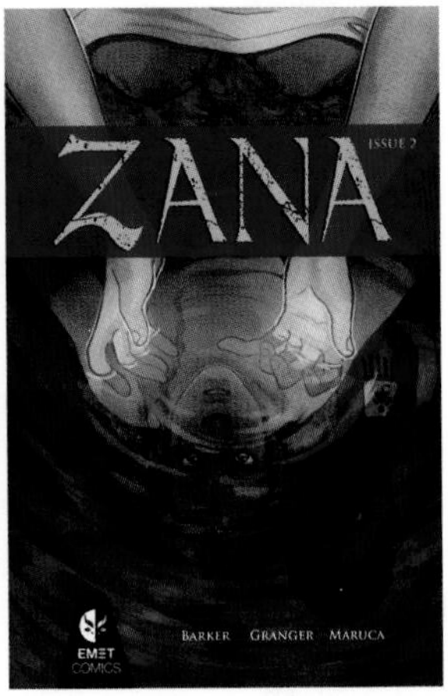

ZANA
ISSUE 2
BARKER GRANGER MARUCA
EMET COMICS

Zana #2

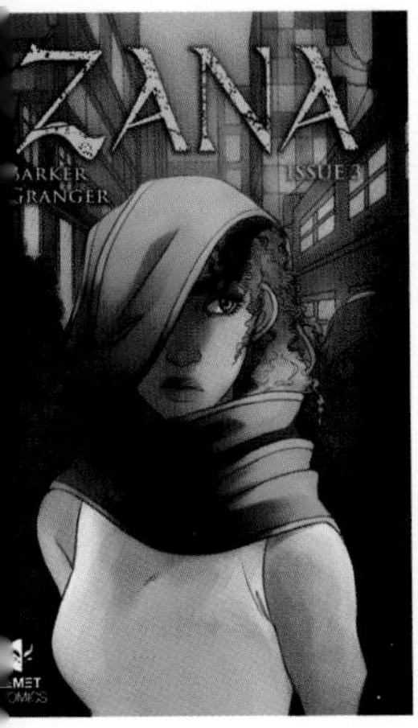

ZANA
ARKER
RANGER
ISSUE 3

na #3

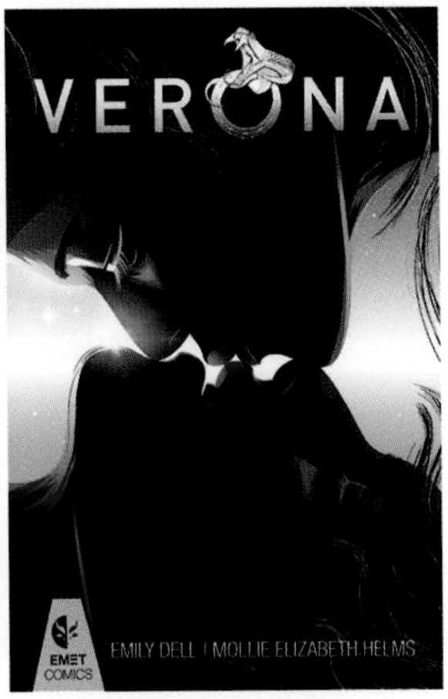

VERONA
EMILY DELL | MOLLIE ELIZABETH HELMS
EMET COMICS

Verona #1 & #2

Like what you see?
Head over to
emetcomics.com
for comics, shirts,
posters, and more!

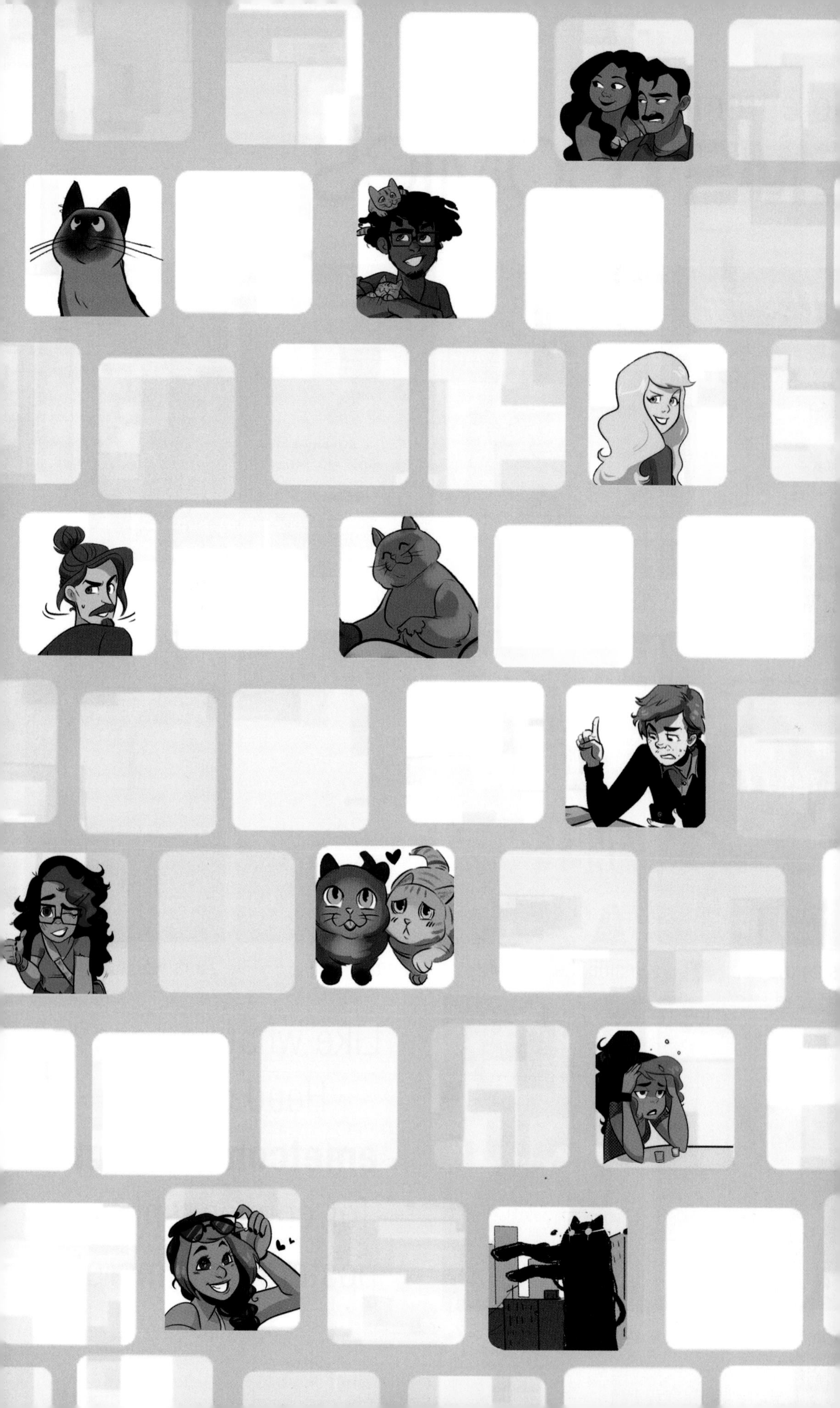

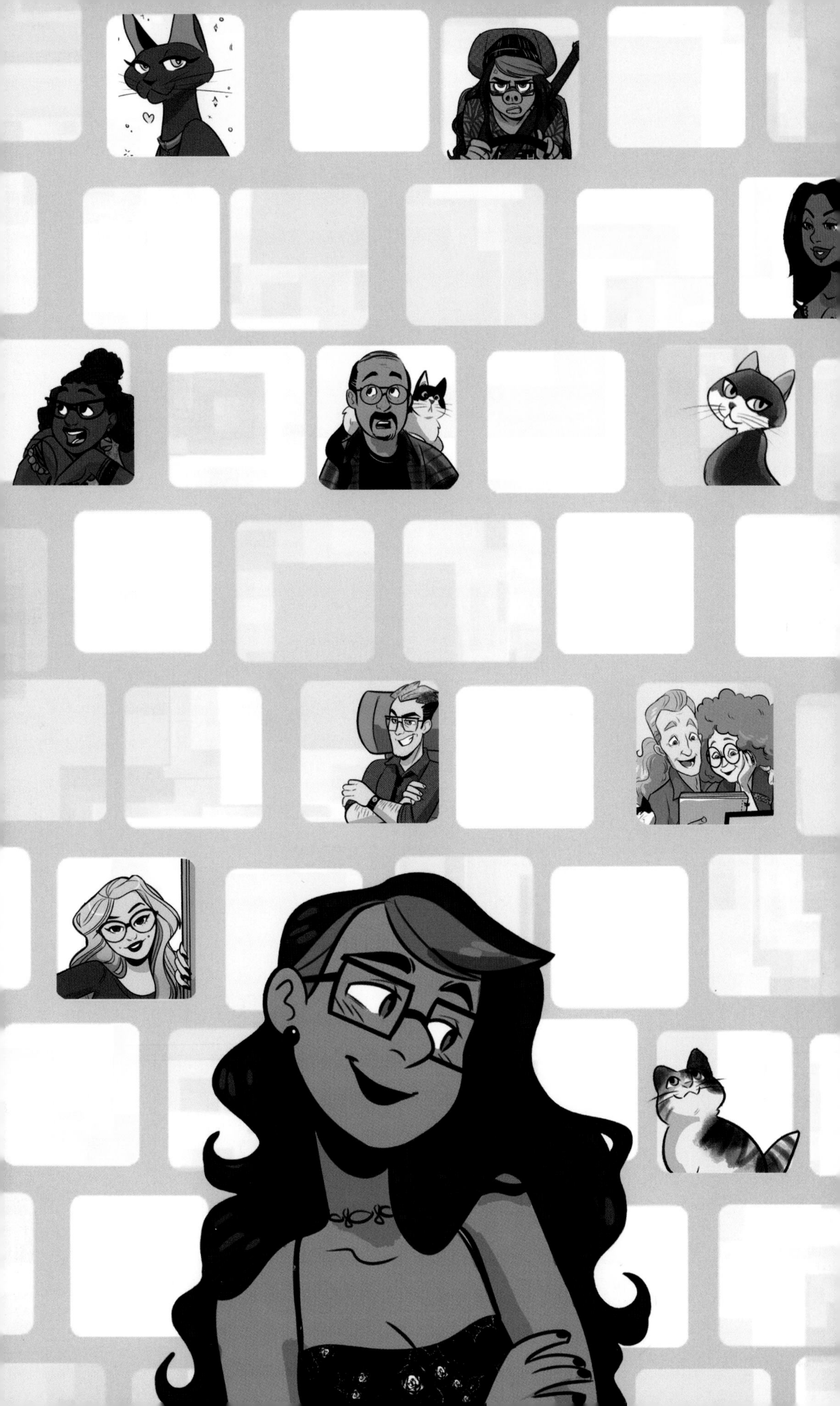